10 0456581 4

UNIVERS

WITHDRAWN

FROM THE

DATE DUE FOR

UNIVERSITY L"

D1448492

PERCEPTUAL AND ASSOCIATIVE LEARNING

OXFORD PSYCHOLOGY SERIES

Editors

Donald E. Broadbent   Nicholas J. Mackintosh

James L. McGaugh   Endel Tulving

Lawrence Weiskrantz

Perceptual and Associative Learning

Geoffrey Hall

Professor of Psychology,
University of York

OXFORD PSYCHOLOGY SERIES

NO. 18

CLARENDON PRESS · OXFORD

1991

100456581[?]

This book has been printed digitally and produced to a standard design in order to ensure its continuing availability

OXFORD
UNIVERSITY PRESS

Great Clarendon Street, Oxford OX2 6DP

Oxford University Press is a department of the University of Oxford.
It furthers the University's objective of excellence in research, scholarship,
and education by publishing worldwide in

Oxford New York

Auckland Bangkok Buenos Aires Cape Town Chennai
Dar es Salaam Delhi Hong Kong Istanbul Karachi Kolkata
Kuala Lumpur Madrid Melbourne Mexico City Mumbai Nairobi
São Paulo Shanghai Singapore Taipei Tokyo Toronto

with an associated company in Berlin

Oxford is a registered trade mark of Oxford University Press
in the UK and in certain other countries

Published in the United States
by Oxford University Press Inc., New York

© G. Hall, 1991

The moral rights of the author have been asserted
Database right Oxford University Press (maker)

Reprinted 2002

All rights reserved. No part of this publication may be reproduced,
stored in a retrieval system, or transmitted, in any form or by any means,
without the prior permission in writing of Oxford University Press,
or as expressly permitted by law, or under terms agreed with the appropriate
reprographics rights organization. Enquiries concerning reproduction
outside the scope of the above should be sent to the Rights Department,
Oxford University Press, at the address above

You must not circulate this book in any other binding or cover
and you must impose this same condition on any acquirer

A catalogue record for this book is available from the British Library

Library of Congress Cataloging in Publication Data
Hall, G. (Geoffrey)
Perceptual and associative learning/Geoffrey Hall.
p. cm. — (Oxford psychology series ; no. 18)
Includes bibliographical references and indexes.
1. Paired-association learning. 2. Perceptual learning
I. Title. II. Series.
BF319.5.P34H35 1991
153.1'526dc21

ISBN 0-19-852182-0

UNIVERSITY LIBRARY
NOTTINGHAM

Preface

According to Gibson's (1969) influential review of the topic, perceptual learning is a process whereby experience with a given form of stimulation allows an increase in a subject's ability to extract information from it. The chief process involved is one of 'stimulus differentiation' by which features and details of a stimulus that initially were not perceived become capable of evoking a response; and the laws governing this form of learning are not, it is emphatically asserted, those of associative learning.

As someone with an interest in associative learning theory and its application to animal discrimination learning, I found Gibson's ideas directly relevant to my own concerns. First, the extent to which the processes involved in animal discrimination learning might include changes in how stimulus-events are perceived (in particular in the degree to which they command attention) has long been a matter for debate. Second (and the debate over discrimination learning is just one aspect of this more general point), learning theorists have often put forward their associative principles as an explanation for *all* instances of learning. The assertion that perceptual learning obeys different laws constitutes a challenge that the associative theorist cannot ignore. It seemed appropriate, therefore, to examine in detail those studies of traditional forms of learning that make contact with the issue of perceptual learning, the questions of interest being: first, can evidence for learned changes in perception be detected in our standard procedures for studying learning? and second, are any such changes the consequence of a Gibsonian process of differentiation? (As an element of suspense is not thought to be essential to a scientific monograph, the reader might want to know now that my answers will be—to the first question: yes; to the second question: perhaps—although associative processes do a remarkably good job of dealing with most of the phenomena suggestive of differentiation.)

What has just been said will make it clear that the 'and' of my title serves a restrictive function and indicates an intention to concentrate on areas of direct overlap between associative and perceptual learning. This has the advantage of reducing the amount of material that needs to be reviewed to a manageable size. But I hope it will not prevent me from reaching conclusions of general applicability. If perceptual changes can be demonstrated in the conditioning experiments discussed here, then we can assume that they will be occurring in conditioning procedures of (almost) all sorts; their possible contribution to the outcome of these procedures will need to be incorporated by our learning theories. And an advantage of the experimental procedures to be discussed is that they are, on the whole, analytically tractable, allowing us to reach conclusions about the mechanisms involved. These mechanisms, we may hope, will be of relevance when it comes to explaining the much wider range of phenomena (such as are discussed by Gibson, 1969) that are taken as instances of perceptual learning.

Even within the restrictions described above, I have not tried to supply a fully comprehensive review of all the topics that are dealt with. Some chapters are more selective than others (that on habituation, for instance, covers only a small fraction of the experimental work available, whereas in Chapter 5 on acquired distinctiveness I thought it useful to provide an account, as none has hitherto been available, of all the important studies that have been done on this issue). But in general, my aim in each chapter has been to review enough material relevant to the important questions raised by the topic to allow definite answers to be proposed and so allow the argument to be carried forward. I have ignored work that seemed to be only marginally relevant to these questions and, on occasion, I have introduced unpublished work of my own when I felt it might help us resolve some issue left open by the review of the published work.

My experimental work on this topic has relied on the help of a number of collaborators. They are referred to in the text, but deserve separate mention here; they have included, over the years, C. Bonardi, S. Channell, R. C. Honey, J. M. Pearce, P. Reed, T. R. Schachtman, and A. M. I. Willis. It is a pleasure to be able to acknowledge the help they have given in designing, conducting, and interpreting experiments. Charlotte Bonardi and Rob Honey have also read the whole of a preliminary version of the present book, as has N. J. Mackintosh. Others who have helped by reading and commenting on earlier versions of some of the chapters include: A. G. Baker, M. E. Bouton, E. M. Macphail, J. M. Pearce, and D. A. T. Siddle. I am very grateful to them all but perhaps the rest will forgive me if I pick out two for further mention. Nick Mackintosh and I have for many years shared an interest in the subject matter of this book. Discussion with him has helped shape my general approach and has determined some or even many of the specific conclusions I have reached. I look forward to a continuing debate with him over those topics on which I have (perhaps unwisely, time will tell) rejected his arguments and gone my own way. Rob Honey and I have worked in the same laboratory for more than five years and have spent some part of almost every day over that time discussing the issues that make up this book. Our collaboration has been so protracted and extensive that I can no longer distinguish with any certainty his contribution from my own. There can scarcely be a page in what follows that does not reflect his influence in one way or another, but wherever the reader detects an argument of particular originality or ingenuity he can be sure that Rob Honey's thinking is showing through.

Finally I must thank V. D. Chamizo, G. Alsonso Martinez, and other members of the Sociedad Española de Psicologia Comparada. At meetings held at the Universidad de Barcelona (organized by Victoria Chamizo) and at the Universidad del Pais Vasco (organized by Sindi Alonso) I was able to discourse at length on the relation between perceptual and associative learning before an audience that was enthusiastic and helpful. The stimulus provided by these occasions played a critical part in generating the present book.

York   G.H.
November 1990

Contents

1. Associative theory and the phenomena of perceptual learning

For at least 300 years, philosophers and psychologists concerned with the mechanisms of cognition in general and of the acquisition of knowledge in particular have given a central place to the notion of association. This is not to say that there has been agreement among them on the topic. Those committed to the view that knowledge can be in some sense 'innate' grant the association a central place only because of their need to demonstrate the inadequacy of a concept on which empiricists rely. And those wedded to the concept have debated endlessly over its details—over what might be the elements that enter into associations (sensations, ideas, stimuli, responses) and over what conditions might be necessary or sufficient for associations to be formed. (Need the elements occur in contiguity, should they be similar or contrasted, and so on.) None the less, it remains true that associative mechanisms of one sort or another form the basis of current theories for the mechanisms of animal learning and are perhaps reasserting their position in certain recent accounts of human cognition (e.g. Rumelhart, Hinton, and McClelland 1986).

The associative account of learning has at its heart just a single concept— the suggestion that the central representations of specified elements can become linked so that activation of one can excite its associate. Any attempt to deal with a major part of cognitive functioning armed with this single explanatory tool may seem naive but this is just what some associative theorists claim to have succeeded in. Thus Pavlov was prepared to assert the 'it is obvious that the different kinds of habits based on training, education and discipline of any sort are nothing but a chain of conditioned reflexes' (Pavlov 1927, p. 395), the formation of a conditioned reflex being taken, of course, as an instance of association formation. Western psychologists, although espousing a different version of associative theory, have been willing to make equally strong assertions. Thus Miller and Dollard (1941, p. 13): 'The field of human learning covers phenomena which range all the way from the simple, almost reflex, learning of a child to avoid a hot radiator to the complex processes by which a scientist constructs a theory. Throughout the whole range, however, the same fundamental factors seem to be involved.' These factors, Miller and Dollard suggest, are those described by Hull (e.g. 1943, 1952) as determining the formation of stimulus–response associations.

The validity of these claims is difficult to assess. In part this is because a full statement of any associative theory, be it Pavlov's or Hull's, or some other, reveals the use of many theoretical mechanisms in addition to that responsible for association formation. Only a close examination (something undertaken in later chapters) will allow us to evaluate the possibility that these supposedly subsidiary concepts in fact disguise the introduction on non-associative learning mechanisms into theories that are proclaimed to be purely associative. A second, more basic, problem is that associative theorists do not give us a detailed and fully worked out analysis of how it is that associative mechanisms underlie the effects produced by education or the processes involved in the construction of a scientific theory. Given the complexity of the phenomena this is not surprising; but in the absence of a precise specification of how the theories apply to them it becomes impossible to refute the suggestion that these phenomena are, in principle, explicable in associative terms.

There are, however, phenomena that go under the heading of perceptual learning that present a very direct challenge to the comprehensiveness of the associative analysis. They can be evident in studies using very simple training procedures for which it should be possible to give a full account of any associative learning that may be occurring. But the associative analysis supplies no ready explanation of the learned changes that occur as a result of these procedures, leading some theorists to the conclusion that perceptual learning cannot, *in principle*, be reduced to the operation of associative processes.

To illustrate these points we may consider the experiment described by Gibson and Gibson (1955; see also Phaup and Coldwell 1959). This experiment investigated for human subjects, both children and adults, the effects of experience of a relatively simple visual figure on a subsequent discrimination task. The only training that the subjects received was that they were shown, for 5s, a 'standard scribble' (the central card depicted in Fig. 1.1). They were then shown, one by one, all the cards depicted in the figure (plus some others) and were instructed to identify the one that was identical to that they had been shown originally. No feedback was given but after the entire pack had been gone through the subjects were again allowed to inspect the standard. Adult subjects initially made some mistakes, wrongly identifying cards as being the same as the standard; but after three runs through the pack their performance became perfect. Children aged from 8 to 11 years took a mean of 4.7 runs to achieve perfect recognition. Children aged from 6 to 8 years were rather less accurate. They responded on average to 13.4 items on the first run, but these too showed an improvement, their score being reduced to 3.9 after a further six or so runs. It seems, therefore, that discriminative performance can be improved without explicit training, seemingly as a result of mere exposure to the stimuli.

It may be that association formation is going on during training with these procedures but it is not apparent how such learning could generate the results obtained. Gibson and Gibson turn instead to a quite different

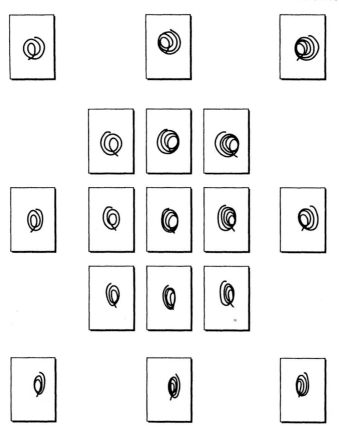

Fig. 1.1 Stimuli used in the experiment by Gibson and Gibson. The central scribble is the standard. The others vary in the number of loops, the degree of compression of the ellipse, and in orientation. (After Gibson and Gibson 1955.)

account—a 'differentiation' theory. Stimuli (like those shown in the figure), they suggest, contain many features or aspects that are not at first fully effective; but with exposure to stimuli, 'percepts change over time by progressive elaboration of qualities, features and dimensions of variation' (Gibson and Gibson 1955, p. 34). Such change will allow improved discrimination between stimuli that previously were perceived as similar or identical. The mechanism responsible for this change cannot, it is asserted, be associative in nature. The grounds for this assertion are stated most clearly by Gibson and Levin (1975). Differentiation occurs, they suggest, as subjects become able to 'extract the relevant information from the manifold stimulation available' producing 'an increase of specificity of discrimination to stimulus input, an increase in differentiation of stimulus information. It is extraction, or "pulling out" rather than adding on' (Gibson and Levin 1975, p. 13). This last point provides the reason for rejecting an associative interpretation. Association formation consists of linking one thing with another but 'this simple and ancient notion does not work for perceptual learning, because what is learned is not addition of something but rather extraction of something' (Gibson and Levin 1975, p. 23).

If this version of the differentiation theory proves to be correct, we have in perceptual learning a form of learning that presents a real challenge to associative theory—learning that clearly has important consequences for the adjustment of the organism to its environment but which, it is stated, cannot be achieved by associative processes. My aim in this book is to assess how well associative theory can meet the challenge, to explore some of the limits of associative theory, and to specify what new mechanisms must be added in order that the theory might deal with perceptual learning. It is possible that these new mechanisms might turn out to be powerful enough to supplant associationism altogether. But we may be sure that a theory that has proved so long-lasting and of such general appeal as has the associative account is unlikely to succumb easily to any assertion that a given phenomenon is quite beyond its scope.

In order to achieve this general aim, certain preliminaries must be undertaken. First it is necessary to specify what should be taken as being the essential features of the associative account. There are many theories of learning that have been called 'associative' but which differ among themselves in many ways. What aspects of these theories should we take as being central to associationism? Second, the example of perceptual learning that we have considered so far has been purely illustrative. It is necessary now to survey the wide range of phenomena that have been regarded as instances of perceptual learning and to select from them particular instances that seem likely to be susceptible to empirical and theoretical analysis. These two issues form the substance of the rest of this chapter.

1.1 The standard associative model

In his discussion of the essential features of an associative theory of learning, Roitblat (1987) identifies what he calls a 'standard associative model'. Critical to this standard model are the following assumptions. The model assumes the existence of associations which are taken to be directional connections between pairs of elements. The elements in question are the central or cerebral representations of environmental events (stimuli) or features of stimuli, and are directly activated by presentation of the appropriate stimulus or feature. The existence of an associative connection allows activity in one element to modify the state of activation of another. All learning consists of the formation or strengthening of such connections.

Some of these features require comment at this early stage. First, although nothing has been said so far about the conditions necessary for association formation, none of our current theories assumes that the two stimuli whose elements are to be linked need to be presented simultaneously and in experiments on conditioning it is usual for one stimulus to precede the other by a short interval (Pavlov 1927). It is often assumed, however, that the representations of the stimuli need to be active simultaneously and accordingly it must be supposed that activation of the first representation will persist (perhaps at a reduced level) during the interval before the presentation of the second stimulus. This is to say that associative theories make use of a notion of (non-associative) short-term memory and to this extent, at least, the claim that all learning consists of the formation of associations is inaccurate. The implications of this inaccuracy are, however, negligible for our present purposes.

Next, Roitblat (1986) identifies the elements that enter into associations as corresponding to environmental stimuli. To do so is to neglect a major class of associative theory which takes the response (or the pattern of central activity that produces a response) as being an element capable of forming associations. We need to acknowledge the existence of such theories although, again, the implications of doing so may be unimportant if, as some have argued (e.g. Mackintosh 1983), the same laws of association apply whatever the elements being associated.

Finally, we need to be more specific about the ways in which activity in one element is supposed to modify activity in an associated element. Perhaps in its strictest form, associative theory should allow only excitatory connections so that the presentation of event A is able to arouse activity in representation B in much the same way as (if to a lesser extent than) the presentation of event B itself. Associative theorists have not been so strict with themselves. Wagner (1981) has suggested that the activity aroused in an element by way of an associative link might differ in kind from the form of activity evoked by the presentation of the stimulus itself. And Roitblat (1987), in company with many others, allows the existence of inhibitory as well as excitatory associations, an inhibitory association being one that prevents or reduces activation in its target element. Theories that accept this latter suggestion cannot describe all acquired knowledge in terms of the patterns of connection between elements—information is also encoded in the link itself and the type of association (excitatory or inhibitory) must also be specified.

Having dealt with the general principles it is appropriate to look at specific examples of theories in which these principles are embodied. The best worked-out of these theories are to be found in the study of classical conditioning in animals, a topic with a tradition of associative theorizing that goes back to Pavlov himself. The most influential of more recent theories is that proposed by Rescorla and Wagner (1972).

1.1.1 The Rescorla–Wagner model

The Rescorla–Wagner (1972) model is chiefly concerned with giving a formal specification of the conditions in which associations are formed and strengthened. The central concept of the model is that of associative strength (often symbolized as V), the strength of a directional connection between elements representing the two stimuli used in studies of Pavlovian or classical conditioning. The first of these stimuli is referred to as the conditioned stimulus (CS) and in most experiments this is usually a neutral event such as the sounding of a tone or the illumination of a light. The second event (the unconditioned stimulus, US, or reinforcer) that is 'paired' with the first (although in practice the US is frequently presented at the offset of the CS) is usually of motivational significance—the presentation of an electric shock, for example, or the delivery of food. The associative strength of a CS–US connection increases when the two events occur in contiguity, which we can take as meaning when the central representations of these two events are concurrently activated. Rescorla and Wagner are not specific about temporal factors but we must assume that the state of activity evoked by a stimulus decays rapidly since increments in associative strength are assumed not to occur when any sizeable delay intervenes between CS and US. The likelihood of a conditioned response (CR) increases with associative strength and such responding can thus be used as an index of V.

The change in associative strength produced by a conditioning trial (a 'pairing' of CS and US) is given by the following equation:

$$\Delta V_A = \alpha_A \beta (\lambda - \Sigma V). \qquad 1.1$$

ΔV_A is the increment in associative strength occurring to a given CS (stimulus A); α_A is a learning rate parameter the value of which depends on the intensity, discriminability, or salience of A; β is a learning rate parameter determined by the nature of the US; λ is the asymptote of associative strength and its value is determined by the magnitude of the US; ΣV represents the summed associative strength of all CSs that are present on that trial and have associations with the US representation.

The course of conditioning with a single CS is straightforward. Here $\Sigma V = V_A$, successive trials cause increases in V_A until the point is reached when $(\lambda - \Sigma V) = 0$ and no further increments are possible. This account has been regarded (Dickinson and Mackintosh 1978) as one which maintains that the US grows less and less effective as conditioning proceeds; that is $(\lambda - \Sigma V)$, which determines the effectiveness of a US presentation in increasing associative strength, tends to approach zero with extended training. The interesting features of this model emerge when we consider training procedures that use compound stimuli in which two or more CSs occur together. Rescorla and Wagner (1972) make the simplifying (and they admit, simplistic) assumption that each of the components of a compound retains its integrity so that, for instance, the associative strength of a tone and light presented together is just the sum of the separate strengths of the two stimuli.

Consider now the consequences of training a subject to asymptote with one CS, A, and then presenting trials in which a compound stimulus, AB, occurs but is not followed by the US. Rescorla and Wagner (1972; see also Wagner and Rescorla 1972) assume that the value of λ is zero when no US occurs. According to (1.1) the change in the associative strength on each of these trials will be negative (($\lambda - \Sigma V$) will be negative) and V_A will decline from the asymptotic level. Applying an analogous equation tells us about the fate of B. Again there will be a decrease in associative strength, and, as the initial strength of a novel stimulus is assumed to be zero, the value of V_B will become negative. Wagner and Rescorla (1972) equate the acquisition of negative associative strength with inhibitory learning. A connection having positive associative strength allows a CS to excite a US representation; negative associative strength means that the CS inhibits the US representation. Rescorla (1979) has suggested that an inhibitory connection might be viewed as acting to raise the threshold below which excitatory connections fail to activate the US representation.

Here then is an example of a theory that departs not at all from Roitblat's (1987) specification for the standard associative model: the elements of association correspond directly to stimuli; associations are forged as a result of contiguous presentation of the stimuli; associations can be only two kinds, excitatory or inhibitory. In spite of this simplicity the Rescorla–Wagner model has proved to be very powerful and capable of explaining a range of phenomena that at first sight seem to be outside the scope of such theorizing. We shall consider two examples.

In an experiment on 'blocking' (e.g. Kamin 1968), the subject is first trained to asymptote with a given CS, A, preceding the US. In a second phase of training a compound stimulus AB is used and US presentations are continued. A test phase in which B is presented alone reveals it to have gained little or no associative strength (i.e., only a weak CR or none at all is evoked). B will gain strength in subjects for whom the first phase of training with A alone is omitted. Thus, pre-training with A is said to block learning about B. An obvious account for this phenomenon (and that originally presented by Mackintosh (1965); see also Sutherland and Mackintosh (1971)) interprets it as being the consequence of perceptual (attentional) processes. Pre-training with A might teach the subject to attend to this stimulus, thus causing the subject to ignore and fail to learn about B during the phase of compound training. But the Rescorla–Wagner model can offer an alternative and simpler explanation that makes use only of associative processes. According to the model, the presence of the pre-trained A will ensure that the value of ($\lambda - \Sigma V$) (see eqn 1.1) will be zero on the compound trials. The reinforcer will therefore be quite ineffective and the associative strength of the B stimulus will remain at zero. The phenomenon of blocking is not enough in itself to require the introduction of an attentional construct.

The second example concerns the ability of animals to learn discriminations involving stimulus patterns. It had long been known (Woodbury 1943) that an animal receiving reinforcement in the presence of a compound AB but not when the individual components are presented will come to emit the CR to AB but not to A or B presented separately (a phenomenon known as positive patterning). Animals can also learn negative patterning, responding to the reinforced components but withholding response to the non-reinforced compound. (For a more recent demonstration of these effects see Forbes and Holland (1980)). Such 'configural learning', as it is sometimes called, challenges the assumption of the Rescorla–Wagner model that the associative strength of a compound stimulus is simply the summed strength of the individual components. It turns out, however, that the challenge can be met by making a minor extension to the model that leaves most of its basic assumptions intact.

As developed by Rescorla (1972, 1973) this extension is the suggestion that when two stimuli, A and B, are presented together some new configural stimulus (X) is created that is unique to the combination of the A and B components. In dealing theoretically with the AB compound it is necessary, therefore, to consider the associative strengths of three elements, A, B, and X. It may be apparent that applying the model summarized in eqn (1.1) along with this assumption generates an explanation for patterning effects. In positive patterning, X will gain associative strength whereas A and B will gain little; in negative patterning, X will gain inhibitory strength to counteract the excitatory effects of A and B. (A fuller account of the application of this model to discrimination learning is given on pp. 14–15.)

Rescorla (1973) has tested and confirmed several other predictions arising from his 'unique stimulus' account of configural learning. It may be objected, with some justice, that the notion of a unique stimulus X implies the operation of unexplained perceptual factors responsible for creating the stimulus out of the conjunction of A and B. But an equally fair response to this objection would be that no new mechanism for learning is being proposed here and that our ignorance about how stimulus X is perceived is no greater than our ignorance of how the simple stimulus A itself comes to excite a given central representation. Within its self-imposed limitations the Rescorla–Wagner model provides us with an exceptionally powerful and elegant account of learning in associative terms. Subsequent developments have increased the power of the theory.

1.1.2 Wagner's SOP model

SOP is a model for 'standard operating procedures' in memory proposed by Wagner (1981; (see also Mazur and Wagner (1982); Wagner and Larew

(1985)). To some extent it can be seen as a development of the Rescorla–Wagner (1972) model in which temporal factors are dealt with and in which the associative structures implied by the earlier model are fully expounded. But it also introduces a set of new concepts that greatly extend the explanatory scope of the basic associative theory.

The elements of association are referred to as a set of 'nodes' in memory (the term 'element' itself being used for the subunits of which a node is composed). It is assumed that any isolable stimulus (i.e., any event that the experimenter distinguishes as such) has its own representative node and 'SOP is expressly noncommittal on the issue of how representative nodes come to have the identities that are assumed' (Wagner 1981, p. 14). It is made clear, however, that there will be no appeal 'to any change in nodal character as a result of learning' (Wagner 1981, p. 14). To this extent the possibility of a form of perceptual learning is acknowledged but the theory in its present form declines to make use of such a process.

The units that enter into associations in the Rescorla–Wagner model can be either inactive or activated to a greater or lesser degree according to the excitatory and inhibitory influences acting upon them. SOP allows for two different forms of activation. The primary state of activation (A1) is produced in some of the elements of a node by the presence of the stimulus to which the node corresponds. The more intense the stimulation, the greater is the proportion of elements in the A1 state. A node having elements in the A1 state represents a stimulus at the focus of attention. Attention is limited and so a restriction is imposed on the number of elements that can be in A1 at given time. The occurrence of a second stimulus while the first is still present will require at least some of the elements in the first-activated node to move from A1 into a secondary state of activation, A2. This secondary state can be equated with short-term memory. Elements in A1 may decay into A2 at any time and do so particularly rapidly as soon as the external stimulus is removed. Somewhat less rapidly, A2 elements then decay into the inactive state (I). Wagner makes nothing of the parallel between his A1, A2 and I states and Freud's notions of the conscious, preconscious and unconscious mind.

As in other associative theories it is assumed that connections can be formed between a pair of nodes when both are simultaneously active. Thus, when two nodes are both in the A1 state, excitatory connections will be formed between them. We need to consider, however, other possible patterns of activation. It is assumed that when both nodes are in the A2 state no associative learning occurs. But when one node is in A1 and the other in A2 an inhibitory connection is formed, with the former inhibiting the latter. In orthodox conditioning procedures the A1 state in the CS node generated by the presentation of that stimulus will overlap both the A1 activity initially evoked by the subsequent presentation of the US and A2 state into which the US node will decay. Accordingly both excitatory and inhibitory

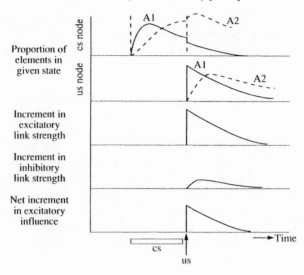

Fig. 1.2 Wagner's 'standard operating procedures' (SOP) model applied to a conditioning trial in which the termination of a conditioned stimulus (CS) is accompanied by the presentation of a brief unconditioned stimulus (US). Presentation of a stimulus moves elements in the corresponding node from I (the inactive state) into the primary state of activation (A1), whence they decay into the secondary state of activation (A2) and back into I. The changes in link strength refer to the excitatory and inhibitory influences of the CS node on the US node. The sudden decline in A1 activity in the CS node on presentation of the US is a consequence of the assumption that only a limited number of elements can be in the A1 state at a given time. (After Wagner 1981).

connections will be formed. The ability of the CS to develop excitatory properties in these circumstances reflects the fact (Fig. 1.2) that there will be much less overlap between the A1 state of the CS and the A2 state of the US than between the A1 state of the CS and the A1 state of the US. The increase in strength of the excitatory link will thus outweigh the increment by the inhibitory link.

It may be noted that, for the stimulus presented second on a conditioning trial (the US of Fig. 1.2), conditions are right for the development of a strong inhibitory connection with the node corresponding to the first-presented stimulus (the CS in Fig. 1.2). The US will acquire some excitatory influence on the CS node (there is, as we have already said, a time when both nodes are in A1) but for the most part the US node will be in A1 when activity in the CS node has decayed into A2. The inhibitory effect on the US node on the CS node is thus likely to outweigh the excitatory influence that will also be acquired. This aspect of the model plays an important part in Wagner's analysis of inhibitory learning (Wagner and Larew 1985). For the time being, however, we may confine ourselves to its terminological implications. It has been convenient to use the term CS to refer to the supposedly neutral stimulus (for example, a light) that precedes or accompanies the presentation of a motivationally significant US (for example, food) in an orthodox conditioning procedure. But any event can be a US, in that any stimulus is likely to evoke some unconditioned response (UR). The UR to a 'neutral' stimulus may be undramatic (a light will evoke no more than a brief orienting response, say) but it will none the less occur. In Wagner's terminology, each stimulus is a US in that it will evoke A1 activity in its representative node (the UR is taken to be a consequence of the A1 state). What makes a stimulus a CS is the acquisition of an ability to modify, by means of excitatory or inhibitory connections, the state of activity in some other node. As we have seen, such an ability is acquired by both the events presented on a conditioning trial.

A further unique feature of Wagner's model concerns the activity induced by way of associative links. We have said that presentation of a stimulus puts its node into the A1 state (and evokes the appropriate UR). Previous associatives theories have assumed that the activation induced in a US node by the presentation of a CS having excitatory links with that node will be similar in kind, if not in intensity, to the activation induced by direct application of the US itself. Accordingly the CR might be expected to be closely similar to the UR. In Wagner's model, by contrast, CS-induced activity is different from that initiated by the US itself. The effect of an excitatory link (and inhibitory links act to oppose this effect) is to move nodal elements from the inactive state into A2—that is, the CS evokes a memory of the US rather than the state (A1) evoked by the presentation of the US itself. The overt behaviour evoked by the presence of (conditioned) A2 activity in a node may or may not be similar to that evoked by A1 activity. Wagner is willing to allow that different nodes may follow different principles—that for some the response evoked by A2 may mimic that evoked by A1 whereas for others the A2 response may be very different. He is thus able to accommodate the sizeable body of evidence (e.g. Siegel 1977; Schull 1979) showing that for some conditioning preparations the CR takes a form that tends to oppose or compensate for the UR elicited by direct application of the US.

Figure 1.3 attempts to summarize the salient features of the SOP model. The upper panel (a) of the figure makes clear what was perhaps obscured by my previous discussion of the simple CS–US association, that nodes can enter into multiple associations forming associative chains and networks. With appropriate training, two or more CSs can come to influence a common US node and that node could itself serve as a CS node having excitatory or inhibitory influence on some further node; and so on. In principle, therefore, the presentation of a single stimulus activating a well-connected node could lead to an extensive spread of activation throughout the system. This spread of activation is kept within bounds by the fact that only nodes

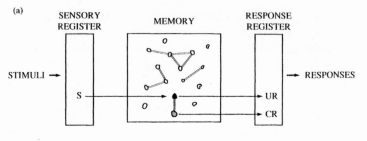

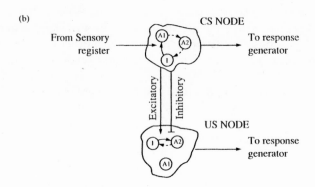

Fig. 1.3 A schematic summary of Wagner's (1981) 'standard operating procedures' model. Panel (a) shows its main feature, memory with nodes corresponding to environmental stimuli. Some nodes are connected by associative links. An external stimulus is present and creating primary (A1) activity in its node and evoking its unconditional response (UR). By way of a an excitatory link, the secondary state of activation (A2) is engendered in another node. Panel (b) shows details of these two nodes. Only one set of links is shown. The node from which they come is designated the conditioned stimulus (CS) node; that to which they go is the unconditioned stimulus (US) node. Symbols within a node represent the three possible states of nodal elements and possible transitions between them. Dashed lines represent decay of activity, solid lines the transitions being brought about by the influences shown acting on the nodes.

directly connected to the first are in contact with a node in the A1 state. They will themselves be put into the A2 state, and Wagner assumes that A2 activity is much less effective than is A1 activity in promoting further (A2) activity in another node.

Wagner's SOP model can accommodate the empirical findings that gave rise to and grew out of the Rescorla-Wagner model; and it also has application to a range of further phenomena. We may exemplify the first of these points by considering the application of the SOP model to the blocking procedure described above (p. 7). It will be recalled that initial training with stimulus A as a CS blocks learning about stimulus B during subsequent conditioning with the AB compound as the CS. According to the SOP model, the initial training with A permits this stimulus to modulate the activity occurring in the US node. A well-trained A stimulus will evoke A2 activity in the US node, thus reducing the number of elements capable of passing into the A1 state when the US itself is presented. Further presentations of A along with the US will thus be capable of producing only very small increments in the net excitatory strength of A, and the same will apply to any other stimulus (such as B) that is presented along with A.

Many of the new phenomena that are addressed by the SOP model need not concern us here because our central interest is not associative learning itself. We shall shortly see, however, that there are some phenomena, traditionally regarded as instances of perceptual learning, to which the theory can be applied with some measure of success. Indeed the central aim of much of the rest of the book will be to evaluate the extent to which models like that proposed by Wagner (1981) can be successfully applied to the phenomena of perceptual learning.

1.1.3 Application to discrimination learning

Our discussion of the standard associative model has concentrated on its application to 'simple' conditioning in which a CS is paired with the US and a change in the likelihood of some CR is measured. Many of the findings to be discussed later, however, come from experiments using discrimination learning procedures and it is important to see how the standard associative model applies to these.

All conditioning implies discrimination in that the CS must be discriminated from the set of background stimuli that constitute the context in which training is given. In explicit discrimination training, however, the experimenter presents (at least) two CSs that differ in the reinforcement they receive. In the simplest case the subject might experience a series of intermixed trials on some of which a high-pitched tone (say) is presented along with the US whereas on others a low tone is presented and the US is omitted. Such training will bring about the development of conditioned responding to the high tone, the positive CS. The non-reinforced (or negative) CS, too, will often evoke CRs early in training (an effect that is particularly marked when the subject has been given initial reinforced training with the positive stimulus before non-reinforced trials are introduced; see Pavlov (1927), pp. 118–20). But with continued training any tendency to respond to the negative stimulus will diminish and a clear-cut discrimination will be formed. Rather confusingly from our point of view, since we shall want to use the term to refer to a particular theory of perceptual learning. Pavlov (1927) described this outcome as 'differentiation'.

The behaviour shown at the end of training—different responding to the two different stimuli—is evidence that at this stage the subject can tell the

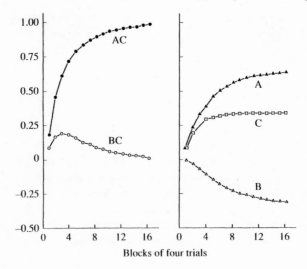

Blocks of four trials

Fig. 1.4   Results of a computation using the Rescorla–Wagner equation (p. 6) for discrimination training with alternating AC reinforced and BC non-reinforced trials. Negative values of V represent inhibitory learning. The right panel depicts the theoretical values of individual components; the left panel the resulting net values of the compounds. (After Rescorla and Wagner 1972).

stimuli apart. The absence of differential responding in the initial stages of training is open to more than one interpretation. One possibility is that the two stimuli were initially perceived as identical and that one effect of the training procedure was to bring about a change in the way in which they are perceived. Konorski (1967, pp. 93–5) refers to this possible process as 'discrimination', distinguishing it from Pavlov's differentiation, a term that he uses to refer to the process by which discriminated stimuli come to control different responses. The second possibility is that discrimination learning might be explicable solely in terms of this latter mechanism without recourse to Konorski's concept of 'discrimination', Such is the interpretation supplied by the standard associative model.

Consider the application of the Rescorla–Wagner model to the acquisition of a discrimination of the sort just described. The positive stimulus (A) and the negative stimulus (B) will have some features in common—both are sudden in onset, are equal in intensity and duration, and so on. We may lump all these common features together and call them stimulus C. The discrimination required, therefore, is between the reinforced compound AC and the non-reinforced compound BC. Applying the appropriate variants of eqn 1, above, tells us about the fates of A, B, and C as training proceeds. Figure 1.4 presents the results of this application over a series of alternating AC and BC trials. As the right-hand panel shows, stimulus A acquires excitatory strength with each reinforced trial, as does stimulus C. But C also experiences non-reinforced trials which reduce its strength and so, by the end of training when the AC compound has reached asymptote, the lion's share of the excitatory strength is governed by A. The presence of the (slightly) excitatory C stimulus on BC trials determines what becomes of stimulus B. Both stimuli experience a decrement in strength but B, which receives no reinforced trials, is reduced below its initial value of zero (i.e., B acquires inhibitory strength). The net effect of these changes is shown on the left of the figure. The AC compound steadily acquires associative strength until asymptote is reached; the BC compound acquires strength initially (perhaps enough to evoke some conditioned responding) but thereafter its net strength declines to zero. Although this analysis has made use of the Rescorla–Wagner (1972) model, Wagner's (1981) model can provide an equivalent account by supposing that in addition to the nodes representing A and B a third (C) node can exist. Neither interpretation requires the assumption that training changes the ability of the subject to tell the stimuli apart.

The application of associative theory to discrimination learning has a long history, and associative explanations have long been available for cases seemingly more complex than the 'successive' discrimination described above. In particular, Spence (1936, 1937), using a version of the standard associative model of which the Rescorla–Wagner model is a direct descendant, was able to supply a satisfactory explanation of the behaviour shown during 'simultaneous' discrimination learning. (In a typical simultaneous discrimination task, two stimulus-objects are presented simultaneously and approach to one but not the other results in reinforcement.) This behaviour is often complex. Rats learning a simultaneous visual discrimination may, during the pre-solution period, show systematic patterns of responding, perhaps always choosing the stimulus on the left for a series of trials, or reliably alternating between left and right. By taking into account the excitatory and inhibitory learning that occur to irrelevant stimuli (such as the cues defining the positions in which the relevant stimulus-objects are presented), Spence (1936) was able to model with some accuracy the behaviour actually shown by the subjects. The fact that simultaneous discriminations can be construed as requiring the subject to make a choice between alternatives in a way that successive discriminations do not required the introduction of no new principle. Spence assumed simply that the subject always approaches the alternative with the greater net associative value.

Spence's (1936) theory of discrimination learning was not without its problems. As Mackintosh (1983, pp. 247–9) has pointed out, it fails to predict correctly the relatively low value of associative strength acquired by stimulus C in a discrimination between AC reinforced and BC non-reinforced (see Fig. 1.3). But this is the sort of issue that the more modern versions of the standard associative model were explicitly designed to deal with, and these theories can be applied to simultaneous discrimination learning just as readily as can Spence's. It seems quite likely that experiments on discrimination learning might introduce complexities and new processes that are not present in studies of simple conditioning. But the basic facts of successive and simultaneous discrimination learning do not in themselves require us to introduce concepts other than those employed by the standard associative model. Evidence for such concepts must come from the investigation of other learning phenomena. It is time to turn to these.

1.2 Some perceptual learning phenomena

Those who have written on perceptual learning have often been unwilling to offer any brief definition of their topic (see, e.g. Gibson 1969; Walk 1978). Those who have done so have quickly gone on to hedge the definition with qualifications. Thus Epstein offers 'modifications of perception which have been attributed to learning' (Epstein 1967, p. 1) and immediately adds a list of perceptual phenomena that might seem to fall within this definition but are not to be regarded as instances of perceptual learning. He is no doubt aware that almost any example of learning could be interpreted as a case of perceptual learning under his definition—although our usual interpretation of Pavlovian conditioning, say, is in terms of the formation of a CS–US association, this is not the only account possible. The Pavlovian training procedure could be regarded as being one that, among other things, brings about a change in the way in which the CS is perceived. The change in the behaviour evoked by this stimulus might then be taken as evidence of such a perceptual change. (This is in fact just the analysis of conditioning offered by Woodworth (1947).)

It may be that a satisfactory definition of perceptual learning will emerge only in the context of a specific theory of perception and of the mechanisms of learning. To get the discussion under way it will be enough, for the time being, to define the general field by sampling some of the issues considered by those who have set themselves the task of reviewing the topic of perceptual learning (e.g. Wohlwill 1966; Epstein 1967; Gibson 1969; Walk 1978).

One set of issues that has received much attention from reviewers concerns the role of early experience in perceptual development. The notion that perceptual learning will be particularly important early in life (Hebb 1949) has promoted study of the perceptual abilities of the newborn and of the refinement of these abilities that occurs during the course of normal development. It has also generated studies in which experimental animals have been reared in controlled conditions: in enriched conditions with stimulus-objects added to the normal environment; and in conditions of deprivation, either total exclusion of stimuli in a given modality or with limited exposure to selected stimuli (see, e.g. Tees 1976). Special attention has been paid to imprinting and related phenomena because of the possible implication that

Poor research background

there might be critical periods early in life during which perceptual learning is particularly likely to occur.

It is not to be concluded from the emphasis given to early experience that adults are deemed to be incapable of perceptual learning—the skilled discrimination performance of tea-blenders and wine-tasters, often mentioned in this context, may be taken as evidence that they can. For the most part the rest of this book will be concerned with studies conducted with adult subjects, if only because analytical experiments designed to determine the mechanisms by which performance on perceptual tasks is modified are most easily conducted with such subjects. It is to be hoped, of course (and shortly I will present some grounds for this optimism) that the mechanisms revealed will be of general relevance.

Epstein's (1967) review of experimental studies of perceptual learning conducted with adult human subjects distinguishes three main types. First there are (the rather few) experiments that have attempted to demonstrate an effect of standard training procedures, the administration of reward and punishment, on perception. As an example, in a study by McNamara (1959), subjects were rewarded (verbally or with money) on occasions when they overestimated the separation between a pair of horizontal lines. Such subjects subsequently showed a tendency to overestimate when they were required to set the length of an adjustable horizontal line to match that of a given vertical line. It has proved difficult, for findings of this sort, to determine whether the effect is genuinely in the perceptual system or reflects the development of a response bias by the subject. This problem of interpretation is less evident in the second class of experiment considered by Epstein (1967).

Experiments of this second type are designed to investigate the 'acquired distinctiveness of cues' (Miller and Dollard 1941). The specific hypothesis put forward by them was that otherwise similar stimuli might acquire distinctiveness if the subject learns to respond with quite different names to them. Whatever the merits of this hypothesis (and Gibson (1969) puts forward a quite different interpretation for what she refers to a 'stimulus predifferentiation') it has provoked much experimental work. A typical example is the study by Ellis and Muller (1964)—although their result, which provided evidence for an acquired distinctiveness effect, has not been the universal outcome of such studies (see, e.g. Robinson 1955; Vanderplas and Garvin 1959). Subjects were exposed to a set of complex geometrical figures. Some learned to associate a different word with each figure; others simply observed the figures without labelling them. In a final test all the subjects were required to pick out the figures they had seen before when these were presented along with other similar but novel figures. Those who had learned the labels showed superior recognition performance.

Epstein's third category consists of experiments in which discriminative performance is assessed during or after mere exposure to the stimuli or stimuli like them. Human subjects may, of course, sometimes engage in labelling the stimuli in these circumstances but no explicit training is given to encourage this. An example of this type of experiment is that by Gibson and Gibson (1955), described above, although this example cannot be assumed to be typical, given the wide range of phenomena that mighty be included in this category. The McCollough effect, for example (the observation that the after-effect of exposure to a colour can become contingent upon the orientation of a pattern presented along with the colour (McCollough 1965) might also be taken as an instance. Perhaps more typical are the many instances, often involving 'visual illusions', in which exposure to a pattern of stimulation allows observers to come to see aspects or interpretations that previously they could not. (For example, see Leeper (1935); Ramachandran and Braddick (1973).)

This very selective sample is enough to make clear how disparate are the various phenomena that come under the heading of perceptual learning. It also makes clear that the procedures used in studies of perceptual learning are often quite remote from those used in traditional experiments on associative learning. This latter fact makes it difficult even to attempt to provide an associative analysis on many of the phenomena. Only the McCollough effect, with its dependence on the pairing of two stimuli (a colour and an orientation), fits readily into the associative framework, and associative explanations for the effect have indeed been proposed (e.g. Siegel and Allan 1985) and debated (Skowbo 1984). The absence of associative explanations for the other phenomena may indicate not that they are, in principle, incapable of being explained in these terms but rather that associative theorists have been unwilling to undertake the labour of attempting to redescribe these unfamiliar procedures in their own terms. The chief challenge to associative theory comes not from the specific findings of these experiments but from the general principles that they have been thought to reveal. We can distinguish two that appear to be particularly challenging.

1.2.1 Effects of discrimination training

According to some theories of perceptual learning, discrimination training serves not only to change the associations that underlie performance but also to modify the way in which the stimuli are perceived. This change in perception should be evident if the subjects are given some new test (a transfer test) involving the pre-trained stimuli. The problem with this experimental design is to ensure that the transfer observed is indeed the result of a perceptual change and not a direct consequence of such associations as may have been formed. Several strategies have been tried.

(a) The acquired distinctiveness of cues

Miller and Dollard's (1941) suggestion was first explicitly investigated in a classic and influential experiment by Lawrence (1949). Lawrence sought evi-

SIMULTANEOUS TRAINING

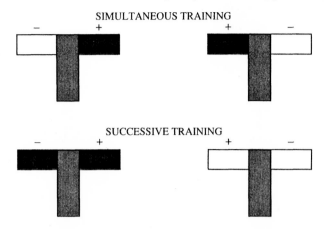

SUCCESSIVE TRAINING

Fig. 1.5 Schematic representation of the training procedures used by Lawrence (1949). In simultaneous training there are two possible dispositions of the cues and reward (+) is correlated with brightness. In the successive conditional procedure shown, choice of the right arm is rewarded when both are black and choice of the left when both are white. (After Sutherland and Mackintosh 1971.)

dence for the acquired distinctiveness of cues, using animal subjects and training procedures of the sort that Spence (1936, 1952) made the basis of his associative analysis. In simplified form, Lawrence's experiment was as follows. Rats in the critical experimental condition were trained on a simultaneous black–white discrimination, receiving reward for choosing one of the stimuli rather than the other. Control subjects received training on a discrimination between alternatives that differed in the texture of the flooring but were both painted mid-grey. For experimental subjects the floor texture was intermediate between the rough and the smooth values used for controls. The training given to the experimental subjects will, according to Spence (1936), establish a tendency to approach the positive stimulus (black, say) and to inhibit approach to the negative (white) and these tendencies will transfer to new tasks involving the same stimuli. But will there also be transfer on the basis of an increase in the discriminability or distinctiveness of the stimuli? In order to answer this question Lawrence devised a transfer test in which, it was argued, the specific associations acquired in the first stage would be irrelevant. The subjects were required to learn a conditional, successive discrimination. In this procedure, the alternatives between which choice was required on a given trial were not different in brightness. On some trials, both were black and response to the right (say) was rewarded; on other trials, both were white and response to the left was rewarded (Fig. 1.5). Thus, having a tendency to approach black rather than white would not aid acquisition of this new task, but an increase in the distinctiveness of black and white might do so.

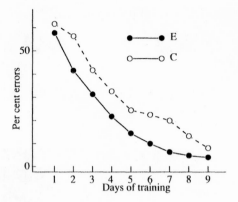

Fig. 1.6 Acquisition of a successive discrimination in Lawrence's (1949) experiment. All subjects learned one task, (say, brightness) with some other cues (e.g. differences in floor texture) present but irrelevant. For such a test, experimental (E) subjects would be pre-trained on a simultaneous brightness task (with no differences in flooring) and control (C) subjects on a simultaneous texture discrimination (with no brightness differences).

The results are shown in Fig. 1.6. Animals in the experimental condition learned the successive discrimination more readily than did controls. Several subsequent experiments (e.g. Jaynes 1950; Mackintosh and Holgate 1967), using versions of this general procedure, have confirmed Lawrence's finding (without necessarily endorsing his explanation, e.g. Siegel (1967).)

Lawrence's (1949) procedure attempted to distinguish between changes in the associative strength of cues and changes in their distinctiveness by changing the nature of the response required in the transfer test. An alternative strategy is to leave the response requirement the same in the two stages but to change the stimuli in such a way as to eliminate the effects of direct associative transfer. Thus, in an intradimensional shift, a subject might initially learn a discrimination between red and green and then be transferred ('shifted') to a blue–yellow discrimination. Generalization of associative strength from the original training cues might endow both blue and yellow with some strength but, with appropriately chosen hues, the two stimuli will not differ in strength. If distinctiveness is acquired in the first stage of training and if (as many theories suppose—Sutherland and Mackintosh (1971); Mackintosh (1975)) distinctiveness generalizes to similar stimuli, this will result in positive transfer from the first to the second discrimination. Such positive transfer has been reported from a range of experiments using both human (e.g. Uhl 1966) and animal subjects (e.g. Mackintosh and Little 1969).

A further strategy employed in attempts to distinguish associative transfer from transfer based on changes in distinctiveness merits brief mention. Reversal learning pits these two sources of transfer one against the other.

When a subject is required to learn the reversal of a pre-trained discrimination (that is, a task in which the previously positive stimulus becomes the negative, and vice versa) transfer based on associations will retard new learning. And indeed, subjects who come to a given discrimination task as a reversal are usually found to perform less well than others who come to it without prior training or after training on some quite different problem (e.g. Kelleher 1956). Interest has focused, therefore, on the observation that subjects given an extended period of training on the original discrimination can sometimes show more rapid reversal learning than those trained only to a moderate criterion of mastery in the first stage (e.g. Reid 1953). This result has been interpreted as showing that the perceptual change induced by discrimination training is so strongly established by overtraining that it can outweigh associatively based negative transfer. Although the conditions in which this overtraining reversal effect will occur are tightly circumscribed, its reality is well established (Mackintosh 1969) and has thus been widely cited as strong evidence that discrimination training does more than merely change associative strengths (e.g. Sutherland and Mackintosh 1971).

(b) Acquired non-distinctiveness

Lawrence's (1949) experiment concentrated on the possibility that discrimination training might enhance the distinctiveness of the relevant stimuli (black and white in Fig. 1.5). Might there not also be a change in the distinctiveness of those other cues that distinguish the alternatives but are not relevant to the solution of the problem? Lawrence's procedure specifically included such cues (the floor textures). But in any simultaneous discrimination task the alternatives differ in spatial position so that the cues in that define left and right are alternatives, being experienced equally often along with reward and non-reward. A number of theorists have supposed that such training might reduce distinctiveness, a supposition supported by demonstrations (e.g. Waller 1970) that learning proceeds rather slowly when previously irrelevant cues are now made relevant in a subsequent stage of discrimination training.

It is also possible to conduct 'irrelevance training' without concurrently training the animals on a soluble discrimination. In this procedure, sometimes called 'pseudodiscrimination' training (Honig 1969), subjects simply experience the same schedule of reinforcement in association with each of the cues. A good deal of the research on pseudodiscrimination training has concerned the possibility that it might modify the subject's level of general attentiveness (e.g. Thomas 1970). But there is some (e.g. Winefield 1978) to show that such training has a particularly deleterious effect on subsequent discrimination learning with the same cues made relevant. As the initial training could not be expected to generate a difference in associative strength between the cues, an explanation in terms of lost distinctiveness seems appropriate.

It is convenient to describe the pseudodiscrimination procedure in this context but strictly it is not an example of discrimination training because the training procedure is not one in which the critical stimuli are reliably associated with different schedules of reinforcement. The procedure could quite appropriately be categorized as an instance of exposure learning. This term is usually restricted, however, to cases in which no reinforcers are present during the initial stage of training. We shall consider examples of such learning next.

1.2.2. Exposure learning

The experimental work reviewed under this heading demonstrates that mere exposure to a stimulus can modify the behaviour that it evokes and the ease with which the stimulus is subsequently learned about in associative procedures. Evidently learning of some sort goes on during exposure and, as no explicit contingency is arranged between the target stimulus and other events during the exposure phase, the scope for explaining these effects in associative terms appears to be limited. The strategies that were required to distinguish associative from other forms of transfer in studies of the effects of discrimination training are less necessary here.

(a) Discrimination learning after stimulus exposure

An experiment by Gibson and Walk (1956) demonstrated positive transfer in rats given previous exposure to the stimuli used in a discrimination task. Subjects in the experimental condition were raised from birth in cages with white walls against which were displayed cut-out black metal shapes, triangles and circles. When they were 90 days old these subjects and control subjects that had not been exposed to the shapes were trained on a food-rewarded discrimination with triangles and circles as the relevant stimuli. The experimental subjects were markedly superior to the controls—15 of the 18 experimental subjects learned the discrimination within 150 trials of training whereas only 1 of the 11 control subjects did so.

Few of the subsequent attempts to replicate this finding have produced effect as dramatic as that reported by Gibson and Walk (1956) (see Hall 1980 for a review) but there seems no doubt that, when the conditions of exposure are right (in particular, when the stimuli are solid objects that the rats can manipulate; Bennett and Ellis (1968)), familarity with the stimuli will facilitate later learning. We can also specify some features of the original experiment that are not necessary for the effect to appear. First, although Gibson and Walk (1956) presented their study in the context of theorizing about the role of early experience in perceptual development (e.g. Hebb 1949), there is no reason to suppose that exposure learning is confined to immature animals. Hall (1979) conducted a study which confirmed that rats given

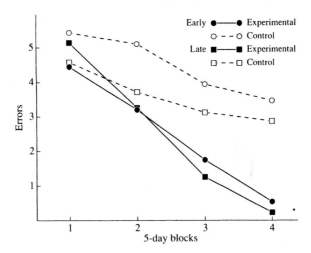

Fig. 1.7 Performance of four groups of rats in learning a discrimination between triangle and circle. The experimental subjects (that had received prior exposure to the stimuli) learned more rapidly than the control subjects, but whether exposure was given early or late in life made no difference. (After Hall 1979.)

exposure early in life (from 40 to 80 days of age) learned the discrimination, beginning at 80 days, more readily than control subjects of the same age (Fig. 1.7) But rats from the same litters that were allowed to grow to full adulthood before being exposed to the stimuli showed exactly the same effect. Second, exposure need not be continuous and prolonged. Channell and Hall (1981) found positive transfer in (adult) rats given exposure for just one hour a day for 40 days (Gibson and Walk gave exposure for 24 h a day for 90 days).

Although the reliability of the Gibson–Walk effect seems to be well established it should be mentioned here that there are a few experiments that are formally equivalent in design to those just discussed (although very different in details of procedure) but which have generated a quite different result. Chantrey (1972), using exposure procedures akin to those used in studies in imprinting, found that domestic chicks given prior experience of a pair of colours were in some circumstances less ready to learn a subsequent food-rewarded discrimination between these colours than were control subjects unfamiliar with the colours. (See also Bateson and Chantrey (1972); Stewart, Capretta, Cooper, and Littlefield (1977).)

(b) Simple conditioning after CS exposure

In contrast to some of the phenomena described above, the effect of prior exposure to the to-be-conditioned stimulus on classical conditioning is clear-cut: acquisition of the conditioned response is retarded. Fig. 1.8 shows

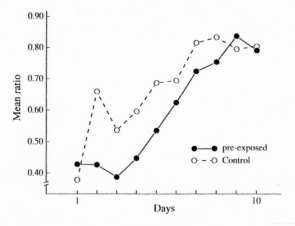

Fig. 1.8 Classical conditioning in rats given light–food pairings. The conditioned response is a tendency to approach the site of food delivery. As subjects sometimes make responses in the absence of the light, a ratio score is used; approaches in the presence of the light/total approaches. Animals that have received prior exposure to the light learn relatively slowly. (After Channell and Hall 1983.)

a typical example of the effect from an experiment using rats as the subjects (Channell and Hall 1983). One group of rats received, over six daily sessions of training, 60 presentations of a 30-s light with an average interval of 4 min between presentations. Control subjects had equivalent experience of the apparatus but no exposure to the light. Both groups then received training in which the light preceded the delivery of food. As the figure shows, control subjects readily acquired the CR. Pre-exposed subjects eventually reached the same asymptotic level of performance but the rate of acquisition was slow, especially over the early sessions of conditioning.

This 'latent inhibition' effect, as it has been called (Lubow and Moore 1959) has proved to be robust, having been demonstrated in a variety of species and for a wide range of stimuli and conditioning preparations (for reviews see Lubow (1973); Weiss and Brown (1974); Lubow, Weiner, and Schnur (1981)). And it is seen not only when the test phase involves excitatory conditioning but also in conditions that are likely, according to the associative theories described above, to produce inhibitory learning. Thus, Rescorla (1971) trained rats on a discrimination in which presentation of a light was followed by the reinforcer whereas presentation of a light-tone compound was not. The formation of this discrimination requires (according to the Rescorla–Wagner model, above p. 7) the establishment of an inhibitory connection between the tone and the US representation. Rescorla (1971) found that subjects given prior exposure to the tone learned the discrimination slowly (see also Reiss and Wagner 1972).

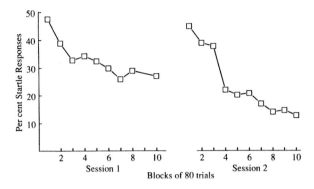

Fig. 1.9 The startle response of rats to a tone presented on average every 7.5 s in each session. There was an interval of 60 min between the sessions. (After Marlin and Miller 1981.)

(c) Habituation and related phenomena

Just as well established as latent inhibition is the phenomena of habituation—the reduction in the vigour or likelihood of a UR produced by repeated presentations of the US.* Figure 1.9 presents a typical set of results. Rats were presented on each of two sessions (separated by an interval of an hour) with a series of brief loud tones, occurring every 7.5 s on average. The behaviour measured was the rat's 'jump' or startle response. It declines in frequency over the course of the first session, recovers to some extent between sessions, and declines again during the second series of presentations. In other training preparations there is sometimes an initial increase in the likelihood of the response during the first few trials (Groves and Thompson 1970) but in all the ultimate result is a loss of responsiveness.

That habituation is not just a short-term, within-session phenomena is suggested by Fig. 1.9, which shows that, on average, the likelihood of a startle response was lower in the second session that in the first. Nor is it confined to stimuli that elicit defensive responses like the rat's startle response. Figure 1.10 shows the result of a study (by Kaye and Pearce 1987) in which rats received 12 daily, 40-min sessions during each of which a small light bulb was lit for 10 s, presentations of the light occurring at 6-min intervals. The rat's behaviour during these trials was observed and those occasions on which it turned toward the light were scored. The percentage of observation periods that included such a behavioural orienting response declined steadily

---

* This empirical definition will serve for the time being. In later chapters a more theoretical definition will emerge so that we may want then to regard habituation as a process that is just one of the factors determining the likelihood of occurrence of a UR.

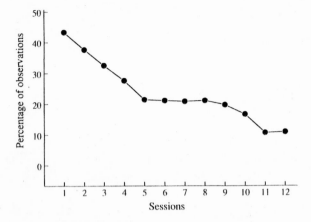

Fig. 1.10 Mean percentage of observations on which rats were recorded as orienting to a light. Sessions occurred daily and contained six presentations of the 10-s light occurring at 6-min intervals. (After Kaye and Pearce 1987.)

from day to day.* It may be noted that the training procedure used here is closely similar to those used in the first (exposure) phase of studies of latent inhibition and indeed Kaye and Pearce went on to show that the rats whose performance is depicted in Fig. 1.10 conditioned slowly when subsequently the light was paired with a reinforcer. The latent inhibition procedure has sometimes been seen as an indirect way of studying habituation in which a different measure is used—loss of effectiveness as a CS rather than loss of effectiveness as an US.

Habituation procedures have also been thought capable of modifying an animal's preferences (Zajonc 1968; Hill 1978). The most obvious instance here is that of avian imprinting in which chicks of a precocial species given exposure to a conspicuous object early in life will show filial responses toward that object and will, if given a choice, tend to approach it rather than some other (e.g. Bateson 1966; Polt 1969). But the effect is not limited to traditional imprinting procedures. Cross, Halcomb, and Matter (1967), for example, investigated the effects of exposing young rats to the works of Mozart and Schoenberg. When tested in a situation in which they could determine the sort of music they heard, those experienced with Schoenberg showed a slight preference for him and those familiar with Mozart showed a marked preference for him. (Musically naive rats show a tendency to choose Mozart rather than Schoenberg).

---

* The orienting response (OR) studied in this experiment is defined purely behaviourly. The relationship between this response and the complex of autonomic and other changes that characterizes the Pavlovian orienting reflex (Sokolov 1963) remains open at this point.

Sadly, but not surprisingly, most empirical work on the effects of exposure on preference has used non-musical stimuli. That done with rats as the subjects has concentrated on exposure-induced changes in taste preference. Rats given a choice between a familiar and a novel food reliably exhibit a preference to the familiar. This 'neophobia' is also evident when rats are presented with just one novel flavour. Domjan (1976) found that thirsty rats given access to water flavoured with saccharin will drink less than 5 ml when they experience it for the first time. But with repeated daily exposure, consumption rises and after about 10 days reaches the level (15–20 ml) shown by rats given unflavoured water throughout. This result is best interpreted as showing that the rat's unconditioned neophobic response will habituate; and the habituation of neophobia is enough in itself to explain why, in a choice test, rats prefer a familiar food over an unfamiliar food that still evokes the neophobic response. Neophobia is not confined to rats and flavours but is a feature of the behaviour of most species when confronted with novel stimuli of all kinds. It follows that changes in preference produced by pre-exposure to a stimulus are quite generally explicable as examples of habituation.

1.3. Conclusion

Although it is commonly identified with a certain set of training procedures (those used in studies of animal conditioning and in some investigations of human verbal learning), the notion of associative learning is a theoretical one. When we describe the results of these procedures in terms of the formations of associations we are subscribing to a theory of a particular type (a specification of which was given earlier in this chapter) that purports to provide an explanation for the results.

The position is rather different when we come to consider perceptual learning. This again is a theoretical term but in this case we lack a well-articulated specification of the theory. Instead we must define the area in terms of a set of phenomena—instances of learning in which perception appears to be modified and which use procedures that appear, at first sight, to be beyond the scope of current associative theories. The studies cited above as instances of perceptual learning are very disparate and have been brought together largely on procedural grounds. It might be felt, therefore, that some of these examples in fact reflect the operation of associative rather than perceptual processes, and indeed that no single principle of learning (perceptual or other) is likely to apply to all of them. Without a well-formed theory, however, it would be impossible to try to trim down the list so as to ensure that the only instances left are those involving 'true' perceptual learning. Rather, we must accept a definition of the field in terms of these phenomena. We can then proceed to investigate whether or not our first impressions were justified by attempting to apply associative theorizing to them. Some of them may succumb to an associative analysis but others may not. If so, we shall have to acknowledge that the association can provide a mechanism for some of the phenomena of perceptual learning. What new theoretical mechanism will be required to explain the rest remains to be seen.

What follows, then, is a detailed analysis of the various perceptual learning phenomena just described. Two chapters (5 and 6) are devoted to a consideration of the possibility that discrimination training might produce not only changes in the overt responses evoked by the trained stimuli, but also changes in the way in which these stimuli are perceived. The remaining chapters deal with the effects of non-reinforced exposure to a stimulus or stimuli. Chapter 7 concerns the effect of prior exposure to a pair of stimuli on a subject's ability subsequently to learn a discrimination between them. Chapters 2 to 4 deal with what is perhaps the simplest case of all—the effect of non-reinforced exposure to a single stimulus on subsequent conditioning (Chapters 3 and 4) and on the ability of the stimulus to evoke its UR (Chapter 2). This last case, that of habituation, has been little discussed in the context of perceptual learning but this neglect is inappropriate. If repeated exposure to a given event allows 'differentiation' to occur, then the effects of this process might be especially apparent in a simple training paradigm that offers little scope for other forms of learning to occur and interfere. I examine this possibility next.

2. Habituation

According to some interpretations, the apparently simple phenomenon of habituation depends on relatively complex processes of perceptual learning. The essence of the 'comparator' theory of habituation developed by Sokolov (e.g. 1963) (see also Konorski 1967) is that the repeated presentation of a stimulus allows the formation of a 'neuronal model' of it. When a stimulus is presented, a comparator looks for a match between the sensory input and a neuronal model. If there is no match, the response (Sokolov was concerned particularly with the behavioural and physiological orienting response, the OR) is triggered. But if the comparator detects a match the OR is inhibited. The neuronal model is held to encode all aspects of the stimulus and to become more precise with repeated stimulation. Accordingly, habituation is total only when a fully accurate model has been formed. It will be apparent that the process of forming an accurate neuronal model might be taken to be an instance of perceptual learning—the process of differentiation can be equated with the formation of a fully elaborated representation of a stimulus. This interpretation of habituation engenders the hope that a study of the phenomenon might be able to reveal a good deal about the mechanisms involved in perceptual learning. There are, however, alternative accounts available that attempt to explain habituation without recourse to the complexities of comparator theory. The central task in this chapter, therefore, is to assess the adequacy of these rival interpretations, to determine whether habituation does indeed depend on a process of stimulus differentiation. The best known of these rivals I shall refer to as S–R theory: the theory that habituation occurs simply because repeated presentation of a stimulus produces a decline in the efficiency of transmission in the direct pathway connecting stimulus (S) to response (R). Such an account has no place for subtle or elaborate changes in the nature of a central representation of the stimulus. Even so, to adopt this theory would be to concede too much for those committed to an entirely associative analysis of learning, based as it is on a non-associative change in the effectiveness of the S–R connection. Attempts have been made to supply associative accounts of the processes by which exposure to a stimulus can produce a relatively permanent change in its ability to evoke a response. I begin, therefore, by considering the possibility that habituation can be explained without departing in any major way from the basic tenets of the standard associative model before turning, in the second part of the chapter, to a direct comparison of traditional S–R and comparator theory.

2.1 An associative theory of habituation

A number of associative theories of habituation have been proposed (e.g. Stein 1966; Lubow, Weiner, and Schnur 1981) but the theory to be considered in detail here is derived from Wagner's (1981) version of the standard associative model. Öhman (1979) has proposed a conceptually similar account expressed in the terminology of human information processing, and Wagner himself originally (Wagner 1976, 1979) expressed the theory in rather different terms from those used subsequently. But the SOP (standard operating procedures) theory is very precisely formulated and leads to a number of clear predictions open to experimental test.

The starting point for the account is that a stimulus is assumed to evoke its unconditioned response (UR) because it induces A1 activity in its corresponding node (see Chapter 1, p. 9). Conditions that reduce the likelihood of elements in the node moving into the A1 state will reduce the likelihood of a UR. Of chief interest here are those circumstances that cause elements to enter the A2 state, since elements in this state are unable to move into A1. The A2 state can be brought about in two ways. First, elements in A1 are held to decay rapidly into A2, the probability of this decay being determined by the limitation imposed on the number of elements that can be maintained in A1. Second, inactive elements in a node will move directly into A2 when a conditioned stimulus (CS) having an excitatory link to that node is presented. A2 activity may itself evoke a response but it is assumed to be less effective in doing so than is A1 activity and that the response might be different in sign from that evoked by A1 (i.e. might be a compensatory response).

These assumptions supply two mechanisms by which habituation can occur. First, although the A2 state produced by the brief presentation of a stimulus will decay (the elements will return to the inactive state), it takes some time to do so. Re-presentation of the stimulus after a short interval will thus not evoke the UR since the nodal elements will not be able to move into A1. In other terminology, short-term habituation will occur because the short-term memory trace created by a previous occurrence of the stimulus is still active. Second, repeated presentation of the stimulus allows associative learning to occur. Excitatory links will be formed between the target stimulus and such other cues as are available—in the typical habituation experiment these will be features of the experimental apparatus or context in which the target stimulus is presented. Consequently, these CSs will evoke the A2 state in the node corresponding to the target stimulus and again the likelihood of a UR will be reduced. Long-term habituation will occur because the contextual cues will allow the retrieval of a representation of the target stimulus from long-term memory.

Although I have referred to Wagner's (1976, 1981) account as being an associative theory, it clearly has things in common with the other theories briefly mentioned above. The mechanism for short-term habituation is non-

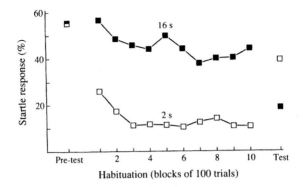

Fig. 2.1 Mean percentage of presentations of a tone that elicited a startle response in rats. Interstimulus intervals on the pre-test and the test varied from 2 s to 16 s for all subjects. Different groups experienced fixed intervals of either 2 s or 16 s during habituation. There was an interval of 60 s between the end of habituation training and the test. (Data from Davis 1970.)

associative and can be viewed as being a more elaborate specification of the S–R account since an important aspect is the decline in the effectiveness of the direct S–R pathway. And the mechanism for long-term habituation has been interpreted as being a version of comparator theory (Mackintosh 1987) because habituation occurs when an incoming stimulus proves to be one that is already represented in memory. None the less, there are clearly some important differences (not least the role given to an associative mechanism) and Wagner's theory generates a number of predictions (some of them unique) that we should consider next.

2.1.1 A preliminary evaluation

(a) Supporting evidence

Wagner (1976) sought support for his theory from three main classes of experiment. The first concerns the effects of varying the interstimulus interval on habituation. Davis (1970) investigated the startle response of rats to a brief tone. Different groups of subjects experienced 1000 presentations of the tone with an interstimulus interval of either 2 or 16 s. As has been found before (see Thompson and Spencer 1966), habituation was more rapid and more profound with the short interval (Fig. 2.1), a result consistent with the suggestion that the A2 state induced by the stimulus persisted from one trial to the next when the interval was short but dissipated between trials at the longer interval. If this account is correct it means that only in the group experiencing the 16-s interval did the stimulus repeatedly evoke a sizeable A1 state in its node. Only in this group, therefore, were the conditions appropriate for the formation of the associative link between the context and

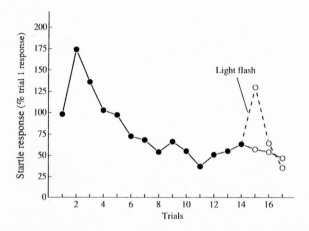

Fig. 2.2 Dishabituation of the rat's startle response. The averaged responding of two groups of subjects is shown for the first 14 presentations of a tone (expressed as a percentage of the initial level). One group received a light flash before trial 15, the other group did not and data are presented separately for these groups for the final three trials. (After Groves and Thompson 1970.)

the target stimulus that is supposed to generate long-term habituation. Figure 2.1 shows the results of a test in which the stimulus was re-presented after the subjects had been allowed a period of a minute without stimulation. On this test, habituation was more evident in the 16-s group than in the 2-s group (and the same pattern was found for other groups of subjects tested after a 24-h rest).

The second line of relevant evidence comes from studies of the effects of presenting a novel salient stimulus between habituation trials with the target stimulus. It is well established that an interpolated stimulus can have a proactive effect causing restoration of an habituated response (dishabituation) when it immediately precedes a trial with the target stimulus (see, e.g. Groves and Thompson 1970; Fig. 2.2). Wagner can explain this effect in terms of the limited capacity of the system—by establishing activity in its own node, the dishabituator limits the extent to which those elements in the target node that have recently been activated can remain active. They will tend to revert to the inactive I state, and the greater the proportion of inactive elements, the greater is the likelihood of a subsequent occurrence of the target stimulus evoking A1 activity and hence eliciting its UR.

Wagner's theory also anticipates that a dishabituating stimulus could have a retroactive effect, modifying the course of habituation when it is presented just after the target event. Whitlow and Wagner (reported in Wagner 1976) demonstrated this effect in a study in which rabbits received habituation training with two tones differing in pitch. A further stimulus (a visual–tactile compound) was also presented, scheduled so that it preceded each of the tones equally often but consistently followed only one of them. After a 15-min rest the two tones were presented again. It was found (Fig. 2.3) that the tone that had been followed by the dishabituator was more likely to evoke the UR (i.e. showed less evidence of long-term habituation). This result was interpreted as showing that the dishabituating stimulus could function as a 'distractor', limiting the extent to which the node corresponding to the target stimulus could stay in the A1 state, and thus limiting the growth of the context–target association responsible for long-term habituation.

The third set of observations to be considered concerns the suggestion that long-term habituation depends upon the presence of some cue that, by virtue of an associative link, ensures that the node representing the target stimulus is in the A2 state when the stimulus is presented. It would be possible to test this suggestion by conducting an habituation experiment in which the target stimulus is reliably preceded by some other and to note the size of the UR to the target on these trials and on test trials when the first stimulus is omitted. Such a training procedure is, of course, Pavlovian conditioning, and Wagner (1976) finds support for his account by noting that experiments on conditioning have sometimes revealed a 'conditioned diminution of the UR'—a decline in the amplitude of the response evoked by the US over conditioning trials that is eliminated when the US is presented alone (e.g. Kimble and Ost 1961). In habituation experiments, of course, there is no explicit CS and the training context assumes this role. For clear-cut, even

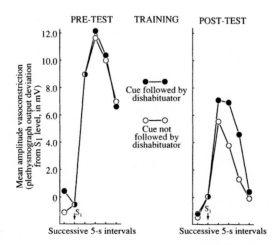

Fig. 2.3 Mean responses evoked in rabbits by each of two auditory cues before and after 16 habituation trials with each. The measure taken is the degree of vaso-constriction recorded in 5-s intervals before and after presentation of the 1-s tone. During habituation training one of the auditory cues was followed by a salient stimulus (the dishabituator). (After Wagner 1976.)

dramatic, evidence that the context can indeed function in this way we need to turn to a quite different habituation procedure—the development of tolerance to a repeatedly administered drug.

When it is injected for the first time, morphine evokes a range of reactions of which a reduction in general activity and a loss of sensitivity to pain are the most easily measured. With repeated exposure to the drug these reactions diminish so that increasingly stronger doses are required to achieve the same effect. A subject that has developed tolerance in this way will accept a dose of morphine that would kill a naïve animal. At the procedural level, the development of drug tolerance constitutes an example of habituation, a parallel that has been pursued at the theoretical level by Wagner and others (e.g. Baker and Tiffany 1985) (see also Eikelboom and Stewart 1982). In terms of Wagner's theory it is necessary to suppose that the various cues associated with the administration of the drug (including the context in which it is given) can come to function as CSs eliciting the A2 state and thus preventing the drug itself from eliciting A1 activity. And certainly, drug tolerance does appear to be context specific. Siegel, Hinson, Krank, and McCully (1982) gave rats a series of heroin injections in a distinctive room. Tolerance was evident in that most of the rats survived a subsequent heroin overdose administered in the same room. In contrast the same overdose proved fatal to a majority of the rats in a group that had received the same initial series of injections but had experienced them in a different room (see also Siegel 1977; Siegel, Hinson, and Krank 1978).

It may be noted that Wagner's (1981) theory (see also Paletta and Wagner 1986) embodies two mechanisms by which tolerance might be produced. The presence of conditioned A2 activity in the relevant node when the drug is injected restricts the ability of the node to enter the A1 state, thus ensuring conditioned diminution of the UR. And in addition, Wagner (1981) allows that the A2 state can produce a response opposite in sign to that evoked by A1. Thus the elicitation of a conditioned compensatory response (see Schull 1979; Siegel 1979) could also contribute to the observed effect.

(b) Analysis

Although consistent with it, the evidence cited above does not compel us to accept Wagner's (1976, 1981) model. Thus, with respect to the effects produced by varying the interstimulus interval, it is open to any theory of habituation to assume that the after-effects of a stimulus will be more evident when the interval is short, without proposing the existence of different mechanisms for short-term and long-term habituation.*

The superior retention of habituation seen after training with a relatively

---

* I shall continue to use the terms short term and long term but only as convenient labels to distinguish the effects seen in a given training session from the decline in responsiveness seen across widely spaced (e.g. daily) training sessions.

long interstimulus interval (Fig. 2.1) can be explained in a variety of ways (Mackintosh 1987). One possibility makes use of the notion of generalization decrement, the observation that stimuli similar to that used in training will tend to evoke the same response as that governed by the trained stimulus but will do so to a lesser extent. The effect was first demonstrated in Pavlovian conditioning but it is now well established that habituation to one stimulus will generalize only incompletely to a similar but different stimulus. Thus, for example, human subjects who have experienced presentations of a tone of a given frequency so that the OR has habituated will respond again when the frequency of the tone is changed (Corman 1967). Now a characteristic of each of the tones (but the first) heard by the 2-s group in the experiment by Davis (1970) was that it had been immediately preceded by another tone. The event to which habituation occurred, therefore, would be the tone that was physically present plus a contribution from the after-effects of the previous tone. The test stimulus presented after a rest interval would lack this latter feature and, being different from the trained stimulus to some extent, might prove able to evoke the UR. Generalization decrement would be less likely in Davis's 16-s group, for whom the test tones would be more similar to those experienced in training.

The phenomenon of dishabituation (the proactive effect of a novel salient stimulus) is no more decisive theoretically. The account offered by Groves and Thompson (1970) has been widely accepted (at least for the effects observed in experiments with non-human subjects; Stephenson and Siddle (1983)) and it makes no use of the limited-capacity mechanism central to Wagner's (1976) interpretation. Groves and Thompson make use of the notion of 'sensitization', suggesting that a salient stimulus will increase the subject's level of arousal and will thus potentiate the response to any subsequently presented event. It is not supposed that the process responsible for habituation is changed by the dishabituating stimulus (and thus the term 'dishabituation' is something of a misnomer); rather it is suggested that even a weak tendency to respond can show clearly in performance when amplified by a high level of arousal. The results shown in Fig. 2.2 have been taken as supporting this account. They show that it is not necessary to present the target stimulus again in order to restore the habituation disrupted by the presentation of a dishabituator. Habituation remains intact; all that is needed is for the sensitizing effect of the dishabituator to decay with the passage of time.

Wagner (1976, p. 116) is willing to allow that the strong (and often noxious) stimuli typically used as dishabituators might indeed have a sensitizing effect, but he does not regard this as invalidating his own interpretation. Both mechanisms may be involved. In order to assess the unique features of Wagner's theory we must turn to the other phenomena mentioned in the preceding section: the effects of distractors and the context-specificity of habituation. Wagner's theory is unique in giving a central role to the formation of a context–stimulus association and thus is unique in predicting that conditions likely to interfere with the formation or effectiveness of this association will influence habituation. We need, therefore, to examine these phenomena more closely both to determine the extent to which they are reliable and the extent to which they are not only predicted by Wagner's theory but actually require us to accept the interpretation offered by this theory.

2.1.2 The effects of distractors

(a) Post-trial distractors

The effect of a post-trial distractor in limiting the development of habituation (Fig. 2.3) has been sought in range of experimental preparations. In rats, the presentation of a salient novel stimulus will suppress ongoing behaviour (such as lever pressing for food or drinking from a water bottle); but after a few presentations of the stimulus this unconditioned suppression will habituate. If the target stimulus is presented followed by some other, it might be possible to see a return of unconditioned supression in a subsequent test session. Several experiments allow investigation of this possibility and their results have been uniformly negative (Szakmary 1977; Baker and Mercier 1982*a*; Mercier and Baker 1985; Honey and Hall 1988) (see also Pfautz, Donegan, and Wagner 1978); that is, animals that have experienced serial presentation of the two stimuli have been no more likely to show unconditioned suppression on the test than control subjects that received exposure to just the target or to uncorrelated presentations of the two events. Although unfortunate for Wagner's (1976) theory, these null results do not provide grounds for rejecting it. There are several reasons why a post-trial distractor might fail to attenuate habituation—the distractor would not be expected to exert much of an effect if it were insufficiently salient or if it were difficult for the subject to discriminate it from the target itself. Our analysis should concentrate, therefore, on an experimental procedure in which the distractor effect has been reliably demonstrated, the habituation of the rat's neophobic response to a novel flavour (Chapter 1, p. 27).

Figure 2.4 summarizes the results of an experiment by Green and Parker (1975). Rats were given initial exposure to a novel flavour (milk) and were then allowed a choice nine hours later between milk and water. Loss of neophobia was evident in the preference for milk shown by the control subjects who received no distractor. But subjects that were allowed to consume a second novel flavour (strawberry juice) shortly after their first experience of milk showed less of a preference. Equivalent results have been reported by others (e.g. Robertson and Garrud 1983; Shanks, Preston, and Stanhope 1986; Kaye, Gambini, and Mackintosh 1988). As Fig. 2.4 shows, the effect of the interpolated flavour was more marked the more closely it followed the first presentation of the target, a result to be expected if this flavour is func-

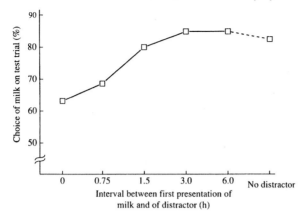

Fig. 2.4   Comsumption by rats of a target flavour (milk) on a test trial occurring 9 h after the first presentation of milk. When no distractor flavour intervened between the two trials, the level of consumption was high. Neophobia remained when a distractor closely followed the first trial. (After Green and Parker 1975.)

tioning as a distractor that interferes with the formation of a context–target association. Further evidence consistent with this position comes from the observation (Shanks *et al.* 1986) that a distractor with which the subjects are fully familiar does not interfere with habituation—a familiar distractor will establish A2 activity in its node and will thus not restrict the extent of A1 activity in the node of the target stimulus.

(b) Pre-trial distractors and compound pre-exposure

Presenting a distractor before the occurrence of the target stimulus should also, according to Wagner, disrupt the course of habituation. The presence of a distractor would limit the extent to which the nodes corresponding to contextual cues could move into the A1 state. Only a weak context–target association would then be formed. As a consequence, contextual cues alone would be unable to establish A2 activity in the target node and the target would be able to evoke A1 activity (and hence the UR) when presented on a test trial in the absence of the distractor.

Signalling the target stimulus in this way has, in fact, usually proved to be ineffective in disrupting habituation when stimuli other than flavours have been used (e.g. Marlin and Miller 1981; Mercier and Baker 1985) (but see also Lantz 1976). Thus, Marlin and Miller monitored the habituation of the rat's startle response to a brief tone (see Fig. 1.9). For one group of subjects each tone was preceded by 1 s by the offset of a light; a second group experienced presentations of this visual cue that were uncorrelated with the tone. Both groups showed the same degree of habituation on a test session given a day later in which the tone was presented alone. But, as was also true for studies of post-trial distractors, a different picture emerges when the stimuli are flavours. Several experimenters (Robertson and Garrud 1983; Kaye, Swietalski, and Mackintosh 1988a) have succeeded in finding a pre-trial distractor effect in studies of neophobia, although the exact conditions necessary for it remain a little unclear. In particular, Robertson and Garrud were able to find a disruption of habituation only when the distractor flavour was similar to the target flavour whereas Kaye, Swietalski, and Mackintosh (1988a) found that a dissimilar distractor produced even more disruption than did one that was similar to the target.

Although encouraging from the point of view of the analysis offered by Wagner (1976, 1981), these pre-trial distractor effects are open to an alternative interpretation. Mackintosh (1987) (see also Robertson and Garrud 1983; Kaye, Swietalski, and Mackintosh 1988a) has suggested an interpretation in terms of generalization decrement. We have already noted how the habituated response to an auditory cue will be restored when the stimulus is changed slightly. Similar effects are seen when neophobia is the target response. Domjan and Gillan (1976) found that familiarization with saccharin of a given concentration produced an attenuation of the neophobic response to solutions similar in concentration but not to solutions that were much stronger or weaker than the original. Now, in the experiments being considered here the stimulus presented on the test trial is supposedly identical to that used in training and no generalization decrement should occur. But, as Mackintosh (1987) points out, that different flavours can interact at a sensory or perceptual level is a fact of common experience. Experience of a distractor flavour immediately before exposure to the target might well alter the perceived taste of the latter. Neophobia will be fully attenuated only when the test stimulus is perceived as being the same as that presented initially; failure to generalize from the training to the test presentation would result in a return of the neophobic response.

The essence of this account is that the two flavours will interact so as to modify the qualities of the target. A distractor effect should be especially apparent, therefore, when things are arranged so as to maximize the extent of this interaction—when for instance the two flavours are presented together as a simultaneous compound. This case has not been investigated for flavour stimuli. James and Wagner (1980, experiment 3B), however, found that a single exposure to a light reduced the extent to which this stimulus suppressed the behaviour of rats licking at a water tube, but that exposure to a compound of light plus tone did not. Unfortunately, other experimenters using this same basic experimental procedure have found no difference between subjects exposed to a compound or to just the target element (Rudy, Krauter, and Gaffuri 1976; Mercier and Baker 1985) and James and Wagner (1980, experiment 2B) themselves failed to find the effect when the details of the way in which the stimuli were presented were changed.

These failures to find generalization decrement after compound pre-

exposure are perhaps not critical for the suggestion that generalization decrement plays an important part in the effect of a distractor on the habituation
of neophobia to a flavour—after all, it seems reasonable to assume that two
flavours might interact at the sensory or perceptual level in a way that a tone
and a light (say) might not. The absence of direct evidence on the habituation
produced when the target flavour is presented mixed with some other during
the pre-exposure phase is thus particularly unfortunate. There is, however,
one study, directed at a rather different issue, that does allow assessment of
the response shown to a single flavour (e.g. saline) in rats given previous
experience of a mixture of saline and saccharin (Gillette and Bellingham
1982). It was found that the subjects tended to shun the saline presented
alone although they consumed the compound quite readily. This effect was
found, however, only in subjects that had received extensive initial exposure
to the compound, a complication that requires further discussion (see below,
p. 60).

(c) Summary

The basic effects of a pre-trial distractor on habituation can be explained
both in terms of Wagner's (1976, 1981) theory and as instances of generalization decrement. In favour of the generalization decrement account it may be
said that the process being postulated is one that must be incorporated in
some form into any theory of habituation in order to deal with the dishabituation produced by a simple change in the stimulus (say from a low- to a
high-pitched tone). This account has the advantage of parsimony. But on the
other hand, it might be felt that the effects of post-trial distractors are not
explicable in terms of generalization decrement and that these effects follow
much more naturally from Wagner's account. Perhaps some new explanation can be offered that can incorporate the best features of both accounts. It
may be doubted, however, that a place will be found for the context–stimulus association as an important source of habituation. The experiments
reviewed in this section do not require us to use this notion; those discussed
in the next section of the chapter speak clearly against it.

2.1.3 Contextual effects in habituation

Distractor effects have relevance to the associative account of habituation
because it is argued that a distractor will restrict the growth of strength of a
putative context–stimulus association. A more immediate way of assessing
the role of this association is to manipulate directly the context itself.

(a) Transfer to a different context

There is no doubt that, in some circumstances, the presentation of a familiar
stimulus in a context different from that used for habituation training can
cause a restoration of the habituated UR. Figure 2.5 (a) summarizes the

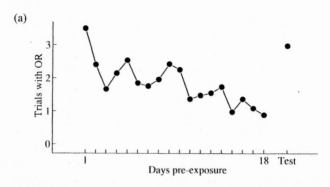

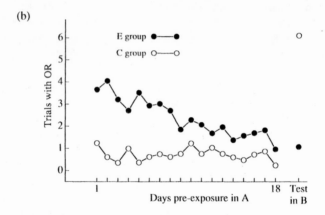

Fig. 2.5   Mean number of trials (out of 8 per day) on which rats showed an orienting response (OR) to a light (or, during pre-exposure for the C group, approached the unlit light bulb). In panel (a) all subjects received pre-exposure in one context and were tested in another. In panel (b) the subjects received two sessions per day, one in context A and one in context B, followed by a single test session in B. The E group experienced the light during pre-exposure in A. (After Hall and Channell 1985*b*.)

results of an experiment by Hall and Channell (1985*b*) in which the rat's orienting response to presentations of a 10-s light habituated over 18 daily sessions of exposure (each of eight trials) but was restored to its original level when the same stimulus was presented in a novel chamber that different from that used for training in its smell and the level of background noise. Figure 2.6(a) presents equivalent results from a quite different training procedure. It shows the habituation of the rat's neophobic response to a strong sucrose solution and the return of neophobia when the subjects were allowed access to sucrose in a new cage, different in size from that used in training and housed in a different room. (See also Archer and Sjödén 1979; Archer, Sjödén, and Nilsson 1985).

The context-specificity of habituation has also been demonstrated in less conventional experimental procedures. Evans and Hammond (1983) monitored the extent to which the recorded squeal of a rat will disrupt the behaviour of another licking at a water spout. They found that the habituated response of suppression of licking will reappear when the squeal is heard in a quite novel context. Peeke and Veno (1973) reported that the habituated aggressive response of a stickleback to a conspecific will return when the eliciting stimulus (another fish) is presented in a new position in the subject's tank. Shalter (1975) reports an equivalent effect for auditory and visual stimuli presented at different positions in the enclosure housing domestic fowl.

But not all attempts to demonstrate context-specificity in habituation have been successful. Thus Leaton (1974) and Baker and Mercier (1982a) found no restoration of the unconditioned suppression of ongoing behaviour evoked by an auditory cue when that stimulus was presented in a novel test chamber; Domjan (1976) found no return of neophobia to a flavour experienced in a training context when the flavour was subsequently presented in the home cage; habituation of the startle response studied by Marlin and Miller (1981) was found to transfer readily to a different test apparatus; and the orienting response (measured in terms of skin conductance changes) remains habituated when the target stimulus is presented along with different contextual cues (Churchill, Remington, and Siddle 1987). But these failures to find an effect pose no real threat to the suggestion that habituation depends upon the existence of a context–stimulus association. If the training

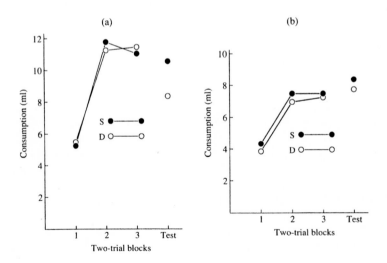

Fig. 2.6 Mean amount of sucrose solution consumed by rats on successive daily 15-min exposure trials and on a trial occurring in the same (S) or a different (D) context. In panel (a) the test context was novel for group D; in panel (b), group D was tested in a familiar context in which they had previously had no experience of sucrose.

and test contexts do not differ in ways that are readily discriminable by the subject (no matter how different they may seem to the experimenter), the test context will be perfectly effective in establishing a representation of the target stimulus and habituation will remain. Our analysis must concentrate on the positive findings.

(b) Interpretation

Although consistent with the associative account, demonstrations of the context-specificity of habituation are open to other interpretations. Two factors require discussion. The first is, again, the role of generalization decrement; the second concerns the response evoked by a novel test context itself.

Habituation could not be expected to transfer to a new context if the contextual change were to modify the nature of the target stimulus. In such circumstances, habituation would suffer generalization decrement. Some of the experiments cited above seem particularly susceptible to explanation in these terms. The contextual manipulation used by Archer and Sjödén (1979) included presenting the flavoured solution in bottles having different drinking spouts, a procedure likely to change some of the cues that constitute the complex referred to as 'a flavour'. (See Holder 1988; Sjödén and Archer 1988). Peeke and Veno (1973) found a reliable restoration of the habituated response by presenting the stimulus in a different position only when the test stimulus was an unfamiliar fish, perhaps a minor stimulus change for us but possibly a major one for a stickleback. And in Shalter's (1975) experiments it is easy to construe the test procedure as involving a change of stimulus rather than a change in context—a black object moving across the bird's enclosure at floor level (the test stimulus) can be regarded as a different stimulus from that used in training (a black object moving at ceiling level).

Wagner's (1976, 1981) theory proposes that dishabituation will occur when the target stimulus is presented in a context discriminably different from that used for habituation training. In the experiments discussed so far the test context has been quite novel but Wagner's theory predicts that dishabituation should be seen even when the test context is familiar, provided that the target stimulus has not previously been encountered there. Further experimental results provide a disconfirmation of this prediction. Figure 2.5(b) presents the results of a second experiment by Hall and Channell (1985b) on habituation of the behavioural orienting response in rats. It is identical in every way to that just described except that in this experiment the subjects received two sessions per day during habituation training, one of exposure to the light in the training context, the other of exposure to the context to be used in the test with no presentations of the light. As the figure shows, presenting the light for the first time in the familiar test context produced no dishabituation.

Figure 2.6(b) shows the results of a formally identical experiment using the flavour–neophobia paradigm. The procedure was the same as that used to generate the results shown in panel (a) of the figure except that, again, the subjects also received a daily session of exposure to the context to be used for the test. Neophobia did not reappear on the test session. (It may be noted that Domjan (1976) similarly found no evidence for the context-specificity of habituation when he used the rat's home cage as the test context, a place with which they were presumably fully familiar.) The null results (the failures to find dishabituation) shown in Figs. 2.5 and 2.6 derive their importance from the fact that they cannot be explained away by supposing that the contexts used in these experiments were not discriminably different to the subjects. The fact that dishabituation does occur when the test context is unfamiliar constitutes clear evidence that the rats could tell the two apart.

We may conclude that habituation is not context-specific in the way required by Wagner's associative account. This is not to say that context--target associations are not formed during habituation training. There is abundant evidence that the repeated presentation of a shock US (Randich and LoLordo 1979; Baker, Singh, and Bindra 1985) or of food (e.g. Rescorla, Durlach, and Grau 1985) in a given experimental apparatus will endow that context with the ability to evoke CRs. Thus, Rescorla *et al.* (1985) report that pigeons given a series of food deliveries in one distinctively coloured Skinner box but not in another come to show high levels of general activity in the first box but not in the latter, an effect indicating that a context–food association has been formed. (See also Marlin 1982, 1983.) There is no reason to doubt that an equivalent association will be formed between the context and the stimulus used as the target event in a study of habituation; what we may doubt, however, is that this association plays a critical role in habituation.

(c) The effects of novel contextual stimuli

It remains to explain why presenting a familiar stimulus in a novel context should bring about a restoration of its habituated response. One possibility offered by Hall and Channell (1985*b*) (see also Mackintosh 1987) is that the effect might be functionally equivalent to the dishabituation seen when a discrete novel stimulus is presented just before an habituated target stimulus. That effect was explained (p. 35) by suggesting that the dishabituating stimulus raises the subject's general level of arousal, amplifying the weak response-tendency controlled by the target stimulus. It requires no great leap of faith to accept that a novel context might also be capable of raising an animal's arousal level. One feature of the results displayed in Fig. 2.5 might seem to cast doubt on this interpretation: the control (C) group in (b) showed an especially high level of response when first presented with the stimulus in a fully familiar environment, a finding that has been confirmed in subsequent studies (Hall and Schachtman 1987). That is, the initial level of the OR was elevated when the stimulus was presented in a context that must be assumed to be not very arousing. The effect can be readily explained, however, if it is accepted that pre-exposure to the context permits the habituation of exploratory responses evoked by the contextual cues themselves. The loss of these responses, which would otherwise compete with the OR to the light, could be enough to allow a high level of orienting to be seen.*

An alternative explanation for the dishabituation seen in a novel context makes use of the notion of 'relative novelty' (e.g. Berlyne 1960; Mitchell, Kirschbaum, and Perry 1975; Lubow, Rifkin, and Alek 1976; Mitchell, Winter, and Moffitt 1980) (see also Hall 1980). According to the version presented by Lubow *et al.* (1976), a stimulus will elicit its response not only when it has absolute novelty (i.e. has never been encountered before) but also (or even especially) when it has relative novelty—when it is a familiar event presented in an unfamiliar context or a novel event presented in a familiar context. The stimuli most effective in evoking ORs in the experiments depicted in Fig. 2.5 were those with a high level of relative novelty.

The evidence that might allow choice between this suggestion and the simpler suggestion (that contextual novelty acts to potentiate responding) is sparse and conflicting. Both accounts agree that a familiar stimulus in a novel environment is likely to evoke its response and both can accommodate the finding that a novel stimulus in a familiar environment is likely to be especially effective—the arousal theory by way of the assumption that competing responses evoked by the context will themselves habituate; the relative novelty theory because of the contrast in familiarity between the stimulus and the context. An adequate test requires the use of a training situation that allows for the possible role of competing responses. Mitchell *et al.* (1980) found that rats given a choice between saccharin solution and water in an environment with which they were fully familiar showed a more marked neophobic response to the novel saccharin than did subjects receiving the test in an environment with which they were less familiar. It is difficult to see how this difference in preference could be engendered by differences in the extent to which the contextual cues evoke competing responses, and Mitchell *et al.* conclude that their result demonstrates the effect of a contrast in familiarity between target and context (see also Sheldon 1969). But two experiments (Kurz and Levitsky 1982; Hall and Channell 1986, experiment 2) have monitored the consumption of a flavoured solution by rats in a novel

---

* This account should be distinguished from that of 'optimal arousal' theory (e.g. Dember and Earl 1957; Berlyne 1960; Mitchell, Koleszar, and Scopatz 1984) that animals seek to maintain an optimal level of arousal and that the tendency to approach or avoid any given stimulus depends both on how novel that event is and the current level of arousal. Optimal arousal theory predicts that a subject familiar with its environment would tend to approach and investigate a novel event presented in that environment but it cannot accommodate the observation that presenting a familiar stimulus in a novel environment reinstates the unconditioned response to that stimulus whether this response be an avoidance (neophobia) or an approach (the OR).

or a familiar context. Both found that consumption was less in the novel context (see also Welker 1959; Bolles and Rapp 1965; Braveman 1978) but failed to detect any effect of whether or not the flavour had been experienced previously; that is, they found no sign of a relative novelty effect. The process by which a novel context has its effects must therefore remain unresolved for the time being.

(d) Compensatory responses

The discussion so far has been concerned to establish that habituation is not context specific in the way required by Wagner's (1976, 1981) account of long-term habituation. It is not disputed that context–stimulus associations can be formed and that the context can thereby come to evoke a CR. It follows that, should the CR be of a type that tends to oppose or compensate for the effects of the US, a diminution in the size of the UR will be observed. We can accept that the development of tolerance to a drug might depend upon the conditioning of a compensatory response to the context without adopting an associative account of habituation more generally.

It is possible that the acquisition of a compensatory CR might play a role when USs other than drugs are employed. Evans and Hammond (1983) found that habituation of the response to an artificial auditory stimulus generalized across contexts but that the UR to the squeal of a rat returned when testing occurred in a different context, even when the test context was one with which the subjects were familiar. Mackintosh (1987) has interpreted this result by suggesting that the compensatory response mechanism is likely to operate only for potent stimuli. The loss of responsiveness to stimuli that elicit only a startle response or an orienting response may be taken to reflect 'true' habituation and will not be context-specific. But the loss of responsiveness to an event of motivational significance (such as the squeal of another rat) will depend upon the acquisition of a compensatory CR which, like any other CR, will be elicited only when its CS (the appropriate context) is present.

Whatever the merits of the opponent–process account, it remains to establish that it provides a complete explanation for the context-specificity of drug tolerance. Wagner's (1981) theory supposes that a drug will be less effective when it is experienced in the usual context not only because the context elicits a compensatory response (by way of establishing the A2 state in the relevant node) but also because the existence of A2 activity prevents the node from moving into the A1 state. Paletta and Wagner (1986) have presented evidence intended to demonstrate the reality of both these processes.

Paletta and Wagner first monitored the URs evoked by an injection of morphine. They found it to produce an initial analgesia that waned after two hours or so, and also a change in the level of general activity that had a biphasic pattern—there was an initial reduction in activity followed, after about six hours, by a period of hyperactivity. They interpreted this pattern as implying that the A2 state remaining when the immediate effects of the drug have worn off evokes a response of opposite sign to that evoked by the A1 state only in the activity measure. It follows that tolerance as indexed by a reduction in the drug's ability to reduce activity might be the consequence of a conditioned compensatory response. The reduction in the drug's ability to produce analgesia, however, must be interpreted as an example of conditioned diminution of the UR.

The critical test of this interpretation is to present the contextual cues assumed to be controlling any compensatory CR in the absence of morphine itself. These cues should be capable of evoking hyperactivity, and this is what Paletta and Wagner found. More critically, these cues should not evoke any compensatory tendency toward hyperalgesia and unfortunately here is a conflict of evidence on this point. Paletta and Wagner found no hyperalgesia whereas Siegel and his collaborators (e.g. Krank, Hinson, and Siegel 1981) have consistently demonstrated the effect. Paletta and Wagner discuss possible reasons for the discrepancy; but until the matter is settled we must withhold judgement.

2.1.4 Conclusions

Wagner's (1976) associative account of long-term habituation predicts that distractors will disrupt the development of habituation and that habituation will be context-specific. Both these predictions turn out to be upheld in some circumstances, but a detailed examination of the evidence shows that the mechanisms involved are unlikely to be those envisaged by Wagner. Most distractor effects can be economically explained by making use of the notion of generalization decrement; contextual effects by noting that contextual change will influence the subject's level of arousal (although the role played by compensatory CRs must also be acknowledged). There seems no evidence, therefore, to support the suggestion that habituation depends on associative processes (at least in the form that these processes are supposed by Wagner to take—another interpretation of the role of associative mechanisms will be offered in Chapter 8). But to reject this associative account does not lead us to accept that habituation depends on the formation of a complex neuronal model; for an elaborated version of the S–R theory has no difficulty in accommodating most of the findings just described.

2.2 S–R and comparator theories

In the 'dual process' version of S–R theory advanced by Groves and Thompson (1970) (see also Thompson and Spencer 1966), the effects of stimulation are held to depend on two independent processes. One is the habituation process responsible for a decline in transmission along the direct S–R pathway; the second is a sensitization process which produces a change in the 'state' of the organism—an initial increase in the general level of activation that declines with repeated presentation, provided that the stimulus is not very intense. The operation of this sensitization process provides a ready explanation for some of the contextual effects described above. And although the theory says nothing about the effects of competing responses evoked by contextual cues or of the possibility that contextual cues might come to function as CSs, there is no reason why it should want to disallow them.

Dual process theorists are also happy that the effects of habituation training should generalize to some extent to other stimuli (Thompson and Spencer (1966) list generalization among the defining features of habituation). The phenomenon is most readily dealt with by conceptualizing the stimulus as consisting of a set of features or elements each of which has its own pathway to the response (and to the state system). After prolonged training, each of these S–R pathways will be non-functional. A different but similar stimulus can be regarded as one having some elements in common with the original stimulus. These common elements will not evoke responding, but the paths between each unique stimulus element and the response-generating mechanism will still be functional and some degree of responding is therefore to be expected. There will be some generalization of habituation, however, since the common elements will not be able to contribute their share in evoking the response. This account of generalization and generalization decrement (which is by no means unique to theories of habituation) can be applied with success to many of the phenomena described in the preceding section of the chapter.

My concern in the rest of this chapter is to determine whether or not this seemingly simple theory can supply a comprehensive account of habituation; or will there be a need to turn to the apparently more complex comparator theory with its neuronal model as a representation of the stimulus and its postulate of a special mechanism that compares representation with input? In order to resolve this issue it is necessary to clarify the important ways in which the two theories differ, for some of the more obvious differences turn out to be merely verbal. It is, in fact, an easy matter to redescribe the basic S–R account in the language of comparator theory. The 'representation' (or 'model') that is established by exposure to a stimulus will consist of that set of S–R pathways that have come to conduct less readily than they did before (Thompson, Berry, Rinaldi, and Berger 1979). And the likelihood of a response occurring depends on the outcome of a comparison between the representation and the input. A match may be said to occur when the stimulus elements presented correspond to the set of S–R pathways previously stimulated; and a mismatch occurs when some of the elements fall outside this set.

What distinguishes the two theories is the different sorts of representation they assume. The neuronal model of traditional comparator theory can be assumed to be capable of encoding complex, higher-order features of the stimulus; that embodied in S–R theory encodes only that certain stimulus elements have been encountered. Factors that change the S–R representation can do so in only one way, by influencing the degree to which the S–R pathway is more or less effective—extra training, for instance, will make the pathway less effective. But the neuronal model can change in other ways. It may be supposed, for example, that initial exposure to a stimulus might establish a model that represents only the more general features of the stimulus but that extra training would allow an increasingly detailed and accurate model to be formed. The representation proposed by S–R theory will vary only in its 'strength' whereas the *nature* of the information contained in a neuronal model can be expected to change according to circumstance.

Evidence that might allow us to choose between these interpretations has been sought in studies of dishabituation. Both theories suppose that when habituation generalizes to a test stimulus this implies that the test stimulus matches the representation. A failure of generalization (i.e. dishabituation), therefore, by showing that the test stimulus does not match the representation, should allow us to make inferences about the information encoded in that representation. The most direct evidence on this issue comes from experiments in which a stimulus different from that used in training is presented on test; these experiments will be discussed shortly. But also relevant are studies in which habituation fails to transfer to a test stimulus that is nominally identical to the training stimulus, and the ability of distractors to produce this outcome will be reconsidered. Before any of this, however, we should consider the special case in which the test 'stimulus' is the complete omission of an event. Some (e.g. Gray 1975; Stephenson and Siddle 1983) have laid particular emphasis on this procedure as a means of distinguishing among theories.

2.2.1 Dishabituation by stimulus omission

According to the S–R account, dishabituation will occur only when the input activates S–R pathways that have not undergone habituation. But comparator theory, it has been asserted, can predict the finding that the habituated response to a regularly presented stimulus will reappear (at approximately the time when the stimulus should have occurred), if one presentation is omitted entirely (e.g. Sokolov 1963). This result may seem to indicate that the representation formed during training is a complex one, incorporating information about the temporal properties of the training procedure. Such a result, it is suggested, requires us to adopt the neuronal model of comparator theory and to reject the S–R alternative. Closer inspection reveals, however, that the phenomenon of dishabituation by stimulus omission is less theoretically decisive than it might at first appear.

First, although the finding seems compatible with the spirit of comparator theory (in that a response occurs when there is a mismatch between input and some model of the environment derived from past experience), it is less clear that current versions of the theory can actually predict it. We can allow that the neuronal model formed during habituation training might incorporate information about the timing of stimuli and thus might detect a mismatch between the model and the stimulating environment when a stimulus is omitted. But it is not usually supposed that this mismatch itself generates the response. Rather, it is the existence of a match that acts to inhibit the response that some incoming stimulus would otherwise have evoked. In this case there is no incoming stimulus and there should therefore be no response. Comparator theory would need to be elaborated in some way in order to explain a missing-stimulus effect, just as would the S–R theory.

Before making any attempt to elaborate the theory to deal with this problem it will be well to consider whether the empirical data merit the effort. For, although the missing-stimulus effect has been widely discussed, there are no more than three or four fully documented studies of the phenomenon (see Siddle, Stephenson, and Spinks 1983, for a review; Foreman and Thinus-Blanc 1987) and these have given equivocal results or have failed to find any effect at all.

What is not in dispute is that omission-induced dishabituation can be observed when subjects are given habituation training with a pair of stimuli, say a tone followed by a light, and are then given a test trial in which the tone occurs but the light is omitted. In these conditions human subjects will show a skin conductance response following the tone when the light should have been occurring (e.g. Siddle 1985; Siddle, Booth, and Packer 1987).* Equally clear is that this finding does not, in itself, constitute strong evidence against an S–R account. In initial training the subjects experience a tone and a light that is compounded with any after-effects that the tone might generate. On the test trial they experience, for the first time, the after-effects of the tone in the absence of the light. Thus the subjects receive training with what is effectively a simultaneous compound (light plus after-effects) and are tested with just one component of the compound. To the extent that generalization decrement occurs in these conditions, responding can be expected to reappear. It is true that one component of the compound (the after-effects of the tone) is present both during training and on the critical test trial, but the S–R theory is quite at liberty to suppose that this component is perceived slightly differently (contains somewhat different elements or features) when the light is present and when it is absent, and that the novel elements occurring on the test trial will elicit some response.

---

* It has also been found that the light generates a particularly marked response on the next trial on which it occurs (Siddle, Remington, Kuiack, and Haines 1983). This outcome is not predicted by our current theories and its explanation remains obscure (see also Siddle, Bond, and Packer 1988).

It is worth adding that this same line of argument could allow S–R theory to supply an explanation (should one be necessary) for the dishabituation produced by the omission of a regularly repeated simple stimulus. This stimulus too can be thought of as being a compound, consisting of the event itself plus whatever cues arise from the fact that an identical event has been presented say 10 s earlier. In this case the absence of the external stimulus must be supposed to modify the nature of the cues produced by the previous trial, giving rise to some novel feature that might be capable of evoking a response. If it is thought that such a mechanism would be likely to generate only a weak response and that only in ideal circumstances, then remember that this is just what the experimental results seem to show.

2.2.2 Distractor effects reconsidered

We have already noted how the principle of generalization decrement can supply a ready explanation for the effects of a pre-trial distractor (or of the effects of training with a simultaneous compound stimulus) in attenuating habituation. The essence of the explanation is that the test stimulus, although nominally identical to that presented in training, will in fact be slightly different because the distractor will modify the way in which the training stimulus impinges on the animal. A mismatch of this sort is quite compatible with the sort of stimulus representation proposed by S–R theory. Training will modify one set of S–R pathways. The test stimulus will contain some novel features that will be capable of activating fully functional S–R pathways. It is not clear, however, whether this S–R interpretation can handle the effects produced by post-trial distractors.

An attempt to explain even post-trial distractor effects in terms of generalization decrement has been offered by Mackintosh (1987) (see also Kaye, Gambini, and Mackintosh 1988), who suggests that experience of a distractor flavour immediately after a target flavour might alter the remembered taste of the latter. The stimulus presented on the test trial would thus differ to some extent from that subjected to habituation training and the UR might be restored. The justification for referring to this possibility as generalization decrement appears to be that here, as in the other cases we considered previously, the UR returns because of a change in the nature of the effective stimulus. It is important to acknowledge, however, that the mechanisms that must be responsible for such generalization decrement will be rather different from those envisaged by orthodox S–R theory.

In the S–R theory, generalization decrement occurs when the test stimulus activates a different set of S–R pathways from those activated by the original. But a given target stimulus will activate a given set of pathways whether or not it is about to be followed by a distractor. Without modification or extension the S–R theory does not expect the post-trial distraction procedure to result in generalization decrement. One possibility is suggested by the

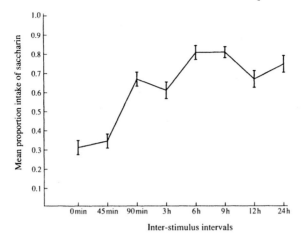

Fig. 2.7 Mean (± SE) proportion of intake that consisted of saccharin solution in rats allowed to choose between saccharin and water. The subjects had received brief exposure to saccharin at various intervals before the choice test. (After Green and Parker 1975.)

results of a study by Green and Parker (1975, experiment 1), who gave rats a brief exposure to a saccharin solution and then tested different groups on their choice between saccharin and unflavoured water, either immediately or after a range of retention intervals ranging from 45 min to 24 h. The results (Fig. 2.7) showed that the neophobic response decreased (i.e. habituation appeared to grow stronger) as the retention interval was increased, at least for intervals of less than 90 min. (See also Nachman and Jones 1974; Bond and Westbrook 1982; Bonardi, Guthrie, and Hall 1991.)

The incubation effect shown in Fig. 2.7 suggests a possible explanation for the effects of a post-trial distractor. Incubation of habituation may occur because the retention interval allows the subject to rehearse, in some way, the features of the stimulus presented on the exposure trial, thus effectively increasing the amount of training it receives. This seems particularly likely when the stimulus is a flavour that will linger for some time in the subject's mouth. The presentation of a further flavour as a post-trial distractor will, of course, directly eliminate this possibility. Perhaps, then, subjects given a distractor show less evidence of habituation simply because they have had less experience of the target stimulus.

There are several reasons to doubt this account. First, it relies on an interpretation of the results shown in Fig. 2.7 that is far from secure. These results may be the product of a process of incubation but other explanations are available (see Bonardi *et al.* 1991). One possibility is that the initial exposure to saccharin produces a short-lived sensitization that will, after a short retention interval, enhance the exhibition of such neophobia as

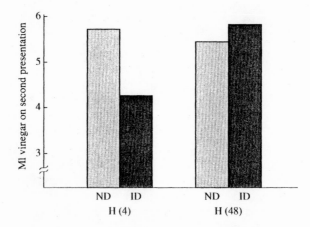

Fig. 2.8   Consumption of a target flavour on a test trial occurring 4 h (H(4) groups) or 48 h (H(48) groups) after the initial presentation. ID groups experienced a distractor flavour immediately after the training trial; ND groups did not. (After Kaye, Gambini, and Mackintosh 1988.)

remains unhabituated but will have dissipated (allowing habituation to be seen) at longer intervals. Alternatively, the fact that exposure to saccharin will leave a bitter aftertaste might contribute to the effect. A second (test) presentation of saccharin given while the subjects are still experiencing the aftertaste of the first might be perceived slightly differently from one given much later. The latter would be perceived accurately and habituation would be evident; the former would suffer from generalization decrement and neophobia would still occur. This second alternative implies that the incubation effect may be less likely when a flavour other than saccharin is used; and an experiment by Kaye, Gambini, and Mackintosh (1988) (Fig. 2.8) found no sign of the effect when rats exposed to vinegar were tested again after 4 or 48 h.

The results reported by Kaye *et al.* (1988) present a further problem for the attempt to devise a simple S–R account of post-trial distractor effects. They included groups that experienced a distractor flavour immediately after their first exposure to vinegar. The distractor abolished the habituation that was otherwise evident when the target flavour was re-presented 4 h later; but when the test occurred 48 h later, habituation was seen both in subjects that had experienced the distractor and in control subjects that had not. Now if the distractor has its effects by truncating some rehearsal process initiated by the first presentation of the target, these effects should be seen whatever the retention interval.

The explanation offered by Kaye, Gambini, and Mackintosh (1988) for the basic post-trial distractor effect can be extended to accommodate these results. Presentation of a post-trial distractor, they suggest, will modify the representation of the target event and thus attenuate habituation which depends on the test stimulus being identified with that remembered from the training trial. The effect of the distractor will be evident only after a short interval, however, because when the interval is long the precise details of the target will have been forgotten (perhaps simply as the result of a decay process) both in subjects that have experienced the distractor and those that have not.*

The representation required by this account must be rather more complex than that implied by basic S–R theory. In particular, it must be assumed that the representation established by exposure to a pattern of stimulation will initially include information that will be lost over time (or become unavailable), either because of some process of decay or because of interference from other events. After this loss, only some, rather general, features of the initial pattern of stimulation will remain. Here then is a result that encourages us to suppose that the nature if the information encoded in the representation can change. For further evidence we may turn to direct studies of the effects of imposing a retention interval between training and test.

2.2.3 Generalization after a retention interval

(a) In habituation

An apparently straightforward implication of the view that the nature of the representation established by habituation training changes over time is that there should be less evidence of habituation when the original stimulus is re-presented after a long interval. Unfortunately the empirical data relevant to this issue are inconsistent and their theoretical analysis turns out to be anything but straightforward. It will be recalled that habituation can often show spontaneous recovery (Fig. 2.1 above) but this effect need not be interpreted as indicating a loss of information from the representation; rather it may be a simple case of generalization decrement with the stimulus presented at the beginning of the test session possessing features that were not present in the stimulus that was thoroughly habituated at the end of the training session. Evidence for spontaneous recovery in studies of long-term habituation is harder to come by. Although Hall and Schachtman (1987) found a recovery of the habituated OR in rats after a retention interval of 14 days, Leaton (1974) found no loss of the habituated UR of suppression to a tone in rats tested up to 21 days after the end of training, and only a very small recovery in subjects tested after 42 days. In flavour neophobia, we have already noted that habituation can sometimes show 'incubation' rather

---

* This analysis leads to the prediction (not confirmed by the results shown in Fig. 2.8) that the UR should return when a lengthy delay is interposed between training and the test. It must be presumed, therefore, that in this experiment some other factor was operating to increase fluid consumption in the groups tested after 48 h.

than 'forgetting' over relatively short intervals; and over longer intervals (24–30 days), perfect retention has been observed (Siegel 1974; Domjan 1977). Only at a very long interval (75 days) was Domjan (1977) able to detect a return of neophobia in his rat subjects.

Perhaps a detailed analysis of these and of related experiments would reveal what conditions must be met if a loss of long-term habituation is to be observed. But such an enterprise is unlikely to yield theoretical dividends since all theories of habituation expect that there will be conditions (e.g. after very extensive initial training) when forgetting of habituation will be difficult to detect. And all can accept that forgetting might occur—a recovery of the UR could just as well reflect a restoration of the efficacy of an S–R pathway as a change in the sort of information encoded in the representation. But these two interpretations make different predictions about the way in which habituation established to one stimulus should generalize to another. According to a simple S–R theory, loss of habituation over a retention interval should influence both the performance shown to the original stimulus and the generalized effect seen with other test stimuli. But if forgetting over the retention interval means that the information encoded in the central representation becomes less specific, then this might mean that generalized habituation will be unaffected. The critical experiment, therefore, is one that shows forgetting of habituation to the target stimulus and which also includes a test of generalized habituation to some other stimulus.

Relevant experimental results have recently been reported by Boakes and Thomas (1988). Their subjects, food-deprived rats, all received initial exposure to a 1 per cent saccharin solution. Separate groups of subjects then received a test session with the original 1 per cent solution, with a 1.5 per cent solution, or with a 2 per cent solution. Some animals received the test session 4 h after pre-exposure; the remainder at the same time on the following day (i.e. 28 h after pre-exposure). The results are shown in Fig. 2.9. After the shorter retention interval a gradient of generalization is evident with subjects drinking the training concentration (1 per cent) more readily than the novel concentrations. Subjects tested after 28 h show a much flatter gradient, a result consistent with the suggestion that a detailed representation of the training stimulus failed to survive the longer retention interval—for these subjects all three test concentrations were treated as being equivalent in similarity to (or difference from) the training concentration.

It may be noted from Fig. 2.9 that (although the effect was not statistically reliable) animals tested after 4 h showed more reluctance to consume the most dissimilar (the 2 per cent) test solution than did those tested after 28 h. That is, subjects tested at the shorter retention interval, although they showed more evidence of habituation to the training stimulus, actually showed somewhat less evidence of habituation with the generalization test stimulus. This seemingly paradoxical outcome can be interpreted as a possible case of dishabituation by stimulus omission (see pp. 48–50). It seems to

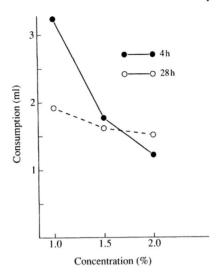

Fig. 2.9 Consumption of saccharin solutions of various concentrations in separate groups of subjects tested 4 h or 28 h after their last pre-exposure session with a 1 per cent solution. (After Boakes and Thomas 1988.)

require the conclusion that the mechanism responsible for generating the UR is sensitive not only to the features that the input and the representation hold in common but also to the extent to which specific features of the representation are *not* matched by the input. To make the argument more concrete, consider the training and test stimuli as each consisting of two feature, flavour (S for saccharin) and concentration (1 or 2). The representation initially formed and present after the shorter delay will encode S-1; after the longer delay only S will remain, information about concentration being lost. Stimulus S-2 will therefore match the one remaining feature of the representation when the delay is long but, when the delay is short, although it will still match S it will fail to match the other feature of the representation. If this discrepancy is capable of evoking a UR then a reduced level of consumption can be expected in subjects tested with S-2 after a short retention interval. The generalization gradient obtained after a long retention interval may be not just flatter than that obtained with immediate testing; rather, the two gradients may actually cross. For further evidence on this possibility it is necessary to turn from simple habituation procedures to studies involving reinforced training.

(b) In conditioning

The processes responsible for stimulus representation formation will presumably operate during conditioning as during habituation training and the

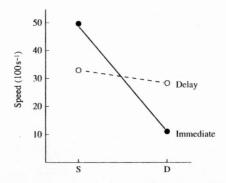

Fig. 2.10 Median running speeds over the first eight test trials for rats tested in the same runway (S) as that used in training or in a different runway (D). The test took place immediately after the end of training or after a delay of 24 h. (After Perkins and Weyant 1958.)

extent to which a conditioned response (CR) will generalize will depend on the match between the test stimulus and the conditioned stimulus (CS). We may thus use generalization of CRs as a further way of assessing how stimulus representations might change over time. It is open to any theorist, of course, to assume that the vigour of the CR will decline over a retention interval. What we are concerned to determine is whether or not the generalization gradient becomes flatter, with the decline being more marked for the original CS than for a different test stimulus. It is even possible that the gradient observed after a delay might be found to cross that obtained in an immediate test. I have argued for habituation that, with a short retention interval and a test stimulus different from that used in training, the failure of some feature of the input to match those of the representation might be a source of unconditioned responding. Such unconditioned responding, if it interfered with the ability of the subject to perform a CR, might act to reduce the likelihood of generalized conditioned responding being seen when the retention interval is short.

The first explicit investigation of the effect of a retention interval on the generalization of a CR was that of Perkins and Weyant (1958) (see also Steinman 1967; Gisquet-Verrier and Alexinsky 1986). Rats were trained to run for food in a runway of a given colour (black or white) and then tested either in the original runway or in the other. Some subjects were tested immediately after the last training trial, others after an interval of 24 h. The results (Fig. 2.10) revealed a steep generalization gradient in the subjects tested immediately and a much flatter gradient in those given the delayed test—flatter both because responding to the original runway was reduced and because that shown in the novel runway was rather more vigorous.

Confirmation of this striking finding has been sought in a variety of other experimental paradigms. Thomas and Lopez (1962) and Thomas and Burr

(1969) investigated the effects of imposing delays of up to one week between the end of training and testing on the generalization gradients of pigeons along the wavelength dimension. Gradients were indeed flatter after the delay. Unfortunately, these investigators report only a relative response measure—the proportion of responding that occurred to the various stimuli presented on the test. This measure is difficult to interpret unambiguously (Lea and Morgan 1972). If a factor (such as a long retention interval) produced the same absolute reduction in the response tendency at all points on the dimension, we would not want to say that the gradient had become flatter. But, given that the absolute rate will be higher to the originally trained stimulus than to the test stimuli, a uniform reduction in the absolute rate would generate a flattening of the relative gradient. We cannot tell whether the gradients reported by Thomas and his colleagues reflect a flattening of the absolute gradient or not.*

There are several studies of aversive conditioning, however, that report absolute response measures and confirm the basic result of Perkins and Weyant (1958). McAllister and McAllister (1963) and Desiderato, Butler, and Meyer, (1966) (see also Gabriel and Vogt 1972) found that the effectiveness of a light trained as a signal for shock in rats was insensitive to generalization decrement (produced by presenting the light in a changed apparatus) when the test occurred after 24 h but that a marked loss of effectiveness was apparent when the test occurred immediately after initial acquisition. And Thomas and Riccio (1979) found that rats were sensitive to a change in the frequency of a tone CS after an interval of a day but not when 21 days intervened between initial acquisition and the next stage of training. After one day the original tone would act to block acquisition by a light when the two stimuli were trained in compound whereas the changed tone did not; after 21 days it proved to be immaterial whether the tone used in compound training was identical to that initially trained or not—all frequencies tried produce the same (rather small) degree of blocking.

Such evidence as is available, then, appears to confirm the widely held notion (see, e.g. Riccio, Richardson, and Ebner 1984) that generalization gradients grow less steep when a delay is imposed between training and testing. It should be acknowledged, however, that although a gradient will become flatter and may sometimes actually cross that determined in an immediate test (as in Fig. 2.10), there are, as yet, no statistically reliable demonstrations of such a crossover in absolute gradients. And in the absence of such a demonstration a relatively uninteresting explanation for the effect remains possible. Certainly imposing a delay between training and test has more of an effect at the training value than with other stimuli but this could

---

* Equivalent problems of interpretation arise with a study of the generalization of conditioned taste aversion by Richardson, Williams, and Riccio (1984), who also use a relative measure, in this case a preference score from a choice test.

arise simply because the higher level of responding maintained by the training stimulus provides a more sensitive baseline against which changes can be detected. This account could not explain a crossover in the gradients but it can explain why the effects of a delay appear to be greatest at the training value. While this account remains viable we can accept only with reservations the view that the flattening of gradients over a retention interval is a consequence of the loss of information from an originally more complete stimulus representation.

2.2.4 Generalization after extended training

According to the S–R theory of habituation, each presentation of the training stimulus produces a decrement in the efficiency of transmission along the S–R pathways corresponding to the elements that make up the stimulus. With extended training, each pathway will become non-functional. The size of the response elicited by a slightly different test stimulus will depend on the number of novel elements it contains and on any residual responsiveness that remains in the pathways stimulated by the elements that the test stimulus shares with the training stimulus. With extended training, this second source of responding will be eliminated and the generalization of habituation will be more nearly complete.

This conclusion does not necessarily follow from the suggestion that the nature of the information encoded in the representation might change. We have allowed that information might be lost with time as a result of decay or interference. Given what we know of learning and memory more generally, it seems reasonable to assume that repeated exposure to the original stimulus will establish more firmly those features that otherwise tend to be lost. It may also allow the encoding of some detailed features that would escape attention when the initial exposure to the stimulus is brief. Accordingly, if only a small amount of habituation training is given, the representation available on a subsequent test trial will be lacking in detail. The habituation evident on a subsequent test trial may not be profound but it should occur not only when the test stimulus is identical to that used in training but also to other stimuli of the same general type—that is, the generalization gradient should be flat. With extended training, however, an exact representation of the training stimulus will be available on the test trial. Re-presentation of the original stimulus will evoke very little responding. The effect of testing with a changed stimulus is more debatable. If extended training allows the encoding of features of the training stimulus that escape attention when little training is given, and if these features happen to be present in the test stimulus, then extra training might be effective in reducing the responding evoked by a changed stimulus. But just as likely is that the test stimulus might again match the representation only in sharing certain general features. If so, responding will be as likely after much training as after little. Indeed, if, as was

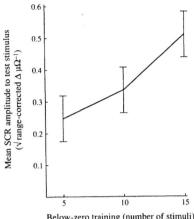

Fig. 2.11 Magnitude (mean ± SE) of the skin conductance response (SCR) elicited by a tone of 1.4 kHz in subjects that had experienced varying amounts of habituation training with a 1 kHz tone. All subjects were trained to a criterion of non-responding, and separate groups then received a further 5, 10, or 15 'below-zero' training trials. (After Stephenson and Siddle 1976.)

suggested above in discussion of the effects of a retention interval, the mechanism responsible for generating the response is sensitive not only to the features that the input and the representation hold in common but also to the extent to which specific features of the representation are *not* matched by the input, then the response to a changed stimulus may be even greater after much habituation training than after little.*

(a) Evidence from studies of dishabituation

In a study of the OR in human subjects, Stephenson and Siddle (1976) gave sufficient presentations of a 1 kHz tone to achieve habituation of the skin conductance response that was evoked initially. (Individuals differed in the number of trials they required to reach a criterion of non-responding, but all were fairly close to the mean of 12 trials.) Separate groups then received 5, 10, or 15 further trials of 'below zero' habituation training followed, after a short retention interval, by a single test trial with a changed stimulus, a 1.4 kHz tone. Fig 2.11 shows the mean amplitude of the skin conductance response for the three groups on the test trial. Dishabituation occurred (i.e. there was some failure to generalize) in all groups but the effect was more

---

* Sokolov's theory can be made to generate these conclusions (see Graham 1973), granted the assumption that increased training results in an increase in the precision of the neuronal model. But Sokolov himself makes little of this possibility, emphasizing instead that habituation will generalize and that generalization will increase across training trials (Voronin and Sokolov 1960).

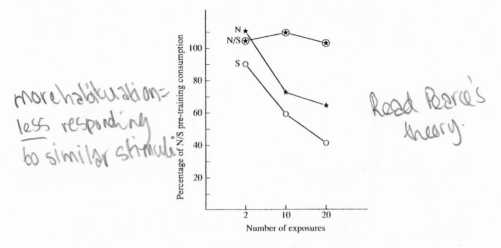

more habituation=
less responding
to similar stimuli

Read Pearce's
theory.

Fig. 2.12   Consumption of a solution of salt (N), saccharin (S), or a compound of both (N/S) by rats given differing numbers of previous exposures to the N/S compound. (After Gillette and Bellingham 1982.)

marked in subjects that had received prolonged initial training. That is, extended training resulted in a steeper gradient of generalization. Essentially identical findings have been reported by Waters and McDonald (1974) and by Smith and Council (1978) in further studies of the OR in humans. And an equivalent effect has been revealed in the study by Gillette and Bellingham (1982) of neophobia in the rat.

Gillette and Bellingham's experiment was directed at what is ostensibly a rather different issue. It was concerned with the possibility that, in some circumstances, subjects given a compound stimulus might perceive it as a unique whole (or configure) rather than as being the sum of its constituent parts. In such circumstances, training with the compound would fail to generalize to the components if these were presented alone. Now we have already noted that the effects of habituation training will show generalization decrement (i.e. dishabituation will occur) when rats are trained with a compound stimulus and tested with the elements of the compound. Gillette and Bellingham set out to show that the magnitude of such generalization decrement would increase with increasing amounts of initial habituation training, their expectation being based on the assumption that a compound will be more likely to be perceived as a configure after extensive experience.

Different groups of rats received 2, 10, or 20 presentations of a compound stimulus, water flavoured with both salt (NaCl) and saccharin. Each of these groups was then divided into three for the test trial: one subgroup received a further presentation of the compound; the others received one of the elements on its own. The results are summarized in Fig. 2.12. They show that the subjects tested with the familiar compound drank it as readily as on

AB ← AB
    A
    B

the last session of pre-exposure. Those tested with one of the elements tended to drink it less readily—habituation did not generalize fully. And critically, increasing the amount of training with the compound increased the extent to which neophobia was shown to the elements presented individually. (See also Forbes and Holland (1985), who in their experiment 2 report a very similar effect.) The procedure is quite different from that used in studies of the OR but the basic finding is the same—habituation is less likely to generalize to a changed stimulus after much training than after little. And although the result is consistent with Gillette and Bellingham's configural hypothesis, other explanations are possible. In particular, the suggestion that only with extended training do subjects become capable of encoding the detailed features of a stimulus can accommodate the results just as readily.

(c) Pre-exposure and generalization in conditioning procedures

The results presented so far can be taken as showing that a discrimination between the test stimulus and the (rather similar training stimulus) is made more readily when the training stimulus has been rendered fully familiar. We have monitored this discrimination by noting the extent to which the loss of responding produced by habituation training fails to generalize to a changed test stimulus. But the effect should occur even when other behavioural measures of discrimination are employed.

Honey and Hall (1989a) investigated the influence of habituation training on the generalization seen after flavour-aversion conditioning. In one of their experiments, rats were given access to 10 ml of a distinctively flavoured solution (e.g. very dilute acid) for 30 min—long enough for them to overcome any initial neophobia and to consume all the fluid. They then received an injection of a nausea-inducing agent (LiCl). The effect of this conditioning procedure is to establish an aversion to the flavour encountered just before the injection (which will be referred to as flavour A). When flavour A was presented again two days later, the subjects drank much less of it (Fig. 2.13), and a further injection of LiCl ensured that on a third presentation, flavour A was rejected almost totally.

Once the aversion to A had been established all the subjects received test sessions in which they were allowed free access to a new flavour (B, e.g. a sucrose solution). For half the subjects (group N, for no pre-exposure) this flavour was novel but the remainder (group B) had received habituation training with flavour B. Before the start of conditioning with A, subjects in group B had been given eight daily presentations of fluid, flavour B (group N experienced only unflavoured water at this stage). An aversion acquired to one flavour can be expected to generalize to some extent to another, and generalization was evident in group N which showed a low level of consumption of flavour B on the test trials (Fig. 2.13). But if the habituation training procedure allows the formation of an exact representation of the stimulus in question, then discrimination between this stimulus and another

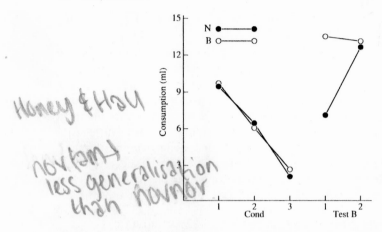

Honey & Hall

*nov (am)
less generalisation
than nov nov*

Fig. 2.13 Amount of a fixed 10 ml of stimulus A consumed on each conditioning trial (cond). On test trials the subjects were given free access to flavour B for 30 mins. For group N, flavour B was novel; group B had received prior exposure to flavour B. (After Honey and Hall 1989a.)

similar stimulus should be enhanced—that is, less generalization should occur. And, as Fig. 2.13 shows, subjects in group B (who had received extensive prior experience of B) showed little generalization of the aversion from A to B, drinking readily on the first test trial. Results similar to those presented in Fig. 2.13 have been reported previously by Domjan (1975) and by Best and Batson (1977).

I have attributed the differing test performance of the two groups of Fig. 2.13 to a difference between them in the extent to which generalization occurs from A to B. But we should consider another and less interesting possibility. For group N the test flavour B was quite novel at the time of test and thus might be expected to evoke a neophobic response; for group B, any neophobia evoked by B would have habituated during the first stage of training. It is in principle possible, therefore, that the test results are a consequence of a difference between the groups in the tendency of the test stimulus to evoke its UR. That they are not, or at least not solely, to be explained in this way is suggested by a further experiment (Honey 1990).

Honey's experiment included the equivalents of groups N and B of Honey and Hall (1989a) but used different training procedures. The stimuli, A and B, were presentations of a tone and a clicker. Subjects in group B received, over the course of eight 1-h training sessions, 48 presentations of the stimulus designated as B. Pre-training for group N consisted of exposure to the experimental apparatus. All subjects the received conditioning trials in which presentations of A were followed by the delivery of food until they developed the CR of approaching the site of food delivery when A was presented. This CR is quite different from the UR evoked by an auditory stimulus in this situation—a novel cue will induce a suppression of ongoing behaviour. Fig. 2.14 shows the extent to which the CR generalized to B when this stimulus was presented in a final non-reinforced test session. It shows that generalization was much less evident in group B than in group N—exactly the same pattern of results as Honey and Hall (1989*a*) found for the flavour-aversion paradigm, in spite of the fact that with this appetitive training procedure a tendency for B to evoke its UR in group N would act to produce the opposite result.

(c) Generalization after reinforced training

In the experiments just described, all subjects received the same amount of conditioning but differed in the extent to which they were familiar with the stimulus used in the generalization test. The experiments to be considered next use the complementary strategy of varying the amount of conditioning given to different groups but testing all of them with equally unfamiliar (novel) test stimuli. These are experiments that assess the extent to which conditioned responding generalizes after varying amounts of reinforced training and they are procedurally quite distinct from studies of habituation. None the less, they are directly relevant to the point at issue here. Prolonged reinforced training means extensive exposure to the stimulus and hence allows the possibility that a fuller representation will be formed. Of course, the extra associative strength acquired during prolonged training will tend to increase the likelihood of generalized responding to a novel stimulus but this

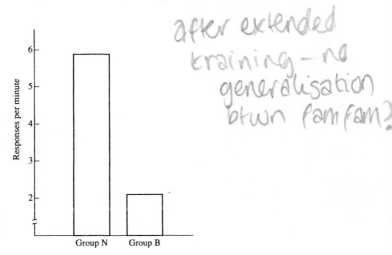

after extended training – no generalisation btwn fam fam?

Fig. 2.14 Generalized responding to stimulus B for groups given appetitive conditioning with stimulus A. For group N, stimulus B was novel; for group B, stimulus B had been pre-exposed. The response measured is that of approaching the site of food delivery in the presence of the stimulus. (After Honey 1990.)

tendency will be opposed by the increased likelihood of the test stimulus being discriminated from the training stimulus. It is possible, therefore, that generalization gradients of conditioned responding might actually become steeper with extended training.

This possibility was considered by Pavlov himself (1927, p. 117) (see also Razran 1949) and was taken up and analysed in some detail by Hovland (1937) for studies of the skin conductance response. Hovland's results showed clearly that over-training led to a sharpening of the gradient when a relative measure was used, that is, when the size of response to the test stimulus after a given amount of training was expressed as a ratio of the magnitude of the response governed by the training stimulus. Increasing the amount of training sharpened the relative gradient because it increased the magnitude of the response governed by the CS but had little effect on responding to the generalization test stimulus. Similar results have been reported for studies of the generalization of operant responding in pigeons (Hearst and Koresko 1968) (see also Olson and King 1962; Taus and Hearst 1972), for salivary conditioning in dogs (Brown 1970), and for generalization by infant children of a simple lever-pull response along a brightness continuum (Spiker 1956a).

Whatever is true for relative gradients, it remains the case that in none of the studies just cited was there convincing evidence of a sharpening in the absolute gradient. To provide such evidence (in this procedure just as in studies of the effects of a retention interval) it is necessary to demonstrate that manipulation of the variable in question can produce a cross-over in the absolute gradients. Fortunately, a number of studies of avoidance learning (Thompson 1958, 1959; Hoffeld 1962) have achieved just this. Figure 2.15 summarizes the relevant results from Hoffeld's (1962) experiment. Cats were trained to respond in the presence of a 250-Hz tone to avoid a shock. There were four groups that received differing amounts of training: to a criterion of 10 responses in 20 trials (50 per cent), 18 in 20 trials (95 per cent), for three sessions beyond the more stringent criterion (the 190 per cent level), or for a further six sessions beyond the criterion (285 per cent). In the generalization test, all subjects received a series of trials with a 500-Hz tone. As the figure shows, although lower levels of training resulted in a fairly high level of test responding, there was very little generalized responding in the group of subjects given extended initial training; that is, extended training led to a reduction in the ability of the 500-Hz tone to evoke the response.

Again (as was the case when we considered the effects of extended training on dishabituation), experimental work aimed at the issue of configuring is relevant here. In attempts to demonstrate 'spontaneous configuring', subjects have been given extensive reinforced training with a compound stimulus followed by test trials with the elements presented individually. Such over-training, although it is likely to enhance the conditioned responding controlled by the compound stimulus, might lead to a reduction in the ability of the individual components to evoke the CR—that is, generaliza-

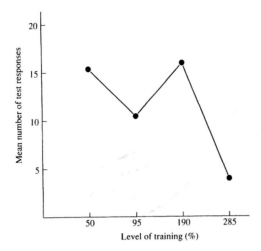

Fig. 2.15 Responding on a generalization test with a 500 Hz tone in cats given different amounts of initial avoidance training with a 250 Hz as the warning stimulus. (After Hoffeld 1962.)

tion from the trained to a changed stimulus might become less evident with over-training.*

Not all studies of spontaneous configuring have been successful in generating the effect (e.g. Rescorla 1972; Bellingham and Gillette 1981a; Forbes and Holland 1985, experiment 1) and those that have (e.g. Booth and Hammond 1971; Gray and Lethbridge 1976) have been criticized for failing to exclude a possible artefact (Kamin and Idrobo 1978). There are, however, some studies (Bellingham and Gillette 1981b; Forbes and Holland 1985, experiments 3 and 4) that seem to provide a satisfactory demonstration of the effect.

The critical results from one of Bellingham and Gillette's (1981b) experiments are shown in Fig. 2.16. Thirsty rats received 100 trials each day on which presentations of a tone–light compound were followed by water. Different groups were tested after varying amounts of training (from as little as 3 days to as much as 39) with presentations of the tone alone, the light alone, or with the light–tone compound. As the figure shows, extended training had little effect on the high level of conditioned responding maintained by the compound stimulus but it produced a marked decrement in the responding that generalized to the components. Bellingham and Gillette themselves

---

* The notion of spontaneous configuring is that the compound stimulus comes to be perceived as a unique configure and that this cue, different from each of the constituent elements, gains associative strength at their expense. Configuring is 'spontaneous' because there is no training on an explicit discrimination between the compound and the elements.

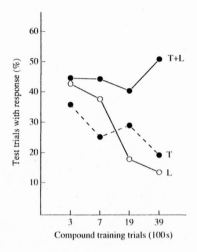

Fig. 2.16   Proportion of trials in which a test stimulus of a tone (T), a light (L), or a tone–light compound (T+L) evoked a response. Different groups of subjects had received varying amounts of reinforced training with the compound prior to the test. (After Bellingham and Gillette 1981*b*.)

allow that this result can be seen as a special case of a decrease in the range of stimulus generalization produced by extended training.

Finally, in this section, it is important to acknowledge that standard associative learning theory might be capable of supplying an explanation for the sharpening of gradients produced by extended reinforced training. As Mackintosh (1974) points out, early in training incidental features of the training situation (background, contextual cues) are just as likely to gain associative strength as is the experimenter's CS. These cues will be able to generate responding on a generalization test, thus producing a flat gradient. Further training will allow the formation of a discrimination between the presence and absence of the CS and the consequent loss of control by contextual stimuli could result in a reduction of the level of responding measured for generalization test stimuli. We may doubt, however, that this mechanism is the sole source of the results described above. In particular the mechanism could not apply to the habituation paradigm where, it will be recalled, just the same sharpening of gradients with extended training is observed; and presumably the mechanism responsible for the effect seen in the habituation case will play a part in determining that seen after reinforced training.

2.2.5. Conclusions

Any account of habituation can be interpreted as being a sort of comparator theory since whether or not a UR occurs must depend on the outcome of some sort of comparison between information about current sensory input and stored information about previous inputs. My concern in the latter part of this chapter has been to evaluate the simplest version of the comparator theory—the version that equates the stored information (the representation of the stimulus) with the extent to which a given set of S–R pathways have been rendered ineffective by prior stimulation.

According to this account, the only dimension along which changes can occur in the representations that of 'strength'. Factors like amount of training or opportunity for forgetting can influence the representation only by changing the degree to which a pathway is more or less effective. But the evidence reviewed above suggests that the *nature* of the representation can change—that the sort of information it holds can be influenced by the presentation of a distractor, the extent of training, or by interposing a retention interval between training and the test. We may conclude that the habituation procedure embodies an important form of perceptual learning in that it involves a change with experience in the nature of a stimulus representation. My aim in the rest of this book will be to determine by what mechanisms such changes occur—perhaps by a Gibsonian process of differentiation, or perhaps in some other way. I shall address this issue directly in the final chapter. The review of various other training paradigms that constitutes the intervening chapters will provide the facts and concepts that will be needed.

3. Latent inhibition as reduced associability

3.1. Habituation and latent inhibition

In a typical experiment on latent inhibition, a stimulus that has been repeatedly presented on its own is used as the CS (conditioned stimulus) in a conditioning procedure and the course of acquisition of the CR (conditioned response) is compared with that shown when a novel stimulus is used as the CS. The procedure can thus be viewed as being an indirect way of assessing the effects of habituation training. Certainly, the habituation process described in Chapter 2 will be engaged during the first stage of a latent inhibition experiment and might be expected to play some part in determining the outcome. What we need to determine now is what further processes, if any, must be assumed to operate during the habituation procedure if the results of studies of latent inhibition are to be explained. The suggestion that pre-exposure to a stimulus establishes an exact representation of it, for instance, is not in itself enough to explain latent inhibition; indeed it seems capable of predicting quite the wrong result. The ability of the CS to evoke the CR after conditioning trials have been given will depend, in part, upon that stimulus being identified with the one that was presented during conditioning. To the extent that this identification is more likely to be made when the stimulus in question is already capable of activating a detailed representation, the likelihood of a vigorous CR may be increased. What we have already seen, however, (p. 24) is that pre-exposure to the to-be-CS results in *retarded* development of the CR. Clearly, this aspect of our account of habituation is not enough in itself to explain the latent inhibition effect. But, whatever its theoretical explanation, the habituation procedure has direct behavioural consequences and their role needs to be considered before we are obliged to accept the suggestion that latent inhibition implies the operation of mechanisms other than those involved in habituation.

3.1.1. The role of the UR

The most obvious possibility is that the waning of the overt unconditioned response (UR) produced by pre-exposure to the to-be-CS might be directly responsible, in whole or in part, for some instances of latent inhibition. Some conditioning procedures (in particular, those that use the suppression of ongoing behaviour as their measure) engender the development of a CR that is similar in form to the UR evoked by the CS when it is first presented.

The summation of these two response tendencies (conditioned and uncondi-tioned) in control subjects, for whom the CS is novel, might be enough to ensure a bigger net response than that seen in pre-exposed subjects, for whom the unconditioned component will be absent. There can be no doubt, however, that there is more to latent inhibition than this because the effect is routinely observed both when the stimulus evokes no very marked UR (e.g. Carlton and Vogel 1967; Domjan and Siegel 1971) and also when the CR required is quite different from the UR. The experiment by Channell and Hall (1983), mentioned in Chapter 1, provides an instance. Here, as Fig. 1.8 shows, the CS when it was first presented to the control subjects tended to suppress responding; but thereafter, these subjects acquired the CR (which involved an increase in responding) more rapidly than did pre-exposed sub-jects.

A somewhat more subtle interpretation of latent inhibition in terms of the known facts of habituation comes from considering the role of orienting responses (ORs). Pavlov (1927) expressed the view that the OR evoked by a novel stimulus constituted an 'obstacle' to conditioning; and indeed, if con-ditioning is seen as a process in which the OR comes to be replaced by the CR, it might be expected that pre-exposure to the CS would facilitate this process. That it does not, requires a different interpretation, and one has been offered by other Eastern European workers, notably by Sokolov (e.g. 1963), who suggested that the functional significance of the OR is that it facilitates the uptake and processing of environmental information. Condi-tioning with an habituated stimulus as the CS requires, it is suggested, that the OR be re-established so that the processing necessary for the formation of an associative link can occur.

Certainly, those experiments in which the occurrence of an overt compo-nent of the OR has been monitored have demonstrated that the response that has been habituated during pre-exposure tends to reappear when the CS–US pairings are begun. An example is shown in Fig. 3.1.

This experiment, by Kaye and Pearce (1984) (see also Pearce, Kaye, and Hall 1982), included a group of rats given a series of presentations of a light, a stimulus that initially evoked a behavioural OR. After habituation had occurred, the light was used as a CS signalling the availability of food. The subjects showed latent inhibition, developing the CR (the response of approaching the site of food delivery when the light came on) less readily than a control group that had not received pre-exposure (Fig. 3.1, lower panel). And, as the upper panel of the figure shows, the introduction of the conditioning procedure was accompanied by a rapid and dramatic increase in the occurrence of the OR. (It is interesting to note that the frequency of occurrence of the OR actually declined during conditioning for the control subjects. This observation, along with the implications of the performance shown by group Partial, will be taken up later, p.100.)

Interpretation of the results presented in Fig. 3.1 is not straightforward. It

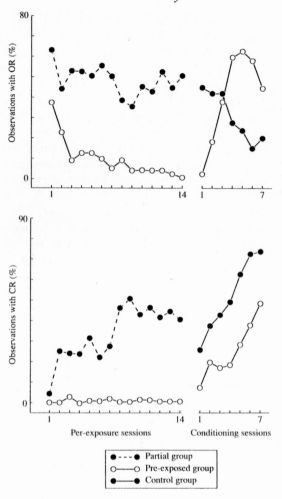

Fig. 3.1   Mean percentage of observations on which rats were recorded as orienting to a light (OR) or showing the conditioned response (CR). The pre-exposed and control groups received continuously reinforced conditioning in the second stage; pre-exposed subjects experienced non-reinforced presentations of the light in stage one. The partial group received pre-exposure in which the light was followed by the reinforcer on half of the trials. (Adapted from Kaye and Pearce 1984.)

is difficult to distinguish cause and effect; and even if we could be sure that the low level of orienting in the pre-exposed subjects was responsible for their retarded conditioning, it would still be necessary to explain why it is that the OR should return when reinforced training begins. None the less, it seems plausible to suppose that the loss of the OR in the pre-exposed group might retard the formation of a light–food association simply because it reduces the likelihood that these subjects will see the light at the start of conditioning. In this case, latent inhibition and habituation would indeed reduce to essentially the same thing. But, in fact, latent inhibition is routinely obtained with stimuli that are diffuse and non-localized and thus seem certain to impinge on the subject's sense organs even in the absence of an overt OR. Stimuli of this sort may still evoke an OR that habituates during preexposure but there is no reason to suppose that the loss of the overt components of this response will prevent the subjects from seeing or hearing the stimulus. Siegel (1972) reports that pre-exposure to a tone in rabbits leads to a loss of the OR (evident as a decline in the likelihood of occurrence of an eye-opening response evoked by the novel tone) but the latent inhibition that was also found cannot be directly attributed to the loss of this aspect of the OR.

In order to explain latent inhibition in terms of the habituation of the OR it is clearly necessary to interpret the latter as being some central response, the evocation of which is necessary for speedy conditioning. (An overt OR might serve as an index of this central change but would not, in itself, be directly responsible for most cases of latent inhibition.) Another way of putting this is to say that habituation training produces a loss of effectiveness by the to-be-CS (a reduction in 'conditionability' or 'associability') and that this loss is determined by the same mechanism as that controlling the loss of overt URs. We need to examine, therefore, those experiments that try to determine if the conditions necessary for stimulus exposure to produce latent inhibition are the same as those that produce the habituation of a UR. Should it turn out that latent inhibition and habituation can be dissociated, two possibilities will emerge. One is that latent inhibition should not be interpreted as being the result of a loss of stimulus associability; Chapter 4 will discuss the most widely considered alternative, 'interference' theory. The other is that latent inhibition does indeed result from a loss of stimulus associability but that the mechanism responsible for this loss is not that that underlies habituation. Later sections of the present chapter discuss this possibility.

3.1.2. Empirical dissociations of habituation and latent inhibition

(a) Cross-experiment comparisons

If latent inhibition and habituation reflect the operation of a common mechanism, then procedural variations that modify the magnitude of one of these phenomena should have a similar effect on the other. Often this has proved to be so. Thus, the extent of habituation increases with the number of exposures to the stimulus and so does the magnitude of latent inhibition (e.g. Lubow 1965; Lubow, Markman, and Allen 1968; Lantz 1973). Again, testing with a stimulus somewhat different from that used for pre-exposure produces generalization decrement both in habituation and in latent inhibition (e.g. Carlton and Vogel 1967; Siegel 1969; Dawley 1979). There are, however, some seeming discrepancies. One of Thompson and Spencer's (1966) list of 'criteria' for habituation is that habituation proceeds most readily with closely spaced trials; but latent inhibition appears to be more profound when the pre-exposure trials are relatively widely spaced (Lantz 1973; Schnur and Lubow 1976; but see also Crowell and Anderson 1972). Again, Thompson and Spencer suggest that intense stimuli habituate only slowly but there is some evidence that they might acquire latent inhibition especially readily (Crowell and Anderson 1972; Lantz 1976; Schnur and Lubow 1976). A further feature of habituation is that it is supposed to show spontaneous recovery after a retention interval; but although some studies of latent inhibition have revealed an equivalent effect (e.g. Best and Gemberling 1977; McIntosh and Tarpy 1977; Westbrook, Provost, and Homewood 1982), others have reported perfect retention of latent inhibition (Siegel 1970; James 1971; Crowell and Anderson 1972).

It might be objected that when the comparison of habituation and latent inhibition gives rise to a discrepancy, it does so because we have failed to compare like with like. In particular, Thompson and Spencer's list of the features of habituation was derived from studies of short-term examples of the phenomenon; it may therefore be unreasonable to expect these features to be found also in latent inhibition (see Lubow, Weiner, and Schnur 1981). There is some reason to doubt that all the discrepancies can be eliminated by taking account of the short-term/long-term distinction: Lantz's (1973) demonstration of superior latent inhibition with spaced trials came from a procedure in which the first conditioning trial followed the last trial of pre-exposure; James' (1971) demonstration of perfect retention used, in training, the interstimulus intervals typical of studies of short-term habituation. None the less, it is surely true that it will be difficult to reach firm conclusions from comparing experiments which, however similar they may be formally, use quite different subjects, stimuli, and training procedures. We need to find examples of experiments in which the habituation of the UR and the development of latent inhibition have been assessed in animals subjected to identical conditions of training. We should acknowledge at the outset that there may be many cases (like that illustrated in Fig. 3.1) in which presentation of a given stimulus has been shown to result in both latent inhibition and the habituation of a UR. Our concern must be, however, to seek out instances in which one effect has been observed in the absence of the other.

(b) *Physiological intervention*

One of the earliest claims to have demonstrated a dissociation of latent inhibition and habituation was made by Weiss, Friedman, and McGregor (1974), who studied the phenomena in rats having surgically produced lesions of the septal area of the limbic system. When presented with a series of tones, these rats showed perfectly normal habituation of the UR (the suppression of a water-licking response); but equivalent pre-exposure produced no latent inhibition when the subjects were required to learn a shock-avoidance task with the tone as the warning signal—animals with septal lesions learned readily whether they were familiar with the tone or not. More recent corroborative evidence comes from Gallagher, Meagher, and Bostock (1987), who investigated the effects of infusions of the opiate agonist levorphanol into the septal region of rabbits. Animals that received infusions during pre-exposure sessions showed normal habituation of the UR (heart-rate deceleration) evoked by the tone used as the stimulus. The response remained habituated on a test session given 24 h after the last pre-exposure session; but when the tone was then paired with shock, conditioned responding developed readily, that is, there was no sign of latent inhibition.

(c) Generalized effects of flavour pre-exposure

Pre-exposure to a novel flavour normally results in both a reduction of neophobia and in a reduction of the ability of that flavour to serve as a CS in flavour-aversion conditioning. If the initial exposure is given to some flavour other than that used for the test phase, then both the habituation of neophobia (Siegel 1974) and latent inhibition (Tarpy and McIntosh 1977) are attenuated but may still occur to some extent—the degree of generalization will presumably depend upon the extent to which the pre-exposed flavour and the test flavour are perceived as similar. With certain flavours, however, it has been found that habituation can generalize perfectly well when latent inhibition fails to do so.

The effect was first shown in an experiment by Braveman and Jarvis (1978) (see also Miller and Holzman 1981; Gilley and Franchina 1985; Franchina and Gilley 1986). They used a saline solution as the test flavour and gave different groups of subjects pre-exposure either to saline itself or to some other flavour or flavours. (The flavours used are listed in Fig. 3.2.) Half the subjects received a test in which their consumption of saline was measured. As panel A of Fig. 3.2 shows, only the subjects pre-exposed to water showed neophobia; pre-exposure to any of the other flavours produced generalized habituation of the neophobic response to saline. But the latent inhibition effect did not generalize. Panel B of Fig 3.2 shows the results for a further set of subjects that received aversion conditioning with saline as the CS before the test session. It is evident that only pre-exposure to saline itself produced latent inhibition and that an aversion was established perfectly readily after all other conditions of pre-exposure.

On the basis of their findings, Braveman and Jarvis (1978) put forward the suggestion that latent inhibition derives from a loss of effectiveness by the specific cues that characterize the CS (and thus requires pre-exposure to that very stimulus), whereas neophobia is taken to be a reaction to the aversive properties of novelty *per se* and can be attenuated by prior exposure to any other novel event (see also Braveman 1978). Support for this interpretation

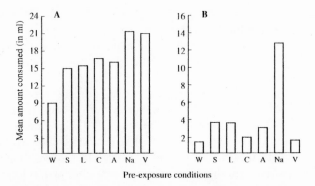

Fig. 3.2 Amount of a saline solution consumed by rats pre-exposed to water (W), saccharin (S), lemon (L), coffee (C), almond, (A), sodium chloride (Na), or to a variety of these flavours. In the neophobia test (panel A) the subjects were allowed access to the saline solution for 10 min. Panel B shows the results of a similar test given after a conditioning trial on which consumption of saline was followed by an injection of LiCl. (From Braveman and Jarvis 1978.)

has been sought in the effects of a procedure in which subjects are given pre-exposure to a variety of flavours. This procedure, it might be supposed, would ensure repeated experience of novelty and should thus be especially effective in reducing neophobia to a test flavour not previously experienced. It should not, however, generate latent inhibition to this test flavour. Figure 3.2 shows such a dissociation between neophobia and latent inhibition, result subsequently confirmed by Miller and Holzman (1981) (Fig. 3.3).*

However suggestive these results may be, they are all open to a rather trivial explanation. As Fig. 3.3 shows, the subjects exposed to a variety of flavours acquired the aversion readily; that is, showed no latent inhibition. But, as the figure also shows, the dose of LiCl used was sufficient to produce an almost total aversion in the subjects naive to the CS, and thus a difference between the groups might have been obscured by a 'floor effect'—by a lack of sensitivity in the test (see also Misanin, Blatt, and Hindenliter 1985). And indeed, Tarpy and McIntosh (1977), using a procedure likely to be more sensitive (involving, among other things, a weaker US and prolonged testing), were able to demonstrate substantial latent inhibition in rats given exposure to a variety of flavours before conditioning. Miller and Holzman (1981) were aware of this possible problem with their procedure and conducted a further study in which a smaller dose of LiCl was used as the US. Although they again found no difference between subjects given no pre-exposure and

---

* Although this dissociation between latent inhibition and habituation is as predicted, one feature of the results does not fit the hypothesis. Exposure to a variety of flavours, although it does attenuate neophobia substantially, is somewhat less effective than repeated exposure to the test flavour itself.

those exposed to a variety of flavours, interpretation of this finding is rendered equivocal by the fact that the two groups drank different amounts of the CS flavour on the conditioning trial. Differences in the amount consumed are capable, in themselves, of determining the magnitude of a conditioned flavour aversion (e.g. Bond and DiGiusto 1975).

Once it has been allowed that the procedure used in these various studies of flavour pre-exposure might have used insensitive measures of conditioning, it becomes inappropriate to place much reliance on them as demonstrating a dissociation of habituation and latent inhibition. Indeed, Braveman and Jarvis (1978), having argued that their results imply separate mechanisms for the two phenomena, go on to acknowledge the possibility that their results might simply reflect the use of a test procedure that was less sensitive as a measure of conditioning than as a measure of neophobia. And, although it arises in a particularly acute form in these flavour-aversion studies, the same difficulty of interpretation vexes all the experiments cited here.

(d) Effects of changing the context

Figure 3.4 shows the results of an experiment by Channell and Hall (1983) in which rats received appetitive conditioning with a light CS—some subjects

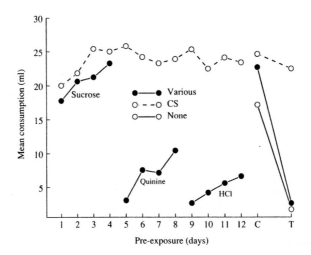

Fig. 3.3 Amount of flavoured solution consumed by subjects given 12 days of pre-exposure to NaCl (CS), no pre-exposure (none), or 4 days each of three different flavours (various). All three groups received NaCl on a conditioning trial (C) and consumption on this trial allowed assessment of the extent of neophobia in groups CS and none. The effects of the LiCl injection given on this trial was assessed on a subsequent test (T) trial. (Based on data from Miller and Holzman 1981, experiment 1.)

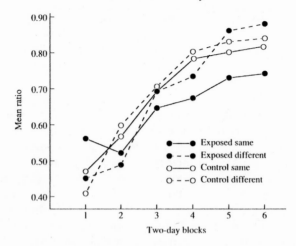

Fig. 3.4 Acquisition of conditioned responding to a light signalling food in rats pre-exposed to the test context (same groups) or to some other context (different groups). Half of the subjects in each of these groups experienced the light during pre-exposure (exposed) and half did not (control). A higher ratio score means a greater tendency to exhibit conditioned responding. (After Channell and Hall 1983.)

in a context to which they had been pre-exposed, others in a novel context, differing in its smell and the level of a background noise from that with which they were familiar. Half of the subjects in each training condition had received presentations of the light during the pre-exposure phase. Those that received pre-exposure and conditioning in the same context acquired the CR slowly (i.e. showed latent inhibition); those that experienced a change of context from exposure to conditioning learned as readily as the control subjects. This failure of latent inhibition to transfer from one context to another is of some theoretical significance, being uniquely predicted by Wagner's (1976, 1981) theory (see below, p. 81), and it has subsequently been sought and found in a variety of other training procedures (e.g. taste aversion, Hall and Channell (1986); conditioned suppression, Hall and Minor (1984), Lovibond, Preston, and Mackintosh (1984), Swartzentruber and Bouton (1986)).

The evidence discussed in Chapter 2 showed that, at least when the test context is familiar, a change of context does not restore an habituated response. Does latent inhibition continue to show context specificity when tested under equivalent conditions? The experiment by Hall and Channell (1985*b*), described in Chapter 2 (p. 40), was designed to allow an answer to this question. Recall that the experimental group (E group in Fig. 2.5(b)) in this experiment received exposure to two distinctive contexts (those used by Channell and Hall 1983), with presentations of a light occurring in only one of them (context A in the figure). The habituated OR to the light did not return when this stimulus was presented in the other context (context B in the figure), that is, habituation transferred across contexts. The status of latent inhibition was assessed in a final stage of training that immediately followed the habituation test. All subjects received two sessions per day of appetitive conditioning with the light as the CS, one session in context A and one in context B. As Fig. 3.5 shows, control subjects, for whom the light was novel, learned readily in both contexts. The experimental subjects acquired the CR only slowly when trained in context A, the context in which the light had been presented during the first stage of habituation training. But no latent inhibition was evident when conditioning was assessed in context B.

Essentially identical results have come from an experiment by Hall and Honey (1989*a*), which used quite different procedures. Two stimuli were used, the offset of a light and the presentation of a clicker, both of which tended on first presentation to evoke a suppression of ongoing behaviour. All subjects received presentations of both stimuli, the light in one distinctive context and the click in another. On the test session, subjects in one group continued with this same arrangement but for subjects in the critical experimental condition the stimuli were presented in the contexts in which they had not previously occurred. As Fig. 3.6 shows, the change of context for the latter group did nothing to restore the ability of the stimuli to evoke the UR. (Bouton (1990) reports an experiment by Bouton, Okun, and Swartzentruber which used closely similar training procedures and generated essentially identical results.) But the change of context did attenuate

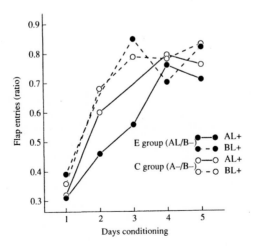

Fig. 3.5 Tendency of rats to perform a conditioned flap-pushing response as a result of light–food (L+) pairings. All subjects received training in two different contexts (A and B). The experimental (E) group had previously received exposure to the light in A; the control (C) group had not. (After Hall and Channell 1985*b*.)

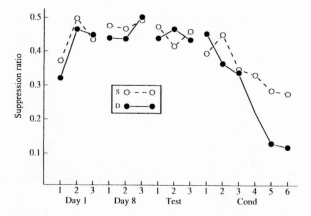

Fig. 3.6 Suppression (ratio score below 0.5) of ongoing behaviour during days 1 and 8 of habituation training, the habituation test day, and the two days of conditioning (cond). Groups S (same) and D (different) received identical treatment during the first stage, experiencing each of the two stimuli three times per day in separate sessions in two distinctively different contexts. (The ratio scores are pooled across stimulus type to produce three trials per day). In the test and for conditioning, group S received the stimuli in the 'wrong' contexts. (After Hall and Honey 1989*a*.)

latent inhibition. Figure 3.6 also shows the results of a final conditioning phase in which presentations of the stimuli continued as in the test session but were followed on each occasion by electric shock. Conditioned suppression was acquired readily only by those subjects (group D in the figure) that received training with the stimuli presented in the 'wrong' context.

(e) Effects of a retention interval

In all the examples cited so far the dissociation of habituation and latent inhibition has taken the form of showing that certain procedures abolish the latter while leaving the former intact. There is, however, one procedure that has been found to produce apparently the reverse effect—Hall and Schachtman (1987) have demonstrated that leaving a long interval between the last session of pre-exposure to the stimulus and the first test session will result in the restoration of an habituated UR while leaving latent inhibition unaffected. In this experiment, which used the same general procedures as those employed by Hall and Channell (1985*b*), rats received 16 days of preexposure to presentation of a light, enough for their tendency to orient to habituate. They then remained undisturbed in their home cages for a further 16 days before experiencing the light again. The frequency of occurrence of the OR returned to its original level. But when light–food pairings were given in the test phase, latent inhibition was observed; subjects given this treatment acquired the CR no more rapidly than control subjects that went straight from pre-exposure to conditioning without an intervening retention interval.

The dissociation produced by this procedure constitutes something of a theoretical puzzle. The account of habituation offered in Chapter 2 held that dishabituation would occur after a retention interval when the input failed to match the (partly forgotten) representation of the stimulus—when the subject failed to recognize the test stimulus. But if subjects failed to recognize the stimulus in the Hall and Schachtman (1987) study (as indicated by the occurrence of dishabituation), how could they show latent inhibition to that stimulus? The suggestion put forward by Hall and Schachtman was that the dishabituation observed in their experiment was not the consequence of a failure of input and representation to match, but rather depended on a change in level of arousal. They suggested that the likelihood of an OR might be determined not only by the specific state of habituation of the target stimulus but also by the extent to which the context is generally arousing (cf. the dual-process theory of Groves and Thompson 1970). It might plausibly be assumed that one of the effects of a long retention interval is to restore the lost arousing properties of a familiar context. If so, the restoration of the OR seen in these circumstances need not necessarily imply a change in the specific ability of the target stimulus to evoke its UR; rather it may mean that even a weak tendency to emit this UR can be amplified substantially by a high level of arousal. (The further implication is that the change in the effectiveness of the stimulus that is responsible for latent inhibition is not susceptible to the effects of heightened arousal.)

Table 3.1 presents the design and results of a study (reported by Hall and Honey 1989*b*) that provides support for this dual-process interpretation. Two groups of rats received 14 sessions of habituation training in context A with a light as the target stimulus. By the end of this training, ORs were occurring on no more than 20 per cent of trials. Both groups received a test session in which the light was presented in a different context (B) but one with which they were familiar in that all subjects had received 14 sessions of exposure to it. For one group (A-L/B in the table) these sessions of exposure to B followed habituation training in A, whereas for the other group (B/A-L) they preceded habituation training, which itself immediately preceded the test. Table 3.1 reveals that the OR was *not* restored after the retention interval when exposure to the test context filled the interval—habituation of the specific response to the light must therefore have survived the retention interval. On the other hand, the effects of pre-exposure to the test context did not survive the 14-day retention interval during which the light was presented in another context—subjects in group B/A-L showed a restoration of the OR similar to that seen in subjects transferred to an entirely new context. It seems that the arousing properties of a context will be re-established over a retention interval and will boost the frequency of occurrence of an habituated response that is otherwise unlikely to occur.

Table 3.1   Design and results of an orienting response experiment

	Stage 1	Stage 2	Test
Group B/A-L	B alone	Light in A 75 → 19 per cent	Light in B 48 per cent
Group A-L/B	Light in A 47 → 10 per cent	B alone	Light in B 23 per cent

A and B represent different distinctive contexts. Subjects received 14 days of training in each of stages 1 and 2 and a single test session. The light, when presented, occurred 10 times per session. Scores are percentage of trials on which OR occurred for the first and last sessions of stages 1 and 2 and the test session.

(f) Conclusions

On close inspection, several of the demonstrations of a dissociation between latent inhibition and habituation turn out to be of less theoretical significance than they first seemed. They consist, for the most part, of demonstrations that a certain procedure can abolish latent inhibition but will leave habituation intact. This finding is open to the criticism that it reflects no more than a difference between the two phenomena in their sensitivity—that the procedure in question disrupts some process common to both phenomena and that the latent inhibition procedure provides a more sensitive measure of this disruption than does the habituation procedure. This criticism is not easy to meet but perhaps the best argument available comes from the experiment described last. Here it was the habituated OR that was sensitive to a change in arousal level whereas latent inhibition was not. To accept the implication of this finding makes it difficult to explain away the dissociation obtained by Hall and Channell (1985*b*) (the observation that latent inhibition is context dependent when habituation is not), which came from an experiment using the same response measures, stimuli, and procedures as were used by Hall and Schachtman (1987). Taken together, these two experiments constitute a double dissociation between habituation and latent inhibition.

The force of the argument just presented may not be overwhelming but it is enough to prompt the tentative conclusion that, in addition to the habituation process invoked by exposure to a stimulus, some other process comes into play and is responsible for latent inhibition. The mechanism responsible for latent inhibition may still be a loss of stimulus associability but we need some new account of how this loss comes about. A range of rival theories is considered next. An important feature of a successful theory will be an ability to explain (since this is where the habituation theory fell down) why latent inhibition should be context-specific. One of the most persuasive interpretations of this fact, and that to be considered next, derives from

Wagner's (1976, 1981) theories. Ironically this account was originally presented as a theory of habituation.

3.2. CS predictability and latent inhibition

3.2.1. Wagner's theory

Wagner's (1976, 1981) theory of habituation, discussed at length in Chapter 2, is also a theory of latent inhibition. It will be recalled that, according to this theory, a stimulus is held to be fully effective only when it is able to generate the A1 (primary activation) state in the node that constitutes its central representation. A node that is in the A2 (secondary activation) state (either because its stimulus has only recently been presented or because it has been activated internally by means of an excitatory associative link) will not be able to move into A1. Accordingly, a stimulus will be relatively ineffective both when it has itself recently occurred and also when it is presented along with cues that have previously signalled its occurrence. (In the case of habituation training, these cues will normally be those that constitute the context in which the stimulus has been presented).

So far we have considered only the extent to which changes in stimulus effectiveness might be revealed by changes in the ability of a stimulus to evoke its UR; but, according to the theory, a loss of effectiveness will have other effects. In particular, a stimulus can come to acquire associative strength as a CS only when it is represented in the A1 state in company with another active node—excitatory conditioning will occur when the US node is in A1; inhibitory conditioning when the US node is in A2 (see Chapter 1). Thus the conditions of training that generate habituation of the UR (i.e. those that put a node into the A2 state) will also result in the stimulus acting as only an inadequate CS—that is, they will also produce latent inhibition. Like habituation, therefore, latent inhibition can be the result of both associative and non-associative mechanisms, since the A2 state can be established both directly (as the after-effect of presentation of the stimulus itself) and associatively (by presentation of contextual cues). In its latter aspect the theory can be seen as a formalization, in associative terms, of the very reasonable suggestion that a stimulus is likely to receive a full measure of processing only when its occurrence is unexpected (i.e. not predictable on the basis of other, usually contextual, cues).

The extensive discussion of the topic in Chapter 2 led to rejection of the account offered by Wagner for habituation, but this may be just as well as far as his theory of latent inhibition is concerned. For the empirical evidence discussed in the first section of this chapter led to the conclusion that habituation and latent inhibition are subserved by different mechanisms; it follows that a theory based on the assumption of a common mechanism must be wrong in one way or another; the fact that Wagner's theory is inadequate as an account of habituation provides no reason to reject its explanation for latent inhibition. I turn next, therefore, to an examination of its two chief predictions about latent inhibition. They are, first, that it should be possible to distinguish different forms of latent inhibition based on associative and non-associative mechanisms, the former being short-lived and the latter more nearly permanent. Second, long-term latent inhibition depends upon the target stimulus being predicted by other cues and should be disrupted when the stimulus occurs in the absence of these cues (in particular, in a new context).

3.2.2. Short-term latent inhibition

Most studies of latent inhibition use procedures in which there are many widely spaced presentations of the target stimulus and there is a long interval (frequently of 24 h) between the last pre-exposure trial and the first trial of conditioning. Such procedures are right for generating the phenomenon in Wagner's associative form—a series of widely spaced exposure trials will promote the formation of a context–stimulus association; and the after-effects of presentation of the target stimulus could not be expected to survive a 24-h retention interval. But it should also be possible to generate a short-lived form of latent inhibition in which the A2 state is an after-effect of the occurrence of the target stimulus. When the interval between exposure and the start of conditioning is short enough to ensure that this after-effect has not dissipated, latent inhibition should be particularly marked having contributions both from the short-term and the associative mechanisms. The size of the latent inhibition effect should decline as the interval is increased and the short-term effect is lost; and when the exposure conditions are poor for association formation (e.g. when there is just a single, brief exposure) there may be only a short-term effect and no latent inhibition at all at the longer interval.

(a) Effect of the interval between exposure and test

In order to test these predictions we need to compare the size of the latent inhibition effect found after a long exposure–test interval (which we may take to be 24 h or more) with that found after a short interval (when conditioning follows exposure immediately or after a few minutes). The matter was first investigated by Siegel (1970) (but see also Lubow *et al.* 1968) who found, using an auditory stimulus and aversive conditioning, that latent inhibition was as substantial with a 24-h interval as when there was no delay between exposure and conditioning. Siegel's result has been confirmed by others using similar training procedures (James 1971; Crowell and Anderson 1972). But evidence consistent with Wagner's account has come from experiments using the flavour-aversion procedure. Figure 3.7 summarizes the design and results of an experiment by Best and Gemberling (1977) (see also

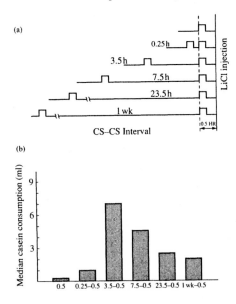

Fig. 3.7 Design (a) and results (b) of experiment by Best and Gemberling (1977). All rats received a conditioning trial in which access to a flavoured solution (casein) was followed after 0.5 h by an injection of LiCl. Some subjects received pre-exposure to the solution at intervals ranging from 0.25 h to 1 week before the conditioning trial. Panel (b) shows the amount consumed by the various groups on a test trial given a day after conditioning. (CS = conditioned stimulus.)

Best and Barker 1977) in which rats were given access to 5 ml of a distinctively flavoured solution at various intervals before a conditioning trial on which consumption of this solution was followed by an injection of LiCl. It is apparent that the aversion developed only poorly with an exposure–test interval of 3.5 h but that conditioning proceeded more readily (latent inhibition was attenuated although not abolished) when the interval was increased.[*]

An attenuation of latent inhibition with a long interval between exposure and conditioning has not always been found, even in flavour-aversion learning—Nachman and Jones (1974) and Siegel (1974) have found the latent inhibition effect to persist in strength at intervals of much more than 3.5 h. Bond and Westbrook (1982) suggest that the source of the discrepancy can

---

[*] The figure also shows that latent inhibition was attenuated when the exposure-conditioning interval was reduced to 0.25 h. This effect is probably not of theoretical significance. It is known that the magnitude of a conditioned aversion can be enhanced by increasing the amount of a flavour consumed on the conditioning trial (e.g. Bond and DiGiusto 1975; Barker 1976). 'Pre-exposure' given shortly before the conditioning trial may amount to giving the animal an especially effective CS.

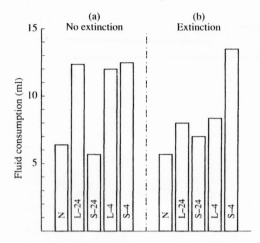

Fig. 3.8 Consumption of water in the presence of an odour conditioned stimulus on a test session following odour–illness conditioning. Some subjects received no exposure (N) to the odour prior to the conditioning trial; others received exposure of long duration (L) or short duration (S) occurring 4 h or 24 h before the conditioning trial. Half the subjects in each condition received a period of exposure to the context in the absence of the odour (extinction) interpolated between pre-exposure and conditioning. (After Westbrook *et al.* 1981.)

be found in the amount of the flavoured substance experienced by the subjects on the pre-exposure trial—Best and Gemberling (1977) gave only brief exposure whereas the other experimenters gave rather more. Direct tests of this suggestion have been conducted in experiments by Westbrook, Bond, and Feyer (1981), by Bond and Westbrook (1982), and by Westbrook, Provost, and Homewood (1982), in which the duration of the initial pre-exposure trial was varied. All three studies confirmed the Best and Gemberling (1977) effect when the exposure duration was brief but also found that more prolonged initial exposure generated latent inhibition both when the exposure–conditioning interval was short (3–4 h) and when it was long (24 h or more). Figure 3.8(a) summarizes the effect seen in the experiment by Westbrook *et al.* (1981).* Westbrook and his collaborators interpreted their results as supporting Wagner's account of latent inhibition, arguing that prolonged experience of the stimulus in the context might be necessary for the

---

* It should be added that although the studies by Bond and Westbrook (1982) and by Westbrook *et al.* (1982) produced the same general pattern of results as is shown in Fig. 3.8(a), an odd feature was that latent inhibition was found to be especially profound at the 24-h interval after lengthy pre-exposure. The source of this discrepancy is obscure.

formation of the association on which long-term latent inhibition is held to depend. A brief exposure will, therefore, produce only the short-lived effect. Longer exposure will produce both this effect and the associative version, making it much more difficult to see any decline in latent inhibition at the longer intervals. It may be noted that the experiments by Siegel (1970), James (1971), and Crowell and Anderson (1972), which failed to find any loss of latent inhibition at longer intervals, all gave repeated presentations of the target stimulus in pre-exposure; that is, they gave training likely to establish a context–target association.

Although these results appear to be consistent with the short-term/long-term distinction inherent in Wagner's theory, they do not *require* us to make the distinction. We can just as readily conclude that there is just one type of latent inhibition; that the change induced by exposure to the stimulus always tends to dissipate during the exposure–test interval; and that the size of the interval required for such a loss of latent inhibition to become apparent grows longer as the strength of the effect induced by the initial exposure phase is increased. An implication of the last point is that even when the initial exposure to the stimulus has been prolonged or has involved repeated presentations, it should be possible to detect some loss of the latent inhibition effect over time, provided the interval before the start of conditioning is long enough. I have already said that a 24-h interval is not enough for such a loss to be seen. But what will be the effect of extending the interval to a period of days or even weeks? Experiments using the flavour-aversion techniques, comparing intervals of 1 day versus 24 days (McIntosh and Tarpy 1977), and of 1 day versus 21 days (Kraemer and Roberts 1984), have found that latent inhibition is diminished at the longer interval. And equivalent results have come from at least some studies using the conditioned suppression procedure (e.g. Baker and Mercier (1982*b*), who compared intervals of 1 day and 5 days; Hall and Minor (1984), who compared 1 day and 8 days; but see also Crowell and Anderson (1972)).

(b) Contextual manipulations

Thus, the observation that brief exposure to a flavour produces latent inhibition only at short retention intervals (say 3–4 h) whereas more prolonged exposure produces latent inhibition at intervals of 24 h or more is not in itself proof of the suggestion that different mechanisms underlie the two cases. What is needed is evidence that the phenomena supposed to reflect different short-term and long-term processes respond differently to various procedural manipulations. Such evidence has been sought by Westbrook *et al.* (1981), with mixed results. They argue that prolonged exposure (to an odour in their experiments) will allow the formation of a context–stimulus association, wholly responsible for the latent inhibition seen at 24 h and partly responsible for that seen at 4 h. A change of context between the exposure phase and the conditioning phase should, therefore, eliminate latent inhibition at the 24–h interval and reduce that seen at the 4–h interval. Westbrook *et al.* found this to be so, and demonstrated also that the latent inhibition produced by brief exposure to the odour was unaffected by contextual change. They argue further that it should be possible to eliminate the long-term effect by a procedure designed to extinguish a context–stimulus association—the procedure they used was that of giving a period of exposure to the context alone between initial exposure to the target and the conditioning phase. (See below, p. 87, for a fuller discussion of the implications of this procedure.) And indeed, they were able to show (see Fig. 3.8(b)) that such a procedure dramatically attenuated the latent inhibition produced by lengthy initial exposure both at 4 h and 24 h but had no effect on the latent inhibition (at 4 h) produced by brief initial exposure.

Interpretation of these findings is not straightforward. The sensitivity to contextual manipulations of the latent inhibition produced by lengthy exposure is certainly consistent with the suggestion that a context–stimulus association is responsible for the effect seen at 24 h and contributes to that seen at 4 h. But an obvious implication of this last point is not confirmed by the observations. As the latent inhibition effect seen at 4 h after lengthy pre-exposure is supposed to enjoy the benefit of contributions from both the short-term mechanism and from the context–stimulus association, this effect should be especially strong. But no such result is found. Westbrook *et al.* (1981) conducted several experiments (Fig. 3.8(a) constitutes an example) that allowed the relevant comparison and all agreed in showing that the latent inhibition seen at 4 h was just as profound after brief exposure as after lengthy exposure. They have no explanation to offer apart from the speculation that there might be an incompatibility between the two sources of latent inhibition allowed by Wagner's account, with the short-term version being developed only in conditions that preclude the development of the associative version. There is no evidence bearing on this suggestion and the matter must remain unresolved for the time being. We can conclude only that unequivocal evidence for the existence of the special short-term version of latent inhibition posited by Wagner's theory has yet to emerge. Such evidence as there is derives from the studies by Westbrook *et al.* (1981) in which contextual cues were manipulated. We need now to examine the role of contextual factors directly and in more detail.

3.2.3. The context-specificity of latent inhibition

The evidence, already discussed in this chapter (pp. 75–8), demonstrating that latent inhibition shows context-specificity constitutes powerful support for Wagner's (1976, 1981) associative interpretation of the phenomenon. Prior to the development of Wagner's (1976) theory, the role of contextual factors had received little attention (but see Anderson, O'Farrell, Formica, and Caponigri 1969; Anderson, Wolf, and Sullivan 1969; Dexter and Merill

1969). The prediction of the theory, that latent inhibition should be diminished when pre-exposure and conditioning take place in different contexts, thus provoked a new line of experimental work and, as we have seen, the prediction has been convincingly confirmed. But, however suggestive it may be, the fact that a given phenomenon is successfully predicted by a theory does not prove the theory to be correct. Alternative accounts of context-specificity are available and they will be discussed in Chapter 4. For the time being we shall concentrate on empirical studies concerned with specific further predictions made by Wagner's theory.

(a) Exposure to the context alone

According to Wagner's theory, a period of exposure to the context alone, given either before or after exposure to the target stimulus in that context, should attenuate latent inhibition. Prior exposure to the context will produce latent inhibition of the contextual stimuli themselves (they will come to be reliably predicted by those cues that signal the start of an experimental session) and so the context–stimulus association will form only slowly, if at all, when presentations of the target stimulus are begun. Exposure to the context alone given after latent inhibition training will, according to the theory, allow extinction of the context–stimulus association that has already been formed. As latent inhibition is held to depend on the integrity of the context–stimulus association, both these procedures should alleviate the retarding effect of pre-exposure to the stimulus.

Investigation of these predictions has yielded mixed results. We have already noted that the experiment summarized in Fig. 3.8 (Westbrook *et al.* 1981) produced results suggesting that the latent inhibition consequent on relatively prolonged exposure to an odour can be abolished by extinction of the context. But experiments using the conditioned suppression procedure have generated doubts about the generality of this conclusion. Baker and Mercier (1982*b*) found evidence of the extinction effect in only two of their six experiments and were able to offer no very convincing account of why these two studies (which used a somewhat different test procedure from that used in the others) should have generated the result they did. And a further set of six experiments by Hall and Minor (1984), which used procedures very similar to those of Baker and Mercier (1982*b*), found no sign of any loss of the latent inhibition effect when exposure to the context intervened between exposure and conditioning.

Hall and Channell (1985*c*) used the same general training procedures as had been employed by Hall and Minor (1984) but they reversed the order of the treatments in the critical condition; that is, they gave exposure to the context alone before the latent inhibition training. Here, as Fig. 3.9 shows, a clear effect was observed. Pre-exposure to the stimulus (a tone) produced latent inhibition but the effect was especially marked (i.e. the acquisition of conditioned suppression was particularly retarded) in subjects given prior

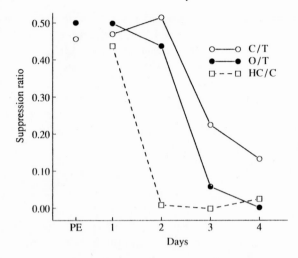

Fig. 3.9 Acquisition of conditioned suppression by three groups of rats given training with a tone signalling shock. Two groups had received latent inhibition training with the tone which had itself been preceded by a phase of exposure to the conditioning context (group C/T) or to some other context (O/T). Control subjects (group HC/C) remained in their home cages during the first phase of training and then experienced the context without any presentations of the tone. PE shows performance on the last session of tone pre-exposure. (After Hall and Channell 1985*c*.)

exposure to the context. Thus, far from attenuating the latent inhibition effect as Wagner's associative theory requires, prior exposure to the context acted to enhance latent inhibition.

Hall and Channell (1985*c*) interpreted their context pre-exposure effect as being a special case of the more basic phenomenon of context-specificity. They argued, first, that pre-exposure to a context will reduce the extent to which a subject is likely to learn about it (see Balaz, Capra, Kasprow, and Miller 1982); second, that presenting reinforcers (shocks in this experiment) in a context in which they had not previously occurred is functionally equivalent to transferring the animal to a physically different context. The first suggestion implies that context pre-exposure should make subsequently acquired latent inhibition less likely to be context-specific—subjects need to be prepared to learn about the context if context-specificity is to occur. Adding this to the second suggestion, it follows that the change of context produced by introducing reinforcers in the conditioning stage will have little effect on subjects given pre-exposure to the context but will limit the degree to which latent inhibition is shown by subjects not given pre-exposure. What remains to be explained, of course, if this account is accepted, is why latent inhibition should show context specificity at all. Although explicable as an instance of context-specificity the results of this experiment have apparently put paid to the only explanation for the phenomenon that we have so far considered.

3.2.4. An alternative associative account

Although we may want to reject Wagner's (1976, 1981) specific formulation, it remains possible that other versions of associative theory might be able to explain the findings on context-specificity. This is what has been claimed for an alternative associative account put forward by McLaren, Kaye, and Mackintosh (1989). This theory develops the convergence (also noted by others, e.g. Sutton and Barto 1981; Gluck and Bower 1988) between standard associative models and connectionist systems of parallel distributed processing (e.g. Rumelhart, Hinton, and McClelland 1986) and it is intended to apply to a range of phenomena in perceptual learning. For our present purposes, however, the important feature of the model is that it develops the implications of the widely accepted notion that even the simplest stimulus will consist of a set (probably a large number) of elements and that only some of these will be sampled (will activate their central representations) on a given exposure (cf. Estes 1950; Neimark and Estes 1967). Latent inhibition is held to be a consequence of the formation of associations among these elements.

More specifically, the model makes the usual associative assumption that excitatory links will be established between representations (of elements) that are activated concurrently. Repeated presentation of a given stimulus, therefore, will allow a network of links to be established among the elements that go to make it up (particularly strong links being formed among those elements that tend to be sampled frequently). After such training a given element will, when the stimulus is applied, be the target both of external input and of internal input by way of the associative links that connect it to other elements. The model assumes the existence of a mechanism (a 'modulator') that detects any discrepancy between internal and external inputs, and, when the external input exceeds the internal, boosts the associability of the element to a degree proportional to the discrepancy. A novel stimulus will lack internal inputs, will have a large discrepancy between external and internal inputs, and thus its elements will enter readily into associations. For a familiar stimulus there will be little discrepancy and associability will be low—that is, latent inhibition will occur.

Contextual cues are given no special status in this scheme. The context consists of a set of elements some of which will be sampled along with elements of the target stimulus on each exposure. The associative network formed will thus include links among contextual elements and between these and elements of the target. These latter, as in Wagner's theory, will play their part in lowering the associability of the target stimulus.

It will be apparent that this model can readily generate the prediction that latent inhibition will be (to some extent) context-specific. Presenting the target stimulus in a new context will eliminate some sources of internal input to the stimulus. Furthermore, as context–stimulus associations are not the sole source of latent inhibition, the model need not be embarrassed by the observation that exposure to the context alone (either before or after exposure to the target stimulus) does not abolish the effect. What remains a problem is to explain why exposure to the context alone given after exposure to the stimulus can be quite without influence on the magnitude of latent inhibition (Hall and Minor 1984) and why pre-exposure to the context should actually enhance the magnitude of the effect (Hall and Channell 1985c).

McLaren *et al.* (1989) acknowledge the reality of these problems for their theory and present additional features of the connectionist model that might allow it to accommodate the findings. One suggestion is that pre-exposure to the context, by preventing the subsequent formation of context–target associations, might enhance latent inhibition because it ensures that particularly strong associations will be formed among the elements of the target itself. A further suggestion is that exposure to the context alone given after exposure to the target stimulus will result not only in extinction of context-stimulus associations but may also serve to attenuate the rate with which associations are forgotten. The latter process will tend to counteract the loss of latent inhibition produced by the former.

These other features of the model have yet to be fully developed and experimental evidence that might allow us to evaluate them is sparse. We can do no more for the time being, then, than acknowledge that a refined version of associative theory might be capable of dealing with features of latent inhibition that constitute problems for a theory which relies solely on the context–stimulus association for its explanation. It may be noted, however, that the connectionist theory is in principle identical to that of Wagner (1976, 1981). Both theories have as their basis the suggestion that a stimulus (or stimulus element) will be low in associability to the extent that it is the subject of excitatory associative influence—to the extent that it is predicted by other stimuli or stimulus elements. Other theories of latent inhibition have taken a quite different view of the phenomenon. They have suggested that the loss of associability suffered by a pre-exposed stimulus is determined not by the extent to which it is predicted by its antecedents but by the relationship it bears to subsequent events. I consider these theories next.

3.3. Stimulus consequences and latent inhibition

3.3.1. Conditioned attention theory

(a) An outline

The theory proposed by Lubow and his collaborators (e.g. Lubow, Schnur, and Rifkin 1976; Lubow, Weiner, and Schnur 1981) starts by assuming that a novel stimulus will evoke an 'attentional response'. This response is not directly equated with the OR or any component of it; rather it is an hypothetical construct evidenced in behaviour by its effect on the rate of conditioning—the associability of a stimulus is determined by the magnitude of the attentional response it evokes.

Repeated presentation of a stimulus is held to bring about a decline in the size of the attentional response. This decline is postulated to be a classically conditioned decrement, with the consistent absence of any effective event following the target stimulus being viewed as the US that supports the conditioning of inattention (see Lubow *et al.* 1981, p. 5). The assumptions about classical conditioning that are implied by this notion must be rather different from those embodied in the standard model. It is necessary to assume, for instance, that the complete absence of an event can function as a US; that some mechanism exists whereby whatever association is formed during conditioning brings about a reduction in the magnitude of the unconditioned response (i.e. the attentional response) initially evoked by the stimulus that is trained as the CS. Lubow *et al.* (1981, p. 8), however, deny the need to specify a theory of conditioning and concern themselves with the empirical implications of the view that changes in attention will be governed by the known laws of classical conditioning. We need to examine, therefore, whether procedures known to influence associative strength in orthodox conditioning will also influence the acquisition of inattention during stimulus exposure.

(b) Overshadowing, blocking, and related phenomena

The considerations just advanced led Lubow *et al.* (1981, p. 14) to maintain that the development of latent inhibition, like the acquisition of associative strength, will be subject to overshadowing and blocking. Overshadowing (the observation that the associative strength acquired by a target stimulus A is reduced when another event, B, is also present on reinforced trials) and blocking (the observation that prior reinforced training with B can effectively eliminate acquisition to A when AB trials are given) are primary characteristics of conditioning, found in all training procedures and in almost all organisms capable of classical conditioning. It is critical for Lubow's general approach, therefore, to demonstrate their presence in latent inhibition.

In order to investigate this matter, Honey and Hall (1988) gave rats pre-exposure to a compound stimulus AB (a mixture of two flavours) followed by aversion conditioning with A alone as the CS. Less profound latent inhibition than that shown by subjects given pre-exposure to A alone would constitute evidence for overshadowing of latent inhibition. Other subjects (in a separate experiment) received pre-exposure to B alone before AB exposure. If the acquisition of latent inhibition by B blocks that by A, then these subjects should show more rapid conditioning to A than those given

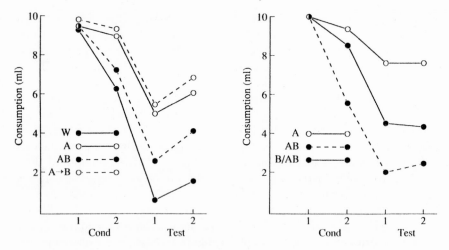

Fig. 3.10 Group mean amounts of a flavoured solution (A) consumed during conditioning (cond) trials and on test trials for groups of rats pre-exposed to water (W), to the flavour (A), or to the target flavour mixed with some other (AB). One group of subjects (A→B) received serial presentations of A and B during pre-exposure. In the right-hand panel, group B/AB received presentations of B alone before exposure to the AB compound. (Adapted from Honey and Hall 1988.)

no experience of B before their AB trials. The results, summarized in Fig. 3.10, show an overshadowing effect (group AB conditions more readily than group A) but far from producing blocking, pre-exposure to B alone allows AB exposure to generate a particularly marked latent inhibition effect.

This pattern of results is enough to make us doubtful about the interpretation of latent inhibition offered by Lubow *et al.* (1981); but it remains to explain why latent inhibition procedures should apparently be capable of producing overshadowing but not blocking. Honey and Hall (1988) offered the following. Latent inhibition will be fully evident only when the subject is able to identify the stimulus used as the CS as being that presented during pre-exposure. If the two are perceived as being different in some way (and with compound, AB, pre-exposure the presence of B might interact with A at a sensory or perceptual level making it discriminably different from the A used in conditioning), then generalization decrement would occur and the transfer of latent inhibition would be incomplete. Thus the overshadowing effect can be explained without recourse to the mechanisms usually supposed to be responsible for it in associative learning (but see Pearce 1987). And the notion of generalization decrement can also explain the effects of prior exposure to B alone if it is allowed that such training will make the B stimulus less effective and thus relatively unlikely to interfere with the perception of A when the two are presented in compound. Pre-exposure to B, therefore, will attenuate or abolish the overshadowing effect.

Evidence in favour of Honey and Hall's interpretation comes from examining the conditions that are necessary for the overshadowing effect to emerge in latent inhibition. In particular, earlier studies using the conditioned suppression procedure have provided little evidence for the effect (Rudy, Krauter, and Gaffuri 1976; Baker and Mercier 1982*a*; Mercier and Baker 1985) (but see also Mackintosh 1973). Thus, Mercier and Baker report a series of experiments in which rats pre-exposed to a compound of a clicker and a light acquired latent inhibition to the click just as readily as subjects pre-exposed to the click alone, and this in spite of the fact that the light was a salient event that was certainly noticed and processed by the animals. Everyday experience tells us that a flavour mixed with some other will be perceived differently from that flavour presented on its own, but a click and a light (perhaps because they come from different modalities) are less likely to interact in this way. If so, a click pre-exposed in compound with a light will be perceived as being identical to the click presented alone, and compound pre-exposure will thus be perfectly effective in producing latent inhibition. In other words, considerations of generalization decrement give reason to expect an overshadowing effect in flavour-aversion experiments but not in the conditioned suppression experiments.

Evidence to support this conclusion comes from a further set of studies by Honey and Hall (1989*b*), who examined the effects of compound pre-exposure in the conditioned suppression paradigm using two auditory stimuli, a tone and a click. Sharing a common modality may be enough to produce generalization decrement and thus, according to the account presented above, an overshadowing effect might be expected with these stimuli. This is just what Honey and Hall (1989*b*) found—compound exposure attenuated the acquisition of latent inhibition by a tone when the other member of the compound was a click; but (as in the Mercier and Baker (1985) study) a salient light was ineffective as an overshadowing stimulus.*

A further implication of this analysis concerns the related case in which the AB compound is used as the CS and pre-exposure is given to the A and B elements presented separately. If A and B interact, then the components of the compound will not necessarily be perceived as being the same as the stimuli encountered during pre-exposure and latent inhibition will be attenuated. Exposure to the AB compound itself will be much more likely to generate latent inhibition. Conditioned attention theory appears to make the

---

* Lubow, Wagner, and Weiner (1982, experiment 2) claim to have shown that a tone will suffer less latent inhibition when exposed alone than when exposed in compound with a salient light. In their experiment, however, conditioning trials were given with the tone–light compound. Accordingly, their result could be the consequence of overshadowing that occurred during the conditioning phase, an effect that might be expected to be more extensive in the group for which the light was novel (see Carr 1974).

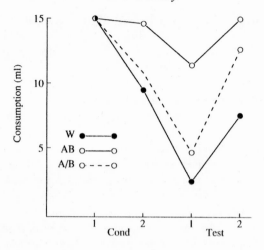

Fig. 3.11   Group mean amounts of a flavoured solution (AB) consumed during conditioning trials (cond) and on test trials for groups of rats pre-exposed to water (W),
to the AB compound itself, or to separate presentations of the elements of the compound (group A/B). (After Baker *et al.* 1990.)

opposite prediction. To the extent that a given CR, separately acquired to
each of two CSs, is likely to be evoked with particular vigour when the two
CSs are presented together so the conditioned response of inattention will be
especially strong when A and B have separately undergone latent inhibition
training.

These rival predictions have been tested in a series of experiments by
Baker, Haskins, and Hall (1990). Figure 3.11 shows a representative set of
results from an experiment using the flavour-aversion paradigm. The stimuli
and procedures were identical to those employed by Honey and Hall (1988;
see Fig. 3.10) except, of course, the CS was the AB compound and pre-
exposure was either with AB itself or with A and B presented separately. As
the figure shows, both pre-exposed groups showed latent inhibition (were
more ready to consume the AB compound on test than subjects not given
pre-exposure) but the size of the effect was much diminished in the group
that experienced A and B separately. Thus the interaction between these stimuli is just what would be expected from considerations of generalization
decrement and is not that predicted by conditioned attention theory.*

---

* It should be added that in none of their experiments could Baker *et al.* (1990) find
   any sign of an effect reported by Holland and Forbes (1980) which seemed to suggest that, at least with certain procedures, element pre-exposure might produce
   more latent inhibition than compound pre-exposure. The source of the Holland
   and Forbes result remains obscure.

(c) Exposure to a serial compound

Although, according to conditioned attention theory, exposure to a stimulus will inevitably lead eventually to a decline in its power to evoke an attentional response, this decline can be postponed (even for a time reversed) if the target stimulus (S_1) is followed by some other (S_2) during initial exposure. The rationale for this suggestion is that, since S_2 will itself initially evoke an attentional response, classical conditioning will ensure that this response comes to be evoked by S_1, summating with the attentional response evoked by S_1 itself. With sufficient training, however, both stimuli will lose the ability to evoke attention. It follows that after a moderate number of trials the amount of latent inhibition accruing to S_1 when presented as part of the serial compound S_1–S_2 is likely to be less than that produced by training with S_1 alone. It may be noted that Wagner's (1976) theory makes the same prediction. The presentation of S_2 will, according to the theory, act as a distractor, limiting the subject's ability to process the target S_1 and thus the development of the context–S_1 association supposedly responsible for latent inhibition.

Experimental investigations of this prediction have produced a mixed set of results. The left-hand panel of Fig. 3.10 (p. 92) contains an example of a study of the S1–S2 procedure (by Honey and Hall 1988) in which the stimuli were distinctive flavours. Subjects in the A→B condition received pre-exposure to the target stimulus A followed by access to another flavoured substance (B). The result in the figure show that this procedure generated just as much latent inhibition as did exposure to A alone. This failure to find any effect of presenting the S_2 during pre-exposure confirms the findings of an earlier set of experiments by Westbrook *et al.* (1982), which, using very similar stimuli and training procedures, similarly found no effect. It is something of a puzzle, therefore, that others using the flavour-aversion procedure (Best, Gemberling, and Johnson 1979; Kaye, Swietalski, and Mackintosh 1988*b*) should have been able to demonstrate an attenuation of latent inhibition. The results of one of the experiments by Kaye *et al.* (1988*b*) are summarized in Fig. 3.12. They show that animals pre-exposed once to vinegar before a conditioning trial with this flavour consumed more vinegar on the test trials than did control subjects not given pre-exposure. But subjects given vinegar followed by sucrose (VS) during pre-exposure showed no latent inhibition, consuming no more vinegar on test than did control subjects.

Although these results are compatible with conditioned attention theory (and with Wagner's theory), Kaye *et al.* (1988*b*) prefer an explanation in terms of generalization decrement. We have already acknowledged that latent inhibition can be expected only when the CS is identified as being the same as the pre-exposed stimulus. If we accept (and the case has been argued in detail with respect to habituation; Chapter 2, pp. 50–3) that the

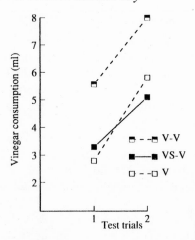

Fig. 3.12 Consumption of vinegar on two test trials in rats given a single condition-ing trial with vinegar as the CS. Vinegar was novel for group V on the conditioning trial; group V-V had received pre-exposure to vinegar; group VS-V, pre-exposure to vinegar followed immediately by sucrose. (From Kaye *et al.* 1988*b*.)

presentation of S_2 modify the representation of S_1 that is formed, then gener-alization decrement will ensure that little latent inhibition will be evident after S_1–S_2 pre-exposure. Kaye *et al.* (1988*b*) support this interpretation by demonstrating that the VS pre-exposure treatment will produce perfectly good latent inhibition when the CS used in the conditioning phase is itself vinegar followed by sucrose, an arrangement that should ensure that the same representation of vinegar is activated on both occasions. They further point out that the likelihood of such generalization-decrement effects will depend upon the exact nature of the stimuli (some pairs will interact more than others) and that not all combinations of S_1 and S_2 can be expected to generate an attenuation of latent inhibition.

Certainly, experiments using more orthodox conditioning stimuli (tones, lights and so on) have produced only scanty evidence that the presence of S_2 during can influence latent inhibition. Mercier and Baker (1985) (see also Baker and Mercier 1982*a*) report the results of an extensive and thorough series of experiments (using the conditioned suppression procedure and a clicker and a light as the stimuli), none of which yielded any indication that the S_1–S_2 procedure diminished the magnitude of latent inhibition. On the other hand, Lubow *et al.* (1976) have found that pre-exposure to a tone and a light presented serially generates less latent inhibition than pre-exposure to the target stimulus presented alone (a result also reported by Szakmary (1977) in a study using a noise and a light as the stimuli). Oddly, however, the S_1–S_2 procedure used by Lubow *et al.* (1976) did not generate reliably less latent inhibition than a control procedure in which the subjects received exposure to S_1 and S_2 presented uncorrelated with one another. Why this control procedure should have attenuated latent inhibition is not clear, but evidently the presence of S_2 can have this effect even when it is not (as is required by current theories) presented immediately after S_1. The source of the effect seen in subjects given the S_1–S_2 treatment is accordingly difficult to interpret.

The issue is made yet more obscure by the results reported by Matzel, Schachtman, and Miller (1988, experiment 1A). Although their procedures were almost identical to those employed by Mercier and Baker (1985), they were able to demonstrate a total abolition of latent inhibition in subjects given S_1–S_2 pre-exposure. I can only speculate about the reasons for their success. One possibility concerns the nature of the stimuli they used—a tone as S_1 and a click train as S_2. I have already suggested (p. 93) that tone and clicker (at least when presented simultaneously) might interact perceptually in a way that an auditory and a visual stimulus do not. If the same applies with serial presentation, then the generalization-decrement argument offered by Kaye *et al.* (1988*b*) for their own results might be applicable in this case too. A second distinctive feature of the experiment by Matzel *et al.* (1988) was that their S_2 varied from one pre-exposure trial to the next. S_2 was always a 3-s train of clicks but the frequency of the train was varied being 3 Hz on some trials and 12 Hz on others. There is a hint here that latent inhibition might be determined by the extent to which the target stimulus has consistent consequences—a notion inherent to the theory (proposed by Pearce and Hall (1980)) that will be discussed next.

(d) Conclusion

Lubow *et al.* (1981) list 15 predictions that they derive from their conditioned attention theory and point out that many of these have received empirical confirmation. If I have concentrated on just a few of these predictions this is, in part, because several of those neglected are not unique to the conditioned attention theory and are readily accommodated by its rivals. The predictions that I have concerned myself with are rather more critical. Lubow *et al.* (1981) themselves place great emphasis on the S_1–S_2 procedure. From their point of view the results are rather disappointing. There is some sign that the presence of an S_2 during pre-exposure might, in some circumstances, attenuate latent inhibition but little to suggest that the mechanism responsible is that envisaged by conditioned attention theory. Even more worrying is the fact that latent inhibition does not suffer from overshadowing and blocking in the way that normal conditioning does. This is enough in itself to make us want to reject conditioned attention theory as it is presently formulated.

3.3.2. The Pearce–Hall model

(a) An outline of the model

Perhaps the earliest statement of the view that latent inhibition depends upon the relationship between the target stimulus and its consequences was that offered by Mackintosh (1973), who argued that the phenomenon was one aspect of a general ability of animals to learn to ignore stimuli that predicted no change in reinforcement. This notion was formalized in the model proposed by Mackintosh in 1975. Recall that the standard associative model (see equation 1, p. 6) makes use of α, a learning rate parameter determined by the properties of the CS. Mackintosh's suggestion was that the value of α (i.e. the associability of the CS) might be determined not only by the intrinsic qualities of the stimulus (such as its intensity) but also by the animal's past experience with the stimulus.

This notion was taken up in the model proposed by Pearce and Hall (1980) (and developed by Hall and Pearce (1982), and by Pearce, Kaye, and Hall (1982)), which was presented originally as an account of classical conditioning. The central assumption of the model is that the α-value of a novel stimulus tends to be high (its exact value being determined by stimulus salience) but will decline with training according to an equation of the following sort:

$$\alpha^n = |\lambda^{n-1} - V^{n-1}| \qquad (3.1)$$

where α^n represents the associability of a given CS after trial n, λ^{n-1} the magnitude of the US presented on the preceding trial, and V^{n-1} the associative strengths of stimuli having associations with the US representation. In a simple conditioning procedure the value of V will grow from trial to trial as a result of CS–US pairings and in consequence the value of α will fall. When α reaches zero (when λ, the outcome of the CS, matches V, what is expected on the basis of the CS), no further conditioning will be possible.

The general principles just outlined apply to latent inhibition training as to conditioning. In such training the values of λ and V will be zero, and α will accordingly fall to zero. Subsequent learning about the pre-exposed stimulus will then be impossible until a discrepancy between the values of λ and V is established (as will happen when the US is introduced at the start of the conditioning phase of a latent inhibition experiment) so that the value of α will be increased for the next trial.

It should be acknowledged that eq 3.1 must be viewed as only an approximation to the true state of affairs. In particular, it is clear that associability is not (as eq 3.1 implies) determined solely by events occurring on the preceding trial. Associability does not fall to zero after just one exposure trial and is unlikely to be fully restored by a single reinforced conditioning trial. Rather,

α needs to be determined by some sort of average of the values for a number of preceding trials as in the following equation:

$$\alpha^n = \gamma|\lambda^{n-1} - V^{n(1)}| + (1-\gamma)\alpha^{n-1} \qquad (3.2)$$

The value of the parameter γ (which will lie between 0 and 1) will determine the extent to which the outcome is weighted in favour of events occurring on the immediately preceding trial.

Returning to the more general picture, the essential notion that this formalization tries to capture is that the associability of a stimulus will be determined by how well the consequences of that stimulus are predicted. A stimulus that is reliably followed by a given consequence (whether this be a US or no event at all) can be ignored. Animals need to attend to and learn about a stimulus only when its implications for the future are uncertain. The unique implication of this view is that associability will *not* be lost when a stimulus is followed by inconsistent consequences. This implication has been subjected to a variety of experimental tests.

(b) Inconsistent reinforcement and transfer

A standard latent inhibition experiment investigates transfer from a pre-exposure phase in which the target stimulus is consistently associated with no subsequent event to a test phase consisting of reinforced training. An experiment reported by Pearce *et al.* (1982) examined the transfer effects produced by a pre-exposure procedure in which the outcome of the target stimulus was inconsistent. Rats were given extensive pre-exposure to a tone which was followed on some randomly chosen trials by a mild electric shock and on other trials by no event at all (i.e. they received a partial reinforcement schedule). It may be evident that eqns 3.1 and 3.2 above imply that a variation in the value of λ (i.e. in the magnitude of the reinforcer) from one trial to another will tend to maintain the value of α. In a second stage of training the tone was followed consistently by a stronger shock and the acquisition of conditioned suppression was monitored. The results, summarized in Fig. 3.13, reveal some evidence of latent inhibition in that these subjects acquired suppression less readily than control subjects that had received initial exposure to a stimulus other than the tone. But the latent inhibition effect was not profound—rats given partial reinforcement during pre-exposure learned much more readily during the test phase than a group of subjects that had experienced the tone followed consistently by the mild shock during pre-exposure.

The slow learning of the group given consistently reinforced pre-exposure can be taken as being a special case of latent inhibition—of associability being lost by a stimulus followed by a consistent consequence. The results for the partially reinforced group show that this latent inhibition effect will be attenuated when the reinforcement presented during pre-exposure to the tone is inconsistent. It will be recalled (see p. 97) that the most convincing demonstration of an S_1–S_2 effect in latent inhibition came from the experiment by

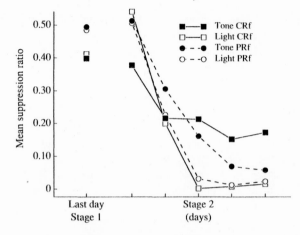

Fig. 3.13 Group mean suppression ratios for subjects given partial (PRf) or continuous (CRf) reinforcement with a weak shock in stage 1. In stage 2, all subjects received conditioning with the tone and a stronger shock. (After Pearce *et al.* 1982.)

Matzel *et al.* (1988), and that these experimenters used an S_2 that changed (being a train of clicks that could vary in frequency) from one trial to the next. The findings of Matzel *et al.* can be accommodated by the Pearce–Hall equations if it is accepted (as seems reasonable) that the different event used as S_2s differed in qualities that determine the value of λ used in these equations.

(c) The orienting response in rats

A transfer test is an appropriate way of assessing the value of α since the Pearce–Hall (1980) model assumes (as do similar models) that the value of this parameter determines the readiness with which a CS will enter into associations. It is possible (although not necessary), however, that other aspects of an animal's behaviour toward a stimulus might be determined by the value of α. One possibility advanced by Kaye and Pearce (1984) is that the behavioural orienting response (OR) shown by rats to a localized stimulus might serve as a direct index of α. Certainly the OR shows some of the right properties—it has a high likelihood of occurrence when the stimulus is first presented and tends to decline with repeated presentation (see Fig. 3.1, p. 70). But such an effect is predicted, of course, by any theory of habituation. More significant, therefore, are the other results shown in Fig. 3.1.

One group of subjects (labelled 'Control' in the figure) experienced only reinforced conditioning trials. Although it occurred more slowly than for subjects given non-reinforced pre-exposure, loss of the OR occurred in control subjects too, a result consistent with the view that α will decline when the CS predicts a consistent consequence and that the OR reflects the value of α. An effect of this sort was reported some years ago by Grastyan (1961), who monitored an electrophysiological correlate (hippocampal slow waves) of the overt OR during conditioning and found that the electrical response diminished as the CR emerged. He concluded that, with conditioning, 'the significance of the stimulus becomes "certain" and as a consequence the "what-is-it reflex" loses its biological usefulness' (Grastyan 1961, p. 245). Öhman (1983) reaches almost exactly this conclusion on the basis of formally equivalent experiments investigating conditioning of the human skin conductance response, as do Svendsrød and Ursin (1974) in their analysis of the acquisition of a conditioned emotional response by rats.

More novel are the results produced by a third group of subjects ('Partial' in the figure). These received exposure in which the stimulus was followed on a random 50 per cent of occasions by the presentation of a reinforcer. In these subjects the OR continued to occur at a high level throughout training, a result suggesting that a stimulus that fails to predict its consequences reliably will continue to receive some form of processing. The essential feature of these results, that partial reinforcement tends to maintain orienting to the light, has been sought in a series of further experiments by Pearce and his collaborators and has been amply confirmed (e.g. Pearce, Wilson, and Kaye 1988).

Swan and Pearce (1988) have attempted to establish the generality of the principle that the strength of the OR will be inversely related to the predictive accuracy of the stimulus by using a procedure other than partial reinforcement. In one of their experiments (the results of which are presented in Fig. 3.14) rats were given a serial conditioning procedure in which presentations of a light were followed, after an interval of either 10 s or 30 s, by food. For subjects in the critical experimental condition the long interval was filled by one auditory stimulus (say a clicker) and the short interval was filled by a different stimulus (such as a tone). Both these auditory cues should become associated with food and acquire conditioned reinforcing properties, but by virtue of its onset occurring in relatively close proximity to the food, the tone is likely to acquire somewhat more power than the clicker. The animals received, therefore, some trials on which the light was followed immediately by a weak conditioned reinforcer and others on which it was followed by a more powerful conditioned reinforcer. This effective variation in reinforcer magnitude should, according to equations 1 and 2 above, maintain the level of α. The results displayed in Fig. 3.14 show that these subjects continued to orient to the light over the course of 16 ten-trial sessions. Control subjects that experienced training in which the immediate consequences of the light did not differ in their reinforcing value from one trial to another (for these the interval between the offset of the light and food delivery was fixed and thus did not depend on whether it contained a tone or a clicker) showed a steady decline in the frequency of the OR.

Using the behavioural OR as an index of the value of α should not be taken to imply a belief that α is the sole determinant of this OR. I have already argued in this chapter (p. 79) that the rat's level of arousal can help

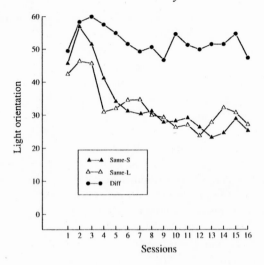

Fig. 3.14 Percentage of observations on which rats were recorded as orienting to a light over 16 ten-trial sessions of conditioning. Each presentation of the light was followed, after a delay filled by an auditory cue, by food. For group same-S the interval was short; for group same-L the interval was long; group diff experienced both long and short intervals, each being associated with a different auditory cue. (After Swan and Pearce 1988.)

determine the vigour of the OR; and, theoretically more important, in this and in previous chapters I have argued that the decline of this investigatory response represents the operation of a process of habituation. The relation between the effects of habituation and those implied by the Pearce–Hall model can perhaps be made clear if we adopt the elaboration offered by Liddell (1950) of Pavlov's notion of the orienting reflex. Liddell suggested that in addition to Pavlov's 'what-is-it?' reflex, the presentation of a novel stimulus will also evoke a 'what-happens-next?' reflex. The first of these reflexes will be subject to the influence of habituation and will decline as the subject becomes familiar with the stimulus, forms an accurate representation of it, or whatever. The second will be evoked when the consequences of the stimulus are uncertain; it is this reflex that tracks the value of α.*

The behavioural OR (or investigatory response) shown by rats in the experiments just described must be presumed to reflect the state of both these reflexes. The initial loss of this response produced by presenting the stimulus repeatedly alone will occur both because of habituation and because of a decline in the value of α, each of these changes influencing one

---

* Having made this distinction it becomes necessary to recast Grastyan's (1961) conclusion—it is the 'what-happens-next?' reflex that loses 'biological usefulness' as conditioning proceeds.

of the reflexes that contributes to the observed behaviour. But once habituation has occurred, there is no reason to suppose that the 'what-is-it?' reflex will play a further role in the experiments discussed here. These can be unambiguously interpreted in terms of the effect of predictive accuracy on the 'what-happens-next?' reflex.

(d) Partial reinforcement in pigeon autoshaping

In the autoshaping procedure, pigeons are confronted from time to time with presentations of an illuminated disc (a response key) signalling the delivery of food. Classical conditioning principles suggest, what is indeed the case, that the bird will come to peck at the lit key. It is well established (e.g. Gibbon, Farrell, Locurto, Duncan, and Terrace 1980) that partial reinforcement generates a higher rate of autoshaped responding than does continuous reinforcement. Collins and Pearce (1985) have offered an interpretation of this effect in terms of the Pearce–Hall model for associability change. They suggest that in pigeon autoshaping the level of associability of a stimulus might determine, in part, the likelihood that it will be responded to. When pigeons attend to a discrete stimulus, it is suggested, they are also likely to peck at it. Partial reinforcement, by maintaining associability (attention), will generate pecks that constitute components of the OR and these, by adding in to the CRs produced by the associative strength of the CS, ensure a high rate of response.

Evidence to support this interpretation comes from a series of studies of partial reinforcement in autoshaping by Collins, Young, Davies, and Pearce (1983), Collins and Pearce (1985), and Pearce, Kaye and Collins (1985). They investigated the rate of autoshaped pecking controlled by the first of two keylights presented serially and were able to show that the rate was elevated when the first element was an inaccurate predictor of its consequences. In a typical experiment the target stimulus (A) was followed, on different trials, by different stimuli (keylights X and Y). For one group of subjects the A–X serial compound was followed by food and the A–Y sequence was non-reinforced; for another group the A–X and A–Y compounds were each equally often reinforced and non-reinforced. Both groups thus experienced equivalent schedules of partial primary reinforcement. But for the first group, stimulus A was sometimes followed by an event (X) having high associative strength and sometimes by one having no strength (Y). For the second group, A was always followed by events having comparable strength (X and Y were both reinforced on 50 per cent of occasions). The former condition generated a higher rate of response. Honey, Schachtman, and Hall (1987) have confirmed this finding and have devised an explanation for it that follows directly from the Pearce–Hall model. They point out that the model predicts that a stimulus will lose associability if it is consistently followed by a reinforcer of a given size but that if the size of the reinforcer varies from trial to trial then associability will be maintained. The extreme case is, of course, a partial reinforcement schedule in which food is sometimes presented and sometimes not. In the serial conditioning procedure we must take account of the fact that stimuli possessing associative strength (and thus conditioned reinforcing power) follow the target stimulus. Thus, for one group of subjects, A is followed on some trials by both primary and conditioned reinforcement whereas on other trials there is no reinforcer at all; for the other group, stimulus A is always followed by a reinforcer of some sort. Accordingly the associability of A (and its tendency to evoke the OR) will be higher in the former case because the differences in reinforcer magnitude that follow the stimulus are particularly marked.*

(e) Conclusion

The notion that the development of latent inhibition might depend (directly or indirectly) upon what follows the target stimulus during pre-exposure is to be found in several theoretical accounts of the phenomenon. What sets the Pearce–Hall (1980) model apart is its prediction that a decline in associability occurs when a stimulus accurately predicts its consequences and that inconsistent consequences will attenuate or prevent the loss. And, as we have seen, there is plentiful evidence from a variety of experimental procedures to encourage the conclusion that this prediction is well founded. The theories of latent inhibition that I considered earlier in this chapter (e.g. that proposed by Wagner) were concerned with phenomena that suggested that latent inhibition depends upon how well the target stimulus is predicted by its antecedents. Clearly, theories of this sort must be extended in some way if they are to accommodate the fact that latent inhibition depends in part on what the target stimulus predicts. But by the same token, theories like that proposed by Pearce and Hall must come to terms with the evidence that has been taken to show that what the stimulus is predicted by can also play a role.

3.3.3. The role of contextual factors

However much we may criticize the details of the explanation they offer (above, pp. 86–9), the clear fact that latent inhibition shows context-specificity (i.e. is most likely to occur when the context predicts the occurrence of the target stimulus) constitutes good support for theories that emphasize the role of stimulus predictability. Theories that suppose latent inhibition to be a function of what the stimulus itself predicts have been

---

* This interpretation deviates from that put forward by Collins and Pearce (1985) themselves, who offer the slightly different suggestion that the associability of a stimulus will be determined by how well it predicts the associative strength of its immediate consequences. Honey *et al.* (1987) have conducted an empirical test of the alternatives and their results support the account presented in the text.

compelled to introduce special explanations to deal with the fact of context–specificity—and, as we shall see, they have done so with rather little success.

(a) Context in conditioned attention theory

Lubow, Rifkin, and Alek (1976) have explicitly investigated the role of the context in a series of experiments concerned with the effects of pre-exposure on discrimination learning in both children and in rats. The procedure used with the rats was as follows. Subjects were exposed to a distinctive odour in one or other of two discriminably different cages. They were then trained to approach the source of an odour to obtain food. Some subjects received a novel odour at this stage, others the pre-exposed odour. Of these two main groups, half the subjects received training in the context with which they were familiar (that used for pre-exposure) and half received training in a novel context. It was found that when the test environment was the same as that used for pre-exposure, the rats learned only with difficulty to approach the source of the familiar odour—that is, latent inhibition occurred. This effect showed context–specificity in that when the familiar odour was presented in a novel test environment, learning proceeded more rapidly. In fact the combination of an old stimulus in a new environment produced more rapid learning than any other arrangement.

In order to explain these results, Lubow, Rifkin, and Alek (1976) accept that the loss of the attentional response produced by pre-exposure must be modified by contextual factors. They put forward a number of suggestions. They suggest (see also Lubow *et al.* 1981) that a novel environment might serve as a dishabituator causing the original attentional response to be reinstated; in addition the novel environment might, quite independently of the stimuli presented in it, have an arousing effect that helps learning. The mechanisms that might be responsible for these effects are in need of fuller specification but the effort would perhaps not be worthwhile since in fact they do not account for the results to be explained. In particular, Lubow, Rifkin, and Alek (1976) themselves have shown that animals pre-exposed in one environment and tested in another can learn more readily than a control group exposed neither to the stimuli nor to the test apparatus. For both these groups the attentional response should be present and the test environment arousing, and thus the considerations introduced by Lubow, Rifkin, and Alek (1976) give no grounds for predicting the result observed. Accordingly it becomes necessary to consider the further possibility that learning might be exceptionally rapid when there is a contrast in novelty between the critical stimulus and the environment in which it is presented. I have already discussed the notion of relative novelty in the course of an analysis of habituation (Chapter 2, pp. 44–5) and failed to come up with hard evidence that might require us to accept its reality. More critical for our present concern (which is the need to explain the context-specificity of latent inhibition) is the fact that latent inhibition can be abolished by a change of context even when the test context is fully familiar, provided that pre-exposure to the test context and the target stimulus have taken place separately. With such a procedure there is no contrast in novelty between stimulus and context.

(b) The Pearce–Hall model

The Pearce–Hall (1980) model faces a further problem in attempting to deal with contextual effects. The extra dimension comes from the fact that the model is based, in part, on experiments that use the likelihood of occurrence of a behavioural OR as a measure of the level of associability of a stimulus. But as we have already seen (pp. 75–8), the OR and associability (as indexed by latent inhibition) can be dissociated. In particular, a change of context will attenuate latent inhibition whether the test context be novel or familiar but will restore the OR only when a novel test context is used. The results for the OR are just what the model expects. There is no reason why a change of context should restore α but given that a novel context is likely to be arousing, some increase in the likelihood of the OR might occur. No increase is to be expected (and none is found) when the test context is itself familiar. The problem for the model is, therefore, to explain why latent inhibition should be attenuated when the value of α apparently remains low.

A possible solution to this problem was proposed by Hall and Honey (1989*b*). They pointed out that the conditioning phase of a latent inhibition experiment involves a treatment (a change in the outcome of the target stimulus—the presentation of a US) that, according to the theory, should produce a change in the value of α. A simple habituation test would produce no change in α. Now the results of experiments on habituation of the OR have been taken as supporting the latter assertion—dishabituation fails to occur if the changed context is familiar. And the latent inhibition results imply that α is very rapidly restored by contextual change. This outcome can be predicted if it is allowed that a change of context causes changes in α to be determined solely or largely by events on the immediately preceding trial (i.e. if contextual change produced an increase in the value of γ in equation 3.2 above). This interpretation amounts to saying that an animal will still recognize an habituated stimulus when that stimulus is presented in a new context but will be prepared to change very quickly its assessment of that stimulus as being of no significance.

However plausible this suggestion, empirical investigation has lent it no support. In a recent unpublished experiment, Honey and Hall gave rats extensive experience of two contexts but presented the target stimulus in just one of them. Subjects in the critical experimental condition then experienced a single conditioning trial in which the target stimulus was presented in the unaccustomed context and was followed by shock. (See also Hall and Minor 1984.) On this single trial the α–value of the target must be assumed to be at the (low) level produced by pre-exposure—however rapidly α tends to change in a new context, the change will require at least one trial to occur.

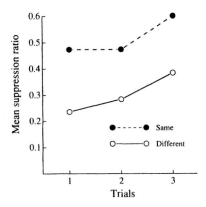

Fig. 3.15 Group mean suppression scores to a tone for rats pre-exposed to the tone either in the same context as that used for conditioning and the test or in a different context. All subjects received just one tone–shock conditioning trial prior to the test trials shown in the figure. (From an unpublished experiment by Hall and Honey.)

Accordingly, this single-trial procedure should eliminate the tendency of the contextual change to attenuate latent inhibition. The results of the test trials (Fig. 3.15) in which the CS was presented again (in the conditioning context) show no such thing. Latent inhibition was still found to be attenuated by the change of context.

It will be evident that the Pearce–Hall theory finds it difficult to deal with the effects of contextual factors. But this difficulty is not enough to make us abandon the theory. The weight of evidence on the effects of predictive accuracy makes it essential to accept some version of the notion that stimulus consequences help determine the level of α. What seems inescapable, since a change of context does not seem to restore α, is the conclusion that a change in the level of α is not the sole determinant of the retardation of subsequent learning produced by prior experience of the stimulus. The next chapter evaluates a range of further possible sources of latent inhibition.

4. Latent inhibition as associative interference

The term *proactive interference* is used to refer to the fact that prior learning can interfere with the acquisition, retention, or use of new information. At the operational level, therefore, latent inhibition is a good example of the phenomenon, and any theory of latent inhibition can be seen as proposing a mechanism by which proactive interference occurs. The theories discussed on the previous chapter were united in arguing that the source of this interference is to be found in a loss of associability (conditionability, effectiveness, attention-attracting power) by the critical stimulus. But in this context the term 'interference' is commonly used more narrowly to designate those theories that try to explain latent inhibition in terms of the interaction of standard (usually associative) processes of learning or performance and without recourse to attentional constructs of the sort employed by the theories discussed in Chapter 3. In this Chapter I shall begin by briefly considering the (rather wide) range of interference theories that have been applied to latent inhibition. Having identified the most likely candidates I shall then consider the critical experimental evidence (which again derives from studies of the role of contextual factors). Finally, I shall attempt to devise a synthesis that can incorporate the successful features of several theoretical approaches (including aspects of the attentional theories discussed in Chapter 3).

4.1. Interference theories

4.1.1. Interference with conditioning

The theories to be discussed in this section of the chapter all suppose that something is learned during the pre-exposure phase of a latent inhibition experiment that interferes with the formation of the CS–US (conditioned–unconditioned stimulus) association during the conditioning phase of the experiment. They differ from the theories described in Chapter 3, therefore, only in that they do not ascribe the poor acquisition to a change in the value of some attention-like process. Interference theories have taken a variety of forms.

(a) Interfering responses

A possibility originally considered by Lubow and Moore (1959) as an explanation for their newly discovered latent inhibition effect was that during pre-exposure the subject might come to perform some response to the stimulus that interfered with the response monitored during conditioning. The

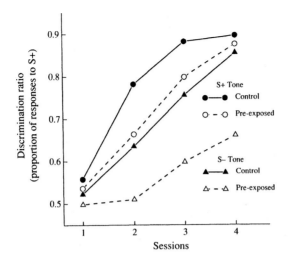

Fig. 4.1 Acquisition of a discrimination between the presence and absence of a tone in subjects pre-exposed to the tone and controls given no pre-exposure. For one pair of groups (S+) the tone was associated with reward; for the other pair of groups (S−) the tone was associated with non-reward. (After Halgren 1974.)

obvious inadequacy of this explanation is that it begs the question of why exposure to a stimulus should allow the acquisition of a new response—we usually suppose only that existing unconditioned responses (URs) will habituate. Furthermore, there are several empirical results (some provided by Lubow and Moore (1959) themselves) that speak against it. Perhaps the clearest instance is that reported by Halgren (1974) and summarized in Fig. 4.1. Rats that had been pre-exposed to a tone were trained on a task in which presses on a lever in the presence of the tone yielded reward but responses in the absence of the tone did not. As the figure shows, the subjects came to respond only when the tone was on, but they formed the discrimination less rapidly than control subjects that had not received pre-exposure. Their slow learning cannot be explained by assuming that the pre-exposed tone tended to evoke a response that interfered with lever pressing. Figure 4.1 shows that the performance of another group of subjects that, after pre-exposure, was required to lever press in the absence of the tone and to refrain from pressing in its presence. These subjects too learned less readily than controls in spite of the fact that the postulated 'interfering' response should actually have proved facilitatory in this case.

(b) Inhibition

According to the theories of associative learning presented in Chapter 1, certain conditions of training (roughly, those in which the CS predicts the omission of a US that might otherwise be expected to occur) allow the formation of an inhibitory CS–US link. A consequence of the existence of such a link is that excitatory conditioning will be retarded when an inhibitory CS is used to signal the occurrence of the US. Our use of the term 'latent inhibition' is a remnant of the suggestion (Lubow and Moore 1959) that simple pre-exposure might allow a stimulus to acquire inhibitory properties.

This suggestion has proved unpopular, in part because simple non-reinforced pre-exposure is not a procedure that, according to most current theories, should be capable of generating inhibition. It has also often been argued that there is empirical evidence that rules the suggestion quite out of court by demonstrating that a pre-exposed stimulus quite lacks the properties that have been taken as defining for an inhibitory CS (Rescorla 1969). But in fact the experimental results turn out to allow of more ambiguity than has commonly been supposed.

One set of results concerns the transfer from latent inhibition training to inhibitory conditioning in which the pre-exposed stimulus is explicitly trained as a CS−, a stimulus that signals the omission of the reinforcer. If pre-exposure endows a stimulus with inhibitory properties then such a stimulus should readily come to serve as a CS− since the inhibition already acquired should give a head start. And as we have already seen, Halgren's (1974) experiment shows that pre-exposure results in retarded conditioning, both when the stimulus is used as a CS+ (signalling reinforcement) and when it is used as a CS−. (See also Rescorla 1971.)

Although unfortunate for the view that latent inhibition can be equated with conditioned inhibition, these results do not in fact constitute a death blow. Hall, Kaye, and Pearce (1985) have pointed out that just as latent inhibition can occur during the CS–US pairings of excitatory training (producing a fully trained CS+ that will form further associations only slowly), so latent inhibition can also be expected to occur during inhibitory training. Hall *et al.* (1985) presented evidence that inhibitory training procedures produce a CS− that is subsequently learned about rather slowly even when the test procedure was one that required further inhibitory learning. They interpreted this finding as showing that associability lost by the stimulus during the first stage of training could outweigh the transfer deriving from the fact that both stage of the study involved inhibitory learning. Whatever the merits of this interpretation, the fact remains that pre-training a stimulus as a CS− has been found, on occasion, to retard further inhibitory learning. Accordingly, the demonstration that latent inhibition training will also retard subsequent inhibitory conditioning can hardly be taken as evidence that latent inhibition is quite different from conditioned inhibition.

A further feature of an inhibitory CS is that it will reduce the ability of a separately trained excitatory CS to evoke its CR when the two stimuli are presented as a compound. There is some doubt as to whether a latent inhibitor can produce this effect. The experimental results are mixed. Rescorla (1971) found that the CR remained undiminished when a latent inhibitor was added to an excitatory CS whereas experiments by Kremer (1972) and by Reiss and Wagner (1972, experiment 2) have both found that the compound tends to evoke less conditioned responding than the excitatory CS alone. The proper interpretation of the latter finding is unclear. It is certainly what would be expected if the latent inhibitor functions like a CS— but it could just as easily be a consequence of generalization decrement—adding another stimulus to the excitatory CS might modify the way in which the latter is perceived and thus reduce its ability to evoke the CR.

The role of generalization decrement in these experiments can be investigated by comparing the effects on excitatory responding of an added stimulus that has had little or no pre-exposure with those produced by a stimulus that has undergone latent inhibition training. The ability of the added stimulus to disrupt normal perception of the excitatory CS should undergo habituation and thus the 'inhibitory' power of the pre-exposed stimulus might be less than that of a novel one. This apparently decisive comparison turns out, unfortunately, to be nothing of the sort. In the first place, there is a discrepancy in the experimental results—Reiss and Wagner (1972) found that a novel stimulus was more effective than a familiar one in disrupting the CR whereas Kremer (1972) found the opposite. And worse, each result is susceptible to an alternative explanation. That from the Reiss and Wagner study may imply only that, in their procedure, generalization decrement completely masks inhibitory effects; the result does not require us to deny the existence of the latter. And the Kremer result does not require us to accept that a pre-exposed stimulus inhibits a CR in the way that a CS— does. His experiment used the conditioned suppression procedure and his critical experimental finding was that a novel stimulus added to a pre-trained excitatory CS evokes more suppression than the compound of CS plus familiar stimulus. An obvious explanation for such a result is that the former compound evokes more suppression simply because the UR (of suppression) evoked by the novel stimulus combines with the CR elicited by the CS+. For a pre-exposed stimulus there will be no such effect since the tendency to evoke unconditioned suppression will have habituated.

Although these experimental results are indecisive, the theoretical point remains—the latent inhibition procedure is not that used to train a conditioned inhibitor. Accordingly it would be surprising if animals learned the same thing about the stimulus in the two cases. At the very least, conditioned inhibition training is likely to differ from latent inhibition training in that the former is likely to convey the information that a given event (a given US) will not occur whereas the latter could only convey that no event will occur. Evidence that illustrates this point come from investigations aimed at the notion of 'learned safety'.

(c) Learned safety

Workers studying the effects of CS pre-exposure on flavour-aversion learning have independently generated an account of latent inhibition that is formally exactly equivalent to the inhibitory notion just discussed. Kalat and Rozin (1973) suggested that subjects given exposure to a novel flavour are capable of learning that the flavour predicts no aversive consequence, that the taste is 'safe'. Such learning would then interfere with a subsequent attempt to teach the subject a taste–poison association.

This hypothesis prompted a series of experiments by Best (1975) in which a given flavour was established as a conditioned inhibitor (or a signal for safety) by an explicit discrimination training procedure in which this flavour was presented along with a previously established CS+ but in the absence of the US. The effect of giving non-reinforced pre-exposure to the target flavour was to reduce the readiness with which it came to function as a safety signal—that is, the outcome was the opposite of that predicted by the suggestion that the pre-exposed stimulus might already have acquired some of the properties of a safety signal. The argument made here is that already applied to Halgren's (1974) results. It is thus, of course, open to the objection that was raised previously—that a loss of associability incurred during pre-exposure might obscure the transfer effect generated by such inhibition as was also acquired.

But Best's experiment included another feature that helps establish the distinction between latent and conditioned inhibition. His procedure for testing the properties of the target flavour was one in which the rats were given a choice between this flavour and some other. He found (see also Batson and Best (1981)) that animals given his discrimination training procedure showed an enhanced preference for the safe flavour (the conditioned inhibitor). Subjects given simple pre-exposure to the target flavour showed no such preference. We must conclude then that, at the very least, a conditioned inhibitor is a stimulus having motivational properties that a latent inhibitor lacks; only in a very restricted sense, therefore, can the latter be regarded as an instance of the former.

(d) Learned non-correlation

Acknowledging the problems inherent in the learned safety hypothesis, Kalat (1977) suggested a revision which he referred to as 'learned non-correlation'. Rather than learning that 'nothing bad' follows a non-reinforced stimulus, the animal might learn that the stimulus predicts nothing at all, that the stimulus is not correlated with another event. Weiss and Brown (1974) have put forward a similar proposal with their suggestion that latent inhibition is a consequence of the subject's learning a 'zero correlation' between the target stimulus and other events.

It is, of course, necessary for these theorists to specify how the learning of a zero correlation produces the effects it does. At one level of analysis, this task poses no special problems. As Weiss and Brown (1974) point out, conditioning occurs when correlations are arranged between pairs of events: excitatory conditioning when there is a positive correlation with the CS predicting the US; inhibitory conditioning when the correlation is negative so that the CS predicts the omission of the US (see, e.g. Rescorla 1967, 1968). An animal that has previously learned that a stimulus is not correlated with other events will have learned something quite incompatible with what is true during conditioning and so negative transfer can be expected.

All this will be perfectly satisfactory to those who are willing to stop their analysis of conditioning at this level and who do not concern themselves with the detailed mechanisms that underlie the subject's sensitivity to these various correlations. Indeed, to some, the account offered by Weiss and Brown (1974) may seem to be over-elaborate. Testa and Ternes (1977) reject even the notion of learned non-correlation. Conditioning, they argue, is determined by the conditional probability of occurrence of the US given the CS, and of the US given no CS. Exposure to the CS prior to the conditioning trials will mean that the conditional probability of US given CS (when assessed over all trials) will be lowered and the likelihood of the CSs being able to evoke a CR will be reduced. (Baker and Mercier (1982a) offer a very similar interpretation.) The mechanism by which animals might integrate these various events, spread out as they usually are over several sessions of training, and by which the critical conditional probabilities might be computed, are not considered.

Kalat (1977), by contrast, makes an attempt to express the notion of learned non-correlation in more traditional, associative terms. He refers to latent inhibition training as producing a CS–US association, the US being described as consisting of 'no event' (see also Hall *et al.* 1985). Odd as this may sound, the idea that an association might be formed between a CS and the absence of some event is not without precedent in associative theorizing. Konorski's (1967) well-developed and influential theory of conditioning deals with inhibitory learning by assuming that an inhibitory CS is one that activates a 'no-US' representation. (See also Pearce and Hall (1980).) The inhibitory CS is supposed to owe some of its behavioural effects to the fact that activity in the 'no-US centre' inhibits that in the 'US centre'. Something of the sort could apply in latent inhibition. Our usual accounts of excitatory conditioning refer to associations between events referred to as CS and US, but in doing so they are guilty of over-simplification. Each of these stimuli has many attributes. An electric shock US, for instance, is an event occurring at a particular time, with a certain duration and intensity, that impinges on a particular part of the animal, and so on. Instead of postulating a single link between CS and US we should perhaps imagine a whole collection of them (the exact number depending on which attributes of the stimuli are noticed and encoded by the animal), all of which play some part in generating the CR. One of these may be a link between the CS and a representation of 'some event'. If so, latent inhibition training that establishes a CS–no event association would retard the course of conditioning.

However elaborate (indeed, contrived) this theorizing may be, it is still not wholly adequate for the task in hand. Applying to the inhibitory case the analysis of conditioning presented above leads to the suggestion that one of the associative links likely to be formed will be between the CS and a representation of no event. The hypothesis that, for a pre-exposed stimulus, this association will already have been formed before the start of conditioning leads to the prediction that pre-exposure should facilitate inhibitory learning. That it does not means that this theory, like the other versions of interference theory already discussed, needs to include some further process (such as a loss of associability) to explain the results.

(e) Concurrent interference

Revusky (1971, 1977) has developed an account of the role of interference effects in associative learning that has proved applicable to a wide range of phenomena. The essence of 'concurrent interference' is the postulate that the formation of an association between the target event and some other will reduce the ability of the target to enter into other associations. The particular case of greatest interest to Revusky is that of conditioning with some interfering event (X) presented in the interval between CS and US. The concurrent formation of CS–X and X–US associations is held to interfere with the formation of the target, CS–US, association.

As the theory is explicitly concerned with *concurrent* interference, its application to latent inhibition (an instance of proactive interference) has not been fully worked out. But Revusky (1971) offers the following possibility in discussing flavour-aversion learning. During pre-exposure, the consumption of a flavoured substance will be followed by certain consequences with which an association could be formed; if the flavour is presented as a fluid, for instance, consumption will be followed by an alleviation of thirst. But the exact nature of the associate does not matter—the mere existence of a CS–X association will interfere with the ability of the pre-exposed flavour to form a new association as is required in both excitatory and inhibitory conditioning.

Although Revusky (1971) does not discuss the matter, there is a second mechanism by which concurrent interference theory might predict latent inhibition. In discussing the effect produced when event X precedes the CS–US pairing of a conditioning trial, Revusky lays emphasis on the interference that results from the formation of an X–US association; but it might also be allowed that the formation on an X–CS association plays a role. If so, an equivalent effect can be expected in latent inhibition. During initial exposure, experience of the flavour will be accompanied by a consistent set of antecedents comprising those cues that characterize the presentation of a container of fluid. The X–CS association that results would then interfere with subsequent attempts to establish the CS–US association. Other interference therories attribute latent inhibition to the effects of an association between the pre-exposed stimulus and its consequences. But concurrent interference theory can also allow that an association between the target stimulus and its antecedents might also contribute to the effect. To this extent the theory can be seen as incorporating the central feature of Wagner's (1976, 1981) interpretation of the phenomenon—the suggestion that further learning proceeds slowly about a stimulus that has formed associations with its antecedents.

The similarity to Wagner's account becomes more marked when we consider the application of concurrent interference theory to procedures other than flavour pre-exposure. Latent inhibition occurs readily with stimuli like lights and tones that have no obvious antecedents or consequences in the way that consumption of a flavoured fluid does. We can suppose, however, that associations might be formed between the stimulus and the context in which it is presented. The source of interference with formation of the CS–US association might thus be the previously established context–CS and CS–context associations. The mechanism by which the context–CS association has its effect is different but the principle is just that adopted by Wagner (1976, 1981). What follows from this analysis, of course, is that concurrent interference as an explanation of latent inhibition is open to the same objections as were raised to Wagner's theory. The evidence in Chapter 3 that was taken as counting against Wagner's analysis of latent inhibition is just as damaging for the interference account developed here.

Although direct associations between the context and the target stimulus can play little part in the effect, it is still possible that associative interference might be responsible, in whole or in part, for latent inhibition. A further possible source of latent inhibition emerges as soon as we accept that any stimulus can be construed as consisting of a set of elements. Stimulus elements that are experienced together will become linked.* Latent inhibition training can be expected, therefore, to establish a network of associations among the component parts that go to make up the stimulus. McLaren, Kaye, and Mackintosh (1989) made use of this suggestion in developing their account of latent inhibition. Their proposal (see Chapter 3) was that the associability of an element activated by external stimulation will be enhanced when this element lacks associative connections. The analysis offered by interference theory is similar, but rather simpler—it is that the existence of these (within-

---

* Such associations are in fact more likely than associations between the stimulus and the context. The elements of a stimulus always occur together and only occur together. The context, by contrast, is often, indeed usually, experienced in the absence of the stimulus—poor conditions for association formation.

stimulus) associations will interfere with the ability of the elements to form new ones.

(f) Conclusions

Several of these attempts to devise an interference theory for latent inhibition fail to explain important features of the data and must be rejected. The notion of a learned non-correlation fails for a rather different reason—it can accommodate the facts but largely because it attempts little more than a redescription of the facts to be explained.

Two accounts remain viable: the suggestion that pre-exposure allows the formation of a stimulus–no event association; and the suggestion that within-stimulus associations interfere with new associative learning involving the same stimulus elements. Neither of these alternatives excludes the possibility that a change in associability might also play a part on generating latent inhibition. The first of these accounts actually requires the additional assumption that associability declines during pre-exposure. Without this the theory would find it difficult to explain why latent inhibition should be seen with inhibitory conditioning in the test phase. The concurrent interference account does not require this assumption but can perfectly well allow that changes in associability might accompany the formation of within-stimulus links. We have seen how McLaren *et al.* (1989) makes use of this possibility but the mechanism involved need not be the one they describe. It could just as easily be that proposed by Pearce and Hall (1980). According to this interpretation, the associability of each stimulus element might be expected to decline as it becomes associated with others, just as a CS as a whole is thought to lose associability as it becomes linked with a US.

4.1.2. Retrieval failure

All the accounts of latent inhibition discussed so far have assumed that what is learned during pre-exposure interferes with the formation of the CS–US association. Revusky (1971) call his theory a *concurrent* interference theory to emphasize just this point and to distinguish it from another commonly held interpretation of proactive interference. According to this alternative view, the target association may be formed perfectly normally but since, on a subsequent test trial, both this and any previously learned association will become activated when the CS is presented, the subjects may fail to retrieve the 'correct' one and the likelihood of the CR will be reduced. Indeed, the effects of retrieval failure may also be evident during the course of conditioning itself because any trial after the first can be viewed as being a test trial on which the subject is required to retrieve information acquired on earlier trials.

Clearly the retrieval-failure hypothesis will make many of the same predictions as other theories of latent inhibition. But if interference effects do indeed operate at retrieval rather than on the formation of the CS–US association, it should be possible to show that an apparently weak association formed after conditioning with a pre-exposed stimulus can be revealed as being perfectly strong in appropriate conditions of testing.

(a) Reminder treatments

Miller and his colleagues (e.g. Miller and Springer 1973; Miller and Schachtman 1985) have shown that certain 'reminder' treatments are capable of restoring lost behaviour, thus demonstrating that the information necessary for the behaviour in question must have been present all along but was merely unavailable to the mechanisms responsible for controlling behaviour. For example, rats given electroconvulsive shock (ECS) immediately after learning a simple avoidance response fail to show this response on a subsequent test, a result that has been interpreted as showing that the ECS destroys the original memory trace. But this interpretation is challenged by the observation that a reminder treatment (foot-shock administered in a different apparatus from that used to train the avoidance response) will allow the avoidance response to appear on a subsequent retention test. Rather than destroying the original trace, it is argued, the effect of the ECS is to make retrieval more difficult.

Kasprow, Catterson, Schachtman, and Miller (1984) have applied this logic to latent inhibition. In their experiment, rats that have been pre-exposed to a noise prior to noise-shock conditioning trials showed latent inhibition in that, on a final test session, the noise elicited only a weak CR. (The results of the test session are shown in Fig. 4.2.) But subjects that experienced a reminder treatment (unsignalled foot-shocks given in a different apparatus) between the conditioning trials and the test session showed almost as much conditioned responding as control subjects that had not been pre-exposed to the noise. Kasprow *et al.* are not able to specify how the reminder treatment produces its effect but they are quite at liberty to use the unexplained phenomenon to make their central point—that the deficit in performance see in the subjects given pre-exposure stems from a failure of retrieval rather than a failure of initial acquisition.

These results certainly require us to take seriously the notion that retrieval process play a part in determining the outcome of a latent inhibition experiment. We must acknowledge, however, that another interpretation is possible. Even those who hold that the latent inhibition treatment interferes with initial acquisition would allow that some association between the CS and US (albeit a weak one) will be formed. It is assumed that so-called reminder treatments act in some way to increase the likelihood that associations (especially weak ones that will be most in need of such help) will be effective in generating overt conditioned responding, then the pattern of results observed can be accommodated. This assumption is arbitrary, but no more so than the assertion that reminder treatments somehow make available information that could not otherwise be retrieved.

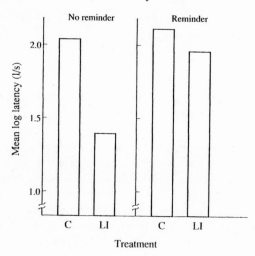

Fig. 4.2 Test responding in the presence of the noise in the experiment by Kasprow *et al.* (1984). A long latency indicates a strong conditioned response. All subjects had received noise–shock pairings; the LI groups had had pre-exposure to the noise; the C groups had not.

(b) Effects of a retention interval

Kraemer and Roberts (1984) (see also Kraemer and Ossenkopp 1986; Kraemer, Hoggman, and Spear 1988) have invoked results from a rather different experimental procedure in seeking support for the retrieval-failure account of latent inhibition. They conducted flavour-aversion conditioning with rats given prior exposure to the substance used as the CS (chocolate milk). The strength of the aversion was then tested; on the day after conditioning for some rats, and 21 days later for others. Although those tested after one day showed only a weak aversion (i.e. latent inhibition was observed in this condition), more of an aversion was evident in those given the delayed test. Apparently the CS–US association must have been formed relatively normally, even in subjects given pre-exposure to the CS, because appropriate conditions of testing (i.e. the use of a long retention interval) were able to reveal the existence of a strong aversion. Kraemer and Roberts (1984) interpreted their results as implying that the pre-exposure procedure and the conditioning procedure establish independent memories and the ability of the former to interfere with retrieval of the latter declines over the retention interval.

We should note that this analysis involves an element of special pleading. Theories of proactive interference (see, e.g. Spear 1978) usually assume that the capacity of the first-formed memory to interfere with that formed second tends to increase as the retention interval is extended. But in this cases it is necessary to assume the opposite in order to explain the results—to assume that what is learned during pre-exposure interferes less after 21 days than after one day. Kraemer and Roberts (1984) offer as justification for this assumption the suggestion that 'important' memories retain the ability to be retrieved even after a long retention interval whereas less important memories do not. If the memory of the association of a given flavour with illness can be taken to be more important than the memory that the flavour has also been experienced without harmful consequences, then the latter memory would interfere after a short but not after a long retention interval. This suggestion is not implausible but it remains to specify the mechanism by which the content of a memory might act to determine its retrievability.

A futher problem arises from the fact that the experimental results of critical importance are far from clear-cut. Although Kraemer and Roberts (1984) were able to demonstrate an apparent loss of latent inhibition over a long retention interval using chocolate milk as the CS, no effect was apparent when saccharin was used. And Kraemer and Ossenkopp (1986), in an experiment formally equivalent to that reported by Kraemer and Roberts, were able to find only a small and statistically unreliable effect using milk as the flavour (see Fig. 4.3). Their results did, however, confirm another effect evident in the original Kraemer and Roberts study—that the effects of a long retention interval can be very apparent when pre-exposure is given to a stimulus different from that used for conditioning and the test. Figure 4.3 includes the test results for a pair of groups given pre-exposure to saccharin before being conditioned and tested with milk. Such pre-exposure is apparently capable of generating latent inhibition since the group tested one day after conditioning (SM-1 in the figure) showed little evidence of having acquired an aversion, consuming just as much of the test substance as those subjects actually given latent inhibition training with this substance (group MM-1 in the figure). When tested after 21 days, however, the latent inhibition effect produced by pre-exposure to saccharin has disappeared. Subjects given this test (group SM-21) now show a strong aversion.* It is not clear why the effect of the retention interval should be especially marked when the pre-exposure flavour is different from that used in the subsequent phases of the study. One possibility is that generalized latent inhibition is likely to be weaker than that produced by pre-exposure to the CS itself and thus is more likely to be susceptible to the effect of the long interval. This suggestion is, unfortunately, no more than speculation at this stage.

---

* Curiously, the subjects in group SM-21 show a stronger aversion even than that displayed by subjects (group M-21) that received no latent inhibition training. The source of this effect, which was not evident in the Kraemer and Roberts (1984) report, is obscure.

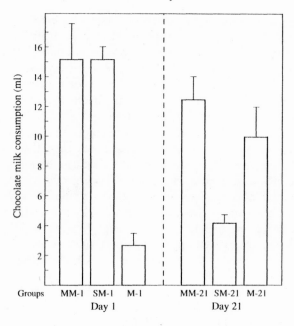

Fig. 4.3 Amount of chocolate milk consumed on a test trial given either 1 day or 21 days after conditioning with this flavour. Some subjects (MM groups) received exposure to the flavour before the conditioning trial, some (SM groups) received pre-exposure to saccharin, the rest (M groups) received no pre-exposure. (From Kraemer and Ossenkopp 1986.)

(c) Conclusions

The evidence summarized above will not be enough to convert adherents of other theories to the view that latent inhibition is a consequence of the subject's failing to retrieve the relevant information about the CS. The evidence is suggestive but not conclusive. It should be noted, however, that to accept the retrieval-failure account of latent inhibition does not necessarily imply a rejection of all other theories of the phenomenon. Those who have espoused the notion of retrieval failure have not usually been much concerned with specifying what it is that is learned during pre-exposure; rather, their experiments have been designed to show that, whatever the source on interference may be, it acts at retrieval rather than on the formation of the CS–US association. The hypotheses considered in the preceding section of this chapter (that pre-exposure allows the formation of a stimulus–no event association, and so on) still remain viable provided it is allowed that the associations they envisage can still be assumed to interfere with retrieval. What is more, the experimental results that have been taken to demonstrate that retrieval plays a part in latent inhibition cannot demonstrate this failure to be the sole source of the effect—these experiments show that a CS–US association is indeed formed after latent inhibition training and can be revealed if the conditions of testing are appropriate; they do not show convincingly that the association is just as strong as that formed in subjects given no pre-exposure to the target stimulus. In other words, pre-exposure to the stimulus may both retard the acquisition of the CS-US association and act to interfere with the retrieval of the information embodied in this association when it comes to a test trial.

Discussion of these various possibilities must remain the merest speculation, however, in the absence of convincing evidence demonstrating competition between associations at retrieval. I have already noted that the experimental results presented so far have not been conclusive. There is, however, evidence from a quite different experimental procedure that can be taken to confirm that retrieval mechanisms play an important role in the phenomena considered here. Evaluation of this evidence requires us to consider once again (see Chapter 3) the role of contextual factors.

4.2. Contextual factors in retrieval

Students of human memory have long recognized that performance on a retrieval task tends to be superior when the test context is similar to that experienced during initial training. This effect, sometimes referred to as 'encoding specificity' (e.g. Tulving and Thomson 1973; Tulving 1983) has been subject to a range of interpretations but what concerns us here is the general possibility that contextual factors might determine test performance by modulating the ease with which stored information is retrieved. This notion has been adopted by a number of animal learning theorists (e.g. Spear 1973, 1981; Hirsh 1980). Its relevance to out present concern is as follows. Latent inhibition shows clear context-specificity—that is, the retardation of conditioning produced by pre-exposure to the stimulus is attenuated when pre-exposure and conditioning occur in different contexts (see Chapter 3, pp. 75–8). Such an effect is readily interpreted in terms of the assumption that the presence of the original set of contextual cues is necessary for the subject to retrieve, during conditioning, information about the stimulus that was acquired during pre-exposure. In other words, the context-specificity of latent inhibition might constitute evidence in favour of the retrieval theories of the phenomenon discussed in the preceding section of this chapter.

In order to establish the retrieval interpretation of latent inhibition it is necessary to demonstrate, therefore, that contextual cues do indeed have their effect by fostering the retrieval of previously acquired information. Most of the relevant experimental evidence on this issue comes not from studies of latent inhibition but from investigations of conditioning itself. Accordingly, I consider next the phenomenon of context-specificity in Pavlovian conditioning. Does conditioned responding fail to transfer from one context to another? If it does fail to transfer, can such context-specificity be established by means of the training procedures typically employed in studies of the context-specificity of latent inhibition? And need a failure of transfer necessarily imply the failure of a contextually mediated retrieval process?

4.2.1. Context-specificity in conditioning

(a) Explicit and non-explicit training

It is well established that explicit discrimination training can render the effects of a conditioning procedure context-dependent. By explicit training is meant a procedure in which the animal is given pairings of a CS and a US in one distinctive context, and presentations of the same CS along with some other event in a different context. The animal can come to emit different CRs in the two contexts. Thus, for example, Preston, Dickinson, and Mackintosh (1986) have demonstrated that rats given alternate sessions in two contexts can come to respond appropriately to a tone that signals the occurrence of shock when it occurs in one of them and the occurrence of food when it occurs in the other. They can also discriminate appropriately when the stimulus signals food in one context and extinction in the other, a result amply confirmed in experiments by Bouton and Swartzentruber (1986). These latter note the parallel with 'occasion-setting' (cf. Holland 1983; Rescorla 1985), a term used to describe the finding that subjects can come to respond appropriately to a CS that is sometimes reinforced and sometimes not according to whether some other event (the occasion setter) accompanies the target CS. Boulton and Swartzentruber urge the acceptance of a common explanation for both phenomena, arguing that contextual cues and explicit occasion setters act not by direct association with other events but by modulating the influence of CS-US associations.

The occasion-setting procedure involves explicit discrimination training; in the procedure known as feature-positive training, for instance, the subject experiences reinforced trials in the presence of the occasion setter and non-reinforced trials in its absence. It is usually assumed (see e.g. LoLordo and Ross 1987; Ross and LoLordo 1987) that such explicit training is necessary for a stimulus to acquire modulatory, occasion-setting properties (but see also Bonardi (1989, 1991)). But what we need to demonstrate is that the context can acquire modulatory properties even in the absence of explicit training—we are seeking to explain the context-specificity shown by latent inhibition and this is evident without any form of initial discrimination training. Latent inhibition will show context-specificity when the only training given has been non-reinforced presentations of the stimulus in a given context. Will conditioning show context-specificity in comparable circumstances? Will a

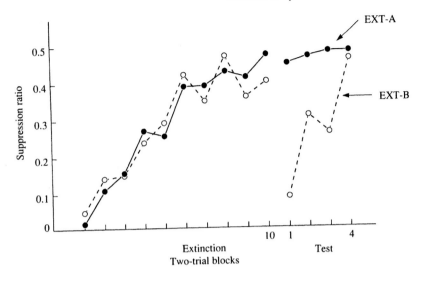

Fig 4.4 Test performance after conditioning in context A. The groups did not differ during the extinction phase whether this occurred in context A (group EXT-A) or in B (EXT-B). In the final test all subjects received conditioned stimulus presentations in context A. (Adapted from Bouton and King 1983.)

subject given reinforced trials in one context fail to respond when the CS is presented in a different context without having had previous experience of non-reinforced trials in the second context?

Bouton and his collaborators have conducted a series of experiments (for reviews see Bouton (1988, 1990)) using the same stimuli and general procedures as those employed by Bouton and Swarzentruber (1986) but differing in that no explicit training was given. They found that conditioned responding transferred readily from one context to another. The results of a typical experiment (by Bouton and King 1983) are shown in Fig. 4.4. After acquiring conditioned suppression to a CS in context A, rats received non-reinforced presentation of this CS in either A or B. It is apparent from the figure that conditioned responding was equally likely in both test contexts—that there was no evidence in this phase of training for context-specificity. Evidence for a form of context-specificity came from a final test stage of the experiment in which all the subjects experience the CS again in the original context (A). Those that had received extinction trials in A continued to show little responding; but those given extinction in B showed a recovery of suppression. Bouton and King (1983) interpret their results as showing that context-specificity will be evident only when there is some ambiguity about the CS that the contextual cues help to resolve. In this case the CS is at one time associated with a US and at another time is not, and for one group of subjects different contextual cues are correlated with these arrangements. Another way of interpreting these results is as showing that explicit training is indeed necessary for context-specificity—in this case the two conditions are presented separately (i.e. there is a block of reinforced trials followed by a block of non-reinforced trials) but the arrangement is formally equivalent to the explicit discrimination procedure used by Bouton and Swartzentruber (1986).

Although Bouton and his collaborators have failed to establish context-specificity after simple conditioning, they would not want to claim that such an effect can never be seen—there is ample evidence from experiments using rather different training procedures that a change of context can produce a performance deficit. In flavour-aversion learning, for instance, Archer and his collaborators (e.g. Archer, Sjödén, Nilsson, and Carter 1979; Archer, Sjödén, and Nilsson 1985) have routinely found that an aversion established in one context is far less marked when the flavour is presented in a different context. Avoidance learning similarly shows a clear decrement (e.g. Gordon, McCracken, Dess-Beech, and Mowrer 1981) as do certain food-rewarded discrimination tasks (e.g. Chiszar and Spear 1969). There are even experiments using the condition suppression procedure (as used in Bouton's own experiments) that have succeeded in showing a loss of the CR with a change of context (e.g. Balaz, Capra, Hartl, and Miller 1982; Lovibond, Preston, and Mackintosh 1984, experiment 1B). The question that needs to be asked about these results is do they demonstrate the function of the context as a retrieval cue or can they be explained away in other terms?

(b) Alternative explanations

The observation that a CR may be less likely when the CS is presented in a context other than that used for training is open to a number of explanations, some of them of little theoretical interest. Perhaps the least interesting is the possibility that the change of context modifies the way in which the CS is perceived, either because of some change in the physical nature of the signal (the properties of an auditory cue, for instance, are likely to change according to the shape of the space in which it is presented) or because there is some change in the way the cue impinges on the animal (if different contexts promote different patterns of orienting behaviour, the same cue, defined physically, may be experienced differently in the contexts). It may even be possible for background, contextual stimuli to interact with the pattern of nervous activity evoked by the target stimulus in the early stages of sensory or perceptual processing (Hull's (1943) notion of 'afferent neural inter-action'). Whatever their source, such generalization decrement effects would mean that a change of context would produce a diminution of the CR. It seems very likely that the context-dependency reported by Balaz *et al.* (1981) and Balaz, Capra, Kasprow, and Miller (1982) is, in part, a consequence of generalization decrement as is that described by Archer *et al.* (1985) (see the discussion of this issue in Chapter 2, p. 42).

A related possibility makes use of the notion of configural conditioning. The stimulus that the experimenter regards as the CS might interact with features of the context in which training is given to form a unique cue that constitutes the effective CS (see Rescorla 1972, 1973). Presenting the nominal CS in come other context would generate some different configural cue and so, in the absence of the trained CS, no CR could be expected. Configural conditioning has been proposed as the likely explanation for the context-specificity observed by Preston *et al.* (1986, experiment 2).

Finally, it proves possible to generate an associative explanation for context-specificity. We may assume that during conditioning associations will be formed between contextual cues and the individual events (the CS and the US) that occur in their presence. Presenting the CS in a test context that lacks those associative links could have several consequences. One possibility that follows from Wagner's (1981) theory is that the magnitude of the CR might actually be enhanced. In the context used for training, contextual cues will be able to establish an A2) (secondary activation) representation of the CS thereby limiting the ability of the stimulus itself to evoke A1 (primary activation). In a different context, however, the CS will be able to evoke A1 and since the A1 state is better than A2 at activating an associative link, the CS will be better able to elicit its CR when the context is changed. There may be other associative effects, however, and these allow the possibility that a change of context might reduce the likelihood of the CR. In particular, associations will also be formed between the context and the US, allowing the former to come to elicit, at least to some degree, the CR evoked by the nominal CS. If the CR observed in the original context depends on a summation of its own excitatory strength with that controlled by the context, then a decline in the vigour of the CR is to be expected in a test context lacking excitatory strength. Bouton (e.g. 1988, 1990) has argued against this summation notion, pointing out that in his own experiments the size of the CR seems to be uninfluenced by the associative value of background cues. But for other experiments the interpretation seems very plausible. Lovibond *et al.* (1984, experiment 1b) gave rats tone–shock pairings in one context, intermixed with sessions of exposure to a second context; the subjects were thus fully familiar with the second context but had no experience of conditioning procedures in it. Presenting the tone in this second context produced a distinct loss of the CR of suppression. But Lovibond *et al.* conducted a further study (experiment 1c) that was almost identical to the first but which failed to yield any evidence for context-specificity. This second study differed only in that during initial training the subjects received conditioning trials with a different stimulus (a light) in the context that was to be used for the test. Lovibond *et al.* point out that this change in procedure will tend to

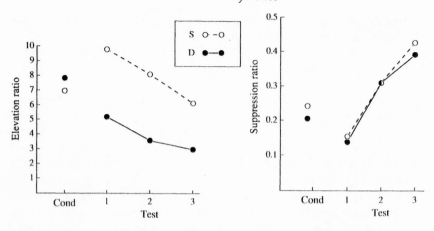

Fig. 4.5 Performance of rats on the last day of conditioning (cond) and on test trials with the conditioned stimulus (CS) presented in the same (group S) or in a different (group D) context from that used for training. In (a) the reinforcer was food and the response measured was the CS-elicited increase in responding to the site of food delivery; in (b) the reinforcer was shock and the response the suppression of behaviour. (Adapted from Hall and Honey 1989*a*.)

equalize the associative statutes of the two contexts and suggest that the context-specificity they observed in their first experiment was solely a result of their failure to equalize the two contexts in this respect.

(c) Eliminating the alternatives

In order to provide evidence for the view that the context can act as a retrieval cue (or exert conditional control over an association), it is necessary, as a first step, to demonstrate context-specificity using the control procedures recommended by Lovibond *et al.* (1984). Hall and Honey (1989*a*) report a study doing just this. Rats received initial training in which presentations of an auditory cue in one context were associated with food, as were presentations of a visual cue in different context. The subjects developed the CR of approaching the site of food delivery in the presence of each of these cues. On the single test day, subjects in the critical group (group D in Fig. 4.5(a)) received sessions in which the cues were presented in 'wrong' context. Group S continued with the usual arrangement. As Fig. 4.5 shows, the change of context experienced by group D produced a substantial loss of vigour in the CR, evident from the very first trial of the test. This result encourages the conclusion that appropriate contextual cues must be present for satisfactory retrieval of the effects of the effects of initial conditioning; but it also poses a number of further questions.

Foremost among these is why the experiment summarized in Fig. 4.5(a) should have revealed context-specificity when formally equivalent experiments (e.g. by Lovibond *et al.* 1984) have failed to do so. The most obvious distinguishing feature of the experiment by Hall and Honey is that an appetitive reinforcer was used rather than the electric shock of the conditioned suppression procedure. There is some evidence to suggest that this difference is critical. Hall and Honey (1989*a*) report a further study (experiment 3) in which the procedures were exactly the same as those used in their appetitive conditioning experiment except for the use of shock as the reinforcer and conditioned suppression as the measure of behaviour. The results are shown in Fig. 4.5.(b). Groups S and D performed identically during the test; using an aversive reinforcer eliminates context-specificity in this preparation and allows the result of Lovibond *et al.* (1984) to be replicated.

The null result of Fig. 4.5(b) is of theoretical significance as it helps rule out several possible explanations for the effect seen in Fig. 4.5(a). Recall that among the possible reasons for a loss of conditioned responding with a change of context was the generalization decrement that might be expected when the event designated by the experimenter as the CS is presented in a different context. Evidently no generalization decrement occurred with the stimuli and procedures used here because there was no loss of conditioned responding in group D. But the stimuli and procedures used in the aversive conditioning experiment of Fig. 4.5(b) were just the same as those used in the appetitive conditioning experiment of Fig. 4.5(a). Accordingly, generalization decrement cannot be held responsible for the context-specificity of the CR seen in the latter case.

(d) Factors determining context-specificity

Having ruled out the alternatives we are left with the conclusion that the context-specificity seen in Fig. 4.5(a) depends in some way on the context functioning as a retrieval cue. It now becomes necessary to determine why such a form of conditional learning should be evident in this procedure and not in others. The evidence just presented seems to suggest that the use of a food-reinforced procedure makes context-specificity more likely, and certainly other successful demonstrations of the effect have used appetitive conditioning (e.g. Honey, Willis, and Hall (1990), who studied autoshaping in pigeons; Peck and Bouton (1990), experiment 2, who measured the 'head jerk' CR of rats trained with a food reinforcer). But the use of a food-reinforced procedure is not in itself enough—Peck and Bouton's (1990) result was not replicated by Bouton and Peck (1989); and Kaye and Mackintosh (1990) who, apart from giving very prolonged initial training, used procedures similar to those of Hall and Honey (1989*a*), were unable to find the effect. Nor can we say that context-specificity will never appear when aversive conditioning is used. Bonardi, Honey, and Hall (1991) found the effect using flavour-aversion learning; and Hall and Honey (1990) were able to demonstrate context-specificity in a conditioned suppression study

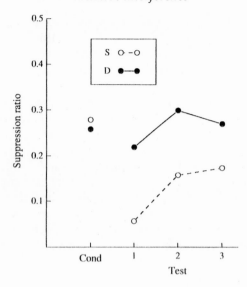

Fig. 4.6 Performance of rats on a single conditioning trial (cond) and on test trials with the conditioned stimulus presented in the same (group S) or in a different (group D) context from that used for training. (From Hall and Honey 1990.)

that differed from the experiment reported by Hall and Honey (1989*a*) only in that conditioning consisted of a single reinforced trial with each CS (Fig. 4.6).

In attempting to explain this last finding, Hall and Honey (1990) offered a suggestion based on the observation (made by many but see, e.g. Schacht-man, Channell, and Hall (1987) that, with prolonged conditioned suppression training, the CR grows up to a point and then begins to decline in magnitude. Apparently a shock that has been experienced often will lose effectiveness as a reinforcer. This effect, Honey and Hall (1990) suggested, might derive from the action of some opponent process that comes into play with the repeated presentation of the shock. In terms of the opponent-process theory of Solomon and Corbit (1974), repeated presentation allows the development of a 'slave process' ('relief') that opposes the state of fear evoked initially by the shock. Whether or not we accept the particular characterization offered by opponent-process theory, it seems that conditioned suppression training is likely to involve more than the formation of a CS-shock association. This association will be formed in the early stages of training but, as training proceeds and the shock loses effectiveness, some form of inhibitory learning can be expected to occur. The magnitude of the overt CR will depend on the interaction of these two forms of learning and can thus be expected to diminish as the contribution of the latter increases.

The relevance of this analysis for out present purposes is that if contextual cues are helpful in retrieving associative information quite generally, then both of the associations formed during conditioned suppression training can be expected to suffer a loss when the context is changed. The effect of the change on the observed level of suppression will depend on the relative contributions of the two associations and any difference between them in their susceptibility to contextual factors. The suggestion put forward by Kraemer and Roberts (1984) (see above, p. 119) that the retrieval of more 'important' associations will be less dependent on contextual cues implies that a change of context might produce a greater loss of effectiveness in the inhibitory than in the excitatory association.

What follows from this account is that the effect produced by a change of context in the conditioned suppression paradigm will vary according to the amount of initial conditioning. In order to see context-dependence in conditioned suppression it will be necessary to devise a procedure in which the contribution of the inhibitory association will be negligible. The one-trial conditioning procedure achieves this since acquisition is over before the shock has a chance to lose effectiveness. The change of context can influence only an excitatory association and thus the result of Fig. 4.6, a loss of the CR, can be expected. With more training, however, the inhibitory association will begin to form. At some point in training, then, the loss of effectiveness of the inhibitory association occasioned by a change of context will counteract the reduced effectiveness of the excitatory association more or less exactly and the outcome will be little or no net change in the observed CR. Thus the null result of Fig. 4.5(b) could occur in spite of the fact that aversive conditioning is context-specific. With yet further training, however, the contribution of the inhibitory association will continue to increase and the effect of its loss when the context is changed is unlikely to match exactly the reduction suffered by the excitatory association. We can expect that a change of context after prolonged training would produce an actual *increase* in the magnitude of the observed CR. It is gratifying to note that Kaye and Mackintosh (1990) have recently reported a series of conditioned suppression experiments in which initial conditioning was prolonged (the subjects received a minimum of 80 shock-reinforced trials in each context during acquisition) showing just such 'supertransfer' when the context is changed.

At first sight the failure of conditioned suppression to show context-specificity (as in Fig. 4.5(b)) looks like evidence against the notion that contextually mediated retrieval is a factor of general importance in associative learning and performance. But this result becomes understandable once it is appreciated that in order to predict the outcome of a change of context it is necessary to know what associations have been formed, how each affects behaviour, and how susceptible each is to the contextual change. By taking all these into account it is possible to explain the varied pattern of context-dependence shown by conditioned suppression after varying amounts of training. The failure of this CR sometimes to show a loss with change of context (and the fact that sometimes the CR is enhanced by such a change) turns out to be evidence in favour of the proposal that appropriate contextual cues can foster the retrieval of associative information.

The same general analysis goes some way toward explaining why context-specificity should be more easily demonstrable in appetitive conditioning. Loss of effectiveness in a shock US is amply demonstrated, for instance by the loss of the CR that occurs with prolonged training. But such effects are much less evident with food reinforcers, implying that our normal procedures for appetitive conditioning will not usually involve an inhibitory component. An appetitive CR must usually be expected to suffer a loss, therefore, when the context is changed. This is not to say that food reinforcers are quite immune from the operation of a mechanism like that supposed in Solomon and Corbit's opponent-process theory. But it may mean that an apparent loss of context-specificity might be found only after very protracted training indeed.

(e) Conclusions

The experimental results described in this section of the chapter allow a number of conclusions. First, conditioned responding can show context-dependence and will do so even without explicit training in which the significance of the target CS is different in different contexts. Second, context-specificity can be observed in conditions that preclude an important role for generalization decrement or other factors that might act by influencing the way in which the CS is perceived. It is also observed in procedures that control for a possible contribution from direct assoications between the context and the US. (It may be added that Wagner's (1981) proposal that direct associations between contextual cues and the CS might limit the ability of the latter to evoke its CR can be rejected with some confidence on the basis of the present results—this hypothesis implies that the CR should always be enhanced when the CS is presented in a different context.) What remains is the suggestion that contextual cues present during associative learning acquire a conditional function allowing the use or retrieval of the information encoded in associative links. Acknowledging that more than one sort of link may be formed as a result of even simple conditioning procedures helps explain the way in which these effects show in behaviour. And although no precise mechanism for contextual retrieval has been given, the parallel with occasion setting has been noted and forms a basis on which we may build.

Finally it is appropriate to say something at this point about the fact, discussed in detail in Chapter 2, that habituation does not show context dependence. In that chapter I treated the habituation experiment as a form of recognition memory task in which subjects compare current sensory input with representations of previous inputs. When the test stimulus is recognized as being the same as one experienced during training (when there is a match between input and representation), no UR is evoked; when the test stimulus is not (or not fully) recognized, dishabituation occurs. The important difference between habituation and conditioning when it comes to context specificity appears to be that the latter involves the recall of associative information whereas habituation requires no more than the recognition of the stimulus as being familiar.

Evidence that recognition of an event can survive a change of context when other forms of learning do not comes from a variety of studies of human memory. An extreme instance is provided by Godden and Baddeley (1975, 1980), who found that the ability of divers to recall a list of words learned either under water or on the beach was much better when the test took place in the same conditions as had prevailed during original learning. But the ability to recognize a word as coming from the original list was uninfluenced by the change of context. An example rather closer to the common experience of most of us comes from studies of face recognition. Young, Hay, and Ellis (1985) asked 22 people to keep records over an eight-week period of difficulties they experienced in recognizing people. In many of these (233 cases) it turned out that a person was recognized perfectly well as being familiar but the subjects reported a difficulty in recalling other details, such as the person's name. Incidents of this type, Young *et al.* report, tend to occur when the person is encountered in an unusual context—that is, efficient recall of semantic information appears to require the presence of appropriate contextual cues whereas recognition does not.

4.2.2. Retrieval and context-specificity in latent inhibition

The experimental work described in Chapter 3 established clearly that latent inhibition is context-dependent; it also pointed, if a little less clearly, to two further conclusions. First, it seems that preliminary exposure to the training context can enhance the magnitude of the latent inhibition effect, perhaps because it retards the development of context-specificity (Hall and Channell 1985c); second, giving animals extensive exposure to the training context alone after they have experienced presentations of the target stimulus in that context does nothing to diminish the size of the latent inhibition effect (e.g. Hall and Minor 1984). Associative theorizing (e.g. Wagner 1976) can deal well enough with the basic fact of context-specificity but is less comfortable with the other phenomena (see also McLaren *et al.* 1989). If, however, we accept that the effects of non-reinforced exposure can become context-dependent in the same way as associative learning itself can, then the entire pattern of results can be accommodated.

First, the effects of pre-exposure will not transfer readily from one context to another because the original contextual cues will be necessary if the information acquired during pre-exposure is to be fully available. Next, there is no reason to suppose that the loss of effectiveness suffered by a cue as a result of non-reinforced pre-exposure will be restricted to the case in which that cue is subsequently required to function as a CS; no doubt the development of an occasion-setting function will also be retarded by exposure to the cue in question. Accordingly, pre-exposure to the context can be expected to attenuate the extent to which latent inhibition will develop context-specificity. And, finally, this interpretation leads to the expectation that exposure to the context after latent inhibition training might be without effect. Certainly it has been argued for a discrete stimulus trained as an occasion setter that subsequently presenting it alone will not produce a loss of occasion-setting power (e.g. Rescorla 1986) (but see also Ross 1983; Holland and Gory 1986). In order to 'extinguish' a cue that signals that a CS and US are associated it may be necessary for the animal to experience uncorrelated presentations of CS and US in the presence of the cue. If the same holds true for contextual cues in latent inhibition, then giving an animal experience of the context alone (i.e. without any presentations of the target stimulus) should not eliminate the ability of the context to activate the associative information about the target stimulus that was established during pre-exposure (e.g. the information that the target is followed by no significant event).

In summary, then, the basic facts of context-specificity in latent inhibition encourage acceptance of the view that the role of the context is to function as a retrieval cue for information acquired during exposure to the target. But before expanding on this interpretation it is necessary to consider some evidence that is apparently directly contradictory.

(a) A dissociation of latent inhibition and associative interference?

Kaye, Preston, Szabo, Druiff, and Mackintosh (1987) report an experiment which makes use of a contextual manipulation in an attempt to demonstrate that latent inhibition is not to be interpreted as a form of associative interference. In the test phase of their study (the results of which are summarized in Fig. 4.7) all the subjects, thirsty rats, received presentations of a CS followed by access to water. Subjects given pre-exposure to the CS in the test context (group LI same in the figure) acquired the CR slowly compared with the control group for whom the CS was novel and with a group of subjects (LI diff) that had experienced the CS previously in a different context. This training procedure evidently generates context-specific latent inhibition, a result that I have interpreted as implying that the effects of exposure to the CS are less likely to interfere with new learning when the context is changed. The challenge to this interpretation comes from the performance of the two other groups shown in the figure. These had received pre-training in which the CS had been used to signal electric shock—pre-training designed to interfere with the final stage of appetitive conditioning. An interference effect was indeed apparent at the start of the final stage (Fig. 4.7) and did not differ in magnitude between subjects that had received their aversive training in the same context as that used for the test and subjects that had received aversive training in a different context. Associative interference is evidently

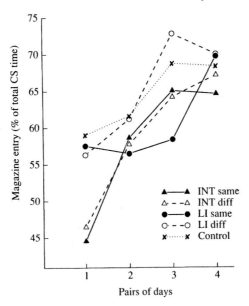

Fig. 4.7 Acquisition of a magazine entry response in rats given conditioned stimulus (CS)–water pairings. For control subjects the CS was novel; LI groups had received non-reinforced pre-exposure to the CS either in the same context as that used for conditioning or in a different context (group LI diff). The INT groups received equivalent pre-exposure but with the CS paired with electric shock. (From Kaye *et al.* 1987.)

not attenuated by a change of context, so Kaye *et al.* (1987) argue, and hence interference cannot be the basis of the (context-dependent) latent inhibition effect.

A recent experiment by Peck and Bouton (1990) failed to replicated the null result of Kaye *et al.* (1987)—that is, Peck and Bouton were able to demonstrate context-specificity in aversive-to-appetitive transfer. Whatever the source of the differing outcomes of these two experiments, it remains the case that the specific procedures used by Kaye *et al.* did achieve an apparent dissociation of associative interference and latent inhibition. These results still constitute, therefore, a direct contradiction of the thesis being developed here. It may already be obvious, however, that even the results summarized in Fig. 4.7 do not require us to conclude that the mechanism responsible for latent inhibition is quite different from that responsible for orthodox associative interference effects. The critical results presented by Kaye *et al.* constitute a demonstration that an aversive CS will interfere with further (appetitive) conditioning, whether the context is changed or stays the same. But a difference between the two conditions (the two INT groups of the figure) could only be found if the effects of aversive conditioning were context-specific; and, as we have already seen, aversive conditioning (at least with a moderate level of initial training and a mild shock as the US such as Kaye *et al.* employed) will transfer from one context to another. The results of Kaye *et al.* constitute a challenge to interference theory only to the extent that this theory is constrained to predict that the aversive CR acquired in the first stage of training should fail to transfer fully to a new test context. But, as we have just seen (p. 127), there are good reasons for thinking that the overt CR evoked by a CS for shock may fail to show context-specificity in spite of the fact that contextual cues can help the retrieval of associative information.

(b) At what stage does interference occur?

The results presented so far imply that the information acquired during non-reinforced exposure to a stimulus, like that acquired as a consequence of other conditioning procedures, requires the presence of appropriate contextual cues if it is to be fully retrieved. To this extent the context-specificity of latent inhibition is to be interpreted as a retrieval phenomenon. What these results do not show, however, is that latent inhibition depends on interference during retrieval in the way postulated by Miller and his colleagues (see above, p. 117). Their version of retrieval theory supposes that information acquired during pre-exposure (that the target stimulus is followed by no event, say) can coexist with information acquired during conditioning (that the stimulus is associated with a US) and will compete with it on a retrieval test. Demonstrations of context-specificity do not in themselves establish the correctness of this view as they can be readily interpreted as showing simply that the effects of pre-exposure interfere less with acquisition when conditioning takes place in different context. What is required is an experiment in which, after non-reinforced exposure in one context and conditioning in a different context, the subjects are tested with the target stimulus back in the original context. Conditioned responding should develop perfectly readily given the context-specificity of latent inhibition; but will it be evident on the final test? If retrieval of the CS-US association depends upon the presence of the cues of the conditioning context whereas the cues of the pre-exposure context allow retrieval of the information that the target stimulus is not followed by any event, then no conditioned responding can be expected when the CS is presented in the latter context.

Experiments aimed at investigating this issue have been reported by many workers (e.g. Anderson, O'Farrell, Formica, and Caponigri 1969; Anderson, Wolf, and Sullivan 1969; Dexter and Merrill 1969; Bouton and Bolles 1979; Lovibond *et al.* 1984; Wright and Gustavson 1986; Wright, Skala, and Peuser 1986). Most of these studies have produced results consistent with the suggestion that interference occurs at retrieval, finding that a CS that has undergone latent inhibition training will be relatively ineffective in evoking

Table 4.1 Design and results of experiment by Bouton and Swartzentruber (1989)

Pre-exposure		Conditioning	Test	
			L in A	L in B
Context A	Context B	Context C		
			0.43	0.29
L	—	L → shock		

L = light; A, B, and C are distinctively different contexts.
Test results: group mean suppression ratios on first test trial.

its CR when it is presented in the context used for pre-exposure. But, as Bouton and Swartzentruber (1989) point out, many of these experiments obtain the effect only in rather poorly controlled conditions, making unambiguous interpretation difficult. The experiment reported by Bouton and Swartzentruber (1989, experiment 3) is more satisfactory. Table 4.1 shows the design and results.

Rats were given repeated exposure to presentations of a light in context A and were also familiarized with a different context (B) in which no stimuli were presented. They then received conditioning trials with the light as the CS in a third context (C). For subjects subsequently presented with the light in A, the suppression controlled by this CS at the end of conditioning in C was much attenuated. To some extent a loss of conditioned responding is to be expected purely on the grounds that conditioning tends to be context-specific. But this is not the sole source of the loss because other subjects that received the final test with the light in context B maintained suppression to the light. A change of context is not enough; what is required is that the subjects receive their test in a context in which they have previously undergone latent inhibition training with the target stimulus.* Bouton and Swartzentruber (1989) conclude that representations of both the latent inhibition treatment and the conditioning treatment are available in the subject's memory at the end of training and that which controls performance depends on retrieval by the appropriate context. The context-specificity of latent inhibition is not be explained (or at least, not entirely) in terms of interference effects that go on during the conditioning phase of the procedure.

---

* This result is compatible with Wagner's (1981) analysis because it may be taken as showing that the existence of the context–CS association makes a CS less effective at evoking its CR. But, as we have already seen, this analysis must be rejected because it predicts the reverse of the context-specificity that is usually seen in conditioning.

4.3. Conclusions

It is now time to attempt to draw together not only the material presented in this chapter but also that considered in Chapter 3. It will no doubt already be apparent that no simple account to latent inhibition is likely to emerge in spite of the seeming simplicity of the basic experimental procedure. None of the theories proposed for the phenomenon is wholly satisfactory but there is evidence that requires us to accept at least some aspects of several of them. Some sort of hybrid theory is likely to result.

The chief conclusion to emerge from the work discussed in this chapter is that retrieval processes contribute to the hybrid—that the latent inhibition effect occurs, at least in part, because subjects tend to retrieve information acquired during pre-exposure to the target stimulus rather than information acquired during conditioning. One advantage of accepting this conclusion is that it provides, with its assumption that the context can act as a retrieval cue, a ready account of the various contextual effects discussed in this chapter and in Chapter 3. The qualification 'at least in part', is necessary because, as I have already noted, the evidence available on the role of inter-ference at retrieval can show only that this process contributes to the effects observed, not that it is the sole source of these effects. It is quite possible that pre-exposure to a stimulus both retards new learning about that stimulus and also establishes a memory trace of its own that interferes with any sub-sequently formed when recall is tested. I shall take up this point shortly.

To endorse the suggestion that information acquired during pre-exposure interferes with the use of that acquired during conditioning requires an attempt to specify the nature of the information acquired in the first phase. The earlier discussion of the various forms of interference theory left us with two main candidates (above, p. 116) and both still remain possible. The first, and perhaps the simplest, was that the formation of within-stimulus associ-ations might interfere with the acquisition of subsequent associations involv-ing these stimulus elements (and, I must now add, might interfere with the ability of subsequently formed associations to influence behaviour). The second candidate—that latent inhibition training might establish stimulus-no event association—is perhaps a little more complex in that this hypothesis requires the addition of a supplementary mechanism to explain why pre-exposure should retard inhibitory as well as excitatory conditioning. The suggestion offered earlier in this chapter was that pre-exposure to a stimulus, as well as allowing certain associations to be formed, might also result in a loss of associability. If this were so, the strengthening of the various associ-ations generated by the inhibitory conditioning procedure would proceed only slowly for a pre-exposed stimulus and this effect could well outweigh any advantage that the existence of a stimulus–no event association might bestow.

The extra complexity of the second hypothesis may seem a good reason for preferring the first, but in fact any theory of latent inhibition will need to find some place for the idea that associability can change if it is to accommodate the chief conclusions to emerge from Chapter 3. Although current theories stressing the role played by stimulus consequence in latent inhibition are inadequate (they are unable to deal with the role of context), there remains a set of empirical findings that such theories alone can accommodate—the various experiments (see pp. 99–104) suggesting that the associability of a stimulus depends on its predictive accuracy. The explanation for these findings offered by Pearce and Hall (1980) was that the associability of a stimulus is determined by how well the stimulus predicts its consequences, declining to zero as the CS–consequence association rises to asymptote. (Inconsistent consequences, such as occur with partial reinforcement schedule, act to maintain associability.) In its original form the Pearce–Hall (1980) model applied this analysis only to the loss of associability that occurs with CS–US pairings, but it is a straightforward matter to deal with orthodox latent inhibition in the same way. Simple pre-exposure may be assumed to be an effective method for reducing associability because it allows the rapid formation either of a strong stimulus–no event association or of associations among stimulus elements, just as consistent reinforcement allows the rapid formation of a strong CS–US association. According to this account the formation of associations during pre-exposure and the loss of associability are not to be thought of as rival interpretations of latent inhibition. Rather they are complementary, with the latter process being a consequence of the former.

To sum up the hybrid theory that has emerged: it is that non-reinforced pre-exposure to a stimulus will allow the formation of potentially interfering associations and bring about a loss of associability. The associative learning that goes on during such pre-exposure will be dependent upon the context in which training occurs, and to this extent latent inhibition will be attenuated by a change of context. The loss of associability suffered by the stimulus will be depend on the extent to which the stimulus, or each of its constituent elements, is able to form strong associations (and will thus be restricted when the consequences of the stimulus change from trial to trial). Both these factors (interference and low associability) may hinder the formation of the association required during conditioning but this new association, when it is eventually formed, will not totally obliterate those formed during pre-exposure and there will be competition between old and new during a retrieval test.

It may seem extravagant to invoke such a range of processes in order to explain the effects of what is perhaps the simplest of training procedures; but in fact the list is as yet incomplete. In addition to the processes just described, repeated presentation of a stimulus also brings about those changes responsible for habituation that I discussed in Chapter 2—changes that were characterized as resulting in the formation of a representation of the stimulus. Given that our primary concern is with perceptual learning it might be argued that this last process is what should command attention and that the processes involved in latent inhibition (apart perhaps from the attentional change it involves) are of marginal importance only. Indeed in subsequent chapters I shall again be concerned almost entirely with the way in which stimulus representations are modified by experience. But a detailed investigation of latent inhibition will not be wasted. Latent inhibition goes on in all experiments aimed at revealing the nature of stimulus representations and often acts to mask the effects under investigation. Only by knowing the mechanisms responsible for latent inhibition will we be able to eliminate its effects allowing other forms of perceptual learning to be revealed.

5. Acquired distinctiveness: mediation and differentiation

In Chapter 1 I distinguished two basic training procedures, one involving discrimination training, the other mere exposure to stimuli, that have been thought to reveal perceptual learning effects. In the exposure learning procedure the subjects are simply exposed to a stimulus (or sometimes to more than one stimulus) without there being any explicit consequences arranged by the experimenter. The effects of this exposure treatment can be assessed in a variety of ways and three were specified in Chapter 1. The first of these, the habituation of the unconditioned response consequent on repeated exposure, was discussed in Chapter 2; the second, the way in which exposure modifies the ability of an event to serve as a classically conditioned stimulus, was discussed in Chapters 3 and 4. The third method for assessing the effects of exposure is one in which the subjects are required to learn a discrimination between pre-exposed stimuli (or between the pre-exposed stimulus and some other). Discussion of the outcome of experiments that have used this method will be postponed until Chapter 7 as a proper interpretation of the results of such experiments requires consideration of the processes revealed by the second of the two basic training procedures outlined in Chapter 1. The next two chapters, accordingly, are concerned with evaluating the effects of reinforced training—in particular, with the suggestion that giving subjects experience of different stimuli associated with different schedules can modify the way in which these stimuli are perceived.

It is common ground that discrimination training will establish associative links that play an important part in generating the changes in behaviour that are observed. Following one stimulus rather than another with food, for example, is likely to establish associations that will cause the subject to approach the former stimulus rather than the latter when both are available. What we need to consider now is the possibility that discrimination training also allows processes to operate that modify the distinctiveness of the stimuli themselves. Changes in stimulus distinctiveness might, indeed, be in part responsible for the development of different patterns of overt behaviour to the different training stimuli, but the mere fact that discrimination learning occurs cannot prove this to be so. That is, the acquisition of a simple discrimination can be adequately explained solely in terms of the formation of stimulus–reinforcer associations and without recourse to any concept of perceptual learning (see Chapter 1, pp. 13–16).

Attempts to demonstrate acquired distinctiveness have, therefore, usually made use of a two-stage procedure in which the effects of an initial stage of discrimination training are assessed in some form of transfer test, often one that requires the learning of a further discrimination. If the stimuli used in initial training have acquired distinctiveness, then this might be revealed in positive transfer to a second task involving these same stimuli. Interpretation of the results of these studies has been an important battleground for theoretical disputes over the nature of perceptual learning. The notion of acquired distinctiveness was originally devised by theorists wedded to an associationist interpretaion of all forms of learning (Miller and Dollard (1941), drawing heavily on the S–R theory of Hull (e.g. 1939)), who were thus seen as offering an associative account of perceptual learning. Gibson and Gibson (1955) responded vigorously to this suggestion, arguing that there were no clear cases in which it was necessary to conclude that the associations formed by cues during discrimination training were responsible for changes in the distinctiveness of those cues. Instead of an associative mechanism (what they refer to as 'enrichment'), Gibson and Gibson (1955) (see also Gibson 1969) advocate an interpretation in terms of their differentiation theory whereby subjects become able to respond to aspects of the cues that were present from the outset but were not initially responded to. This account provoked an immediate riposte from Postman (1955), who objected that no mechanism had been specified to explain the process by which differentiation occurs and argued that associative processes constituted a possibility.

Consideration of these two theoretical positions—the non-associative notion of differentiation and the associative account (to be referred to as 'mediation')—will occupy the latter part of this chapter. It is already clear, however, that the notion of acquired distinctiveness is of central importance in discussions of perceptual learning. We need now, therefore, to consider the empirical work that has been done on the topic of acquired distinction (and on acquired non-distinctiveness or equivalence*). The aim of the review that constitutes the next two major sections of this chapter is largely methodological. Its purpose is to examine in detail the various experimental procedures that have been said to demonstrate acquired distinctiveness and to determine which generate reliable effects that are not to be explained away in other terms. It is against the results produced by these procedures that the theories can be assessed.

---

* The use of this term is not meant to imply necessarily that the stimuli in question have become equivalent in the mathematical or logical sense of the term and may therefore be contrasted with the suggestion (e.g. Sidman and Tailby 1982) that just such formal equivalence can emerge from certain forms of discrimination training. It remains possible, however, that the mechanisms of acquired equivalence to be discussed later in this chapter play some part in generating the phenomena described by Sidman (see Hall 1990).

5.1 Experimental studies with human subjects

The first explicit investigation of acquired distinctiveness was that conducted by Lawrence (1949), using rats as subjects. (Lawrence was a student of Miller who, with Dollard, was responsible for formalizing and popularizing the notion of acquired distinctiveness: Miller and Dollard (1941); Miller (1948); Dollard and Miller (1950). Most of the experiments on this topic have, however, been conducted with human subjects and I shall begin by reviewing this work before turning to an analysis of the relatively few further studies that have used animal subject to pursue the phenomenon revealed by Lawrence. Previous reviews of some of this material have been supplied by Spiker (1956*b*), Arnoult (1957), Vanderplas (1958), Cantor (1965), and Gibson (1969).

5.1.1. Transfer between verbal and motor tasks

(a) Preliminary demonstrations

The first publication reporting an explicit test of the Miller–Dollard hypothesis with human subjects was by Rossman and Goss (1951), although their procedure and findings were anticipated by Gagné and Baker (1950) in a near-identical experiment conducted for slightly different reasons.[*] In both experiments, subjects were trained initially to respond with different verbal labels to a set of visual stimuli and then received training on a motor task with these same stimuli. In the Gagné and Baker task, the subjects had to learn to respond with a particular letter of the alphabet when a light of a given colour in a given position was presented; there were four different lights, each to be associated with a different letter. In the test the subjects were required to learn to press a given switch out of four available in response to a given light. Subjects given extensive pre-training in applying labels to the stimuli learned the motor task more readily than others given little or no pretraining. They quickly learned to respond more rapidly and pressed the incorrect switch relatively infrequently (Fig 5.1). The superiority of subjects given preliminary training in applying labels over control subjects given no pre-training has been repeatedly confirmed by experimenters using procedures closely similar to those just described (Goss 1953; Smith and Goss 1955; Battig 1956; Holton and Goss 1956; Goss and Greenfield 1958). (Arnoult's (1953, experiment 2), failure to find an effect was probably a consequence of giving too little preliminary training.)

The rationale for this experimental design is identical to that underlying Lawrence's (1949) experiment. An initial phase of discrimination training will establish a tendency to make certain (different) responses to the critical

---

[*] Early studies of the role played by verbalization in the discrimination learning abilities of children (e.g. Pyles 1932) perhaps constitute the first experimental demonstrations of acquired distinctiveness in this paradigm.

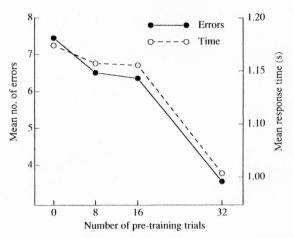

Hall argued the pre-training may not prove acquired equivalence but another reason

evidence for Pre-training

Fig. 5.1 Performance on a motor task of four groups of subjects given varying amounts of pre-training with the relevant stimuli (After Gagné and Baker 1950.)

stimuli, but the change in the nature of the task for the second phase should mean that the specific response patterns acquired in the first phase will be irrelevant. It would be premature to conclude, however, that the transfer seen in such an experiment depends on the acquisition of distinctiveness by the critical cues as a consequence of phase-one discrimination training. Results of the sort shown in Fig. 5.1 could arise simply because the initial training produces general facilitatory effects (by allowing the subject to become accustomed to the situation, and so on). They do not require an appeal to effects specific to the discriminative stimuli.

An essential first step is to demonstrate that pre-training must be given with the same stimuli as are used in the test phase. Some experimenters, therefore, have made the comparison with a control group given initial training in applying labels but to stimuli different from those used in the motor task. There have been some exceptions (again, perhaps because insufficient phase-one training was given) (Arnoult 1953; McAllister 1953; McCormack 1958) but for the most part the test performance of control subjects has turned out to be inferior to that of subjects pre-trained with the relevant stimuli (G. Cantor 1955; J. Cantor 1955; Cantor and Hottel 1957; Smith and Means 1961; Hendrickson and Muehl 1962). Experiments by Murdock (1958) and Reese (1961) have confirmed these findings using a within-subject design. They showed that subjects given verbal pre-training with one set of stimuli learn the appropriate motor response more rapidly to these stimuli than to a further set introduced for the first time in the test phase.

The experiments just mentioned not only introduce a much-needed control procedure but they also extend the generality of the effect. Cantor and Hottel (1957) obtained their results with mentally retarded subjects;

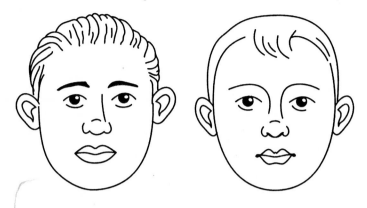

Fig. 5.2 Line drawings used as stimuli in some studies of acquired distinctiveness in children (From Norcross and Spiker 1957.)

G. Cantor (1955) and Reese (1961) used young children. Stimuli other than the onset of a light have been used along with more meaningful verbal labels—G. Cantor (1955), for example, used line drawings of faces (versions of those shown in Fig. 5.2) with the labels being names (Jack and Pete). This study also introduced a different test task using not a successive but a simultaneous discrimination in which the subjects had to choose (for the reward of a marble) one of the two faces. The experiment by Hendrickson and Muehl (1962) constitutes an even more radical departure in that, uniquely, the order of the training phases was reversed.* The children in this experiment were pre-trained on a motor task (they had to push different levers in response to two stimuli, the letters 'b' and 'd') before being tested on a verbal paired-associate task involving these stimuli. Here too, such pre-training produced better test performance than did training on an equivalent motor task with quite different stimuli.

(b) Further control procedures

I have established that the initial phase of training must be given with the stimuli that are to be relevant in the test phase. It remains to show, however, that this training must be discriminative, with the different stimuli being associated with different events. Gibson's (1969) account of these effects

---

* This study is an exception to the usual procedure of establishing verbal labels for the stimuli prior to training on a discrimination requiring quite different (usually overt motor) responses to the same stimuli. There are other exceptions. Murdock (1958) and Smith and Means (1961) included conditions in which pre-training was on one motor task and testing on a different motor task. Both found positive transfer (although the effect was small in Murdock's experiment). Other studies, to be discussed later, have required the learning of verbal labels in both phases of the experiment (Hake and Ericksen 1955, 1956; De Rivera 1959) (see also Kurtz 1955).

suggests that discrimination training may not be necessary but the same con-clusion can be derived from more prosaic considerations—it might be argued, for instance, that the results described so far reflect no more than a disruption in control subjects confronted by novel stimuli at the start of the test discrimination.

In an attempt to deal with this issue, Goss (1953) introduced a control procedure in which subjects were simply allowed to observe the stimuli (in one case being instructed to attend to them, in another given no special instructions) during the first phase of training. It was found that these con-trol subjects performed just as well in the test as did subjects trained initially to make different verbal responses to the stimuli. Subsequent experiments using these control procedures have produced inconsistent results. Some (e.g. Smith and Goss 1955; Holton and Goss 1956; Vanderplas, Sanderson, and Vanderplas 1964) confirmed that subjects made to observe and attend differed little from experimental subjects. But others (G. Cantor 1955; Goss and Greenfield 1958; Katz 1963; Ellis and Muller 1964, experiment 2), found that such controls showed inferior performance. Pfafflin (1960) was able to generate both results by changing details of the stimuli used and the nature of the labels supplied to the experimental subjects.

A close examination of these various experiments might reveal the reason for their discrepant findings. But rather than undertaking such an analysis it will be enough to demonstrate that this control procedure is in principle inadequate for our present needs. First, there is the possibility, acknow-ledged by several of the experimenters just cited, that subjects told merely to observe the stimuli might actually come to attach their own labels to them. Such subjects, as a consequence, might not differ in their test performance from those who were explicitly trained to apply labels. This outcome could not, of course, justify the suggestion that discrimination training is unnecessary for positive transfer to occur, as the control subjects would have supplied for themselves what may be the critical feature of such training.

The other possible result of an experiment of this design is equally ambiguous. However strict the instructions about attending to the stimuli, subjects in the control condition might fail to do so. In the limiting case, therefore, this control condition reduces to that in which no pre-training is given. We have already seen that subjects given no pre-training do less well in the test phase than those given initial discrimination training and we have acknowledged that unambiguous interpretation of this difference is impossible. What we need to arrange is that control subjects perform some sort of task in the first phase—not one, of course, that requires them to attach dif-ferent labels to the critical stimuli, but one that guarantees that attention to these stimuli is maintained. Ideally the control task would be one that required some sort of discrimination learning, thus ensuring that both groups came to the test phase having had the experience of learning one pre-vious discrimination problem.

Unfortunately, although not surprisingly, it has proved difficult to devise a suitable control discrimination. Some use has been made of a control suggested by Kurtz (1955), in which the subjects received pre-training on a same–different task. The stimuli to be used in the test phase were presented two at a time and the subjects were asked to describe the pair as 'same' or 'different' as appropriate. Such training, Kurtz argued, means that the subjects learn a discrimination and must attend to the stimuli although they are not required to label them differently. Kurtz's own experiment demonstrated positive transfer (to a verbal paired-associate task) in subjects given same–different pre-training, but unfortunately the comparison was made only with a group given no pre-training at all. But Norcross and Spiker (1957) (see also Spiker 1956*b*) found, using stimuli like those shown in Fig. 5.2 and a simultaneous discrimination test, that children given training in applying different names to the two faces were superior in their test performance to controls pre-trained on a same–different task. This finding has been confirmed by Spiker and Norcross (1962). It constitutes the best evidence we have come across so far that training in which the critical stimuli become linked to different events generates a unique source of transfer to further discrimination learning. But even here a sceptic might find reason to challenge this conclusion. The problem is that the same–different task and the labelling task are unlikely to be matched in the demands they make on the subjects. A difference in the difficulty of the pre-training tasks might be enough in itself to generate a difference between the groups in the ease with which the test problem is learned, and there would then be no need to suppose that the learning of specific distinctive labels is the critical factor.

A similar objection can be raised to the procedure used by Katz (1963). Here the control group learned an initial discrimination in which one verbal response was required for each of two stimuli (A and B), whereas a different response was required for C and D. Experimental subjects were required to learn a different label for each of the four stimuli. The superiority of this latter group on a test task which involved choice between A and B could well depend on their having learned different labels (and on the control group having learned the same label) for these stimuli. But it could equally well be a consequence of a difference in difficulty between the two pre-training tasks.

(c) Within-subject procedures

Perhaps the most satisfactory solution to the problem of devising an adequate control procedure is to make use of a within-subject experimental design of the sort employed by Norcross (1958) and Reese (1972).

The design and results of the critical aspects of Reese's experiment are summarized as Fig. 5.3. All the subjects (young children) were trained with three 'nonsense' figures as the stimuli, learning to apply one verbal label to two of them and a different label to the third. There was no question, therefore, of different groups receiving different amounts of exposure

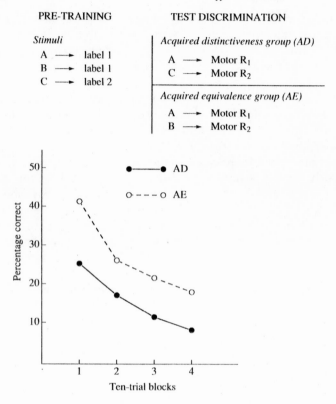

Fig. 5.3 Design and test results from the experiment by Reese (1972). A, B, and C represent different nonsense figures; R1 and R2, different responses.

to the stimuli or receiving training on discrimination differing on difficulty. The children were divided into two groups for the test phase in which they received successive discrimination training, learning to press one button in response to one of the pre-trained cues and a second button in response to another. For subjects in an 'acquired distinctiveness' group, the two stimuli had been given different labels in pre-training; for those in the 'acquired equivalence' group the two stimuli used were those that had been given the same label. As the figure shows, subjects in the distinctiveness condition learned the test discrimination more readily than those in the equivalence condition. The experiment by Norcross (1958), which used a slightly different version of this procedure, produced essentially the same outcome. Four stimuli were used: two of these were given very different labels, thus approximating to the A and B stimuli of Fig. 5.3. Norcross found that the acquisition of a button-pressing task proceeded more rapidly with the first pair of stimuli than with the second.

Table 5.1 Generalization tests for acquired distinctiveness and equivalence: experimental designs

Pre-training	Acquisition	Test
Between-subjects comparison		
AE: A → X and B → X	A → R	B
AD: A → X and B → Y	A → R	B
Within-subjects: single test stimulus		
A → X		
and B → Y	A → R1	C
and C → Y	and B → R2	
Within-subjects: two test stimuli		
A → X		
and B → X	A → R	B and C
and C → Y		

A, B, and C are the critical stimuli, X and Y are different outcomes (e.g. verbal labels)
with which they can be associated; R is the test response; AE = acquired equivalence
condition; AD = acquired distinctiveness condition.

The obvious problem with the designs of these experiments is that it is
impossible to know whether the difference observed in the test depends on
positive transfer in the distinctiveness group, negative transfer in the equivalence group, or both of these. This uncertainty seems a small price to pay for
the comfort of knowing that at least one of these effects must be a reality.

5.1.2. Transfer to a generalization test

Traditionally, acquired distinctiveness effects have been assessed by requiring the subjects to learn a test discrimination between the stimuli experienced in the first phase of training. Typically the various stimuli are
presented concurrently, each associated with a different outcome or requiring a different response. An alternative and, in some ways, simpler procedure is to establish some new response to one of the pre-trained stimuli
and then, in a separate test phase, to present the other pre-trained stimuli.
(Simplified representations of versions of this experimental design are displayed in Table 5.1.). If there is little generalization of the new response to
the test stimuli, we may conclude that the stimulus used in acquisition and
that used in the test are readily discriminated.
   Malloy and Ellis (1970) conducted a study which included the conditions
shown in Table 5.1 as involving between-subjects comparisons. The critical
(A and B) stimuli were six-pointed geometrical shapes; X and Y were nonsense syllables learned as responses to these shapes. In the acquisition phase,

subjects learned to say a particular noun (R) to shape A. The test showed that training in the acquired equivalence (AE) condition was more likely to produce generalization of this response to a B stimulus than was acquired distinctiveness (AD) training. Wickens and Briggs (1951) report the same result from an experiment using a quite different procedure. Stimuli A and B were a tone and a light; X was the verbal response of saying 'now' when one or the other was turned on, and Y that of saying nothing. Training on a task in which the subjects had to learn to make a finger movement in order to avoid shock generalized readily to B for the AE group but poorly for the AD group.

These experiments confirm the results obtained from studies using a discrimination task in the test phase, and, like those previous studies, they are unable to discriminate between acquired equivalence and distinctiveness effects. Malloy and Ellis (1970) included in their experiment control procedures of the sort I have already discussed (groups given no pre-training, allowed simply to observe the stimuli, and so on) but the proper interpretation of the results from such control procedures is no more secure in this experiment than in any other. It is also true of this experimental procedure, as of the use of a discrimination task, that it can be strengthened by a modification to allow a within-subject comparison. If the AE and AD groups differ in the ease with which they acquire the target response to A (as they well might), then differences in test performance might reflect only that there was more conditioned responding to generalize in one case than in the other. The within-subjects designs shown in Table 5.1 avoid this problem.

The first of these designs was used by Jeffrey (1953). Children learned to make the same response (X) to the visual stimuli A and B, and a different response (Y) to stimulus C. (For some subjects X and Y were different verbal labels, for others they were different hand movements.) All subjects then learned to push a handle (R1) in response to A and to pull it (R2) in response to B. The test phase showed that stimulus C tended to evoke R2, that is, to evoke the response acquired to the training stimulus that had received equivalent pre-training.

What is perhaps a simpler within-subjects design, that shown last in Table 5.1, has been employed by Eisman (1955) and in a series of experiments by Grice and his colleagues (Grice and Davis 1958, 1960; Grice and Hunter 1963) (see also Grice 1965). Eisman's subjects were children, the stimuli (A, B, and C) were coloured blocks for which verbal labels (X and Y) had to be learned. After being rewarded for choosing A in the middle stage of training, the children were asked which of B and C they thought might bring reward. They chose B, the block that had shared a common label with A. Grice's experiments, using adult subjects and a classical conditioning procedure, generated equivalent results. In one set of studies stimulus A was the onset of a light and the target response acquired to it in the intermediate phase of

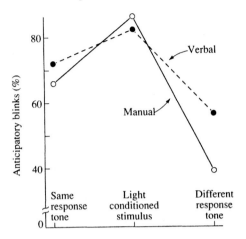

Fig. 5.4 Generalization to two different tones of an eye-blink response conditioned to a light. In a preliminary stage of training the light and one of the tones were trained to elicit the same response (a manual response for one group of subjects, a verbal response for another). (After Grice 1965.)

training was a conditioned eye-blink reinforced by an air-puff uncondi-tioned stimulus. The final phase tested generalization to two auditory sti-muli, tones differing in frequency. In the first stage of training the subjects had received instructions to emit a given response (a key-press in one study, a word in another) to one of the tones and to the light, but to emit a different response to the other tone. The result of Fig. 5.4 show, especially for the manual-response case, that generalization from the light CS (conditioned sti-mulus) occurs more readily to the same-response tone than to the tone pre-trained with a different response.

The advantage of the design of these experiments is that the critical com-parison is made within-subjects. Generalization to both test stimuli (to B and to C) has its origin in a common source (the responding governed by A), thus eliminating the problem identified with the between-subjects design of Table 5.1. As with similar studies using a discrimination test, however, the results do not distinguish acquired distinctiveness from acquired equiva-lence. The response conditioned to A might generalize more to B as a result of the first stage of training; or this training might reduce the extent to which generalization occurs to C; or both of these effects could be occurring.

5.1.3. Transfer from verbal to perceptual tasks

The study by Arnoult (1953), mentioned in the preceding section of this chapter, included a condition in which the subjects were tested not on a discri-minative motor task but on a task which required them to make a judgement about whether two stimuli presented together were the same as or different from one another. Initial training in applying labels to these stimuli did not influence test performance, and this prompted Robinson (1955) to suggest that pre-training might be ineffective when the test task is 'perceptual' rather than 'motor'.

Recognition memory tests

The grounds for the same–different tasks being categorized as 'perceptual' appear to be that, unlike the 'motor' tasks discussed so far, it seems not to require further associative learning. However this may be, Robinson (1955), in common with most subsequent investigators of transfer from verbal pre-training to a perceptual task, made use of a quite different task procedure—a test of recognition memory in which the subject had to respond in one way to stimuli that had been presented in pre-training and in a different way to novel stimuli.* What is of importance here is not so much whether or not the label 'perceptual' is appropriate as whether this task is susceptible to the effects of pre-training in the same way as the motor tasks discussed earlier. Robinson's (1955) results seemed to suggest that it is not.

In Robinson's (1955) experiment the stimuli used were 10 fingerprints. Subject in the distinctiveness condition learned separate names for each of them ('Duke', 'Slim', and so on); subjects in the equivalence condition learned to call five of them 'cops' and five of them 'robbers'. The test required subjects to identify pre-trained stimuli when they were presented among new but similar stimuli. Both groups were superior to a control given no pre-training but they did not differ from each other. Using stimuli of the sort depicted in Fig. 5.5, Vanderplas and Garvin (1959) similarly found no effect on a recognition test of having learned distinctive labels. These results led Ellis and Muller (1964) (see also Katz 1963; Vanderplas *et al.* 1964) to make a direct comparison between a recognition memory test task and one involving the learning of a motor response. For six-pointed shapes of the type shown in Fig 5.5, Ellis and Muller found that subjects who had learned labels for the various shapes out-performed controls (who had simply observed the stimuli in the first phase of training) on a motor task that required pressing one switch rather than some other in response to these stimuli. There was no such difference on a recognition memory task where, if anything, the control group did a little better than the group given distinctiveness training.

---

* It is worth noting that Arnoult's (1953) failure to find an effect with the same–different task is of little consequence since his training procedure also failed to reveal an effect on transfer to a motor task. Subsequently, Katz (1963) has been able to show that children who have been trained to apply common labels to a set of figures do less well on a same–different task than others who have learned distinctive labels.

Training

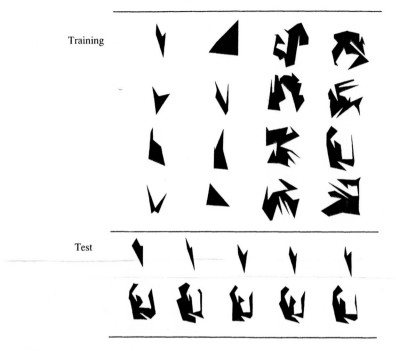

Test

Fig. 5.5 Random shapes used as stimuli by Vanderplas and Garvin (1959). The columns labelled 'training' contain examples of different possible shapes at a given level of complexity. Each of the rows labelled 'test' contains one example of a pre-trained stimulus and four variations on this prototype.

We should be cautious about using these results to argue that verbal pre-training does not influence performance on a recognition memory test. First, the failure of Robinson's (1955) study to reveal an effect was not necessarily a consequence of the test procedure as DeRivera (1959), who used stimuli and a pre-training procedure closely similar to those used by Robinson, was similarly unable to find an effect on test in spite of using a test procedure that required further associative learning. Second, although Ellis and Muller found no difference between their distinctiveness and observation training conditions, there was evidence for a superiority of the distinctiveness group over one given equivalence training in which they had to apply one label to half of the shapes and another label to the rest. The difference in recognition memory-test performance between subjects given these two forms of verbal pre-training has been amply confirmed in several other experiments (e.g. Ellis, Bessemer, Devine and Tafton 1962; Ellis and Feuge, Long and Pegram 1964). Some experimenters indeed (including Ellis and Muller (1964) themselves when they made use of the more complex 24-pointed shapes as their stimuli) have been able to demonstrate a superiority of distinctiveness training over the observe-only control condition (see also Kurtz and Hovland 1953; Ranken 1963; Ellis and Feuge 1966; Ellis and Homan 1968).

Why some of these experiments should be more successful than others at revealing group differences has been the subject of some experimental investigation. There is some evidence to suggest that among the important determinants should be numbered the complexity of the stimuli (Ellis and Muller 1964), whether or not the stimuli look like recognizable objects (Ellis, Muller, and Tosti 1966), and the extent to which the labels match critical features of the stimuli (Segal 1964). I need not pursue these issues further here, however, as the results already cited are enough to establish that, given appropriate circumstances, verbal pre-training can influence performance on a recognition task just as it can on a motor task involving discrimination among the pre-trained stimuli. The experiments reviewed in this section do little to advance out understanding of the mechanisms involved (often important control conditions are lacking) but they do allow the conclusion that there is no fundamental difference between the so-called perceptual and motor test tasks in their susceptibility to acquired equivalence/distinctiveness effects. It will not be necessary, therefore, to devise separate theoretical interpretations for the results of the two test procedures.

5.2. Studies with non-human subjects

I have already considered in some detail the starting point for these studies— Lawrence's (1949) experiment. I begin here, therefore, with a discussion of the relatively few reports of attempts to replicate and extend his findings.

5.2.1. Transfer in discrimination learning

Studies which like Lawrence's (1949) experiment allow investigation of the transfer between simultaneous and successive discriminations involving the same stimuli have been reported by Mackintosh and Holgate (1967, experiment 1), Siegel (1967), and Winefield and Jeeves (1971, experiment 1). The last of these produced negative rather than positive transfer but, in that study, the shift was from a very difficult successive task to a simultaneous discrimination, and comparison was made with a control group that received no prior training. It seems possible that the extensive exposure to the stimuli experienced by the experimental subjects in the first stage of training might have resulted in a latent inhibition effect that would obscure any other source of transfer. Positive transfer was, however, observed by Mackintosh and Holgate and by Siegel, the comparison being made in each case with control subjects that received initial training on a discrimination between stimuli other than those that were relevant in the transfer task but with the latter stimuli being present but irrelevant.

Other experimenters have varied the procedure, following Lawrence in training subjects on two discrimination tasks involving the same stimuli but changing the response requirement not by changing from the simultaneous to the successive arrangement but in some other way. Thus Mackintosh (1964) trained rats on an 'absolute' brightness discrimination in which choice was between black and grey on some trials and between white and grey on other trials. For some subjects, grey was the positive, for others grey was the negative, but neither type of training should establish a difference in associative strength between black and white. The positive transfer that occurred to a subsequent, simultaneous black–white tasks must, therefore, derive from some other source such as an increase in the distinctiveness of the cues.

In a pair of experiments by Jaynes (1950), rats were required in the first-stage task to lift one of a pair of flaps bearing distinctive cues in order to obtain food. Different groups had to lift the positive flap just a little (half an inch) or rather more (up to seven inches); thus the groups differed not in whether they had received pre-training with the cues but in the magnitude of the response acquired. When required to learn a further discrimination involving these same cues but a different response (for example, a reversal in which a simple push to the previously non-rewarded cue now yielded reward) the animals pre-trained with the larger magnitude response learned more readily. Jaynes attributed the transfer to an increase in the distinctiveness of the cues, an increase that was directly dependent on the magnitude of the response first learned to them.

These relatively complex experimental designs are certainly open to more than one interpretation. Unfortunately, the same has proved to be true of experiments using Lawrence's original design. In particular, Siegel (1967) found that a close examination of his results led to the conclusion (see also Riley 1968) that it was unwarranted to assume that responses learned in the first stage could not be the source of the transfer seen in the second. He noted that his rats tended to adopt a strategy for sampling the stimuli in the first stage of (simultaneous) training in which they consistentlly looked into one arm of his T-maze, withdrawing and turning to the other arm only if confronted with the negative stimulus. This strategy was transferred to the successive discrimination, and for at least some of the animals allowed immediate solution of that test—an animal that had learned to turn away from white in the left arm, say, would already be equipped to solve a successive discrimination in which it was rewarded for turning left when both arms were black and right when both were white. In this case, at least, there was no need to assume that the transfer obtained depended on changes in the distinctiveness of the cues.

We may doubt that Siegel's is a complete theory. It needs elaboration, for instance, to deal with the case in which the response strategy learned in the first stage does not accord with the behaviour required in the second. And although Siegel's results demonstrate convincingly that response strategies can indeed transfer from one discrimination to another, they cannot show that such strategies are the sole source of the transfer effects seen in his experiment. Nor can they show that response strategies are responsible for the results reported by others. Indeed, as Sutherland and Mackintosh (1971) have pointed out, Siegels's training apparatus was specifically arranged so as to ensure that the rats would adopt response strategies of the sort they did. Other experimenters have used different forms of apparatus with layouts that seem very unlikely, as far as one can tell, to induce such strategies. Nonetheless, Siegel's arguments have undermined the belief that simultaneous to successive transfer can allow an unambiguous demonstration of an acquired distinctiveness effect. Perhaps better evidence for such an effect comes from experiments using procedures quite different from those employed by Lawrence (1949), procedures in which response strategies of the sort considered by Siegel (1967) could play no role.

5.2.2. Other procedures

(a) Reinforcement history and generalization

I have already discussed (see Table 5.1) how acquired distinctiveness effects can revealed by means of a generalization test. One of the pre-exposed stimuli receives reinforcement as a separate phase of training prior to a test phase in which the other is presented. Lack of generalization to the test stimulus indicates that the two stimuli are readily discriminated from one another.

Honey and Hall (1989c) investigated the influence of an initial phase of discrimination training on such a generalization test, using rats as the subjects and a version of the between-subjects design shown in Table 5.1. In order to distinguish the conditioned response (CR) of the test stage from that acquired in the first stage of discrimination training, the nature of the reinforcer was changed, from appetitive to aversive. Two groups of rats received initial Pavlovian training with two auditory stimuli, A (a burst of white noise) and B (e.g. a tone). For one group, both of these cues signalled the presentation of food; the second group received discrimination training in which B was followed by food and A was not. The effect of this preliminary training on generalization between A and B was examined by establishing A as a CS for some new response and then testing the ability of B to evoke this response. Thus, A was next trained as a signal for shock in both groups. The generalized ability of B to evoke the newly trained CR (of suppression) is displayed in Fig. 5.6. Little generalized suppression was shown by the group given initial discrimination training; that is, these subjects showed a superior ability to discriminate B from A.

In a series of experiments using infant rats as the subjects, Spear and his colleagues (e.g. Spear and Molina 1987; Spear, Kraemer, Molina and Smoller 1988) have investigated acquired equivalence using a design formally identical to that of Honey and Hall (1989c). In one of their paradigms, subjects in

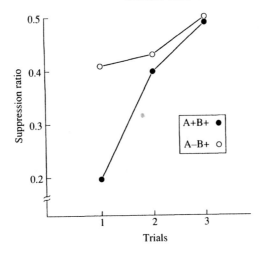

Fig. 5.6 Conditioned suppression shown by two groups of rats on test trials with stimulus B after aversive conditioning with stimulus A. One group (A+B+) received pre-training in which both A and B were associated with food; the other group (A−B+) had food associated with stimulus B only. (After Honey and Hall 1989c.)

the experimental condition were exposed on separate occasions to an odour and to a tactile cue (the texture of a flooring). In the presence of each they received an infusion of a sucrose solution. Control subjects experienced the critical cues but not the sucrose. The odour was then paired with shock for all subjects. The effects of this training were found to generalize to the texture cue in experimental subjects, who tended to avoid contact with that particular flooring whereas control subject showed something of a liking for it.

A problem with the design used by Spear is that there is no guarantee that the two groups learned equally readily during aversive training with the odour cue. Accordingly, the difference between the groups on the generalization test might reflect only a difference in the amount of associative strength acquired in the aversive conditioning phase. The same issue arises with respect to the critical comparison shown in Fig. 5.6, as this depends on the assumption that stimulus A acquired associative strength equally readily in the two groups during the aversive conditioning phase. Honey and Hall (1989c) conducted a direct test of the conditioned suppression controlled by stimulus A and found no difference between the groups. But in order to avoid having to rely on a null result, Honey and Hall (1989c) conducted a further study which attempted to eliminate problems of this sort by making use of the second of the within-subjects designs presented in Table 5.1.

Two groups of rats received initial training in which presentations of each of three auditory stimuli occurred. For both groups, B and C (a tone and a clicker) had different consequences, one being consistently followed by food

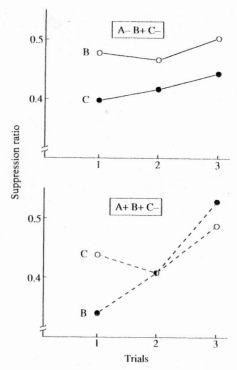

Fig. 5.7 Conditioned suppression to stimuli B and C after aversive conditioning with stimulus A. Group designations show the different pre-training conditions with, some stimuli being associated with food (+) and others not (−). (After Honey and Hall 1989c.)

and one not. The groups differed in the treatment given to the third stimulus, A (a noise). For one group the noise was also reinforced (symbolized as A+B+C− in Fig. 5.7) whereas for the second group (A−B+C−) it was not. Thus the first of these groups learned a discrimination between A and C but not between A and B; the second learned a discrimination between A and B but C and A received the same treatments. All subjects then received A–shock pairings followed by a test session assessing the generalization of conditioned suppression to both B and C. Suppression on this test was not profound but, as Fig 5.7 shows, each group showed more suppression to the stimulus that had received stage-one training equivalent to that given for A.

As I have noted before, an apparent disadvantage of this design is that there is no obvious way of distinguishing acquired equivalence from acquired distinctiveness. That is, the results shown in Fig. 5.7 may occur because rats generalize readily between stimuli that have had the same consequence in prior training; but equally it may be that they generalize less readily between stimuli that have had differing consequences; or both processes may be operating. The advantage of the design is that it allows us to exclude other explanations. The critical comparison made in this experiment (between test responding to B and to C) is made within subjects. Generalization to both test stimuli thus has its origin in a common source (the associative strength acquired by stimulus A during aversive conditioning), eliminating the possibility, inherent in the between-group comparison made for the results in Fig. 5.6, that differences in the associative strength of stimulus A might be responsible for the outcome.

Comparison of the results of the two groups shown in Fig. 5.7 also allows us to reject an explanation in terms of changes in associability or in terms of the transfer of some specific response that directly modifies test performance. The Pearce–Hall (1980) theory (see Chapter 3) allows that the associability of A, B, and C will change during pre-exposure and that the magnitude of this change might depend on whether or not the stimulus was associated with food in stage one (Pearce and Hall 1980). Further, the tendency of a stimulus to evoke an appetitively conditioned response might directly influence the level of responding shown to this stimulus during conditioned suppression training and testing. But the results of Fig. 5.2 show that the degree of suppression evoked by a test stimulus does not depend upon whether or not it was appetitively reinforced during the first stage. What determined the suppression shown to a test stimulus was whether or not its stage-one treatment matched that given to stimulus A.

(b) The differential outcomes effect

All the experiments discussed so far have made use of a two-stage procedure—an initial phase of discrimination training intended to render the cues distinctive, followed by a test in which the nature of the task is changed but which still requires discrimination between these same cues. Experiments investigating the 'differential outcomes effect' (DOE; Peterson and Trapold 1980) can be seen as collapsing these two stages.

First, consider this design for a two-stage experiment with rats. In initial discrimination training a tone signals the occurrence of another event (the onset of a light for 5 s), whereas no event follows presentations of a clicker. Control subjects receive training in which the light is equally likely after the tone and the clicker. In the test phase all subjects are required to learn a new task in which presentation of the tone signals that the left-hand of two levers will yield food and presentation of the clicker signals that a response to the right-hand lever will do so. A difference between the groups on this test (with the subjects given initial discrimination training being superior) would constitute a classic demonstration of acquired distinctiveness/equivalence. Friedman and Carlson (1973) report just such a difference in a one-stage experiment employing the equivalent of this design. Rats were tested on a food-rewarded (conditional go left/go right) discrimination between tone and clicker. Those in a correlated condition experienced the light only after a

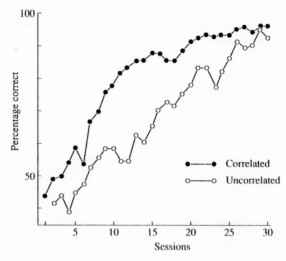

Fig. 5.8 Performance of two groups of rats on a conditional discrimination in which choice between two levers was signalled by an auditory cue. Light presentations following correct responses were correlated with a given auditory cue for one group but uncorrelated for another. (After Friedman and Carlson 1973.)

correct response in the presence of one of the cues (and thus, as the task was learned, increasingly often along with this cue); those in an uncorrelated condition received the light after 50 per cent of rewarded responses whether these were in made in the presence of the tone or of the clicker. As Fig. 5.8 shows, accurate choice performance developed more readily in the correlated group.

The difference between the groups shown in Fig. 5.8 has been called a differential outcomes effect because the superior performance of the correlated group depends on the fact that the outcome of a correct response is reliably different for the two trial types (tone trials and clicker trials). Although in this case the two outcomes are differentiated by the presence or the absence of a neutral event (see also Fedorchak and Bolles 1986), there are several other ways in which such a differentiation can be arranged. Results almost identical to those shown in Fig. 5.8 have been produced by experiments in which the two reinforcers differ in their nature (Trapold (1970) used sucrose pellets and standard food pellets), in their timing (Carlson and Wielkiewicz. (1972) used immediate versus delayed reinforcement), or in their magnitude (one food pellet versus five, Carlson and Wielkiewicz (1976)).

DOEs have also been obtained in experiments investigating matching to sample (MTS) in pigeons. In MTS, the bird is first presented with one stimulus, say a red light, as the sample; two 'comparison' stimuli, say red and green, are presented (often after a delay) and response to the matching stimulus is rewarded. This procedure is formally equivalent to the conditional choice procedure use with rats. It differs in that the alternatives offered for choice include one that is physically identical to the conditional cue (the sample). But this is not an essential feature of the procedure. In 'symbolic' MTS, the bird might have to choose between horizontal and vertical as the comparison stimuli, choice of one being rewarded after a red sample, and choice of the other after green.

Brodigan and Peterson (1976) (see also Peterson, Wheeler and Armstrong 1978) report just such an experiment in which two types of reward (food and water) were available. Subjects for whom trial-type (i.e. whether the sample was red or green) and reward-type were correlated learned more readily than subjects for whom there was no consistent relation between type of trial. A similar DOE has been found in experiments by Edwards, Jagielo, Zentall and Hogan (1982), who used different types of grain to differentiate the outcomes, and by Peterson and Trapold (1984) who presented (in the correlated condition) food after a correct response for one trial-type and just a feedback tone for a correct response for the other type of trial.

The DOE has been interpreted as showing that expectancies can act as effective cues in the control of choice responding (e.g. Peterson and Trapold 1980). The correlated procedure allows each sample (or conditional) cue to become associated with a different outcome. The different expectancies generated by these cues can then, it is supposed, themselves serve as cues.* One reason why the ability of the conditional cues to evoke such expectancies might facilitate learning comes from theories of animal working memory. Some accounts (e.g. Honig 1981) assume that a reinforcer expectancy is more likely to persist in memory than is a representation of the sample stimulus itself. Support for this interpretation can be derived from studies of delayed MTS in pigeons, which have found that the magnitude of the DOE diminishes as the length of the delay is reduced, there being no effect when there is no delay (Brodigan and Peterson 1976; Edwards *et al.* 1982) (see also DeLong and Wasserman 1981). It may be doubted that memory mechanisms form the sole basis of these effects, however, given that formally equivalent conditional discriminations using rats as the subjects have regularly found a DOE using a procedure which makes no demand on memory because the conditional cue remains present until the choice response is made.

Studies of working memory in animals may seem to be rather remote from

* I shall not debate here how expectancies come to be formed nor alternative formulations that stress not expectancies but the different patterns of overt responding that the different samples might come to evoke. Instead I shall simply assert that Pavlovian conditioning will allow the formation of a sample–outcome association, that this association can be thought of as embodying an expectancy, and that the existence of the association probably will (but need not) evoke a characteristic form of responding.

the standard, acquired distinctiveness procedure. It is appropriate to restate, therefore, the formal parallel between DOE studies and acquired distinctiveness experiments (a parallel hitherto ignored by all but Edwards *et al.* (1981)) and to note the possibility (to be taken up shortly) that the mechanisms responsible for the DOE may in fact be responsible for the effects that have been observed in orthodox studies of acquired distinctiveness.

5.2.3. Conclusions

Although Lawrence's original (1949) experiment has not been replicated exactly, the work of his successors (conducted both with animal subjects and with humans) has confirmed the validity of his central contention—discrimination training, in which each of a pair of cues becomes associated with a different outcome, enhances performance on a further discriminative task involving the same cues. This is not to say, necessarily, that the trained cues acquire distinctiveness or that discrimination training is the source of the effect. My conclusions come from experiments in which comparison is made between subjects given discrimination training and subjects given a control procedure of some sort (or sometimes, in the studies done with human subjects, no pre-training at all). Many of these comparisons produce results that can be explained without appealing to the idea that the pre-trained cues become more distinctive.

There are, however, several studies (some conducted with human subjects, others with animals) that allow a comparison between the effects of distinctiveness training and those of equivalence training. The difference found in these is difficult to explain away and I shall accept the conclusion that it derives from a change in the distinctiveness of the pre-trained cues. What these experiments cannot reveal is whether both the equivalence and distinctiveness treatments are effective in producing changes in the discriminability of the cues—clearly the observed difference could be obtained if just one of these treatments worked. This is a pity for, as we shall soon see, the two main theoretical interpretations of the effect differ on this issue. The mediation theory is founded on the notion of acquired equivalence and only with difficulty can predict an acquired distinctiveness effect. Differentiation theory, on the other hand, was constructed as an account of distinctiveness and finds no place for equivalence. But both theories can accommodate the basic effect and we shall need to give both full consideration in the next part of the chapter.

5.3. Theoretical interpretations

5.3.1. Mediation theory

(a) Background

James (1890) was perhaps the first to offer what amounts to an associative account of the acquired distinctiveness of cues. This account can be illustrated by considering his analysis of how discrimination training might increase the ease with which one can distinguish burgundy from claret.

When we first drank claret we heard it called by that name, we were eating such and such a dinner etc. Next time we drink it, a dim reminder of all these things chimes through us as we get a taste of the wine. When we try burgundy our first impression is that is it a kind of claret; but something falls short of full identification and presently we hear it called burgundy. During the next few experiences the discrimination may still be uncertain—'which', we ask ourselves, 'of the two wines is this present specimen?' But, at last the claret-flavor recalls pretty distinctly its own name, 'claret', 'that wine I drank at so-and-so's table', etc.; and the burgundy-flavor recalls the name 'burgundy' and someone else's table . . . After a while . . . the adhesion of each wine with its own name becomes more and more inveterate, and at last each flavour suggests instantly and certainly its own name and nothing else. The names differ far more than the flavors, and help to stretch these latter further apart.

James 1890, p. 511.

James does not discuss the matter, but the process he postulates could also, in some circumstances, make stimuli more difficult to discriminate. If two initially rather different cues are made to adhere to the same name or to closely similar names, then rather than being stretched apart the two cues might be forced closer together. This was the notion taken up by Miller and Dollard (1941) as the acquired equivalence of cues. Miller and Dollard make only brief mention of the idea (on which James concentrates) of acquired distinctiveness; but Miller (1948) explicitly acknowledges both possibilities, expressing them in terms of S–R theory.

According to stimulus–response theory, learning to respond with highly distinctive names to similar stimulus situations should tend to lessen the generalization of other responses from one of these situations to another since the stimuli produced by responding with the distinctive name will tend to increase the differences in the stimulus patterns of the two situations. Increased differentiation based on this mechanism has been called the acquired distinctiveness of cues. On the other hand, if the individual learns to respond to two quite different situations with the same verbal response, the stimuli produced by this response will be a common element mediating an increased amount of generalization from one stimulus to the other. This has been called acquired equivalence of cues, or secondary generalization.

Miller 1948, p. 174.

Although both James and Miller concern themselves with the effects of attaching verbal responses to the cues to be discriminated, there is no reason to restrict the analysis they offer to such responses. It can be applied just as readily to cases in which the associates are non-verbal responses or (as may happen with classical conditioning) not necessarily responses at all but representations of other stimuli.

(b) The acquired equivalence mechanism

Although at first sight the quotations reproduced above may seem to have said all that needs to be said, it will be worthwhile trying to specify exactly

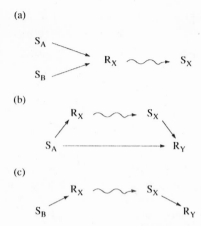

Fig. 5.9 Hull's (1939) account of secondary generalization. Conditioned links (S–R) are shown by straight arrows. S_X represents the various response-produced cues elicited by R_X. In (a) both S_A and S_B come to elicit R_X; in (b) acquisition of R_Y to S_A also produces an S_X–R_Y connection; (c) shows that S_B is now capable of evoking R_Y.

the mechanisms by which associative mediation theory generates the effects that need to be explained. The mechanism supposed by Miller (1948) to underlie acquired equivalence is that introduced by Hull (1939) with his notion of secondary generalization. Primary generalization will occur between stimuli that are similar, presumably because they have features or elements in common. But secondary or learned similarities can mediate generalization between otherwise quite dissimilar stimuli. Hull's S–R version of this idea is presented in Fig. 5.9. The case considered is that in which a subject is trained to make the same response (R_X) to each of two different stimuli, S_A and S_B. When this response occurs, it will elicit a set of feedback cues (S_X) and these will thus be evoked whenever either S_A or S_B subsequently occurs. Training the subject to make some new response (R_Y in the figure) will allow the formation of an S_X–R_Y association. S_B which, like S_A is capable of evoking S_X, will thus be capable of eliciting R_Y in spite of the fact that the S_B–R_Y link has not been trained directly. This analysis applies directly to generalization tests for acquired equivalence of the sort depicted in Table 5.1. And a tendency for the responding acquired to S_A to generalize to S_B will also explain why discrimination learning which requires the subject to make different responses to the two stimuli should be retarded.

Although the S–R terminology seems well fitted to the case in which R_X is a verbal label, it is possible to dispense with the reliance on the notion of response-produced cues that is central to S–R theory. As we have seen, modern theories of Pavlovian conditioning assume that stimuli can activate

(a) Acquired equivalence

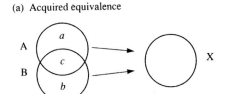

(b) Acquired distinctiveness

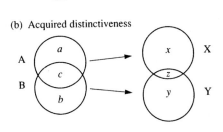

Fig. 5.10 The circles represent stimuli A, B, X and Y; arrows represent associative links. Each stimulus can be thought of as consisting of a set of features or elements. Similar stimuli share elements, the degree of overlap between the circles indicating the proportion of elements shared. Thus A and B have a set of common elements (represented by the area *c*); *a* represents the elements unique to stimulus A and *b* the elements unique to B.

the representations of other events. Such theories can therefore allow that an associatively activated representation may support generalization between stimuli that share the ability to elicit activity in this representation. Thus both A and B could become directly linked with a representation of stimulus X as shown in Fig 5.10(a). Subsequent training with A followed by an unconditioned stimulus (US) might allow the formation of an association between the associatively activated representation of X and the US. Thus B would become capable of activating the US representation (and of evoking a CR) by way of its ability to activate the X representation. A and B might well have features in common from the outset (the *c* elements in the figure) and these will produce primary generalization—training on A will give associative strength to stimulus elements that are present also in B. The X representation functions in just the same way as the *c* elements in producing generalization except for the fact that the ability of A and B to activate X is based on prior conditioning.

It should be acknowledged that not all theories of Pavlovian learning are entirely happy with the suggestion that an associatively activated representation can form an excitatory link with the (directly activated) representation of some other event. In particular, Wagner's (1981) theory (see Chapter 1) asserts that the state of activation produced by an associative link (A2) is different from that produced by the stimulus itself (the A1 state). When one

...tation (node in Wagner's terminology) is in A2 and another in A1,
...ter may form an inhibitory link with the former. It is not supposed,
...ever, that an excitatory connection will form between the two.

There are experimental findings to suggest that Wagner's theory needs to be modified in this respect. Direct evidence that an associatively activated representation (such as X) can acquire associative strength when its CS is associated with a US has been produced by Holland (1981). Rats were given orthodox conditioning with a tone as the CS and a distinctively flavoured food as the US. In a second phase of training presentation of the tone preceded a nausea-inducing injection of LiCl. In a final test the rats, although hungry, proved unwilling to consume the food. Holland's interpretation was that in the second phase of training an association was formed between the illness produced by the injection and a CS-evoked representation of the food that preceded it. (See also Holland and Forbes (1982*a*, *b*), who provide further evidence to suggest that the CS-evoked representation of an event can act as a substitute for the event itself.)

It is appropriate to add a few words at this point that might help avert the possibility of becoming involved in any extensive debate about whether associative changes of the sort described here should really be thought of as instances of perceptual learning, producing changes in the perceived similarity of the stimuli. Certainly these associative processes can just as readily be interpreted as constituting an associative mechanism for categorization or concept formation in that they allow physically different stimuli to come to be treated in the same way. Indeed, some (Bhatt and Wasserman 1989) have argued that the ability of an animal to respond in the same way to a range of different stimuli should be ascribed to the operation of a conceptual category only when mediated generalization can be demonstrated among these stimuli. Following Lea (1984), they suggest that true conceptual categories involve equivalence classes of stimuli that are *not* tied together by perceptual similarity. Mediated generalization is clearly not to be regarded, according to this view, as making the stimuli perceptually more similar. Should acquired equivalence, then, be interpreted as concept formation rather than perceptual learning?

Fortunately it turns out to be impossible to give a simple answer to this question and possible to give a more complex answer allowing both possibilities. Stimuli A and B may be regarded as physically similar to the extent that they share common, *c*, elements. The mechanism responsible for mediated generalization does nothing to increase the number or proportion of such elements and thus those wanting to cite mediated generalization as a characteristic of concept formation can assert that, in a very real sense, the similarity of the stimuli has not been changed. But when it comes to the issue of how a given physical stimulus is actually perceived, we have chosen to represent this in terms of the central representational elements that it activates. The percept initially evoked by A, therefore, must be equated with the *a* and *c* elements that it activates unconditionally. After training, however, presentation of A activates not only these but also elements that in other circumstances are unconditionally activated by stimulus X. The pattern of central representation (and thus, by one definition, the percept) is changed by experience, making the phenomenon an instance of perceptual learning.

(c) Acquired distinctiveness mechanisms

It might seem that a simple complement of the analysis offered above for acquired equivalence would supply us with a mechanism for acquired distinctiveness. The two cues to be discriminated, A and B, are associated in pre-training with different events represented by X and Y in Fig. 5.10. (X and Y would be response-produced cues in the S–R version of the theory.) Subsequent discrimination training thus occurs between the compound of A and its associate X and of B and its associate Y. If the events used as X and Y differ from each other more than do A and B (see Fig. 5.10(b)) then it might be supposed that the compounds would be discriminated more readily than would an untrained A and B. Certainly most proponents of an associative account for acquired distinctiveness effects have taken their analysis no further, implying that the phenomenon follows directly from what has just been said. In fact, closer inspection reveals that further mechanisms must be introduced if the associative structure shown in Fig. 5.10(b) is to generate acquired distinctiveness.

Consider why it should be that A and B are difficult to discriminate in the first place. The interpretation offered by Fig. 5.10 is that they hold many elements (*c* elements) in common. Training with A will allow both its unique *a* elements and the *c* elements to acquire associative strength. Stimulus B will then be able to evoke the response because it too possesses *c* elements. The only way in which the discrimination between A and B can be enhanced is by some process that reduces the role of the *c* elements in producing generalization from A to B. It is not apparent that establishing associations between A and X and between B and Y will do this, even though X and Y themselves hold rather few (*z*) elements in common. The existence of the A–X association may mean that training with A will allow the associatively activated representation of X to gain associative strength; but as long as the *c* elements still gain strength, generalization to B will still occur and discrimination will not be improved. Indeed, to the extent that X is perceived as being similar to Y (i.e. to the extent that these events hold elements in common), the acquired equivalence mechanism will operate, with these common elements (the *z* elements) mediating generalization from A to B.

Consideration of the phenomenon of overshadowing provides one possible way by which the associative structure shown in Fig 5.10(b) can be made to predict acquired distinctiveness. If animals are given Pavlovian conditioning with a compound CS consisting of separable components, the amount of strength gained by one of these components after a given number of training trials will be less than would be acquired if that component had been trained alone. The presence of the added component 'overshadows' learning about the other. This effect is well established empirically and is dealt with by all modern versions of the standard associative model. Thus the Rescorla–Wagner (1972) model (see Chapter 1) envisages conditioning as being a process in which stimuli present on a conditioning trial compete with each other for a limited amount of associative strength. To the extent that one component of a compound gains strength, the other will not. Other theorists (e.g. Mackintosh and Reese 1979) (see also Wagner 1981) attribute the effect to competition between stimuli at a perceptual level, suggesting that because of some limited capacity mechanism, attention can be paid to one component only at the expense of that paid to the other.

Now, one consequence of establishing the A–X association shown in Fig. 5.10(b) is that subsequent training with A presented alone is supposed to allow the associatively activated X representation to gain strength. It follows that X should to some extent overshadow A, restricting the amount of associative strength gained both by its *a* elements and its *c* elements. This last point is critical—if the associative strength of the *c* elements is low there will be little generalization from A to B, that is, discrimination between A and B will be enhanced.

A second possible way in which the existence of A–X and B–Y associations might facilitate the discrimination between A and B follows if it can be allowed that different associations might differ in the ease with which they are remembered. We have supposed that once the A–X association has been established, further training with A will endow both A itself and the associatively activated X with associative strength. Now suppose that the strength acquired by A tends, for some reason, to be lost over a retention interval whereas that controlled by X is retained. On a subsequent test, A will still be able to evoke the conditioned response, but only or chiefly by virtue of its ability to evoke the X representation. There will be little generalization to B, however; there is no reason for generalization to occur between X and B (they have no elements in common, Fig. 5.10(b)), and the *c* elements of B itself will, we are assuming, have lost their strength over the retention interval. Compared with the case in which A and B have not been pre-trained, the consequence of A–X and B–Y associations having been pre-established would be that a new response could be acquired very readily by stimulus A without any increase in the extent to which generalization occurs to stimulus B.

It may seem wholly arbitrary to assume that the association acquired by A should lose its effectiveness when that acquired by the X representation does not. There are, however, circumstances in which this assumption looks secure, or at least justifiable. If X were much more salient than A, for instance, then the required outcome can be anticipated. A version of this suggestion has already been met with as a possible explanation for some

DOEs when it was suggested (p. 159) that an expectancy of a reinforcer evoked by a sample stimulus will be more likely to persist in memory across the delay of a delayed MTS experiment than will a representation of the sample stimulus itself. For experiments with human subjects when X is a verbal label for stimulus A, the important feature could well be not that X is very much more salient than A but that the mechanisms of human memory are especially adept at maintaining verbal information. Thus, when in G. Cantor's (1955) experiment the subjects had to learn over a series of trials a simultaneous discrimination between faces of the sort shown in Fig. 5.2, the task required them to carry over information from one trial to the next. Subjects given appropriate pre-training would be able to bridge the interval by rehearsing some version of the information 'Jack is to be chosen', perhaps an easier task than retaining information about some direct representation of the visual cue itself.

A third possibility that we should consider makes use of the notion of generalization decrement. It is accepted that there may be interactions between supposedly distinct stimuli when they are presented simultaneously. These interactions (which may be peripheral or central) will modify the way in which the stimulus is perceived, producing generalization decrement when a stimulus trained in compound with another is presented on its own, or vice versa. It is a small step to suppose that such effects might also operate when a stimulus is presented in compound not with another that is physically present but with the associatively activated representation of such an event. An untrained stimulus A may be perceived in one way; one that evokes the representation of X in a different way; and one that evokes a representation of Y in a different way yet again. Establishing A–X and B–Y associations will mean, therefore, that the perception of A will be changed in one way and that of B in a different way. These effects will presumably operate both on unique features of the stimulus and also on those features that, for untrained subjects, are perceived as being common to both stimuli. This last point is critical since it means that the number of common elements will be reduced and accordingly that discrimination between A and B will be enhanced.

There is no reason why these various possible mechanisms for acquired distinctiveness—the memory hypothesis, the overshadowing hypothesis, and generalization decrement—should be seen as rivals. Activation of the representation of an X cue might overshadow learning about A, might reduce the number of elements perceived as being common to A and B, and might be especially good at controlling behaviour after a retention interval. It is quite possible that all three mechanisms might operate. And, I should add, it is also possible that none does so. All three suggestions follow directly from, and indeed seem to be required by, our current understanding of the mechanisms of associative learning. But it might well be that an associatively activated X is simply not salient enough to produce effects of a measurable size. As the best evidence for the effects under consideration comes from experiments demonstrating a difference between the acquired distinctiveness and acquired equivalence procedures, it is not essential for the theorist to devise a mechanism for both. The whole of the difference could be a consequence of the operation of the acquired equivalence mechanism, with the acquired distinctiveness procedure constituting no more than a neutral control procedure. It would also be open to the theorist, of course, to devise a mechanism for acquired distinctiveness and to attribute the whole of the effect to this, denying the reality of acquired equivalence. This is just the approach taken by the second theory to be considered.

5.3.2. Differentiation theory

(a) Background

In an analysis of verbal learning, Gibson (1940) argued that much of what must be learned in a paired associate task involves establishing discrimination among the items. The improvement in performance that occurs with training was held to depend not just on the strengthening of the association between the stimulus–word and the response–word but also on a reduction in the extent to which the various words tend to be confused. This process of stimulus differentiation was equated by Gibson with a steepening of the gradient of generalization surrounding each stimulus.

Gibson (1940) also assumed that stimulus differentiation, once it had occurred, would transfer to and facilitate performance on a new task involving the same stimuli. And although Gibson's initial concern was with verbal learning, subsequent experimental investigations of 'stimulus pre-differentiation', as it came to be called, were conducted in a range of transfer paradigms. One of the earliest was the study by Gagné and Baker (1950) with which I began this chapter (Fig. 5.1), this study being designed to show that training in applying a different verbal label to each of the various stimulus lights would produce differentiation among them that would transfer to a subsequent motor task.

(b) Mechanisms

Gibson's (1940) account of differentiation in paired-associate learning was expressed in part in the S–R terminology then current. Training with a list of stimulus words was regarded as an instance of discrimination learning in which each S comes to evoke an R different from those evoked by other stimuli. The sharpening of the generalization gradient around a stimulus was in some way a consequence of the processes responsible for the formation of the S–R links but was not thought to be itself associative in nature.

The non-associative nature of the phenomenon was emphasized by Gibson and Gibson (1955), who made a firm distinction between their own account and the associative interpretation, which they referred to as 'enrichment'. Associative theories of acquired distinctiveness (and of perceptual learning more generally) assume, they argued, that 'percepts change over time by acquiring progressively more memory images' (p. 34), thereby becoming enriched. (Stimulus A of Fig. 5.10 might be said to be enriched, if only a little, by virtue of its ability to evoke the image of X.) The differentiation theory, in contrast, holds that 'percepts change over time by progressive elaboration of qualities, features and dimensions of variation' (Gibson and Gibson 1955, p. 34), that is, by an elaboration of aspects of the stimulus that are present in it from the outset. 'Perceptual learning, then, consists of responding to variables of the physical stimulation not previously responded to' (Gibson and Gibson 1955, p. 34). In particular, with practice and exposure, a subject will become better able to detect the distinctive features that distinguish one environmental event from another, and also become better able to detect the invariant features that a given event displays from one occurrence to the next.

Gibson (1969) expands on these notions at some length but is not in fact very forthcoming about the mechanisms involved. She emphasizes again their non-associative nature and puts forward three possibilities. The first is a process of 'abstraction', the process responsible for discovering invariants. Little is said about how this process works apart from the suggestion that a number of presentations of a given object or event may be needed if invariant aspects are to be distinguished from incidental features that may vary from one occasion to another. The next two processes discussed by Gibson may be considered together—they are central and peripheral mechanisms of attention. These mechanisms allow a subject to ignore irrelevant aspects of stimuli, irrelevant aspects being those that fail to distinguish one stimulus from others. Again, no formal theory of attention is developed and indeed it is unclear that some mechanism other than that involved in abstraction is necessary—the distinctive features of an object or event are likely to be the invariants and the irrelevant aspects those that vary from presentation to presentation.

In the original exposition of the theory, Gibson (1940) assumed that explicit training, which allowed the formation of associations between stimuli and different distinctive consequences, might be necessary for differentiation to occur. This notion was soon abandoned, along with any use of the S–R framework (see, e.g. Gibson and Gibson 1955), to be replaced by the suggestion that perceptual learning can go on quite independently of any associative processes. This is not to say that the procedure employed in studies of discriminative learning will be quite without effect. Rather the assertion is that explicit training is not necessary to produce discrimination, that the need to extract information from the environment is enough to do so, independently of any externally imposed rewards or punishments or of knowledge of results more generally. It follows that this account finds no place for a notion of acquired equivalence. All the forms of training used in the experiments

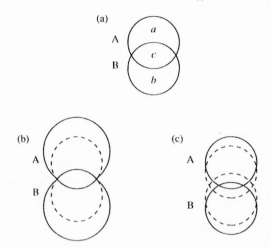

Fig. 5.11   Circles represent the set of elements activated by stimuli A and B. Unique elements are represented by areas *a* and *b*, common elements by *c*. Panel (a) depicts the situation before training; (b) and (c) show two possible ways in which differentiation might reduce the extent of generalization between A and B. Dotted lines superimpose the original arrangement shown in (a).

described earlier in this chapter will produce stimulus differentiation. We cannot suppose, however, that discrimination training is quite without effect—to do so would eliminate any possibility of explaining why acquired distinctiveness training should be superior to acquired equivalence training in producing differentiation. We must assume, therefore, that explicit discrimination training will enhance the size of the effect, presumably because it will compel the subject to attend to distinctive and invariant aspects of each stimulus, and to ignore irrelevant aspects. I NO ME ?

  Leaving the question of what mechanisms produce differentiation, we may turn now to the separable issue of the mechanisms by which discriminative performance is enhanced once differentiation has been achieved. The central question in terms of the diagram used in Fig. 5.11(a) (see also Fig. 5.10) is why experience of A and B should reduce the effectiveness of the *c* elements in producing generalization between these stimuli. The critical aspect of differentiation theory in this context is its assertion that exposure to A and B will lead to an increase in the number of distinctive features that can be detected. This must mean, in terms of the figure, an increase in the number of *a* and *b* elements activated by the stimuli, something that can be represented diagrammatically in more than one way. Figure 5.11(b) shows an increase in the areas *a* and *b* with a consequent reduction in the proportion (although not the absolute number) of *c* elements activated by a stimulus. Figure 5.11(c) presents a slightly different possibility in which the sizes of the A and B circles have not been changed. There is no net increase in the number of elements activated by a given stimulus but the circles have been moved apart, indicating not only an increase in the number of unique elements activated by a stimulus but a corresponding decrease in the number of common elements activated.

It is not clear if either of these possibilities accurately represents the full implications of Gibson's (1969) differentiation theory, but both are capable of predicting the required result.* Comparing the scheme shown in Fig. 5.11(b) with that of Fig. 5.11(a), we might expect that the presence of the extra active *a* elements would produce more effective overshadowing of the *c* elements during training with A. Generalization to B would therefore be reduced. Generalization would also be reduced given the scheme shown in Fig. 5.11(c). There would again be an increase in the ability of *a* elements to overshadow *c* elements, but in addition the reduction of the number of *c* elements activated by A would mean that relatively few of them would be capable of acquiring associative strength in the first place.

5.3.3. Evaluation of the theories

The interpretations of acquired distinctiveness/equivalence effects offered by mediation theory and differentiation theory differ markedly on two (related) issues. First, they differ about the role of explicit discrimination training. The account of acquired distinctiveness supplied by mediation theory (Fig. 5.10) requires that each target stimulus become associated with some different event, and a reliable correlation between each stimulus and its outcome is needed for this to be established. Differentiation theory, by contrast, asserts that merely observing target stimuli will be enough to produce some effect. Second, differentiation theory as developed here envisages no mechanism for generating acquired equivalence, whereas secondary generalization between two stimuli on the basis of their both having associations with some other, common event is at the heart of the mediation theory.

However clear-cut the differences between the theories may be, direct tests of these issues lead to no very clear conclusions. As we have already seen, the results of experiments comparing the effects of mere observation of the stimuli with those produced by explicit discrimination training have turned out to be inconsistent and open to a range of interpretations. And attempts to demonstrate empirically the operation of an acquired equivalence

---

* In particular, the figure represents how exposure leads to an increase in the detection of distinctive features and ignores the postulated increase in the ability to detect invariants. Distinctive features may very well often be invariants, but sometimes they may not—that is, sometimes the invariant features of A may be the same as those of B. In such a case an increased ability to detect invariants might hinder subsequent discrimination.

Acquired distinctiveness: mediation and differentiation

:hanism distinct from that responsible for acquired distinctiveness have proved unsuccessful. It is difficult to devise the neutral control condition that such a demonstration would require. By far the most satisfactory demonstrations of changes in the discriminability of cues with training come from experiments in which the comparison is made between acquired distinctiveness and acquired equivalence conditions; a difference between these conditions could, of course, be entirely the consequence of an acquired distinctiveness effect. Given the failure of these direct tests we need to turn to some slightly less obvious empirical implications of the differences the theories noted above.

(a) Varying the difference between the associates

In acquired distinctiveness training, subjects experience target stimulus A, along with one outcome, X, and target stimulus B along with a different outcome, Y (Fig. 5.10). Mediation theory requires that X and Y be rather different from each other if the formation of A–X and B–Y associations is to lead to an increase in the discriminability of A and B. If X and Y are made more similar, the effect will be reduced (the limiting case, when X and Y are identical, being that in which acquired equivalence is held to occur). Differentiation theory does not predict that the magnitude of the acquired distinctiveness effect will depend on the similarity of X and Y. This theory might suppose that some form of discrimination training will be superior to none if only because such training will ensure that the subjects attend to relevant aspect of the situation. But there is no reason to suppose that the effectiveness of discrimination training in maintaining attention will differ according to the similarity of the events used as X and Y.

Such results as are available tend to support the associative view. In the experiment by Norcross (1958), briefly mentioned above, young children were shown four pictures of different faces, two boys and two girls, and were taught a different name for each. For one pair of faces (say, the boys) the names were rather similar ('zim' and 'zam') whereas for the other pair they were dissimilar ('wug' and 'kos'). Acquisition of a button-pressing task (a separate button was assigned to each of the four faces) proceeded significantly more rapidly for members of the pair given dissimilar names than for members of the pair given similar names.

The experiment by Jaynes (1950) (see above, p. 153) can be taken as demonstrating an equivalent effect in rats. Recall that transfer was good for subjects trained in a simultaneous discrimination to raise a flap bearing the positive stimulus through seven inches but was less good for subjects trained to raise the flap only half an inch. Given that the subjects were trained not to raise the negative flap at all, we may say that the difference between associates established to the two stimuli was greater in the case in which the more extensive motor response was required—that is, in the condition that produced superior transfer to a test discimination involving the same stimuli. The interpretation put forward here is not fundamentally different from that offered by Jaynes when he suggested that a tendency to emit (a fractional version of) the response acquired in the first stage would serve as a mediating process in the second, and that the salience of the mediator would depend on the magnitude of the initial response of which it was a fraction.

(b) Disrupting the associations formed during distinctiveness training

According to mediation theory, discrimination training produces distinctiveness because it establishes A–X and B–Y associations. Differentiation theory, on the other hand, while allowing that these associations are likely to be formed during training, gives them no special role in acquired distinctiveness. An implication of the latter view is that the enhanced discriminability of A and B should survive the introduction of procedures that act to eliminate or disrupt the associations formed during training. A phase of extinction training, for instance, in which A and B are presented in the absence of X and Y, or of reversal training in A–Y and B–X pairings are introduced, should not influence the differentiation established by an initial phase of discimination training. The associative theory makes a different prediction—to the extent that these procedures (extinction and reversal) mean that A and B will no longer be firmly associated with distinctively different events, this theory must expect that the consequence will be an attenuation of the acquired distinctiveness effect.

There are no published experiments that allow a direct assessment of the effects of interpolating a phase of extinction or reversal between the normal training and test phases of an acquired distinctiveness experiment. However, a study of the DOE by Carlson (1974) can supply the information we require. Recall (see p. 157) that I characterized the DOE procedure as collapsing the two stages of the orthodox, acquired distinctiveness design. The test discrimination between tone and clicker (say) is aided by the fact that the two stimuli evoke different expectancies (are associated with different reinforcers), these expectancies not being pre-trained but being formed during the course of the discrimination itself. Carlson (1974), however, reverted to a two-stage design. Rats in one condition received initial Pavlovian discrimination training in which the tone was used to signal food and the clicker to signal a compound reinforcer consisting of food plus a mild electric shock. They were then shifted to an instrumental discrimination in which presentation of the clicker signalled that choice of one lever would be reinforced (with food) and presentation of the tone signalled that choice of the other lever would be reinforced (with food plus shock). The Pavlovian training produced positive transfer to the test discrimination. As Fig. 5.12 shows, these subjects learned the test more readily than did control subjects that were trained on the same task but had received initial Pavlovian training in which the tone and clicker were uncorrelated with reinforcer type. The

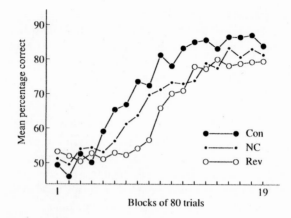

Fig. 5.12   Performance of two groups of rats reinforced for pressing one of two levers in the presence of a tone and (with a different reinforcer) for pressing the other lever in the presence of a clicker. Group Con received prior Pavlovian training in which the pairing of auditory cue and reinforcer type was consistent with that experienced on the test; for group Rev the pairing was the reverse of that experienced on the test. For group NC there was no correlation between auditory cue type and reinforcer type in Pavlovian training. (After Carlson 1974.)

comparison between these groups amounts to a comparison between subjects given acquired distinctiveness training and controls given a form of acquired equivalence training and confirms the result found elsewhere. The novel finding, of central importance here, comes from the behaviour shown by a third group of subjects.

Carlson's third group of subjects received initial Pavlovian training in which the auditory cues were correlated with reinforcer type, but the relationship between cue and reinforcer was the reverse of that in effect during the test stage. In initial training the tone was established as a CS for food, but in the test task a correct response in the presence of this cue yielded food plus shock; the clicker was initially trained with food plus shock in the first stage, but in the test a correct response in the presence of this cue yielded just food. This reversal of the relationship between cue and reinforcer produced poor learning of the test discrimination, performance being retarded with respect to that of both the other groups (Fig. 5.12).

Associative theory has, in principle, no problem in accommodating these results. The solution of this, rather difficult, test task is critically dependent on the rat forming associations between the cues and their differential outcomes. These associations serve to promote discrimination in one or other of the way described above. Clearly, training that allows the subjects to come to the task with these associations ready formed will be of help; and equally clearly, reversed pre-training will have just the opposite effect. But these results run counter to the differentiation theory. According to this theory, initial discrimination training should produce differentiation of the stimuli and the fact that the associations formed during this stage of training do not accord with those likely to be formed during the test phase should be of no consequence. The stimuli having undergone differentiation should be, and remain more, discriminable, regardless of the fate of the associations they may have acquired.

(c) Absence of positive transfer after distinctiveness training

Differentiation theory in its basic form seems constrained to predict that distinctiveness training should produce transfer to any test task that requires discrimination between the differentiated stimuli. But the associative theory can predict that the mechanisms that normally produce acquired distinctiveness might fail to do so, or might even produce negative transfer with certain sorts of test task. An experiment by Tetewsky and Garner (1986) can be interpreted as demonstrating such a failure.

Two groups of undergraduate subjects were compared, a group that had learned to read Hebrew and a group that had not. Familiarity with Hebrew was taken to approximate to having had distinctiveness training with this alphabet. Hebrew letters might, therefore, have undergone differentiation for the former group and would certainly have become involved in some associations. In particular, the symbol for *gimmel* would have become associated with some name or sound equivalent to that associated with the Roman 'G'; the *mem* symbol and the Roman 'M' would also have acquired a common associate. All subjects were tested on tasks in which they had to sort cards bearing these letters in various ways. In one, *gimmel* and G had to go in one pile and *mem* and M in another; a further task required the subjects to put *mem* and G together and to put *gimmel* with M.

If the symbols for *mem* and *gimmel* have become differentiated for Hebrew readers during the course of their previous experience with this alphabet, these subjects should be at an advantage on both test tasks—an enhanced ability to discriminate between the two Hebrew symbols should be helpful in both cases. The associative theory, on the other hand, predicts an advanatage only on the first task, the associations being of no help, or perhaps even hindering, when symbols having a common associate require different responses. The outcome was that predicted by associative theory. Those who knew Hebrew took significantly less time to sort the pack than those who did not in the condition that required symbols having the same name to be put together. The groups did not differ in their card-sorting times on the other task.

(d) The specificity of the effects of discrimination training

In experiments using the within-subjects designs of Fig. 5.3 or of Table 5.1 (e.g. Grice 1965; Reese 1972; Honey and Hall 1989c experiment 3), initial training involves three stimuli, two, A and B, being treated in the same way and the third, C, being associated with a different outcome. Subsequent tests show discrimination between A and C to be superior to that between A and B.

The explanation for this result offered by mediation theory depends on the fact that the initial phase of discrimination training establishes links between both A and B and a common associate (X in Table 5.1), and between C and a different associate (Y). According to my account of differentiation theory, however, the effect of discrimination training depends not on the associations it creates but on the fact that it concentrates the subject's attention on distinctive features of the stimuli. It is difficult to see how this latter analysis can predict the results obtained. Consider the experiment by Honey and Hall (1989c) in which X was the delivery of food and Y its absence. In order to establish the appropriate conditioned responses (or expectancies) during the first stage of training, the subjects would have to attend to and discriminate those features that distinguish A from C and those that distinguish B from C. Any plausible mechanism capable of allowing a subject to do this would also endow the subject with an enhanced ability to discriminate between A and B because it would involve the animal in coming to respond to the distinctive features of each of the three stimuli. Thus, discrimination training of the sort considered here must be predicted to have general effects, enhancing the discriminability of all the stimuli. But the results show, as we have seen, that the effects are specifically determined by the nature of the associations formed.

It is worth adding, as something of an aside, that the experimental result just described not only gives reasons for preferring the associative account but also seems to demand an explanation in terms of acquired equivalence rather than acquired distinctiveness. At the empirical level, all we can observe is a difference between the acquired equivalence condition (good generalization from A to B) and the acquired distinctiveness condition (poorer generalization from A to C). But, given that we must interpret this difference in terms of the mechanisms postulated by mediation theory, certain conclusions follow. First, good generalization from A to B can be readily explained in terms of mediation by the associate. Conditioning with a pre-trained A allows the associatively activated representation of X to acquire associative strength and thus B will be able to evoke responding by virtue of its association with the X representation. C, lacking an association with X, will be able to evoke the test response only to the extent that, without any special training, it holds elements in common with A. Now, for acquired distinctiveness to occur, for the generalization between A and C to be reduced, it is necessary for the training procedures to reduce the extent to which these common elements acquire strength. I allowed in discussion of the mechanisms of acquired distinctiveness that the acquisition of strength by a representation of strength by a representation of X might restrict the strength acquired by A itself during acquisition of the test response. There is no reason, however, why the restriction should apply only to the elements that A holds in common with C and not those that it holds in common with B. That is, the overshadowing mechanism, if it operates, should reduce generalization both from A to C and from A to B. It cannot, therefore, be responsible for the result obtained. This is not to say that the overshadowing mechanism is not operating here or to deny that such a mechanism may be responsible in other cases for observed acquired distinctiveness effects. We can say, however, that whatever *may* be true of acquired distinctiveness, the reality of acquired equivalence must be accepted.

(e) *Conclusions*

The evidence discussed in this final section of the chapter has been uniformly in favour of the associative account of acquired equivalence and distinctiveness. We can conclude that an associative mechanism is required in order to explain these findings. (In some cases we can be more specific and assert that the associative mechanism in question must be that responsible for acquired equivalence. This is not to deny the possibility that an associative acquired-distinctiveness effect may also operate in other cases.) There is no evidence that requires us to accept differentiation theory.

What remains possible, however, is that differentiation occurs alongside the associative processes. In standard acquired-distinctiveness experiments, of course, the two mechanisms will work toward the same outcome. The various experiments just discussed use procedures specifically chosen to ensure that differentiation effects and mediation effects tend toward different outcomes. The fact that in these experiments there is no evidence for differentiation may mean only that differentiation produces less powerful effects than does mediation. A subject trained with both A and B each followed by event X may come to perceive the distinctive features of A and B, something that might reduce generalization between them. But to accept this does not make it necessary to deny that A–X and B–X associations may be formed and that X could thus act to mediate generalization between A and B, perhaps outweighing the effects of differentiation.

Whatever the theoretical possibilities, it is clearly more parsimonious to explain acquired distinctiveness and equivalence solely in terms of associative mechanisms. Is there any positive evidence that might prompt us to adopt the more complex position that differentiation occurs as well? Three lines of argument merit our attention.

First, it may be recalled that in Chapter 2, I concluded discussion of habituation by allowing the possibility that simple exposure to a stimulus might result in the formation of an increasingly detailed and well-specified representation of it. This possibility is, of course, an important aspect of what has been described in this chapter as stimulus differentiation. However different they may be from those involved in habituation, the training procedures used in studies of acquired distinctiveness necessarily involve the

SUCCESSIVE   SIMULTANEOUS

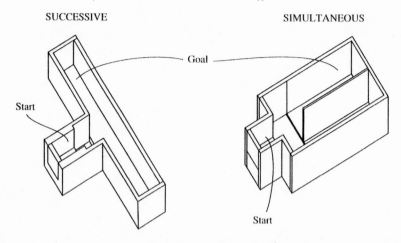

Fig. 5.13 The two pieces of apparatus used by Lawrence (1949) for successive and simultaneous discrimination training. Three different T-mazes were available for the successive discrimination, black, grey and white. The goal boxes of the simultaneous apparatus were lined with card of various brightness, the floor covered with mesh of various sizes, and the width of boxes varied by inserting false side walls.

subjects in receiving repeated exposure to the critical stimuli. The processes underlying habituation training will presumably go on during distinctiveness training and thus, if we accept the interpretation of habituation discussed in Chapter 2, we must also accept the possibility that stimulus differentiation plays a part in acquired distinctiveness.

The second argument is based on the conclusion derived in Chapter 4 that associative learning tends to be context-dependent. In contrast, acquired equivalence/distinctiveness effects seem to transfer quite readily from one context to another. In many of the experiments described in the earlier parts of this chapter, the context was changed substantially from pre-training to the test. Perhaps the most dramatic example is provided by Lawrence (1949) himself. Figure 5.13 shows the apparatus used by Lawrence in each phase of his study. The stimuli may have remained the same but almost all other aspects of the training situation were radically altered in the shift from the simultaneous to the successive procedure. If acquired distinctiveness depends on associative mechanisms, we might expect it to be attenuated or abolished by a change of context that renders these associations less effective. The fact that the effect survives a contextual change so readily encourages acknowledgement of the possibility that a non-associative process (such as differentiation is presumed to be) may be in part responsible for it.

Finally, we may return to the fundamental difference between the mediation and differentiation theories of acquired distinctiveness—for the former the associations formed during distinctiveness training play a critical role, whereas for the latter these associations are essentially irrelevant. An implication of differentiation theory but not of the associative theory, therefore, is that mere exposure to a pair of stimuli without their being followed by any special consequences should be enough to enhance their discriminability. Discussion of the various phenomena of 'exposure learning' in Chapter 1 revealed just such an effect—rats given prolonged exposure to a pair of stimuli presented in their home cages learned a subsequent simultaneous discrimination between these stimuli more readily than subjects for whom the test stimuli were novel (Gibson and Walk 1956). This single observation is not enough in itself to make us accept the assertions of differentiation theory—there are, it turns out, a number of possible interpretations. But it is certainly enough to make us want to persist with our exploration of this theory and to examine in some detail (in Chapter 7) the various possible explanations for the effect.

6. Acquired distinctiveness: attentional factors

The discussion in Chapter 5 of experiments on acquired distinctiveness of the type pioneered by Lawrence (1949) led to the conclusion that the phenomena could be explained without recourse to any non-associative process of perceptual learning—that changes in the discriminability of the stimuli could be mediated by associative mechanisms. There is, however, a widely held view that discrimination training might induce perceptual changes rather different from those embodied in the notion of differentiation. Ever since the pioneering work of Lashley (1929) initiated the development of what has been called 'non-continuity' theory, there has been no shortage of theorists willing to argue that discrimination learning involves changes in attention. Indeed, although Lawrence (1949) described his experiment as being concerned with the acquired distinctiveness of cues, the sort of interpretation he favoured was different from either of the rival theories discussed in the previous chapter. When he refers (see also Lawrence 1950) to the possibility that discrimination training might modify the *discriminability* of the stimuli, he is not suggesting, as his use of this term might seem to imply, that learning a black–white discrimination (say) increases the ease with which a rat can tell black from white. Rather he holds that such training can modify the ease with which these cues will enter into further associations—that after training brightness will come to command the animal's attention more successfully than it did previously.

The present chapter sets out to evaluate the suggestion that an additional effect of discrimination training (additional to those described in Chapter 5) is that it modifies the attention that the subject pays to stimuli present during training. Unlike some other possible varieties of perceptual learning, this one has been the subject of detailed theoretical analysis, and several more or less well formulated models of attention in learning are available. The first main section of this chapter describes what I take to be the two main current theories. The theories differ over the conditions they suppose to be effective in modifying attention but they share the view that the degree of attention paid to a stimulus is to be equated to its level of associability (or conditionability). Experimental tests of the theories have concentrated for the most part, therefore, on transfer studies in which subjects are required to learn two tasks one after the other. Any change in the associability of stimuli generated by the first task should be revealed as positive or negative transfer to a second task involving these same stimuli. The transfer seen in these experiments will no doubt be directly influenced by the associative links formed in the first stage of training; but, with a little ingenuity, experiments can be devised in which direct effects are eliminated (or attenuated). Analysis of the theoretical implications of such experiments will concern us in the second part of the chapter.

6.1 Theories of attention in discrimination learning

6.1.1. Analyser theory

(a) The original theory

Attempts to formalize Lawrence's suggestion that discrimination training might produce a change in stimulus associability have been made by many theorists including Lawrence himself (1963). But perhaps the best-developed of these attempts is the analyser theory proposed by Sutherland and Mackintosh (1971). In this theory, discrimination learning is envisaged as being a two-stage process. One stage is that involved in forming the associations that are responsible for the subject coming to respond to one cue rather than another. But this associative learning mechanism can only work on the representations of events supplied to it by a preliminary stage of perceptual processing. Sutherland and Mackintosh (1971) concur, therefore, with the judgement offered by a number of earlier workers in the field of animal discrimination learning perhaps most clearly by Lashley (e.g. 1941) that in order to have a satisfactory theory of learning it is necessary also to provide an accompanying account of some basic aspects of perception. Analyser theory concentrates on the perceptual processes responsible for changes in attention.

Consider a simple simultaneous discrimination task in which a rat is confronted with two objects that differ in brightness (one is black and one is white) and in spatial position (one is on the left, the other on the right). Over a series of training trials the rat receives reward for approaching black regardless of its position. This training will establish associations that we may characterize—although this is not the precise formulation offered by Sutherland and Mackintosh themselves—as being between black and food and between white and no food. These associations allow a consistent choice of black.* But in addition, according to analyser theory, the acquisition of

---

* Sutherland and Mackintosh (1971) specify the associative component of their theory in terms of 'response attachments'. The strength of an attachment (of an approach response say) to the output of an analyser is increased by reward and decreased by non-reward. This interpretation of their theory can be seen as a version of traditional S–R theory with the S being an analyser output. The notion of the response attachment is not, however, essential to the theory, which would work just as well if it assumed direct associations between stimulus and reinforcer (i.e. as a Pavlovian theory with the CS being the output of an analyser).

such a discrimination involves a strengthening to the tendency to attend to brightness (also referred to as strengthening of the brightness analyser) along with a reduction in the strength of the tendency to attend to the other dimension along which the cues differ, the position dimension. It must be assumed that the brightness dimension has some minimal tendency to attract attention right from the start of training (without this the discrimination would never be learned), but the effect of training will be greatly to strengthen this tendency. The consequences of this process of attentional learning should be evident in subsequent tasks involving the same relevant dimension—the brightness analyser will come to dominate attention and its outputs will be readily learned about in the future.

The feature of discrimination training that is critical in bringing about this strengthening of the brightness analyser is, according to the theory, that the outputs of the analyser are consistently related to certain consequences— black reliably predicts food, white its absence. Sutherland and Mackintosh (1971) draw a contrast between this strengthening process (which depends on the analyser consistently making correct predictions about consequences) and that involved in simple associative learning.

The mechanism whereby the analyser detecting an irrelevant stimulus dimension (position, in the present example) loses strength has been the subject of debate. Sutherland and Mackintosh considered the possibility that an analyser might lose strength when its outputs failed to make correct predictions about outcomes (as, for instance, when reward and non-reward are both equally likely to follow the response guided by each output of the position analyser) but found no firm evidence that required them to accept the reality of such a process. They did suggest, however, that irrelevant analysers might suffer a loss in strength as a consequence of the increase accruing to the relevant analyser. The strengths of all analysers are assumed to sum to a constant amount (an assumption designed to capture the notion that attentional capacity is limited), and accordingly an increase in the strength of one (an increase in the attention paid to one aspect of the situation) necessarily means a loss by others (a reduction in the attention paid to other aspects).

The attentional notions expressed in analyser theory apply readily enough to the basic changed-response procedure of Lawrence (1949). In this procedure the first stage of simultaneous discrimination given to the experimental subjects (see Figs. 1.6 and 1.7) will endow the black and white cues with those associative connections that generate the tendency to approach black (the stimulus correlated with reward) rather than white. There will also be an increase in the animal's tendency to attend to the relevant dimension (brightness) and a reduction in the strength of analysers sensitive to irrelevant dimensions. Upon transfer to the successive discrimination of the test phase, the specific response tendencies acquired in the first phase will be without significance as the subject will be required (on different occasions) to approach both black and white. A tendency to attend to brightness will, however, be relevant and will promote learning of the new task. Control subjects trained initially on some other task (see Fig. 1.7) will have a weakened brightness analyser and will thus do correspondingly poorly on the test discrimination.*

It should come as no surprise to find that analyser theory applies so readily here—the theory was, after all, explicitly devised to accommodate these phenomena. We have seen, however (in Chapter 5), that Lawrence's (1949) results, in common with those of other experiments using his general procedure, are susceptible to explanation in other terms. A proper assessment of the theory requires the rather different experimental designs to be discussed later in the chapter.

(b) Mackintosh's (1975) version

The form of analyser theory proposed by Sutherland and Mackintosh (1971) proved able to account for a wide range of data produced by studies of animal discrimination learning; but a number of difficulties, concerning chiefly the way in which blocking (see Chapter 1, p. 7) should be explained, led Mackintosh (1975) to propose a revised version. Again, two learning processes were proposed, one of them associative, the other producing changes in the attention-getting power (more precisely, the associability) of stimuli— the basic two-stage principle of the original analyser theory was thus retained. Three main amendments were introduced. First, and least important, it was proposed that changes in associability are specific to particular stimuli—to black and white, say, rather than to the entire brightness dimension. This amendment does not eliminate the prediction available to analyser theory that training with one set of cues will influence the attention commanded by others differing along the same dimension. Mackintosh's theory allows this possibility by assuming that a change in the associability of one stimulus will generalize to other stimuli, the degree of generalization being determined by the similarity of these others to the trained stimulus.

Second, Mackintosh proposed a new set of rules governing the conditions in which the associability of a stimulus will change. The spirit of the earlier theory was retained, however. Thus he proposed that the associability of a stimulus will be increased when that stimulus successfully predicts its consequences; specifically, associability (given by the learning-rate parameter α in

---

* Although Lawrence's (1949) results accord well with analyser theory, there is room for debate about the exact mechanisms responsible for the effect. Mackintosh and Holgate (1967) point out that Lawrence's successive task requires subjects to make use of position information. A tendency to disregard the position dimension (present but irrelevant during the first stage of training) would hinder both experimental and control subjects. Experimentals may be at an advantage, they suggest, because their tendency to attend to brightness cancels out this effect.

the formal version of the model) will increase when the target stimulus predicts reinforcement more accurately than such other stimuli as happen to be present (when the associative strength of the target exceeds that of the other stimuli). More of a departure is the introduction of a parallel rule specifying conditions in which α might be reduced below its base level. Associability will decline, it is suggested, when the target stimulus predicts reinforcement less accurately than such other stimuli as are present.* Put less formally, it is suggested that animals will learn to attend to stimuli that are good predictors of their consequences but will come to ignore irrelevant stimuli.

The third amendment can be seen as following from the second. Having introduced an independent mechanism for the loss of associability there is now no need to suppose that increase in attention to some stimuli are responsible for the decline in attention to others. And indeed, Mackintosh's (1975) model discards the notion that attention might be limited in capacity—changes in associability proceed independently (according to the rules just described), and there is no suggestion that the probability of attending to one is inversely related to the probability of attending to others.

In spite of these various amendments, Mackintosh's (1975) theory of attention retains many of the important features of its predecessor. Of particular relevance to our present concern is that both theories accept as a central principle the assumption that cues that are good predictors of their consequences will acquire extra associability. The two theories will be treated together below and referred to together as analyser theory.

6.1.2. The Pearce–Hall model

The Pearce–Hall (1980) model was presented (as an account of latent inhibition) in Chapter 3, and only a brief summary of its essentials is needed here. Like the model proposed by Mackintosh (1976), it identifies associability with the value of the learning-rate parameter α and it supposes that the value of α will change according to how well the stimulus in question predicts its consequences. But the rule it proposes as governing the value of α is quite different from that adopted by Mackintosh. The intuition at the heart of the model, it will be recalled, was the idea that a stimulus will require a full measure of attention only when its consequences are uncertain (as will be the case, for instance, when the stimulus is novel or when its consequences vary from one presentation to the next). An organism needs to learn about such a stimulus and thus associability should be maintained at a high level. A stimu-

---

* The original (1975) statement of this rule suggested that α for a stimulus will decline when that stimulus predicts reinforcement *no better than* other stimuli. The formulation given in the text was one introduced subsequently (Mackintosh 1976).

lus that has been reliably followed by a given outcome, however, requires no such special processing and the amount of attention paid to it can be reduced.

The equations proposed by Pearce and Hall (1980) as a formalization of these notions (see Chapter 3) assume that the starting value of α for a novel stimulus will be high and that the effect of training will (usually) be to reduce it. As the ability of the stimulus to predict its consequences grows (i.e. as the stimulus develops associative strength as a conditioned stimulus (CS), so α will decline. Increases in α occur only when the consequences of a stimulus change from one trial to the next. Thus a stimulus having good predictive accuracy is thought to lose associability—quite the opposite of the principle underlying analyser theory.

6.2. Evidence from studies of transfer

Given this stark divergence between the theories it might be supposed that devising an experiment that allowed a choice between them would be a simple matter. But, as we shall shortly see, any experiment that we advise is certain to introduce a range of other processes in addition to those deemed to influence the value of α. The complications that follow from this make a clear-cut decision difficult to reach. To anticipate on one point, however, it can be said now that, although the data do not allow a fully confident choice of one theory rather than the other, they do provide good reason for concluding that attentional changes of one sort or another are indeed induced by discrimination training procedures.

6.2.1. Negative transfer after conditioning

Although attentional theory arose initially out of studies of discrimination learning, its principles apply just as well to simple conditioning and, as we have seen, more recent theories of associability have been developed in this context. Experiments on discrimination learning will be discussed later in this chapter but we may begin by considering conditioning experiments that attempt to assess the readiness with which a fully trained CS will enter into a further association. The rival theories make clear and divergent predictions. Mackintosh's (1975) theory predicts that, provided there is no intereference between the first-trained conditioned response (CR) and that required subsequently, there will be positive transfer from the first conditioning episode to the second on the basis of the high value of α established in stage one. The Pearce–Hall (1980) model maintains that α will be low after stage one and that stage-two conditioning should proceed relatively slowly, provided the first-trained CR does not act to facilitate acquisition or performance of the second. The problem in conducting such a test, of course, is that of finding two conditioning procedures that evoke CRs that are quite independent of each other.

(a) Changing the nature of the reinforcer

One technique that might allow us to see further learning when the CS has already been trained in a preliminary stage of conditioning is to change the nature of the reinforcer in a way that will permit the acquisition of new CR. A change from appetitive to aversive, or vice versa, has often been used but has produced, for the most part, results that have been rather difficult to interpret (Dickinson and Pearce 1977). It seems well established that initial aversive conditioning will retard the subsequent development of an appetitive CR to the same CS, and that this retardation will occur even when the two CRs are sufficiently dissimilar as not to interfere with each other at the peripheral level (Scavio 1974; Krank 1985). This result is certainly not that predicted by Mackintosh's (1975) theory and might seem to suggest that the associability of a pre-trained CS is low. There is a complication, however, in that the motivational states engendered by the different reinforces might interfere with one another (Konorski 1967; Dickinson and Dearing 1979) even when the overt CRs do not. It could be the case, therefore, that motivationally based negative transfer is obscuring the positive transfer predicted by the analyser version of attentional theory.

It is even possible that motivational interaction might be responsible for certain cases of positive cross-reinforcer transfer. A series of experiments by Fowler and his colleagues (e.g. Fowler, Fago, Domber, and Hochhauser 1973; Ghiselli and Fowler 1976; Goodman and Fowler 1976) were put forward initially as showing that a CS that reliably predicts shock can acquire both affective and 'signalling' functions. A stimulus that has acquired the latter function will, it was proposed, be better able to signal other events (i.e. will be high in associability). The critical finding exploited by Fowler in his various experiments was that rats were better able to learn a food-rewarded T-maze discrimination when a stimulus that had previously been trained as a CS for shock was presented in the correct arm. The affective properties of this CS, it was argued, might tend to retard learning, but its signalling properties evidently outweighed any retardation. An alternative explanation can be derived, however, from the fact that a CS for shock seems in some ways functionally equivalent in its motivational properties to a CS that predicts the absence of food (e.g. Dickinson and Dearing 1979). Fowler's rats, therefore, received food in a maze arm in the presence of a CS that specifically predicted that no food would be available. Such a procedure, it has been suggested (Rescorla and Wagner 1972), is likely to endow the cues of the maze arm with a very strong association with food. Discriminative performance based on these cues would therefore be enhanced. This account of Fowler's results now seems to be accepted by Fowler himself (Fowler, Goodman, and Zanich 1977) (see also Dickinson 1977).

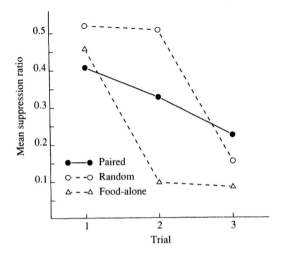

Fig. 6.1 Acquisition of conditioned suppression by rats given prior conditioned stimulus (CS)–food pairings (paired), uncorrelated presentations of CS and food (random), or experience of food without the CS (food alone). (After Dickinson 1976.)

Studies of appetitive-to-aversive transfer have produced even less decisive results. Sometimes there have been no detectable transfer effects (e.g. Jackson 1974), but some studies have found negative transfer (e.g. Hall and Pearce 1978; Mellgren, Hunsicker, and Dyck 1975) and yet others have produced positive transfer (e.g. Overmier and Payne 1971). It seems very likely that the effects observed in many of these experiments reflect peripheral response interactions (O'Neill and Biederman 1974). With the rather complex designs and procedures used in many of these experiments, the various possible sources of transfer have been difficult to disentangle. The problem is eased in experiments that use simple Pavlovian procedures in both stages of training (e.g. Dickinson 1976; Scavio and Gormezano 1980).

The relevant results of Dickinson's (1976) experiment are summarized in Fig. 6.1. The figure shows the acquisition of conditioned suppression in rats given tone–shock pairings after an initial stage of appetitive training. Subjects given orthodox appetitive conditioning in which the tone had preceded the delivery of food (the paired group) learned less readily than control subjects (food-alone) for whom the tone was novel during aversive training. The performance of the paired group was somewhat superior to that of subjects given unpaired presentations of tone and food in the first stage. To this extent, therefore, the initial conditioning procedure can produce a sort of positive transfer. There is no suggestion that the initial training can actually increase the associability of the tone above the level controlled by a novel stimulus (compare the paired and food-alone groups). Rather, initial

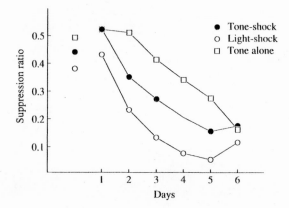

Fig. 6.2 Three groups of rats received stage-one treatment as shown in the figure. The isolated points on the left of the figure show group mean suppression scores for the last day of this stage. In stage two all subjects received six days of training with the tone by a stronger shock. (After Hall and Pearce 1979.)

experience of the stimulus in a conditioning procedure appears to do no more than attenuate the loss of associability suffered by a stimulus experienced on its own. This is the outcome predicted by the Pearce–Hall model. We cannot, however, reject analyser theory on the basis of these results. It is possible that the results shown in Fig. 6.1 are the product of the interaction of two sources of transfer—a negative effect based on motivational processes and a positive attentional effect, with the former outweighing the influence of the latter. The experiments to be described next, which avoid the complications introduced by changing the nature of the reinforcer, go some way toward ruling out this possibility.

(b) Changing the magnitude of the reinforcer

Results formally identical to those of Dickinson (1976) have come from similar experiments in which the change in the reinforcer from stage one to stage two has been merely in its size. Subjects can be trained to asymptote in stage one but an increase in reinforcer magnitude will allow new learning to be seen and thus the state of associability at the end of stage one to be assessed.

Figure 6.2 presents the results of the second stage of such an experiment by Hall and Pearce (1979). It shows the acquisition of conditioned suppression in rats (group tone-shock) that had received prior training in which the CS had been paired with a much weaker shock unconditioned stimulus (US). Any associative strength acquired in the first stage should help stage-two learning and this, combined with the increased associability postulated by Mackintosh (1975), should result in very rapid stage-two learning. But, as the figure shows, this form of pre-training merely attenuated the latent inhibition effect evident in subjects pre-exposed to the tone alone and conditioning was retarded with respect to that shown by subjects for whom the tone was novel at the start of stage two. (These subjects, group light-shock, had received prior experience of the weak shock US but signalled by a light, not by the tone.) The occurrence of negative transfer from training from a weak US to a further stage of conditioning with a stronger US and the same CS has been confirmed in a number of subsequent studies using aversive USs (e.g. Hall and Pearce 1982; Ayres, Moore, and Vigorito 1984; Kasprow, Schachtman, and Miller 1985; Swartzentruber and Bouton 1986; Schachtman, Channell, and Hall 1987) and an equivalent effect has also been found using autoshaping procedures with pigeons (Hall, Kaye, and Pearce 1985).

(c) Interpretation

The results just described allow the conclusion that in general there tends to be negative transfer from one conditioning episode to another when the same event is used as the CS. This conclusion is what the Pearce–Hall (1980) model would expect. Analyser theory, on the other hand, is constrained to suppose that the first stage of training will increase associability and thus, in order to explain the results it needs to introduce other mechanisms that act to oppose the effect of transfer based on enhanced attention. In some procedures these other mechanisms might depend on inhibitory interactions between motivational systems; but there is another possibility with more general and fundamental implications.

As it stands, the version of analyser theory being considered here lacks an explanation for the basic latent inhibition effect. It might be supposed that latent inhibition would occur because of a decline in α during pre-exposure. But the rule for changing α given above does not allow for this. A decline in α will occur when a stimulus is presented uncorrelated with reinforcement, but there is no reason why it should do so when the stimulus is presented alone (such a stimulus does not predict reinforcement less accurately than such other stimuli as are present). Accordingly, it is necessary to graft some further process onto the Mackintosh model in order to deal with latent inhibition. One possibility is that proposed by McLaren, Kaye, and Mackintosh (1989; see p. 89), who suggested that the α-value of a given stimulus will be low when that stimulus has entered into association with other events such as contextual cues. (To be precise, a stimulus element that is not the target of associative input from other elements will have its α-value boosted.) There will thus be two determinants of α: what the stimulus predicts, which will determine α according to the rules given above; and how well the stimulus is predicted by other events (operating according to the principles put forward by McLaren *et al.* (1989)). Both these processes will operate during any conditioning experiment and the net change in the conditionability of the CS will depend on the relative influence of the two. The negative transfer effects described here can be explained if it is assumed that in these experiments the latent inhibition mechanism is outweighing the enhancement in associability consequent on the high predictive accuracy of the CS.

The extra flexibility acquired by analyser theory as a result of the addition of this mechanism for latent inhibition means that no simple transfer of conditioning experiment is going to be able to disconfirm the theory. Some evidence that might cause us to doubt it, however, comes from experiments presented in Chapter 3 on the effects of inconsistent reinforcement. The results presented in Fig. 3.13 came from a version of the experiment summarized in Fig. 6.2 but on which, during stage-one training, the tone was followed, for some subjects, only inconsistently by the weak shock. These animals learned readily when the increase in shock intensity in stage two allowed further suppression to be acquired. In order to explain this effect, analyser theory needs to be able to convince us that the inconsistent reinforcement procedure pushes the balance away from latent inhibition and in favour of the mechanisms responsible for boosting associability.* But it is not easy to see why this should be so (if anything, the rules given above suggest that associability should decline with inconsistent reinforcement). The Pearce–Hall (1980) model, on the other hand, was explicitly devised to incorporate the notion that attention will be paid to a stimulus that has uncertain consequences; and this model therefore finds an important source of support in the effects produced by inconsistent reinforcement.

6.2.2. Transfer after discrimination training

If simple conditioning experiments tend to produce results favouring the Pearce–Hall (1980) model, analyser theory can find comfort in studies of explicit discrimination training. Here the transfer tends to be positive and it is the rival theory that is compelled to introduce supplementary processes in order to deal with the findings.

(a) A survey of the findings

Lawrence's (1949) experiment attempted to distinguish direct associative transfer from transfer based on acquired distinctiveness (increased associability) by changing the nature of the response and thus (it was hoped) eliminating direct transfer effects. But, as was mentioned in Chapter 1, this is just

---

* An alternative is to introduce a further source of transfer—to propose (along with Revusky 1971) that interference occurs between any association and any other, making it difficult for subjects that have acquired an association between CS and weak shock to form one between CS and stronger shock. Partial reinforcement might then be expected to produce less negative transfer than continuous reinforcement if it results in a weaker association at the end of stage one. The fact that the negative transfer effects discussed here tend to be context-specific (Swartzentruber and Bouton 1986; Peck and Bouton 1990) might be taken to favour this analysis (but see Kaye, Preston, Szabo, Druiff, and Mackintosh 1987).

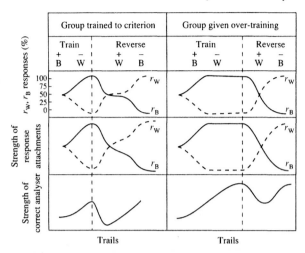

Fig. 6.3 Attentional analysis of the overtraining reversal effect. Subjects are trained initially on a simultaneous discrimination between black (B) rewarded (+) and white (W) non-rewarded (−). Choice of W is represented by r_W and of B by r_B.

one of several possible procedures for distinguishing attentional from associative transfer. In reversal learning, direct transfer is allowed, and its effect will of course be to retard subsequent learning. But according to analyser theory (see also Lawrence 1950) there will also be a source of positive transfer from initial training to a reversal. As the same stimuli are relevant in both stages of training, the attentional changes established in acquisition should be beneficial during the reversal. If conditions of training can be arranged that maximize the contribution of this attentional effect, it may be possible to see net positive transfer to a reversal.

One such set of conditions may be those produced by over-training. Reid (1953) demonstrated that rats given extended training (an extra 150 trials) on a simultaneous black–white discrimination learned the reversal of this task more rapidly than subjects trained only to a moderate criterion of mastery in the first stage. Although the circumstances in which the over-training reversal effect will occur are tightly circumscribed, its reality has been well established by subsequent work (e.g. Mackintosh 1969). Attentional theory supplies a ready explanation for the effect by assuming that over-training is more effective at strengthening the relevant analyser than it is at strengthening specific associations (Fig. 6.3). In consequence, the attentional change induced by the discrimination training is so strongly established that it can outweigh associatively based negative transfer.

Another strategy for distinguishing associative from attentional transfer was outlined in Chapter 1. This is to leave the response requirement the same in the two stages of training but to change the stimuli in such a way as

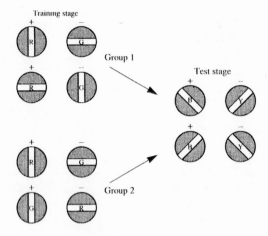

Fig. 6.4 Schematic representation of the experiment by Mackintosh and Little (1969). On each trial the pigeon chooses between two complex stimuli displayed side by side. For each condition both possible displays are shown. The + designates the rewarded alternative. In the test stage the blue–yellow difference is relevant. Group 1 comes to this as an intradimensional shift; for Group 2 it is an extradimensional shift. (After Hall 1983.)

to eliminate the effects of direct transfer but to allow attentional transfer. In an intradimensional shift (IDS) the specific stimuli are changed when a subject is transferred ('shifted') from one discrimination task to another, but the dimension along which the stimuli differ remains the same for both discriminations. With appropriately chosen stimuli there will be no reason for associative transfer to give the subject a preference for one shift stimulus over the other. But if the first stage of training increases the strength of the analyser sensitive to the relevant dimension, then there should be positive transfer from the first task to the second.

In order to demonstrate positive transfer it is necessary to find an appropriate control condition against which subjects receiving an IDS can be compared. Conceptually the simplest is the extradimensional shift (EDS), in which subjects are trained on a quite different discrimination before being shifted to the test problem. A simplified version of the design of such an experiment, conducted with pigeons as the subjects by Mackintosh and Little (1969), is shown in Fig. 6.4. Both groups of subjects saw the same stimulus displays in the first stage, but for Group 1 the colour of the stripe was correlated with reward and its orientation was irrelevant, whereas for Group 2 orientation was relevant and colour irrelevant. In the test stage all subjects learned a discrimination with colour relevant and orientation irrelevant. Group 1, for whom the test constituted an IDS, learned the test problem more readily than Group 2, for whom the test constituted an EDS. The superiority of the IDS condition in such experiments has been cited as being 'perhaps the best evidence that transfer between discrimination problems may be partly based on increases in attention' (Mackintosh 1974, p. 597).*

It should be pointed out, however, that an EDS–IDS difference is not a robust finding (at least in non-human animals) and attempts to determine the conditions necessary for its occurrence have proved unsuccessful. One possibility, that the effect reflects the operation of a learning process available only to so-called 'higher' animals seems to be supported by the clear demonstration of an IDS superiority in monkeys (Roberts, Robbins, and Everitt 1988) and the absence of the effect in fish (Tennant and Bitterman 1973). But the equally clear demonstration of an effect in the honeybee (Klosterhalfen, Fischer, and Bitterman 1978) puts paid to this notion. Turrisi, Shepp, and Eimas (1969) conclude from their experiments with rats that the effect will not occur when the EDS training problem does not include cues from the test dimension as irrelevant features (cf. Shepp and Eimas 1964). This cannot be a general principle, however, as Hamlin (1975) found an IDS superiority in birds trained under just such conditions (see also Durlach and Mackintosh 1986). Furthermore, Couvillon, Tennant, and Bitterman (1976) and Hall and Channell (1985a), using pigeons as subjects, were unable to find any difference between EDS and IDS groups in spite of employing designs and procedures nearly identical to those of Mackintosh and Little (1969) (Fig. 6.2).

Lawrence himself pioneered a rather different procedure for looking at intradimensional transfer with his study (Lawrence 1952) of 'transfer along a continuum', also known as the easy-to-hard-effect (see, e.g., Singer, Zentall, and Riley 1969). The stimuli were shades of grey ranging from light (A) to dark (G) with five intermediate values. Figure 6.5 shows that rats trained from the outset on a difficult discrimination between stimuli lying close together on the continuum (D–E) learned rather slowly. Others (group 2 in the figure), given 30 initial training trials on the easiest task (A/G) performed very well when given the IDS to the D/E task and their terminal level was superior to that of Group 1. Thus 30 preliminary trials on the easy problem produce better performance on the difficult problem than do 30 trials on the D/E problem itself. The attentional interpretation of this result is that initial training with stimuli that differ substantially from each other strengthens the relevant analyser more effectively than does training with stimuli lying close together on the dimension. There will thus be positive transfer from the easy to the hard task.

Lawrence acknowledged (Lawrence 1955) that the easy-to-hard effect does not require explanation in attentional terms. An alternative explanation

---

* In fact it is not clear from this experimental design whether the superiority of Group 1 reflects an increase in attention to the relevant dimension, a decrease in attention to the relevant dimension, or both.

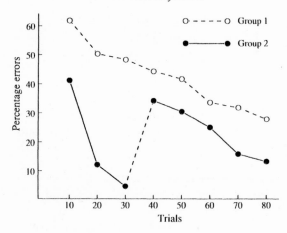

Fig. 6.5 Acquisition of a simultaneous brightness discrimination between two similar shades of grey. Group 1 was trained with these throughout; Group 2 received the first 30 trials with greys further apart on the brightness continuum. (After Lawrence 1952.)

(developed in detail by Logan (1966)) can be derived purely from considerations of the way in which associative strength is likely to generalize from one stimulus to another. With highly similar stimuli such as D and E the associative strength acquired by one will tend to generalize to the other, reducing the net difference between them. But for appropriately spaced stimuli, the excitatory associative strength acquired during initial training with A as the positive stimulus will generalize along the continuum as far as D but may not reach stimulus E; the inhibitory strength acquired by G may reach E but not D. In consequence, the tendency to choose D rather than E could be better established by training with A and G than by training with D and E themselves.

Logan's (1966) theory has been tested in a number of ways (e.g. Marsh 1969; Singer *et al.* 1969) but perhaps the most decisive evidence against it comes from a study by Mackintosh and Little (1970). Their subjects were pigeons that were ultimately required to learn a hard wavelength discrimination. They were given easy pre-training but with the values of the stimuli reversed. Thus, if the shorter of the two 'hard' wavelengths was to be positive they were pre-trained with the longer 'easy' wavelength as positive. Generalization of associative strength should put these birds at a disadvantage. Mackintosh and Little found this to be so at the beginning of the test phase; subjects given reversed pre-training were inferior to those trained on the hard discrimination from the outset (Fig. 6.6). But as training continued, the pre-trained group overcame its disadvantage and overtook the group

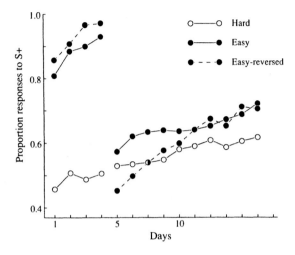

Fig. 6.6 Acquisition by pigeons of a hard colour discrimination after pre-training on an easy colour task, on an easy task in which the significance of the colours was reversed, or on the hard task itself. (After Mackintosh and Little 1970.)

trained only on the hard task. Mackintosh and Little concluded that easy pre-training bestows an advantage by firmly establishing the relevant analyser and that this effect is powerful enough to outweigh negative transfer from the generalization of associative strength.

(b) Additional sources of transfer

These instances of positive transfer after discrimination training accord with the interpretation offered by analyser theory. But the Pearce–Hall model supposes that once a discrimination has been solved so that each stimulus accurately predicts its consequence, the associabilities of the stimuli involved will fall in zero. This latter theory can be maintained only if it is allowed that additional sources of positive transfer are operating in these experiments and that these outweigh the negative effects of lost associability. There is evidence from studies of over-training that indicates the existence of further sources of transfer.

If over-training produces positive transfer to a reversal solely because it increases attention to the relevant stimuli then over-training should convey no benefit when the test problem involves quite different stimuli (i.e. when it is an EDS). Mackintosh (1962) argued (and produced evidence to support his argument; see also Hall 1974) that over-training on one dimension might actually retard the acquisition of an EDS. But subsequent studies have found that over-training either has no effect (e.g. Tighe, Brown, and Youngs 1965;

Siegel 1967; Basden 1970) or actually enhances EDS learning (e.g. Mandler 1966, 1968; Sutherland and Andelman 1969; Waller 1970, 1971). This last set of experiments is enough to demonstrate that over-training can generate some source of transfer that is not a consequence of an enhanced tendency to attend to the stimulus dimension relevant during training. This transfer effect may also have been operative in those studies that found no net positive transfer from over-training. A characteristic of the design of all these experiments was that the relevant stimuli from the first stage of training were present but irrelevant during learning of the EDS. Given that over-trained subjects tended to perseverate in responding to the stimulus that had been the positive in stage one, it is not surprising that the beneficial effects of over-training were not able to show through.

In general, the facilitatory effects of over-training on reversal learning require the conclusion that there is some source of positive transfer deriving from over-training that can be sufficient to compensate for the specific negative transfer that also occurs. But the positive effect need not be an enhancement of attention to the relevant dimension, and the results of studies of the EDS indicate that some more general process if indeed involved. A similar analysis can be applied to the easy-to-hard effect. The generalization of associative strength produced by initial training on the easy problem will help the learning of the hard problem but this cannot be the sole source of transfer because, as Mackintosh and Little (1970) have shown, the effect is still seen when the stimulus values of the easy problem are reversed. There is no need, however, to identify this second source of transfer with heightened attention to the relevant dimension. What will be the effect of pre-training on an easy rather than a hard problem when the test task is an EDS?

Mackintosh and Little (1970) included a group of subjects given easy pre-training (on horizontal against vertical) followed by an EDS (a difficult colour problem) and did not find any facilitation. However, they presented the horizontal and vertical stimuli in compound with the colours in the first stage. This procedure would produce 'overshadowing', prevent the colours from gaining associative strength, and (according to Pearce and Hall 1980) be particularly effective (more so than training with the hard colours alone) in causing a decline in the associability of these cues. These factors would act to obscure any positive general transfer produced by training on the easy problem *per se*. Experiments that avoid this complication (Singer *et al.* 1969; Seraganian 1979) have found that pre-training on an easy problem helps EDS training. The critical results from Seraganian's experiment are shown in Fig. 6.7. One group of pigeons learned an easy discrimination and were then shifted to a hard orientation task. Their performance was initially inferior to that of subjects trained for an equivalent number of sessions on the hard task itself; but the subjects pre-trained on the colour task showed a rapid improvement and ultimately out-performed those trained throughout on the hard task. These results cannot prove that strengthened attention to the rel-

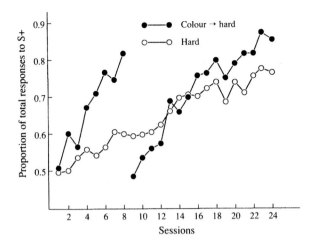

Fig. 6.7 Discrimination performance of pigeons trained for eight sessions on an easy colour discrimination prior to training on a hard orientation discrimination compared with that of pigeons trained on the hard task throughout. (After Seraganian 1979.)

evant dimension plays no part in the intradimensional version of the easy-to-hard effect but they make it unnecessary to adopt such a hypothesis.

It remains to specify the mechanisms by which over-training (as opposed to training to a criterion on the same task) and training on an easy task (as opposed to training for the same number of trials on a difficult task) come to produce positive transfer to an EDS. There are several possibilities, one of which is entirely compatible with the tenets of analyser theory. This theory asserts, as we have seen, that training with one set of relevant stimuli could cause a loss in the associability of irrelevant stimuli that happen to be present, either because of the operation of a limited-capacity constraint or because of a direct effect of the lack of correlation between these stimuli and reinforcement. Now irrelevant stimuli are present in all of the experimental procedures considered here. In every simultaneous discrimination, for example, the positive stimulus will sometimes be on the left with the negative on the right and on other occasions the positions will be reversed. The cues defining left and right are thus irrelevant and will lose associability.* This fact will have implications for the learning of any subsequent task (even an EDS) in the presence of these cues. As irrelevant cues, having lost associa-

---

* A distinction is sometimes made between such irrelevant stimuli and *incidental* stimuli by which is meant stimuli common to both the positive and the negative. But such cues are also irrelevant as predictors of reinforcement and they too will, according to the theory, suffer a loss of associability.

bility, will not be able to gain (or lose) associative strength, changes in the strength of the relevant cues will be able to occur more easily and the new discrimination will be resolved readily.

Direct evidence that over-training and training on an easy task are especially effective in 'neutralizing' irrelevant cues is not available, but there is plentiful evidence to support the implication that some preliminary discrimination training rather than none will help further discrimination learning when the same irrelevant cues are present in both tasks. Bainbridge (1973) found that rats shifted from one discrimination to another (an EDS) involving the same apparatus but quite different discriminative stimuli learned more readily than controls given no previous training. But his result might have occurred simply because the first stage of training allowed the subjects to become less fearful, more accustomed to the working of the apparatus, and so on. What is needed is to include controls given approximately equivalent preliminary training but with no discrimination contingency. Such controls might experience just one of the training stimuli, sometimes reinforced and sometimes not; alternatively they might be given pseudo-discrimination (PD) training (Honig 1969), experiencing both of the stimuli but with reinforcement associated equally often with each. It has been reliably found that animals given initial discrimination training learn an EDS more readily than such controls (e.g. Eck, Noel, and Thomas 1969; Keilitz and Frieman 1970; Frieman and Goyette 1973). Superior performance is also seen when the test task is not a simple discrimination between two new stimuli but consists of a phase of reinforced training to one of these stimuli followed by a generalization test with the other (Honig 1969; Thomas 1970; Mackintosh 1977).

Having acknowledged that a possible source of the transfer seen in the EDS can be derived from analyser theory, it is now time to redress the balance and point out that the evidence does not require us to accept this interpretation. Indeed there is evidence for transfer effects that cannot be explained in terms of a loss of associability by irrelevant cues. An example comes from an experiment by Rodgers and Thomas (1982).

The critical comparison in their study was between two groups of pigeons that both received initial discrimination training on an orientation task before being shifted to a colour task. Incidental and irrelevant cues should therefore be neutralized in both groups. The groups differed in that for one the response requirements of the two tasks were the same whereas for the other they differed. In the latter case, subjects might be trained, for instance, on a standard successive (go/no-go) discrimination and transferred to a successive conditional task in which they had to respond to the left when given one colour and to the right for the other. Animals that stayed with the same task type learned the EDS more readily than those given a change. Rodgers and Thomas concluded that transfer can occur because animals will learn 'task-appropriate response tendencies' (see Bitterman and McConnell

(1954); Wodinsky, Varley and Bitterman (1954), for an early statement of this suggestion). In most transfer experiments, in which the task-type is not changed, these tendencies will, of course, be a source of positive transfer. It could well be that over-training and initial training on an easy problem have their effects because they are especially effective in establishing such tendencies.

The exact nature of the strategies acquired in the Rodgers and Thomas experiment remains to be specified. It has often been suggested, however, that training on a long series of discrimination tasks that differ only in the specific stimuli used will induce in animals, particularly in primates, a 'win-stay, lose-shift' strategy (e.g. Restle 1958). That is, animals given learning-set training, as it is called, will learn to repeat the response to a stimulus that has just been rewarded and to shift to an alternative stimulus when that just chosen has failed to yield reward. There is evidence to suggest that experience of a single, simple discrimination, even for a non-primate species, can foster the development of such a strategy. Hall (1975) trained two groups of rats on a simultaneous discrimination in which the rewarded stimulus (black or white) was alternated from trial to trial. One group came to this task without any prior training. They performed rather better than subjects that had previously learned an orthodox simultaneous discrimination between horizontal and vertical stripes. There is thus some transfer effect produced by discrimination training that is sufficiently strong that it can overcome the beneficial effects of such training (produced by habituation to the apparatus, and so on) and result in overall negative transfer. A tendency to stay with a rewarded stimulus and shift from one followed by non-reward would of course produce negative transfer to a test requiring alternation. And although the transfer will be negative in this special test procedure, the same process will be operative when the transfer test is a simple EDS where it will act to facilitate learning.

(c) Summary

Discrimination training will produce positive transfer to a subsequent discrimination involving the same or similar stimuli. This is the result predicted by analyser theory. It turns out, however, that positive transfer will occur when the test task involves quite different stimuli (is an EDS). Analyser theory can supply an explanation for the transfer seen in this case, too, in terms of a loss of associability in irrelevant cues that are present in both stages of training. The next section of this chapter looks directly at experimental results that have been taken to demonstrate the operation of a process of learned irrelevance. But whatever the outcome of this review, there is nothing to compel us to accept that the effects described above are an outcome of such a process. An alternative is available and this alternative, that discrimination training fosters the development of generally helpful 'response strategies', might allow us to explain the effect of over-training and the easy-to-hard effect without recourse to the mechanisms proposed by analyser theory.

The arguments just advanced do not apply, however, to experiments making a direct comparison between EDS and IDS. In these experiments the two groups of subjects receive equal amounts of training on initial discriminations of approximately equal difficulty. Both groups must be assumed, therefore, to have developed helpful response strategies to the same extent. None the less, shift performance is superior in subjects for whom the same dimension is relevant in both stages of training. Analyser theory derives powerful support from this result. But even here an alternative interpretation is possible and will be taken up after the effects of non-discriminative training have been considered.

6.2.3. Effects of irrelevance training

(a) In discrimination learning

The arguments for analyser theory presented in the preceding section were largely based on the notion that irrelevant stimuli will lose associability. Direct evidence for this suggestion has been sought in studies of simultaneous discrimination learning (e.g. Babb 1956; Jeeves and North 1956; Waller 1970). The last of these will serve as an example. Various groups of rats were tested on a discrimination between rough and smooth floor textures in a T-maze, both arms of the maze being painted grey. Control subjects given prior training on a black–white task with both arms of the maze having a floor texture intermediate between the rough and the smooth showed good performance on the test. But subjects pre-trained on black and white with the rough and the smooth cues present but irrelevant learned the test problem rather slowly. Analyser theory can explain this effect by asserting that the initial stage of training reduces the attention paid to the textural cues. But an alternative is that the training given to the control subjects means that the rough and the smooth cues will be novel and high in associability; for this reason, if for no other, these subjects will be capable of outperforming those given irrelevance training in the first stage, for whom (according to either of the theories being considered here) the associabilities of these stimuli will be low.

The term 'irrelevance training' may also be applied to the case in which subjects experience what amounts to an insoluble discrimination task with reward and non-reward occurring equally often in association with the two stimuli of interest and in the absence of a relevant set of cues (the case referred to above as pseudo-discrimination training). Such training will undoubtedly retard later learning when the conditions are changed so that the previously irrelevant cues now become relevant (e.g. Galbraith 1973; Winefield 1978). This negative transfer may imply that the associability of the critical stimuli at the end of such irrelevance training is somewhat below that of novel stimuli (the comparison has usually been made with control subjects given no prior training). As before, this possibility is allowed by both of the theories under discussion.

There is reason to think, however, that some more general source of transfer is at work—transfer based perhaps on changes on the properties of incidental cues common to both the training and the test situation, or on the acquisition of some more general strategy such as a tendency to persist with a given behaviour in the face of sporadic non-reward. It has even been suggested that subjects given irrelevance training might have some way of encoding the information that events are generally unpredictable, knowledge that might well interfere with subsequent discrimination learning (see e.g. Overmier and Wielkiewicz 1983). These sources of transfer would have influence, even when the test problem was an EDS. And indeed, initial training on an insoluble discrimination has been found to retard the acquisition of a quite different (soluble) test problem (Mandler 1966; Bainbridge 1973; Mullins and Winefield 1977, 1978), comparison again being made with subjects given no prior training.*

To show that irrelevance training with a given pair of cues specifically retards the subsequent learning of a discrimination between them requires comparison with a control group given initial irrelevance training in the absence of these cues (ideally in the presence of quite different cues), a group which thus would come to the test problem as an EDS. There have been surprisingly few experiments that allow this comparison and their results generate no very clear conclusion. Winefield (1978) tested rats on a simultaneous black/white discrimination after irrelevance training with these same stimuli. The rats received a choice between black and white on each of 300 trials of stage-one training; reward was presented on half the trials but its availability was not signalled by these or any other cues. These subjects learned the test discrimination rather poorly compared with other subjects that had received equivalent training in stage one but in the absence of black and white (two grey stimuli were presented). In a series of experiments of similar design, however, Bitterman and his colleagues found either that pre-training in the presence of the to-be-relevant cues produced no special effect (Bitterman, Elam and Wortz 1953; Calvin 1953; Billingsley, Feddersen and Bitterman 1954) or actually facilitated subsequent discrimination learning (Bitterman, Calvin and Elam 1954; Bitterman and Elam 1954).

A feature of the experiments by Bitterman that sets them apart from the others discussed so far is that during pre-training reinforcement occurred on every trial with the subjects receiving reward whichever of the cues they

---

* We have already seen that animals given an EDS after PD training learn less well than others given initial training on a soluble discrimination. The results mentioned here show that the effect is not to be attributed solely to some positive factor operating in the subjects given discrimination pre-training.

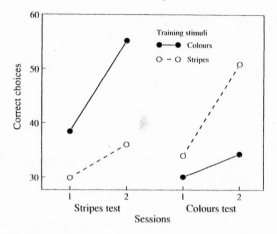

Fig. 6.8 Simultaneous discrimination performance of two groups of pigeons given previous non-differential training with stimuli differing in either colour or orientation (stripes). All subjects received two 60-trial sessions on the orientation discrimination followed by two sessions on the colour discrimination. (After Hall and Channell 1980.)

responded to. This procedure (sometimes referred to as non-differential training) is, like irrelevance training, non-discriminative in that the critical stimuli are not associated with different schedules of reinforcement. It may be, however, that the use of consistent rather than inconsistent reinforcement during pre-training introduces some new process that is capable of producing positive transfer. A set of experiments by Hall and Channell (1980), although it does little else to resolve the issue, does at least rule out this possibility. In these experiments (Fig. 6.8) pigeons were tested on a simultaneous discrimination between stimuli differing in colour (for example) after non-differential training with these same stimuli or with a different set (e.g. different line orientations). Test performance was markedly worse after pre-training with the test stimuli; that is, non-differential training can produce negative transfer just as irrelevance training can. What determines for a particular situation whether these various forms of non-discriminative training will produce positive, negative, or no net transfer remains obscure.

(b) Learned irrelevance in conditioning procedures

The complexities of design, procedure, and interpretation that have emerged during our consideration of experiments employing discrimination training procedures can perhaps be attenuated by devising a conditioning procedure in which the same theoretical issues can be explored. Mackintosh (1973) introduced the use of a Pavlovian conditioning procedure for studying 'learned irrelevance'. An instance of the effect is presented in Fig. 6.9. These results come from an experiment by Baker and Mackintosh (1977). Rats acquired a conditioned licking response in the presence of a tone signalling the availability of water after various types of pre-exposure. The figure shows that pre-exposure to uncorrelated presentations of the tone and of water dramatically interfered with subsequent conditioning, much more so than did either pre-exposure to the tone alone or pre-exposure to water alone. A similar retardation of conditioning as a result of uncorrelated presentations of a CS and a US has been demonstrated in many other studies using a range of different conditioning procedures (e.g. conditioned suppression in rats, Baker (1976); autoshaping in pigeons, Tomie (1976); eyelid conditioning in rabbits, Siegel and Domjan (1971)). The effect is readily interpretable in terms of Mackintosh's (1975) theory. During the pre-exposure phrase, the tone, although it will occasionally occur along with water, will predict the occurrence of water less well than other stimuli that are present (e.g. stimuli arising from the training context itself). Accordingly the associability of the tone will decline, making for slow subsequent conditioning with the tone as CS.

Although it is consistent with (indeed, predicted by) Mackintosh's attentional theory, the phenomenon of learned irrelevance does not require us to accept this theory. In particular, as Mackintosh (1983) himself acknowledges, the learned irrelevance effect might represent no more than the sum of a latent inhibition effect and a separate negative transfer effect produced

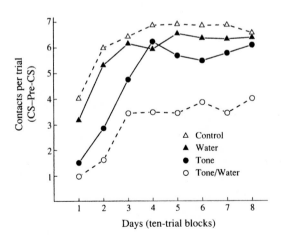

Fig. 6.9 Acquisition of a conditioned response (licking at a drinking spout) to a tone signalling water. Subjects were pre-exposed to uncorrelated presentations of the tone and water, to the tone alone, to water alone, or to neither. (After Baker and Mackintosh 1977.)

by prior exposure to the US. Possible mechanisms for latent inhibition have already been described (Chapters 3 and 4). That pre-exposure just to the event to be used as the US will retard subsequent conditioning is well established empirically (Randich and LoLordo 1979), and there is no shortage of reasons why this should be so. Pre-exposure might establish a context–US association that would block the development of a CS–US association (e.g. Tomie 1976; Randich and Ross 1984); or the habituation process activated by repeated presentations of the US might cause it to lose effectiveness as a reinforcer (Wagner 1981). A further reason why presentations of the US during pre-exposure should produce a particularly marked retardation of later learning comes from considerations of context-specificity. The introduction of the US for the first time during the conditioning stage of a standard, latent inhibition experiment can be seen as constituting an effective change of context—presentations of the CS after the first occur in the novel context generated by the after-effects of the US. A change of context for the conditioning phase of a latent inhibition experiment will attenuate the size of the effect (see Chapter 3, pp. 86–9). The learned irrelevance procedure arranges for the US and its after-effects to be present during exposure to the CS; it thus minimizes the extent to which the transition from pre-exposure to test involves a contextual change and should therefore maximize the degree of negative transfer.

Attempts have been made to show that the various learning processes just described cannot give a full account of the effects of irrelevance training and that there is therefore still scope for a separate mechanism for learned irrelevance (Baker and Mackintosh 1979; Matzel, Schachtman, and Miller 1988). On the whole, however, these attempts have failed to convince. Matzel *et al.* (1988) were able to show that a small learned irrelevance effect persisted even when the pre-exposure conditions were arranged so as to minimize latent inhibition and US–pre-exposure effects. They want to take this finding as an indication of a separate learned irrelevance process; but they prudently acknowledge that they might, even in this study, be observing only the summation of two weakened (but not absent) subsidiary effects.

In a further experiment, Matzel *et al.* (1988) investigated the effects of a change in context from pre-exposure to conditioning on the learned irrelevance effect. They found that the deficit produced by learned irrelevance training transferred across contexts much more readily than did latent inhibition. But this result is to be expected given that we have already said about the context-specificity of latent inhibition—the change of context experienced by the subjects exposed to the CS alone will consist both of the new physical environment and of the introduction of USs. It will thus be more dramatic than that experienced by the subjects given learned irrelevance training and will be more effective in attenuating the effects of pre-exposure. We may conclude that experiments on learned irrelevance do not, as yet, require us to propose any new mechanism for changes in stimulus associability in addition to those already adopted as an explanation for latent inhibition.

6.2.4 Conclusions

It would be difficult to construct an explanation for the various transfer effects reviewed in this chapter that made no use of the concept of attention, of the notion that discrimination training (and conditioning) produce changes in the associability of stimuli. We have not arrived at a consensus, however, about the mechanisms that govern such changes. The Pearce–Hall (1980) model deals with the phenomena described in this chapter in just the same way as it deals with latent inhibition—all are instances of stimuli losing associability when their consequences are reliably predicted. The version of the Mackintosh (1975) model that I have been considering treats latent inhibition as a separate phenomenon distinct from the processes whereby the consequences of a stimulus can bring about a change in its associability. The first of these theories receives support from the negative transfer seen in conditioning studies; the second finds support in the positive effects found in some studies of the transfer of discrimination learning. But in each case, the alternative theory can find a way to explain away the apparent success of its rival.

Are there any other grounds on which a choice between the alternatives might be made? An attraction of the Pearce–Hall (1980) model is the support it receives from the body of data reviewed in Chapter 3. The model predicts that an orienting response (to the extent that it reflects the α-value of the stimulus) will wane as the associative strength of the stimulus grows, and that manipulations that reduce the predictive accuracy of the stimulus should maintain or restore the vigour of the orienting response (OR). These predictions are unique to the model and are amply confirmed by experiment.

If we are to accept that associability is determined in the way described by the Pearce–Hall model, it becomes necessary to find alternative explanations for certain transfer experiments—in particular, for those that demonstrate that animals will learn an IDS more rapidly than an equivalent EDS. Perhaps an explanation can be found in terms of the acquired distinctiveness and acquired equivalence mechanisms discussed in the preceding chapter. These mechanisms must be presumed to be operating in the discrimination tasks described in this chapter, acting to reduce the extent of generalization between stimuli that have been associated with different consequences and to increase generalization between stimuli that have shared common consequences. Is it possible that the EDS/IDS difference occurs because the test stimuli (or stimuli very like them) have been associated with very different consequences (for the IDS group) or similar consequences (for the EDS group) in the first stage of training? Perhaps no very sizeable effect can be expected on these grounds but remember that my review of the experimental findings showed that IDS superiority is by no means a robust effect. It would be foolish to pretend that the analysis just offered is anything more than exceedingly tentative and the only argument to add support is that to adopt it, however tentatively, allows us to provide a fairly coherent account for a wide range of phenomena, including not just transfer effects in discrimination learning but the various features of latent inhibition discussed in Chapters 3 and 4.

7. Discrimination after stimulus exposure

After discussing in Chapters 5 and 6 the effects of explicit discrimination training on the discriminability of stimuli, I return in this chapter to a discussion of the effect of mere pre-exposure on later learning. Chapters 3 and 4 were concerned with the retarding effect of such pre-exposure on subsequent simple conditioning (i.e. with latent inhibition). It is now time to consider the consequences of such pre-exposure for discrimination learning. There is clearly more to be said for, as the discussion in Chapter 1 of the work of Gibson and Walk (1956) showed, there are some circumstances in which pre-exposure facilitates subsequent discrimination learning. It is this observation that encourages the view that stimulus differentiation might go on during pre-exposure. My central concern in this chapter is to evaluate this suggestion.

I shall proceed, first, by reviewing experimental studies that have investigated discrimination after pre-exposure, the purpose being to extract some empirical generalizations about the circumstances that must be met if an enhancement of discrimination is to be found. Next I shall consider a range of theories that might be able to accommodate these basic facts, following this with a discussion of further experimental work intended to allow choice among the theories.

7.1. A survey of the experiments

The procedure used by Gibson and Walk (1956) incorporates several features that make it unique among the studies of stimulus pre-exposure discussed so far. In particular, the subjects were immature animals, exposure was prolonged, and the stimuli were presented in the animals' home cages rather than in the context subsequently used for the discrimination test. I have already mentioned some evidence (Chapter 1, p. 23) indicating that these features of their procedure are not essential in producing the facilitatory effect of pre-exposure. Accordingly it is appropriate to widen the scope of our survey and to include not only studies that adhere more or less closely to the Gibson–Walk procedure but also evidence from a range of different procedures in which a comparison is made of the discriminative performance of subjects allowed to grow familiar with the relevant stimuli with that of subjects for whom the stimuli are novel. I shall begin, however, with a closer look at experiments using the Gibson–Walk procedure.

7.1.1. Exploration of the Gibson–Walk procedure

(a) The nature of the stimuli

Having demonstrated the basic effect, Gibson and Walk and their collaborators set about investigating what features of their procedure were responsible for the outcome. Unfortunately, several of these follow-up experiments failed to reveal any effect at all, even in subjects trained by procedures closely similar to those used in the original study (see Gibson, Walk, and Tighe 1959). These failures of replication appear to be a consequence of changing the exact nature of the stimuli. Gibson *et al.* (1959) exposed animals to painted, two-dimensional figures whereas Gibson and Walk (1956) used cut-out, three-dimensional objects. Walk, Gibson, Pick, and Tighe (1959) presented evidence that this difference is crucial in an experiment directly comparing the two types of stimuli. Bennett and Ellis (1968) confirmed this finding and presented further evidence to suggest that the critical feature of the cut-outs is that the rat can manipulate them (see also Bennett, Rickert, and McAllister 1970). It remains the case, however, that some experimenters (e.g. Kawachi 1965) have been able to demonstrate a facilitatory effect of pre-exposure when the objects were inaccessible to the subjects, or even of pre-exposure to painted two-dimensional figures (e.g. Forgus 1956, 1958a,b).

Clearly the effect is to be found only with some stimuli, but what feature or combination of features these stimuli should possess is less clear. One possibility is that the difficulty of the discrimination required may be important. Oswalt (1972) investigated a range of stimuli in a single experiment, one group of subjects being trained with triangles and circles, a second with objects having stripes that differed in orientation, and a third group with panels bearing U-shaped figures, upright or inverted. These three discrimination tasks differed in difficulty and it was only with the most difficult (the triangle–circle task) that pre-exposure to the stimuli was found to facilitate learning. Other experiments allow the conclusion that the facilitatory effect is not to be found only using the cut-out triangles and circles of the original study, as successful replications have used, among other stimuli, horizontally and vertically striped objects (Channell and Hall 1981), a painted triangle and cross (Forgus 1956), and a globe and a pyramid (Kawachi 1965).

Gibson (1969) expressed concern that the effects observed in these various experiments might reflect some general consequence of exposure rather than a change in the way in which the specific stimuli were perceived. This concern seems to be misplaced. Although it is true that the pre-exposure stimuli need not be identical to those used in the discrimination test—rats exposed to a circle and an equilateral triangle will show positive transfer to a discrimination between an ellipse and an isosceles triangle (Gibson, Walk, Pick, and Tighe 1958) (see also Forgus 1958a,b; Bennett, Anton, and Levitt 1971)—

exposure to quite irrelevant objects does not facilitate subsequent discrimination. For instance, Bennett *et al.* (1971) found no effect of exposing rats to random patterns of crosses and other geometrical figures on a subsequent triangle–circle discrimination.

(b) Exposure to just one stimulus

Prior exposure to a pair of appropriately chosen stimuli can, therefore, facilitate later discrimination learning. What is the effect of exposure to just one of the stimuli? Franken and Bray (1973) found that the result depended on whether or not the pre-exposed stimulus was the positive or the negative in the test discrimination—performance was facilitated in the latter case but retarded in the former. Their interpretation, that rats have a tendency to approach the novel stimulus, highlights a complication in experiments of this design. Unconditioned responses will have habituated to only one of the critical stimuli and may thus play a part in determining the outcome in a way that they cannot with the procedure in which the subjects are pre-exposed to both stimuli. There are, however, two further studies (by Walk, Gibson, Pick, and Tighe 1958; Bennett, Levitt, and Anton 1972) which found that pre-exposure to one stimulus produced facilitation, both when it was used as the negative and also when it was used as the positive. Franken and Bray's 'novelty effect' may have been operating in these experiments too (Walk *et al.* (1958) report that subjects with the pre-trained as the negative were marginally superior to those with the pre-trained as the positive), but clearly, the stimuli and procedures employed were such as to allow some other process to outweigh this effect. As Walk *et al.* (1958) and Bennett *et al.* (1972) used procedures known to generate the basic Gibson–Walk effect (Franken and Bray (1973) did not), we may adopt the conclusion that, under the conditions currently of interest to us, discrimination learning is facilitated by exposure to just one of the stimuli.

(c) Timing and duration of the exposure period

In all the experiments discussed so far, stimulus exposure has been given when the rats were immature. We have already seen, however, that this is not a critical feature of the experimental procedure. In an experiment mentioned in Chapter 1 (see Fig. 1.7), Hall (1979) demonstrated that rats allowed to grow to full adulthood before being given exposure to the stimuli in their home cages show just the same positive transfer to the test discrimination as is seen in rats given exposure in infancy.

A further feature common to the experiments discussed so far is that the stimuli have been presented continuously for 24 hours a day for long periods—for two weeks at least and in some experiments for very much longer. How prolonged exposure needs to be is not certain, but there is some evidence to show that shorter periods can be perfectly effective. Kerpelman (1965) found a facilitation after exposure for two hours a day over a period

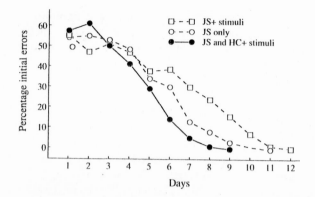

Fig. 7.1 Acquisition of a simultaneous horizontal–vertical discrimination in a jumping stand (group mean daily error scores). All subjects received prior exposure to the apparatus (JS); for one group the stimuli were present in the apparatus; for a second the stimuli were presented in the home cage (HC); the third group received no prior exposure to the stimuli. (After Channell and Hall 1981.)

of 90 days (although the effect was statistically reliable only in food-deprived subjects for whom the presence of the stimuli coincided with their daily feeding time). But using a more orthodox procedure in which food was continuously available, Channell and Hall (1981) (see also Hall and Channell 1983) were able to demonstrate reliable positive transfer in subjects given pre-exposure for just one hour per day over 40 days. The size of the effect obtained by Channell and Hall (1981) for subjects given restricted exposure was every bit as substantial as that observed in a further group exposed for 24 hours a day, encouraging the conclusion that facilitation of discrimination learning could well be found after even shorter exposure periods.

(d) The role of home-cage exposure

Continuous prolonged exposure to the stimuli requires that pre-training take place in the home cage. But the procedure used by Channell and Hall (1981), in which the stimuli are experienced for only one hour each day, allows of other arrangements. Channell and Hall (1981, experiment 3) gave one group of rats exposure to the stimuli for one hour a day, not in their home cages but in the apparatus that was to be used subsequently for the discrimination task. Control subjects received exposure to the apparatus with no stimuli present, and a third group received home-cage exposure to the stimuli. (This third group also experienced the apparatus, in the absence of the stimuli, for one hour each day; thus all three groups were equally familiar with the apparatus when it came to discrimination training.) The test performance of the three groups is shown in Fig. 7.1. Home-cage exposure produced the facilitation (with respect to the nonpre-exposed control) that we have come to expect. But pre-exposure to the stimuli in the test apparatus did not—performance was actually somewhat worse than that shown by control subjects.

Proper interpretation of the results shown in Fig. 7.1 would be easier if we knew the effects of pre-exposure given in some place that was neither the home cage nor the test apparatus. Channell and Hall (1981) offered the suggestion that the Gibson–Walk effect requires that there be a change of context between pre-exposure and the test, implying that pre-exposure anywhere other than in the test apparatus should produce facilitation. It is conceivable, however, that positive transfer might occur only after home-cage pre-exposure—the home cage is, after all, an environment likely to have many special properties that distinguish it from all others. And Channell and Hall interpreted the retardation consequent on exposure in the apparatus as being a case of latent inhibition, suggesting, given the known context-specificity of this effect, that the fact that exposure was given in the test apparatus was critical to the outcome. It remains possible, however, that with these stimuli and procedures a retardation might be found wherever pre-exposure occurs (provided, of course, that it is not given in the home cage).

Although it uses quite different procedures, we should mention here an experiment by Lubow, Rifkin, and Alek (1976), as this study appears, at first sight, capable of shedding light on some of the issues just raised. Lubow *et al.* (experiment 2) gave rats pre-exposure in their home cages to a distinctive odour and then required them, in the same cages, to learn to approach the source of the odour in order to obtain food. The rats failed to learn this response at all well, indicating that home-cage pre-exposure is not in itself sufficient to facilitate further learning. (Subjects pre-exposed to the odour in their home cages but tested in a different environment learned readily.) Unfortunately, however, it seems likely that the mechanisms responsible for the effect reported by Lubow *et al.* are quite different from those engaged by experiments using the Gibson–Walk procedure. The test task used by Lubow *et al.* requires not discrimination between two cues but the simple conditioning of an approach response to one. Animals both pre-exposed and tested in their home cages appear to learn rather poorly, simply because any tendency to investigate the cue has been thoroughly habituated—the approach response is never made and thus cannot be rewarded. Transfer to a novel context will (as we saw in Chapter 2) allow the return of an habituated response and thus conditioning can be effective when the context is changed.*

---

* This does not constitute a complete account of all the results reported by Lubow *et al.* (1976). In particular, the subjects given the pre-exposed odour in a novel context learned more readily than subjects for whom both the odour and the context were novel. Lubow *et al.* attribute the superiority of the former group to a 'relative novelty' effect (but see Chapter 2, p. 44).

7.1.2. Studies of avian imprinting

It is a short step from the original Gibson–Walk experiment to studies of imprinting in which birds have been exposed to a conspicuous stimulus early in life and have been required to learn a discrimination between this stimulus and some other. Bateson (1964) suggested that such an imprinting stimulus, as well as supporting filial responses, might also acquire distinctiveness, and that subsequent discrimination learning might therefore be facilitated.

It seems well established (e.g. Kovach, Fabricius, and Falt 1966; Polt 1969) that facilitation is indeed found when the test discrimination requires the subject to approach the pre-exposed stimulus; but assuming that the initial exposure was effective in establishing imprinting (i.e. the following response), any other outcome would be most unexpected. We should concentrate, therefore, on test procedures in which an approach to the pre-trained stimulus is the incorrect response. Here the results are mixed. Kovach *et al.* (1966) found that birds imprinted on a flashing light learned readily to move away from the light to escape shock. Using a food-rewarded simultaneous discrimination between red and blue as the test procedure, Chantrey (1972, experiment 5) found that birds exposed initially to red learned the task more readily than controls exposed to some other colour, even when red was the negative stimulus. But no facilitation was evident in another experiment by Chantrey (experiment 1), which used only marginally different training procedures; and Polt (1969) found that birds given the imprinting stimulus as the negative made more errors than untreated controls. It is impossible to identify the reasons for these discrepancies. Perhaps, however, given the powerful effect that the following response is likely to exert, it is enough that, in some circumstances at least, a facilitation has been observed in these experiments.

It should be easier to interpret experiments in which the birds are given exposure to both the stimuli that are to be used in the subsequent discrimination task, as if imprinting occurs to both stimuli there should be no special preference for one stimulus over another at the start of the discrimination. Chantrey (1972) (see also Bateson and Chantrey 1972) exposed domestic chicks in the experimental condition to two objects differing in colour presented in quick succession for one hour a day for the first five days after hatching. Control subjects experienced only a third colour. From days 8 to 12 all subjects were taught a food-rewarded simultaneous discrimination between the first pair of colours. Subjects pre-exposed to the test stimuli took significantly longer to learn the discrimination than did controls, the reverse of the result that studies using Gibson–Walk procedure have led us to expect. Chantrey (1974) went on to show, however, that in some circumstances exposing chicks to both stimuli might result in positive transfer. He varied the interval between stimulus presentations during pre-exposure and found that when this interval was increased to five minutes or more the experimental group learned more rapidly than the single-stimulus group.

It is unfortunate, given this intriguing pattern of results, that attempts at replication have not been wholly successful. Stewart, Capretta, Cooper, and Littlefield (1977) conducted a series of nine experiments and found that the retardation reported by Chantrey (1972, 1974) could be obtained only under the exact conditions employed in the original experiments. There was no sign, however, of the retardation changing to facilitation as the interstimulus interval employed during pre-exposure was increased. It is clear then that only tentative conclusions are justified—perhaps the most we can say is that imprinting on a single stimulus can help facilitate discrimination between this stimulus and some other, whereas exposure to two stimuli tends to hinder subsequent discriminative performance.* The discrepancy between this last finding and the results of experiments using the Gibson–Walk procedure is something that any adequate explanatory theory will have to be able to deal with.

7.1.3. Latent learning

A classic procedure for investigating the effects of prior exposure on subsequent discrimination learning is the latent learning experiment used by Tolman and his colleagues (Tolman 1932) in their studies of maze learning. A typical experiment is that reported by Blodgett (1929). Rats were allowed to explore a maze, the floor plan of which is shown in Fig. 7.2, once a day for six days. On the seventh day, food was made available in the exit box and the rats were allowed to eat before being removed from the maze. Learning then occurred very rapidly so that just one more rewarded trial was enough to allow these subjects to reach a level of performance that rats not given initial pre-exposure took seven days of rewarded training to reach (see Fig. 7.2).

The parallel between this result and those produced by the Gibson–Walk procedure is evident; and so also are the differences between the two procedures. It is certainly possible to regard a maze of the type used by Blodgett as constituting a task that requires a series of simultaneous discriminations between those sets of cues that distinguish the left and right alternatives at each choice point, and thus to interpret the result as showing that pre-exposure to these cues facilitates such discrimination learning. But there are obvious alternative interpretations. Pre-exposure might be helpful in Blodgett's procedure simply because it allows the subjects to become habituated to the rather complex experimental apparatus. Or the reinforcement

---

* Bateson and Chantrey (1972) and Bateson (1976) briefly report experiments suggesting that the same pattern of results can be obtained with rhesus monkeys—that exposure to one of the to-be-discriminated stimuli facilitates later discrimination whereas pre-exposure to both will hinder.

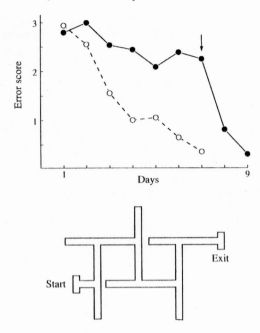

Fig. 7.2   Floor plan of the maze used by Blodgett and the daily error scores of two groups of rats. For one group, food was always presented in the exit box; for the other the arrow marks the day on which food was available there for the first time. (After Tolman 1932.)

of being removed from the exit box might be enough to allow the rats to learn the true path through the maze, either as a sequence of turns or as a sequence of cues that must be followed. The insertion of food in the goal box would then merely serve to allow this learning to be translated into performance—an interesting phenomenon in itself but not one that could apply to the various exposure learning procedures that we have been considering. Subsequent studies of latent learning introduced the use of a variety of control procedures designed to rule out these alternatives. Unfortunately, the effects that remained turn out to be explicable in terms of known conditioning processes rather than in terms of changes in the distinctiveness of the critical stimuli.

An example is the experiment by Seward (1949). Rats were required to learn a single-unit T-maze (i.e. a maze with just one choice point), choosing one distinctive goal box rather than the other. (The goal boxes were not themselves visible from the choice point of the T.) Pre-exposure to the maze produced positive transfer to this task in that pre-exposed subjects when given food in one of the goal boxes and then returned to the start box of the maze, showed a reliable tendency to turn down the arm of the T that led to the goal box containing food. Such a result could be a consequence, in part, of an enhanced ability to discriminate between the cues defining the two arms of the maze; but clearly, as such an ability could not in itself generate correct performance on the very first choice test, there must be something more to it. And indeed, all that we need assume to explain the results is that pre-exposure will allow animals to form an association between each set of choice point stimuli and the goal box it leads to. It follows from what we know of the phenomenon of sensory preconditioning that presenting food in a given goal box will cause the rat to tend to approach the appropriate set of choice-point stimuli. In sensory preconditioning (e.g. Brogden 1939; Rizley and Rescorla 1972), subjects receive initial training designed to allow the formation of a Pavlovian association between two neutral stimuli. If one of these stimuli is then associated with a conventional reinforcer so that it comes to evoke a conditioned response (CR), the other proves to be capable of evoking this same CR. Thus in Seward's (1949) procedure, associating a goal box with food will cause one set of goal-box cues to come to evoke an approach response. The choice-point stimuli that have previously become linked with the goal-box cues will then control an approach response too.

The associative mechanisms at work in Seward's experiment are less adequate as an explanation for a more recent series of latent maze-learning experiments reported by Chamizo and Mackintosh (1989). Rats were tested in a Y-maze in which the two goal arms were distinguished by the nature of their flooring (sandpaper versus rubber). Features of the room itself (extra-maze cues) were visible but not systematically related to which of the arms should be chosen. During pre-exposure the animals experienced both goal arms but one at a time, an arrangement of doors preventing access to other parts of the maze. It is difficult to see how sensory preconditioning occur-ring during such exposure could act to facilitate test performance. Control subjects received equivalent treatment except that for them the maze-arm presented during pre-exposure was always covered with an irrelevant floor-ing, plastic; they were thus allowed to habituate to the test apparatus, much as the experimental subjects were. These two groups differed very little in their test performance (see Fig. 7.3(a)), that is, the latent learning effect was almost eliminated in these conditions. The fact that controls were somewhat worse than pre-exposed subjects is perhaps to be explained by pointing to the fact that these subjects were tested in a situation different from that to which they had become habituated—for control subjects the maze was sur-rounded during pre-exposure by black curtains that were removed during the test phase.

Chamizo and Mackintosh did produce a further result, however, that defies explanation in terms of general habituation or the sensory precondi-tioning process described above. They found that in certain conditions pre-exposure can *retard* later learning. Rats were tested, as before, on the rubber/sandpaper discrimination but to these cues a further (presumably

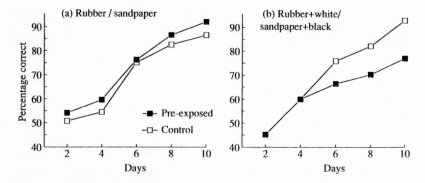

Fig. 7.3 Discrimination performance of rats in a Y-maze after pre-exposure to the critical stimuli. In (a) the choice lay between arms differing in their floor covering; in (b) a redundant brightness difference was also present. (After Chamizo and Mackintosh 1989.)

salient) difference was added—the walls surrounding the sandpaper goal-arm were painted black and those surrounding the rubber arm were painted white. Experimental subjects were pre-exposed to these compound cues; control subjects, as before, experienced the plastic flooring and a maze-arm with unpainted walls. The results, shown in Fig. 7.3(b), revealed a marked superiority in the control condition.

This brief survey of latent learning experiments allows the conclusion that the positive transfer from pre-exposure to maze learning that is evident in classic studies of the phenomenon may often depend on processes other than those usefully regarded as perceptual learning. But our survey has also thrown up a further example of the (rather rare) finding that discrimination learning can be hindered by prior exposure to the cues. A satisfactory account of perceptual learning will need to be able to explain this retardation as well as the more usual facilitatory effect.

7.1.4. Discrimination learning in human subjects

The published record on perception and cognition in humans abounds with instances of experimental studies in which subjects receive pre-exposure to stimuli that are subsequently to be used in some task that involves an element of discrimination. Most of these studies, however, use procedures sufficiently different from those employed in the experiments discussed so far as to make their results of doubtful relevance to the issue at hand. Accordingly I shall restrict consideration to one set of studies in which the procedure used presents what seems to be a rather close parallel to those used in the studies with non-human animals that I have already discussed.

I noted in discussion of acquired distinctiveness (Chapter 5, p. 144) that several experimenters had made use of a control condition in which the subjects were required simply to observe a set of stimuli before being asked to discriminate among them. The focus of attention in these experiments was the difference in test performance (if any) between these subjects and others who learned labels for the stimuli in the first phase of training. But some of these experiments also included a control condition in which subjects were given no experience of the stimuli prior to the test. We can thus make the comparison of central interest in this chapter, comparing the test performance of these controls with that of those allowed to observe the stimuli in initial training. The outcome is almost always that prior observation of the stimuli facilitates subsequent discrimination.

The experiment by Goss (1953) constitutes a typical example. Pre-exposed subjects (undergraduates) simply observed a series of light presentations. Four different intensities were used. They were then trained on a motor task in which a given light intensity signalled which of four switches should be operated. Their performance was superior to that of subjects not previously exposed to lights. Essentially identical results have emerged from similar experiments by Smith and Goss (1955), Holton and Goss (1956), Goss and Greenfield (1958), Pfafflin (1960), and by Vanderplas, Sanderson, and Vanderplas (1964), although in some of these studies the difference between the groups has been reliable only when the pre-exposed group was given specific instructions to attend to the stimuli during pre-exposure.

It is unfortunate that none of these experiments included the control procedure necessary to demonstrate that the positive transfer produced by pre-exposure depends on a mechanism specific to the pre-exposed stimuli. A version of such a control procedure is included in one experiment by G. Cantor (1955), which allows a comparison between subjects pre-exposed to the relevant stimuli with others trained to apply labels to a set of irrelevant stimuli. That these two groups did not differ in their test performance may mean that any sort of pre-training that engages the subject's attention will be sufficient to produce positive transfer. But as the subjects (children) and stimuli (drawings) were quite different from those studied by Goss (1953) and others, it would be inappropriate to extend this conclusion to the experiments discussed earlier and the matter must remain unresolved.

The experiment by Malloy and Ellis (1970; see above, p. 147) avoids some of these problems of interpretation at the expense of introducing others. The design and results of the relevant aspects of their complex experiment are shown in Fig. 7.4. (Omitted from the figure are details of discrimination training with other stimuli that was given concurrently with observation pretraining on the stimuli shown.) Student subjects were allowed to observe two similar geometrical shapes A and A'. They then learned to make R_1 (to say a given word) in response to one of these figures (A), and to respond with a different word (R_2) when presented with a different geometrical

Pre-training	Acquisition	Test
A and A'	$A \rightarrow R_1$	A and A'
	$B \rightarrow R_2$	B and B'

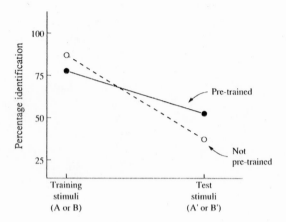

Fig. 7.4 Design and results of part of the experiment of Malloy and Ellis (1970). A and A', B and B' represent stimuli; R_1 and R_2 represent different responses. The test results for the pre-trained case show the percentage of occasions on which R_1 was made to A and A_1; the results labelled 'not pre-trained' show the percentage of occasions on which R_2 was made to B and B'.

figure, B. The test phase assessed the extent to which the response acquired to A generalized to A' and that acquired to B generalized to an equivalently similar figure, B'. Subjects were required to respond with the correct noun for the pre-trained figures, and to respond with 'no' for A' and B'.

Figure 7.4 shows that the A and B stimuli on the whole were identified correctly but that the subjects also showed a tendency to apply the A response to stimulus A' and the B response to stimulus B'. There was, however, substantially more generalization between A and A' than between B and B'. In this procedure, therefore, pre-exposure to the stimuli appears actually to reduce the discriminability of the stimuli rather than to enhance it. Given the many differences between the procedure employed by Malloy and Ellis (1970) and that used in the experiments by Goss (1953) and others, it is impossible to specify at this stage the source of the discrepancy in outcome. We can, however, rule out the possibility that the reduced discrimination observed by Malloy and Ellis is a necessary consequence of their use of a generalization test procedure. The experiments to be discussed next include several examples of enhanced performance after pre-exposure using just this test procedure.

7.1.5. Experiments using conditioning procedures

I have already discussed at some length (in Chapters 3 and 4) the fact that non-reinforced pre-exposure to a stimulus to be used as a conditioned stimulus (CS) will retard subsequent conditioning, that is, will produce latent inhibition. But how will such pre-exposure affect subsequent discrimination? We can attempt to answer this question by investigating the extent to which the conditioned response, once it has been acquired will generalize to another stimulus. And if the experimental subjects are given initial exposure to both the stimuli (both that to be used as the CS and the test stimulus), then a comparison of the generalization shown by these subjects with that shown by controls for whom both stimuli are novel will constitute a very fair parallel to the Gibson–Walk procedure.

Honey and Hall (1989*a*) report just this comparison for rats given flavour-aversion conditioning. Pre-exposed subjects (group A/B in Fig. 7.5(a)) received separate presentations of each of two distinctively flavoured solutions (stimuli A and B). Control subjects (group N) received only water at this stage. All subjects then received a series of trials in which stimulus A was followed by an injection of LiCl. Acquisition of the aversion developed rather more slowly in group A/B than in group N—an instance of the latent inhibition effect—but by the end of the conditioning phase it was firmly established in both groups. Discrimination between A and B was assessed by a final test phase in which B was presented and its generalized tendency to

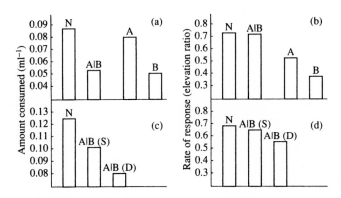

Fig. 7.5 Generalization tests in flavour aversion (panels (a) and (b)) and in appetitive conditioning (panels (c) and (d)) for rats conditioned with stimulus A and tested with stimulus B. Subjects had received pre-exposure to neither (N) stimulus, both (A/B), or to just one of the stimuli. Groups labelled D (in (c) and (d)) received conditioning and test in a context different from that used for pre-exposure; those labelled S were treated identically but did not experience the change of context. (Data from Honey and Hall 1989*a*, from Honey 1990, and from unpublished experiments.)

evoke a CR was measured. As the figure shows, animals in group N tended to reject flavour B, whereas those in group A/B showed little generalization from A to B. Pre-exposure, although it slows initial acquisition to A, appears to enhance the ease with which A and B are discriminated.

Not all conditioning procedures produce this effect. Honey (1990) reports an experiment having the same design as that just described but employing appetitive training in the acquisition phase and using tone and clicker as the two stimuli, A and B. Figure 7.5(b) summarizes the test responding to B shown by groups N and A/B. It is apparent that group A/B shows no less generalization than is shown by group N. This outcome prompted further work using this general training procedure in an attempt to determine if there were any circumstances in which pre-exposure to tone and clicker might reduce generalization between them. In an unpublished study, Hall and Honey investigated the effects of giving the pre-exposure to A and B in one context and conducting conditioning to A and the test with B in a different context. Recall that Channell and Hall (1981), in their exploration of the Gibson–Walk effect, demonstrated that it was necessary to give pre-exposure in the home cage and that pre-exposure to the stimuli in the test apparatus itself (which was the procedure used by Honey (1990)) actually produced a retardation of later discrimination learning. Whatever the source of this latter effect, the general pattern of findings reported by Channell and Hall (1981) prompts the speculation that a facilitation of discrimination after pre-exposure might be observed more readily when there is a change of context.

The results of Hall and Honey's experiment are shown in Fig. 7.5(d). The groups labelled N and A/B(S) match the N and A/B groups of Honey's (1990) experiment. (S stands for same context. These subjects also received experience of a second, distinctively different context, but no presentations of the stimuli occurred in this context.) As before, pre-exposure to A and B did nothing to restrict generalization from A to B. The new results are for group A/B(D). These subjects were treated in the same way as group A/B(S), except that conditioning and the test took place in the other context (D for different). As the figure shows, group A/B(D) animals showed a reduced tendency to generalize from A to B; with a change of context, therefore, pre-exposure to A and B appears to increase the ease with which they are discriminated.

The flavour-aversion results of Fig. 7.5(a) demonstrate that in some circumstances pre-exposure can reduce generalization between the pre-exposed stimuli without there being any change of context. But even here contextual factors still play a part. In an unpublished study, Honey, Coon, and Hall investigated the A/B(D) condition, using flavours as the stimuli. The test performance of these subjects is shown in Fig. 7.5(c), along with that of subjects that experienced no change of context (group A/B(S)) and subjects that had had no pre-exposure to the flavours (group N). The performance of the two latter groups replicates the findings of Honey and Hall (1989*a*) but the reduction in generalization from A to B produced by pre-exposure is even more marked in group A/B(D) than in group A/B(S).

I shall discuss the mechanism by which context change might have this effect later in the chapter. At this point all I need do is discuss two immediate implications of the finding that context change appears to enhance the pre-exposure effect. First it helps to rule out the possibility that the habituation of unconditioned responding is the sole source of the effect. It is no doubt the case that pre-exposure to A and B allows the unconditioned responses (URs) evoked by these stimuli to habituate. The A/B groups in these experiments, therefore, are tested with a familiar B, but the N groups are tested with a novel B that will still evoke its UR. To the extent that the UR mimics the conditioned response of interest, we might be misled into thinking that generalization is more extensive in group N than in group A/B. Habituation of the UR may well contribute to some of the results produced by these experiments (see Honey 1990), but it cannot explain the enhanced pre-exposure effect seen in the A/B(D) groups—there are neither theoretical nor empirical grounds (see Chapter 2) for thinking that a change of context might enhance the degree of habituation produced by pre-exposure elsewhere.

A second implication of these context-change results (Fig. 7.5(c) and (d)) is that they allow an answer to the question raised in discussion of the Channell and Hall (1981) findings. There it was noted that pre-exposure in the home cage helped later discrimination whereas pre-exposure in the apparatus did not. We could not determine whether it was critical that the pre-exposure should occur in the home cage or whether any change of context would do. In neither of the context-change experiments just described was the home cage used as a training context. Contextual change is advantageous even when the pre-exposure context is not the home cage.

Finally, the experiments by Honey and Hall (1989*a*) and by Honey (1990) supply some further evidence on the effects of pre-exposure to just one stimulus. Both of these experiments included groups of subjects that were given pre-exposure either just to stimulus A (the to-be-conditioned stimulus) or just to stimulus B (the test stimulus). The results, shown in Fig. 7.5(a) and Fig. 7.5(b), were essentially the same in both cases. Neither group A nor group B showed as much generalization on test as did the group given no pre-exposure (group N), but the effect produced by pre-exposure to A was small and not statistically reliable, unlike that produced by pre-exposure to B, which was substantial. Again, it is possible that habituation of URs during pre-exposure might have a direct influence on the responding recorded on the test session. In particular, pre-exposure to flavour B would allow any initial neophobic response to habituate and might thus cause animals in group B to consume more of this flavour on test, thereby producing an apparent failure of generalization from A to B (Fig. 7.5(a)). The results from the appetitive conditioning procedure (Fig. 7.5(b)) indicate that habituation of URs is unlikely to be the sole source of the effects observed. In this procedure the UR that habituates during pre-exposure is one that will tend to interfere with the animal's performing the CR. In this case, therefore, pre-exposure to B might be expected to enhance the apparent extent to which generalization occurs. But, as we have seen, here too group B showed rather little tendency to emit the required response. (See Chapter 2, p. 62, for a further discussion of these findings.)

7.1.6. Summary

The effects of non-reinforced pre-exposure on subsequent discrimination have been investigated in a range of species and in a variety of training procedures. Most often these experiments have involved giving pre-exposure to both the stimuli that subsequently are to be discriminated, but in some studies the subjects have been pre-exposed to just one. Usually the test phase has involved discrimination training, with presentation of the reinforced and non-reinforced stimuli occurring concurrently, but in several experiments a two-stage procedure has been used, consisting of a training phase in which a target response is established to one stimulus followed by a generalization test in which the other is presented. These procedural differences do not seem to influence in any systematic way the nature of the results obtained, which may be summarized as follows.

First, exposure to just one stimulus tends to facilitate subsequent discriminative performance. Although habituation of the UR may sometimes contribute directly to the result (as, for instance, when the UR would otherwise tend to compete with the response required in the test phase), such habituation cannot account for many of the cases in which a facilitation has been observed. Studies using a generalization test procedure have detected an asymmetry in the effect. Pre-exposure to the stimulus to be trained as the CS produces a much less dramatic facilitation (when it produces any at all) than does pre-exposure to the stimulus used in the generalization test.

Next, pre-exposure to both the to-be-discriminated stimuli has often been found to facilitate subsequent discrimination, at least when appropriately chosen stimuli and effective training procedures have been used—deficiencies in these can, of course, generate null results. There are, however, several well-established cases in which such pre-exposure has actually resulted in negative transfer to the test task. These cases are very varied. They comprise the experiment by Channell and Hall (1981), which used the Gibson–Walk procedure but gave pre-exposure in the apparatus rather then in the home cage; the report by Chantrey (1972, 1974) of retarded discrimination learning in chicks after some forms of pre-exposure; the study by Malloy and Ellis (1970), showing enhanced generalization of a verbal response in human subjects pre-exposed both to the training and the test stimulus; and finally,

Chamizo and Mackintosh's (1989) demonstration that pre-exposure to distinctively different maze arms can hinder the acquisition of a subsequent simultaneous discrimination between them. Any satisfactory account of pre-exposure effects needs to be able to accommodate these instances of negative transfer as well as the more usually obtained result of positive transfer.

Finally, in procedures that do produce positive transfer, there is some evidence to suggest that the effect is more likely to be found when the stimuli used are difficult to discriminate. And perhaps rather better established is that the likelihood or magnitude of positive transfer is increased when there is a change of context from pre-exposure to the test phase. These factors too will constrain and guide the theories to be described next.

7.2. Theoretical interpretation

The differentiation theory discussed in Chapter 5 assumes that mere exposure to a stimulus will allow subjects to come to detect features of that object that initially were incapable of evoking a response. Given certain further assumptions, this suggestion is capable of predicting that exposure will enhance the discriminability of pre-exposed stimuli (see Fig. 5.11), and thus of accommodating the most common outcome of the experiments just described. There are, however, several other possible explanations for the effects of pre-exposure, most of which rely on learning processes that are well known from studies of other procedures and that must (it can be assumed) be operating in these experiments too. Evaluation of the differentiation notion can best be achieved by assessing the validity of its (rather better specified) rivals. In fact, proponents of differentiation would probably not deny that other processes occur during stimulus exposure—extra processes will be needed to explain the details of the conditions under which positive transfer occurs and why, in some circumstances, the effect of pre-exposure should be deleterious. But once these other processes have been explored to the full, will there be anything left for differentiation to explain?

7.2.1. The role of novelty and familiarity

(a) Novelty and familiarity as stimulus elements

The ease with which two stimuli can be discriminated (or the degree to which generalization occurs between them) we have assumed to depend on the extent to which they have effective features or elements in common. In the representation used in Figs. 5.10 and 5.11, each stimulus is taken to possess a number of unique features and a set that it holds in common with the other. The elements are usually taken to be intrinsic properties of the objects or events in question—a triangle and circle might have a common feature in their colour; having straight edges or a curving contour would be unique elements. But it has been suggested by a number of theorists (perhaps most recently and explicitly by Honey (1990); see also Best and Batson (1977)) that the property of being novel should be regarded as being a feature of a stimulus, equivalent in most functional respects to any intrinsic feature. The feature of novelty, however, would obviously be lost as a result of experience with the stimulus to be replaced, we may assume, by a property that we can call familiarity. A loss of novelty would, of course, be reflected in (or be paralleled by, or might be a consequence of) the habituation of the UR. Discussion of the experiments described above raised from time to time the possibility that changes in the strength of the UR might directly contribute to some of the effects observed. My concern is no longer with such direct effects but with the consequences of the proposal that novelty (and familiarity) can function as stimulus features like any other.

An implication of this proposal is that animals should be able to discriminate between novel and familiar stimuli, that is, perform adequately on tasks of recognition memory in which the correct response to a stimulus is determined by whether or not that stimulus has been encountered before. The usual way of assessing the abilities of non-human animals in this respect has been to make use of a version of matching to sample (see above, p. 158). Subjects are exposed to a sample stimulus and then given a choice between the sample and some other stimulus, their task being to respond to the pre-exposed stimulus. The actual events used as the stimuli are changed from time to time so that adequate performance requires that novelty and (or) familiarity be used as the cues. This technique has been used successfully to demonstrate novelty/familiarity discrimination in a range of species (e.g. Wright, Santiago, Urcuioli, and Sands 1983; D'Amato, Salmon, and Colombo 1985; Wilson, Mackintosh, and Boakes 1985). A rather different and in principle somewhat simpler procedure has been used by Macphail and Reilly (1989) to demonstrate the phenomenon in pigeons. The stimuli used were drawn from a large pool of different photographic slides depicting a variety of natural scenes. Each slide was presented on only two occasions—on the first, pecks to the slide were reinforced and on the second they were not. As Fig. 7.6 shows, over the course of training with many slides (in each session, 24 new slides were presented) the subjects came to respond reliably more rapidly on a first presentation than on a second, implying that they had learned, in essence, that novel slides were associated with reward and familiar slides were not.

It may seem surprising that subjects so apparently lacking in highly developed intellectual powers as pigeons should be able to form what appears to amount to a 'same–different' concept. But the abilities required perhaps involve little more than those involved in simple habituation. On first presentation a stimulus will evoke its characteristic UR but on subsequent presentations the UR will be less vigorous or even absent; in some cases, indeed, it may be replaced by some other response, as when an initial defensive response gives way to exploratory behaviour. A novel stimulus therefore

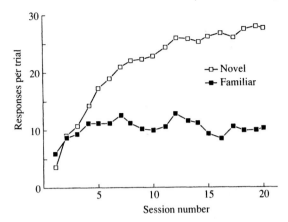

Fig. 7.6 Performance of pigeons on a discrimination in which a given pictorial stimulus is presented only twice, pecks to it being rewarded on the first presentation but not on the second. (After Macphail and Reilly 1989.)

incorporates a set of cues (perhaps central events associated with emitting the UR, perhaps feedback stimuli from the response, perhaps both) that a familiar stimulus lacks. These differences between novel and familiar stimuli may be a product of habituation but there is no reason to suppose that they will be any less able to support discrimination learning than a difference that is present from the outset. Discrimination may very well not be easy, as the stimuli, being physically identical, will have a lot of elements in common; but this fact introduces no special factors—the essence of all discrimination learning is that behaviour comes to be controlled by unique features of the stimuli rather than by features that they hold in common.

(b) Novelty as a general process

The notion of novelty put forward here has something in common with that considered in Chapter 3 in the course of the discussion of flavour neophobia. It differs, however, in the extent to which novelty is taken to be general process. My account of the results of Macphail and Reilly (1989) identifies the novelty of a stimulus with its ability to evoke its UR. The effects of training will therefore be specific to stimuli that tend to evoke the same UR (presumably, all pictorial slides tend to evoke more or less the same UR). Some analyses of flavour neophobia, however, have argued that novelty should be regarded as a general process, not necessarily tied to the specific properties of the stimuli being used (e.g. Braveman 1978; Braveman and Jarvis 1978; Miller and Holzman 1981; Franchina and Gilley 1986). Evidence taken to favour this latter interpretation has come largely from studies of the generalization of habituation.

Pre-exposure to one flavour can attenuate the neophobia shown to another (Siegel 1974), a result that is readily interpreted by assuming that the test flavour has elements in common with the pre-exposed flavour and that these elements, as a result of habituation, make no contribution to the neophobia shown on test. But if novelty is a general process, then pre-exposure to one flavour might influence the neophobia shown to a second, even when the two have no elements in common. In the formulation offered by Braveman and Jarvis (1978), neophobia is interpreted as being a reaction to the aversive property of novelty *per se*, and experience of any novel event reduces the aversiveness of novelty and thus will attenuate the neophobia evoked by another. This account is clearly less parsimonious than one that directly equates loss of neophobia with habituation of the UR evoked by a novel flavour; and further, it runs the risk, as Miller and Holzman (1981) have noted, of making the unfortunate prediction that thorough exposure to one event might eliminate any tendency to show neophobia to any other stimulus. Unless the experimental evidence dictates otherwise, it seems prudent to remain with our original, more specific, interpretation of novelty.

The relevant evidence comes from studies that try to demonstrate a loss of neophobia in a test flavour consequent on pre-exposure to a supposedly quite different stimulus presumed to have no (physically defined) elements in common with it. Sometimes several pre-exposure stimuli are used so as to ensure that exposure to novelty is maximized (the implicit assumption being that exposure to a stimulus not only causes novelty to lose aversiveness but also causes a loss of novelty). The extent to which we are likely to be impressed when a loss of neophobia is produced by such pre-exposure procedures will depend on the extent to which we are convinced that the pre-exposed and test stimuli do not share orthodox, common elements. Attempts to establish that they do not have largely relied on demonstrations that these pre-exposure procedures do not induce latent inhibition in the test stimulus (the assumption here being that only exposure to 'real' common elements, rather than the common element of novelty will be capable of retarding conditioning to the test stimulus). But, as the review of these experiments in Chapter 3 (pp. 73–5) concluded, the failure to find latent inhibition after such pre-exposure may reflect nothing more than the insensitivity of the latent inhibition test procedure.

Braveman (1978) presented a series of experiments which made no attempt to demonstrate that the pre-exposure and test stimuli did not share common elements (other than novelty itself). But the choice of stimuli was such as perhaps to render this possibility implausible. In one of the experiments, for instance, the test stimulus was saccharin and the pre-exposure procedure involved the subjects (rats) in being transferred for a brief period each day for 21 days to a cage that was rather different from the home cage. Rats given this experience showed less neophobia to saccharin than did others that had remained at home during the pre-exposure phase. This result is consistent with the notion that novelty should be regarded as a general process but there is an alternative interpretation. As Braveman acknowledges, his pre-exposure procedures might have their effects by reducing the rat's general level of emotional reactivity (in the way that early handling has sometimes been thought to do; e.g. Levine (1957); Denenberg (1964)). This latter interpretation does not need to suppose that the novelty of the pre-exposure stimuli is critical in their producing the effects they do on test performance, and thus does not require the assumption that the rat is capable of detecting a highly abstract property of novelty common to physically very different events.

An experiment by Franchina and Gilley (1986) approaches this issue in a slightly different way, making use of a flavour-aversion conditioning procedure. They demonstrated that rats conditioned to one flavour (A) showed an aversion to a different test flavour (B) but that for other subjects, given preliminary exposure to a third flavour (C), the magnitude of this generalized aversion was somewhat reduced. Franchina and Gilley interpret the tendency of rats to shun flavour B as an instance of poisoning-enhanced neophobia—prior conditioning to A, they suggest, augments the rats' normal reaction to the novel B (Franchina and Fitzgerald 1983). But pre-exposure to a distinctive novel C will attenuate the aversiveness of novelty *per se* and thus restrict the degree of neophobia governed by B. As novelty is taken to be a general process, it will not matter, according to this account, that this habituation process is occurring to the novelty evoked by a stimulus quite different from that used in the test phase. An alternative interpretation emerges, however, if it is allowed (as seems quite likely given the specific flavours used by Franchina and Gilley) that the three stimuli were not all quite dissimilar from one another. If it is assumed that the CS A and the test stimulus B hold elements in common, then the aversion controlled by B can be taken to be an orthodox instance of stimulus generalization. The pre-exposure stimulus C and the CS A were clearly rather different from one another because pre-exposure produced no sign of latent inhibition during conditioning to A; but C and B might well have had elements in common, in which case habituation of neophobia to C would have had a direct effect on the performance shown to B, attenuating the extent to which consumption was suppressed.

Whatever the merits of these various arguments, it seems safe to conclude that there is, as yet, no requirement to suppose that novelty should be regarded as a general process. Accordingly we may stay with the simpler hypothesis, which interprets a novel stimulus as being one that evokes its UR and a familiar stimulus as one that does not. Our concern now is with the implications of the suggestion that the cues associated with novelty and familiarity (defined in this way) can acquire associative strength and mediate generalization between stimuli in just the same way as can elements that are unconditionally present in the stimuli. This assumption is, of course, no different from that underlying the associative account of acquired distinctive-

Table 7.1 Elements present in stimuli A and B after various forms of pre-exposure

	A (CS)	B (test stimulus)
No pre-exposure	*a,c,n*	*b,c,n*
Pre-exposure to A and B	*a,c,f*	*b,c,f*
Pre-exposure to A	*a,c,f*	*b,c,n*
Pre-exposure to B	*a,c,n*	*b,c,f*

A and B are stimuli; lower case italic letters represent notional elements of which they are composed. Elements unique to A are labelled *a*, those unique to B are labelled *b*; *c* represents common elements apart from those deriving from novelty (*n*) or familiarity (*f*).

ness and equivalence of cues (see Chapter 5). It differs only in that the mediating elements are not assumed to be the direct product of associative learning.

(c) Implications of this analysis

The most obvious implication of this analysis for our present concerns is that pre-exposure to just one of the stimuli to be discriminated can be expected to facilitate discrimination because it will establish a difference between the stimuli along the novelty/familiarity dimension. For a control subject trained with stimulus A as a CS (see Fig. 7.5), stimulus novelty will be one of the features that gains strength (at least during the early trials of conditioning). A novel test stimulus, B, will thus be able to evoke the same response by virtue of the common element of novelty. Pre-exposure to B before the start of conditioning will, however, deprive the stimulus of its novelty and thus remove this source of generalization.

On the face of things, it might seem to be a problem for this account that pre-exposure to A, which should also establish a difference between A and B in novelty/familiarity, is less effective than pre-exposure to B in reducing the degree of generalization between the stimuli. Reasons why such an asymmetry might occur become apparent when we consider Table 7.1, which attempts to represent the important stimulus elements that are responsible for generalization between A and B in these procedures. It shows that what we need consider in our analysis is the associative strength gained by the features 'novelty' (*n*) and 'familiarity' (*f*), and by the elements that are unconditionally common to both stimuli (*c*). The unique features of the two stimuli (*a* and *b*) are, by definition, not responsible for generalization between them. Now generalization between A and B, when neither has received pre-exposure, will occur on the basis both of the *c* and *n* elements; pre-exposure to B, which removes the *n* element from the test stimulus, will thus restrict generalization to that mediated by the *c* elements. But why should not pre-exposure to A, which removes the *n* element from the CS, also produce this effect?

One possible answer to this question emerges when we consider the role of overshadowing. It is known (Carr 1974) that pre-exposure to one element of a compound stimulus reduces the extent to which that element is capable of overshadowing the other when the compound is used as a CS. The same effect can be presumed to occur for conditioning to the compounds shown in Table 7.1. Thus pre-exposure to A will reduce the ability of the pre-exposed *a* elements to overshadow the other elements present during conditioning; the relevant consequence is that the *c* elements will gain more strength in this case than after exposure to B which will, of course, be ineffective in reducing the ability of the *a* elements to overshadow. If the *c* elements have higher associative strength, generalized responding to B on test will be more likely.

There is a further reason why overshadowing of the *c* elements might be more profound after pre-exposure to B than after pre-exposure to A. Although no more than an assumption at this stage, it is at least plausible that novelty is a more salient stimulus element than is familiarity, particularly so, perhaps, if novelty is equated with the ability of a stimulus to evoke its UR. The more salient a stimulus, the more effective it is at overshadowing when it is trained in compound with some other (Mackintosh 1976). It follows that the salient *n* element present after pre-exposure to B should be more effective at overshadowing *c* than the less salient *f* element that is present after pre-exposure to A itself. The consequence will again be that *c* will gain more associative strength in the latter case and thus generalization to B will be more substantial.

The notion that novelty might be much more salient than familiarity is of special importance in that it allows the possibility of explaining what is, after all, the basic effect of interest—the facilitation of discrimination produced by pre-exposure to both A and B, compared to the case in which no pre-exposure is given. As neither of these training conditions generates a difference between A and B in novelty/familiarity (see Table 7.1) it might be thought that no explanation is available in these terms. But if it is allowed that *n* is a very salient element, then generalization from A to B will be more likely when neither has been pre-exposed (both have the *n* element) than when both have been pre-exposed and generalization depends (at least in part) on the associative strength acquired by *f*. If this effect is large enough to overcome the various overshadowing effects (on *c*) that will also be operating here, then an overall facilitation of discrimination in the group pre-exposed to both stimuli might result.

In spite of these successes it cannot be supposed that generalization on the basis of novelty or familiarity is the sole source of all the various pre-exposure phenomena—it supplies no explanation, for instance, of the effects of context or of why pre-exposure should sometimes hinder subsequent discrimination. Further processes must be involved.

7.2.2. Latent inhibition

Prior non-reinforced exposure to a stimulus to be used as a CS will retard subsequent conditioning, in part because the stimulus suffers a loss of associability and also because associations may be formed that will interfere with the formation of the new association or compete with it when retrieval is required (see Chapter 3 and 4). We can assume that the processes responsible for latent inhibition will be operative during the pre-exposure phase of the experiments discussed in this chapter. We must consider, therefore, what their effect will be when the test procedure involves not simple conditioning but a discrimination task.

The simplest case to analyse is that in which the subjects are pre-exposed to A and B, given conditioning to A and are then tested for generalization to B.* As Table 7.1 shows (but ignoring now the stimulus elements n and f, whose role has already been discussed), conditioning occurs to elements a and c, and testing occurs with b and c. The extent of generalization will be determined by the associative strength acquired by the c elements. We need to consider, therefore, how pre-exposure to A and B will influence the strength acquired by these elements.

For subjects not given pre-exposure, both a and c will acquire associative strength, the amount acquired by each being determined, according to current associative theory, by their relative saliences. After pre-exposure, conditioning will proceed more slowly because of latent inhibition. Eventually, however, the same asymptote will be reached as in the nonpre-exposed case but the associative strength will be distributed differently between the elements. The c elements will be particularly poor at acquiring strength, as they will have undergone twice as much latent inhibition training as the a elements. The a elements undergo latent inhibition only when A is exposed but the c elements, by definition, are present both when A occurs and also when B occurs. Because pre-exposure to A and B limits the acquisition of strength by c, generalization from A to B will be restricted, that is, the discrimination between the stimuli will be enhanced. It may be apparent that pre-exposure to just stimulus A or to just stimulus B will also be capable of reducing generalization between A and B by way of reducing the associability of the c elements. It will also be clear that the effects will be smaller than those produced by exposure to both A and B.

The analysis just offered is one of the mechanisms for perceptual learning proposed by McLaren, Kaye, and Mackintosh (1989). As evidence in its favour they point out that it can provide an explanation for the negative transfer effect demonstrated by Chamizo and Mackintosh (1989). Their

---

* The situation is a little more complex when the test involves discrimination training with concurrent reinforcement of A and non-reinforcement of B, but arguments in principle the same as those about to be outlined can apply in this case too.

results showed (see Fig. 7.3) that pre-exposure to the two maze arms to be discriminated hindered later learning when the arms differed both in the texture of their floors and in the colour of their walls; but the retarding effect of pre-exposure was abolished (indeed, marginally reversed) when the maze arms differed only in texture. Chamizo and Mackintosh interpret the procedure of eliminating the colour difference as being one in which the proportion of common elements is increased—the salient black–white difference may be presumed to suppress or eliminate the processing that common elements would otherwise receive. When black and white are present, therefore, the only significant consequence of pre-exposure is that each of these cues would undergo latent inhibition and test performance would be hindered. When common elements are present (i.e. when black and white are absent) the pre-exposure processes that tend to facilitate later learning can come into play. That is, the fact that the c elements receive a double measure could compensate for the latent inhibition accruing to unique elements in the condition where many c elements are present.

In spite of these successes, a problem for the analysis offered here arises from the fact that latent inhibition shows context-specificity. We have noted that the effects of pre-exposure on discrimination survive and are even enhanced by a change of context. How then can these effects be determined by a process that does not readily survive a change of context? One approach to an answer to this question comes if we note that latent inhibition may often be only attenuated and not totally abolished by a change of context. A change of context can be expected to eliminate the contribution of associative interference to the effect, but the consequences of a reduction in the α-value of the pre-exposed stimulus should still be evident. To the extent that some degree of latent inhibition transfers across contexts we can still expect that conditioning to c will be particularly slow after prior exposure to A and B. In order to explain why a change of context might actually enhance the effects of pre-exposure, we need to consider the implications of the fact that the associative component of the latent inhibition effect will be abolished by a change of context.

7.2.3. Acquired equivalence and the role of context

In the experiment by Malloy and Ellis (1970), subjects showed *more* generalization between the pre-exposed stimuli A and A' than between the novel stimuli B and B' (see Fig. 7.4.). Malloy and Ellis explain this negative transfer effect as a case of acquired equivalence. Their subjects, they suggest, come to make the common response of 'no response' to both A and A'. Now, we have already seen (Chapter 5; see Fig. 5.10(a)) that a common associate can act to mediate generalization between two stimuli. The common associate of A and A' could be expected to reduce the discriminability of these cues. What makes this account particularly plausible is that during pre-training the subjects received not just pre-exposure to A and A' but also experience of other stimuli to which specified verbal responses had to be made. The stimuli A and A.' were thus unique in that no verbal response was required, and it may well have been necessary for subjects to learn to inhibit a tendency to say something in response to them.

The effectiveness of a pre-exposure procedure in generating acquired equivalence and negative transfer will presumably depend on the salience of the event that acts as the common associate. A procedure that endows both the stimuli with inhibitory properties might be especially effective in this respect. It is quite possible, however, that even conditions of pre-exposure that are unlikely to generate inhibitory learning might establish a common associate for the two stimuli. I have considered the possibility that latent inhibition might derive, in part, from the effects of a stimulus–no event association. Although unlikely to be salient, this associate, too, might be capable of mediating generalization to some extent. The negative transfer so produced might not be sufficient to outweigh other factors tending to produce positive transfer but it would limit the size of the latter effect.

Whatever the nature of the associate, acquired equivalence can be expected only when the associative learning that occurs during pre-exposure carries over to the test phase. Now the evidence presented in Chapter 4 showed that associative learning tends to be context-specific—it was argued that appropriate contextual cues must be present for a subject fully to retrieve associative information. It follows that the acquired equivalence effect generated by pre-exposure to pair of stimuli will be attenuated or abolished if the discrimination task is conducted in a context other than that used for pre-exposure. It is in such conditions, therefore, that the facilitatory effects of pre-exposure on discrimination are likely to prevail; and this, of course, is what the experimental results show.

An implication of the analysis presented here is that changing the context from the pre-exposure phase to the test phase should have different effects when the subjects have been pre-exposed to one of the test stimuli from those it has when both stimuli have been pre-exposed. In the latter case, to repeat, a change of context will, by attenuating acquired equivalence, increase the probability that a facilitation of discrimination will be observed. In the former case, however, the facilitatory effect of pre-exposure might well be reduced. Pre-exposure to B, I have argued, facilitates the A/B discrimination by establishing a difference between the stimuli along the novelty/familiarity dimension (by habituating the UR to B) and by reducing the associability of the c elements. These effects should survive a change of context. But the pre-exposure procedure will also allow associative learning that might give rise to an acquired *distinctiveness* effect ——B will also have entered into an association with a no-event representation whereas A will not. And if acquired distinctiveness contributes to the enhanced discrimination seen after pre-exposure, the magnitude of the enhancement should be

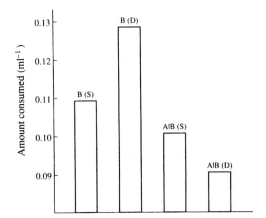

Fig. 7.7 Generalization test in flavour aversion for rats conditioned with A and tested with B. Subjects had received pre-exposure to both stimuli (A/B) or just to flavour B. Groups labelled D received conditioning and test in a context other than that used for pre-exposure; groups labelled S did not experience a change of context. (From an unpublished experiment by Honey, Coon, and Hall.)

reduced by a change of context which will attenuate the acquired distinctiveness effect.

Figure 7.7 presents the results of an experiment (conducted in collaboration with R. Honey and R. Coon) designed to investigate these suggestions. Rats were pre-exposed either to two flavours A and B (presented separately) or just to flavour B. They then received aversion conditioning with A as the CS, followed by a generalization test with B as the test stimulus. For half the subjects in each pre-exposure condition the context was changed for conditioning and the test; for the remainder the context stayed the same. As the figure shows, subjects pre-exposed to both A and B showed better discrimination (worse generalization) when the context was changed (and thus the effect shown in Fig. 7.5(c) is replicated here). But for subjects pre-exposed to B the reverse was true; that is, discrimination was somewhat poorer (generalization was more substantial) in the condition in which the context was changed. This pattern of results appears to be uniquely predicted by the analysis of pre-exposure effects in terms of context-dependent acquired equivalence and distinctiveness.

7.2.4. Sensory preconditioning

In sensory preconditioning (SPC) the subject is given pre-exposure to two neutral events (say A and B) that are presented close together in space and time (sometimes as a simultaneous compound). One of these (A) is then established as a CS and the extent of generalization to B is assessed. As noted in discussion of latent learning (p. 215), studies of discrimination after non-reinforced preexposure can often be interpreted as being versions of the SPC procedure. We need to consider, therefore, the explanations that have been put forward for SPC and how these might apply to the procedures of primary interest in this chapter.

The usual outcome of SPC is that pre-training with A and B permits generalization to occur from A to B. It is possible to distinguish two types of explanation for this result, perceptual and associative. Discussion of the perceptual account will be postponed until the end of the chapter. The most straightforward associative account holds that pre-exposure to A and B permits links to be formed between them under the same conditions as, and obeying the same laws as, those formed during orthodox Pavlovian conditioning. Conditioning with A establishes an A–US association and presentation of B is then able to make contact with the US representation by way of the associative chain B–A–US. Stimulus B is thus able to evoke the CR.

It will be recalled (from Chapter 5) that the associative account of acquired equivalence and distinctiveness was based on the suggestion that associatively activated representations are capable of entering into associations. Applying this principle to the SPC procedure reveals a further way in which associative processes might generate the result observed (see Rescorla and Cunningham 1978). The A–B association formed during pre-exposure might allow A to activate a representation of B during the conditioning phase. If so, an association between this representation and the US will then be formed at this stage, allowing the presentation of stimulus B on test to contact the US representation directly. This mechanism will operate only if A is able to evoke the B representation, and thus will probably not apply to those SPC experiments that arrange for B to precede A in the initial phase of training—most theories of conditioning (Chapter 1) assume that this arrangement will allow the formation on an excitatory link from B to A but not from A to B. But most associative theorists are content to assume that presenting A and B as a simultaneous compound will allow both A–B and B–A associations to be formed (see, e.g. Rescorla and Durlach 1981). The conditioning of associatively activated representations thus constitutes an additional way in which the SPC effect might occur after such pre-training.

(a) Between-stimulus links and negative transfer

If during the pre-exposure phase of an experiment of the Gibson–Walk type, the subject formed an association between the two critical stimuli, the consequence would be a retardation of subsequent discrimination. The associative strength acquired by stimulus A in the test phase would transfer to B by one of the SPC mechanisms just outlined, making it difficult for the subject to come to emit different responses to the two stimuli. That discrimination is not usually retarded by pre-exposure must mean that this SPC process does not usually make a major contribution to the outcome. And this is to be expected. The A and B stimuli are not in these experiments presented as a simultaneous compound. Sometimes they are presented successively (e.g. Honey and Hall 1989) and when they are presented simultaneously (as in the original Gibson–Walk procedure) it is open to the subject to inspect them separately at widely spaced intervals (see Bateson and Chantrey 1972). These are not conditions likely to induce the subject to form an A–B association.

There is, however, one procedure in which the conditions seem right for the formation of an A–B association. In one set of experiments, Chantrey (1974) (see also Chantrey 1972) arranged for chicks to receive pre-exposure in which the critical stimuli (distinctively coloured cylinders) were passed repeatedly in front of their pens, one after the other in quick succession. Stimulus A moved across the birds line of sight for 7 s and then was followed, after a gap of 8 s, by 7 s of stimulus B, and so on. The result of this treatment was that the birds learned a subsequent food-rewarded discrimination between the two cylinders less well than did subjects for whom the colours were unfamiliar—just the results that would be expected on the basis of SPC.

The explanation offered by Chantrey himself (see also Bateson and Chantrey 1972; Bateson 1973), although it uses different terminology, is not fundamentally different from that to be derived from considerations of SPC. He suggested that when animals experience two objects in the same context occurring in close temporal contiguity they tend to 'classify them together' in some way. Such a tendency would, it is argued, interfere with subsequent discrimination learning in which the subjects presumably have to classify the two stimuli apart in order to make different responses to them. Bateson's (1973) chief concern is with the functional implications of thus possible process for a phenomenon like imprinting in which a chick must learn that the various aspects of a rapidly changing object (such as the various views it sees of its mother as she moves about) share the same identity. There is less concern with the mechanism by which classifying together might be achieved and have its effects; but clearly, SPC is a very plausible candidate.

Although it is perhaps the most obvious case, the possibility that pre-exposure might allow the formation of excitatory A–B associations is just one of the ways in which SPC might influence the outcome of these experiments. As SPC can occur when the stimuli are presented as part of a simultaneous compound (Rescorla and Durlach 1981), we must also consider the role played by within-stimulus associations (i.e. among the various features of A itself and of B itself). We shall see, to anticipate, that this possibility has a long tradition as a theory of perceptual learning but that it fares rather poorly as an explanation of the effects of pre-exposure on discrimination learning.

(b) The role of within-stimulus links

One of the earliest attempts to provide an analytic account of the phenomena of perceptual learning, that proposed by Hebb (1949), relies on what amounts to an associative interpretation of the SPC that occurs during exposure to a simultaneous compound. Objects of the sort referred to as 'stimuli' by an experimenter consist, according to Hebb, of a number of identifiable features. Hebb considers the example of a triangle, its features being corners, straight edges, and so on. It is assumed that animals have an unconditional ability to detect such features and a tendency to scan them. Detecting a feature activates its central representation ('cell assembly' in Hebb's terminology) and the various representations of the various features will thus be activated together as the animal scans. Excitatory associations are formed between cell assemblies that are activated together (they become 'mutually facilitatory' in Hebb's phrase) and these links establish a 'super-ordinate structure' that constitutes the cerebral representation of the entire stimulus. As Hebb remarks: 'the idea that one has to learn to see a triangle sounds extremely improbable' but in fact 'the perception of simple diagrams as distinctive wholes is not immediately given but slowly acquired through learning' (Hebb 1949, p. 35).

The notion that pre-exposure to a stimulus will allow the formation of links between its constituent parts has implications for the course of simple conditioning. It is commonly assumed that of the many elements of a complex stimulus only some will be sampled on a given trial; that is, only some features will activate their representations (see, e.g. Estes 1950; McLaren *et al.* 1989). If this trial is a conditioning trial, then only the sampled elements will form associations with the reinforcer. Accordingly, if on the next presentation of the stimulus the subject happens to sample a different set of elements, no conditioned responding will occur; or at least, no responding will occur in subjects not given initial pre-exposure to the stimulus. But for a subject that has received pre-exposure, links are likely to have been formed between the elements conditioned on the first trial and those sampled on the second. The associative accounts of SPC discussed above allow the prediction that in this case conditioned responding could still occur. Pre-exposure, therefore, should speed the course of acquisition.

There is little to suggest that the process just outlined plays anything but a minor role in our usual training procedures. Pre-exposure to a stimulus usually results in latent inhibition, and even when attempts are made to reduce the contribution of this effect by changing the context between pre-exposure and conditioning, there is no good evidence to show that conditioning can actually be enhanced. It may be, of course, that a change of context reduces the effectiveness not only of the mechanisms responsible for latent inhibition but also fo the within-stimulus associations responsible for the SPC effect. It could also be that the stimuli that have been used in the relevant experiments have been too simple for SPC to exert much of an effect—after all, if a stimulus is so simple that all its features can be sampled on every trial, the existence of within-stimulus links will bestow no advan-

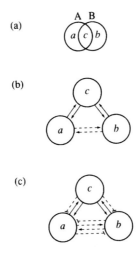

Fig. 7.8 The circles in panel (a) represent the stimuli A and B with their common elements, *c*, and their unique elements, *a* and *b*. Panels (b) and (c) show the associative links that can be formed among these elements. Solid lines represent standard excitatory links; dashed lines represent links formed when one of the elements is activated associatively rather than directly. A stopped end indicates an inhibitory link and an arrow an excitatory link.

tage on the pre-exposed subjects.* This last point is of interest, given the hint, presented by my survey of the experimental work, that pre-exposure is more likely to produce positive transfer to a discrimination task when the stimuli to be discriminated are complex.

Our main concern is not with simple conditioning but with the effects of pre-exposure on discrimination. Here, as we have noted before, the critical factor is the role played by the (possibly many) features or elements that the two stimuli to be discriminated might share. Figure 7.8(a) reproduces the representation used earlier of two stimuli A and B having unique elements (*a* and *b* respectively) and common elements (*c*). No matter how much pre-exposure facilitates the acquisition of associative strength by A, discrimination will not be improved unless it also acts to prevent generalization of this strength to B. On the face of things, pre-exposure might be expected to make things worse.

Figure 7.8(b) represents the within-stimulus excitatory associations that will be formed during pre-exposure, lumping together all the *a*, *b*, and *c* elements and treating them, for the sake of convenience, as single stimuli. Exposure to A will create excitatory *a–c* links and exposure to B, excitatory

---

* Fanselow (1990) has recently produced results consistent with the suggestion that preexposure to a complex cue (in his experiments, the context itself) might promote conditioning to that cue.

b–c links. As a consequence, a conditioning trial with A will allow *c* to gain strength, even if the subject happens to sample *a* on that trial; and B will be capable of evoking the trained response even if only the *b* elements are sampled, because these will be able to contact the *c* elements too. And there are two further reasons why the associative structure shown in Fig. 7.8(b) should produce poor discrimination. First, presentation of A will be able to activate the representation of *b* on a conditioning trial by way of the associative chain *a–c–b*, thus allowing *b* to gain associative strength directly. Next, we accepted in discussion of acquired equivalence (Chapter 5) that an excitatory association can be formed between the associatively activated representation of a stimulus and some other event. In this case, therefore, presentation of B will activate *a* associatively (by way of *c*), will activate *b* directly, and an *a–b* association will form. Similarly, presentation of A will produce a *b–a* link (see Fig. 7.8(b)).* The presence of these links will then act to promote generalization between A and B even when the conditions of exposure are not such as to allow the formation of a direct A–B association.

It seems clear that the formation of within-stimulus associations during pre-exposure is only going to hinder subsequent discrimination. Indeed, given the profusion of mechanisms tending to generate poor discrimination, it may seem little short of a miracle that those processes that tend to facilitate discrimination can so often win out. One possibility is that factors not yet considered might act to limit the role of these within-stimulus associations. In particular, the usual pre-exposure procedure may actually be rather a poor one for establishing strong associations between unique and common elements. Although, for instance, *a* and *c* elements always occur together then A is presented, the *c* elements also appear in the absence of A (when B is presented). An imperfect correlation of this sort will limit the growth of the *a–c* association. (Similar considerations apply, of course to the *b–c* association). To this extent at least, the role of associations, involving the *c* elements in producing generalization from A to B might be limited. Some theorists, however, have gone further than this. MacLaren *et al.* (1989) introduce a new process which allows the possibility that associations among elements *a*, *b*, and *c* might in some circumstances help to promote discrimination between A and B. I consider their proposal next.

(c) Between-stimulus links and positive transfer

If 'classifying together' can be responsible for the negative transfer that occurs after some forms of pre-exposure, then it seems worth pursuing the possibility (also put forward by Bateson and Chantrey, (1972)) that when positive transfer occurs it is the result of a process of classifying apart. Inter-

---

* For the sake of completeness it should be added that analogous processes will mean that the presentation of A will strengthen the *b–c* link, and presentation of B will strengthen the *a–c* link.

preted in terms of SPC, the suggestion is that some pre-exposure procedures might result in the formation not of excitatory but of inhibitory links between aspects of A and B. Conditioning with A would not, therefore, endow the representation of B with associative strength as any tendency for the B representation to be activated on conditioning trials would be inhibited by the presence of A. And any tendency for B to activate the A representation on test (and thus evoke the conditioned response) would be suppresed in subjects having inhibitory A–B links. In these ways, generalization between A and B would be reduced and positive transfer from pre-exposure to the A/B discrimination would be observed.

Such inhibitory effects could put pre-exposed subjects at an advantage only to the extent that they acted to combat the effects of the excitatory associations shown in Fig. 7.8. No such associations will be present when the stimuli are encountered for the first time at the start of discrimination training but it is likely that, during the course of training, *a* may acquire the ability to activate the *b* representation (and vice versa) either by way of the mediation provided by the *c* elements (as discussed above) or directly. A direct association might be formed when, for instance, a subject is required to learn a simultaneous discrimination with A and B displayed side by side. The temporal and spatial contiguity of the two stimuli would encourage the information of A–B links. Such links would be difficult to form, however, in subjects with pre-existing inhibitory links and thus pre-exposure can be expected to facilitate discrimination.

It remains to explain why inhibitory links should be formed during pre-exposure. Bateson and Chantrey (1972) (see also Chantrey 1972, 1974) simply assume that conditions of pre-exposure in which the stimuli are experienced widely separated in space or time or both will foster a tendency to 'classify apart'. McLaren *et al.* (1989) take things further, demonstrating that the formation of inhibitory links is a necessary consequence of the assumptions of standard associative learning theory. Figure 7.8(b) shows the associative structure that pre-exposure will produce initially—direct excitatory links between *a* and *c* and between *b* and *c*; links between *a* and *b* formed by virtue of the fact that one of these features will be associatively activated when the other is presented. But this will not be the whole story. The figure shows only the excitatory links produced by presenting a stimulus when some other representation is associatively activated. There will, however, be associations formed in the other direction and these will be inhibitory. In terms of Wagner's (1981) theory, as may be recalled from Chapter 1, an inhibitory connection is formed when the CS is in the A1 state and the US representation in the A2 state. In other words, an inhibitory connection is formed when the one representation is directly activated by the presentation of a stimulus, and its target representation is activated associatively. The outcome, for the case we are considering, will be the formation of the inhibitory links added in Fig. 7.8(c). When stimulus A is presented, *b* will be activated associatively (e.g. by way of *c*) and thus an inhibitory *a–b* link will form. Similarly, presentation of B alone will engender the formation of an inhibitory *b–a* link. These links will continue to strengthen until they cancel out any tendency of *a* to excite *b*, and vice versa.*

Given the complex associative structure depicted in Fig. 7.8(c), it is difficult to know whether pre-exposure to A and B (which generates such a structure) should be expected to hinder discrimination or to help it. The excitatory links will tend to hinder, the inhibitory links to help, and the overall result will depend on the balance between these two. McLaren *et al.* (1989) suggest that the facilitatory effect will dominate. Figure 7.8(c) represents the associative structure achieved by the end of pre-exposure. We need to compare this with that generated in control subjects during the course of discrimination training. Now McLaren *et al.* point out that the formation of inhibitory associations is dependent on, and therefore occurs subsequent to, the formation of the excitatory associations. It follows that at some stage during discrimination training the associative structure of control subjects will look like Fig. 7.8(b) rather than Fig. 7.8(c). Control subjects will be at a disadvantage having only excitatory links, whereas the effects of these links will be counteracted in pre-exposed subjects by the pre-existing inhibitory connections.

With these assumptions, then, it is possible for this version of associative theory to predict the required result. To determine whether or not such mechanisms do in fact play an important part in determining the result requires empirical test. The issue was first addressed in an experiment by Hall and Channell (1983). They used rats as the subjects and a version of the Gibson–Walk procedure (home-cage exposure followed by simultaneous discrimination learning) with stimuli (H and V, horizontally and vertically striped plaques) that had previously (Channell and Hall 1981) been shown to generate the effect. It must be assumed, therefore, if the associative theory is to apply, that pre-exposure with these stimuli and procedures generates the associative structure of Fig. 7.8(c). It should be possible, then, to devise other ways in which this associative structure should reveal itself and this is what Hall and Channell (1983) attempted. Instead of requiring their subjects to learn an orthodox, simultaneous, H/V discrimination as the test, they trained them on a task in which choice lay between one of these stimuli and a third stimulus (a plain grey plaque). On half the trials the subject was required to choose between H and grey and on the remainder between V and

---

* Also shown in Fig. 7.8(c), again for the sake of completeness, are further inhibitory links that can be expected to form between *c* and *a*, and between *c* and *b*. Presentation of A alone will activate the *b* elements associatively and the *c* elements directly; presentation of B alone will activate the *a* elements associatively and the *c* elements directly. These links will contribute to the net inhibitory influence of *a* on *b* and of *b* on *a*.

grey. Now this is a task that requires the subject to classify H and V together. The existence or formation of excitatory links between H and V should facilitate performance, whereas the existence of pre-established inhibitory links should be a hindrance. With this test procedure, pre-exposure should, if it establishes inhibitory links, produce *poorer* discrimination learning.

The results of the test phase of the experiment (Hall and Channell 1983, experiment 2) were clear-cut. Pre-exposure was found to facilitate discrimination in this case, just as it does when the test is a standard simultaneous discrimination. Such transfer is perhaps to be expected on the basis of considerations of novelty and familiarity. Control subjects were required to choose on each trial between two stimuli that (at least at the start of the discrimination) were both novel. Pre-exposed subjects chose between one that was familiar (H or V) and one that was novel. We have already seen how a difference in novelty/familiarity can aid discrimination between stimuli. If inhibitory links are playing any role here their effect must be rather weak— much too slight to have any impact on the other processes that are acting to enhance the performance of pre-exposed subjects in this study. We must conclude that although between-stimulus inhibitory links may very well contribute to the effects of stimulus pre-exposure, we still await firm evidence that they do so.

(d) Perceptual processes in SPC

Although SPC has usually been explained associatively, an alternative, perceptual, explanation has been proposed, at least for versions of the procedure in which the pre-trained stimuli (A and B) are presented initially as a simultaneous compound (see, e.g., Rescorla 1980, 1981; Resorla and Durlach 1981). In such circumstances the subject might perceive not (or not only) the A and B elements but some unique configural cue. Repeated exposure to the AB compound might establish a unitary representation of this cue, different from the separate representations activated by A and by B but having something in common with each of them. In the absence of this unitary representation there might be no generalization between A and B, but, once formed, it could mediate between them. If associative strength acquired by A could generalize to AB and thence to B, this would explain the basic SPC effect (see also Pearce 1987).

The perceptual interpretation is as well able to explain cases of negative transfer from pre-exposure to discrimination as is the associative analysis— indeed as an account of 'classifying together' it might in fact capture rather more of the intuition offered by Bateson and Chantrey (1972). We need only suppose that experiencing A and B repeatedly in close temporal and spatial contiguity will establish the representation of the AB configure. Generalization between A and B, and thus retarded discrimination learning, is the direct implication.

To explain instances of positive transfer in these terms is more of a problem—the notion of classifying apart does not lend itself readily to a configural analysis. But it is worth considering the implications of the possibility that exposure to a complex stimulus A induces not (or not only) the formation of within-stimulus links (e.g. between *a* and *c* elements) but the formation of a separate unitary representation (which we may symbolize as **A**). If the formation of the **A** representation meant that the *a* and *c* elements were less likely to be activated by the presence of A, then generalization between A and B on the basis of the *c* elements would be reduced. And if the **A** and **B** representations were very dissimilar so that little generalization occurred between them, then the net effect of pre-exposure to A and B would be to improve discrimination between them.

However plausible this explanation may seem, the last assumption it necessitates (that little generalization occurs between **A** and **B**) proves to be difficult to justify. The perceptual account of the basic SPC effect requires that conditioning to one stimulus (A) will generalize to the configural (AB) representation (and thence to the test stimulus B)—it requires, that is, generalization between the configure and its components. It follows that generalization should occur between a configure *A* and its components *a* and *c*; also that generalization should occur by way of *c* to the other configural representation **B**. The formation of **A** and **B** representations could not, then, enhance the A/B discrimination. This is not to deny that configural representations may be formed as a consequence of prolonged exposure to a compound stimulus (this is one of the issues to be taken up in the next chapter). Rather it is merely to make clear that the formation of configures does not in itself generate a direct explanation for important phenomena in perceptual learning.

7.2.5. Conclusions

At the end of Chapter 5 I concluded that the results of traditional acquired distinctiveness/equivalence procedures were most readily explained in associative terms. It was in part for this reason that, in pursuit of evidence that might confirm the existence of a differentiation process, I turned to experiments on discrimination after non-reinforced pre-exposure. The assumption was that associative learning was not likely to be the source of any transfer produced by such pre-exposure. Enhanced discrimination could then be attributed to a process that made subjects better able to detect the unique features of each of the pre-exposed stimuli, thus reducing the impact of the elements they hold in common (as in Fig. 5.11).

It will probably have come as no surprise to discover that the use of non-reinforced pre-exposure does not in fact exclude the operation of associative mechanisms. I have argued that associations may be formed between a pre-exposed stimulus and its consequence (even when this consequence is no event) and that the acquired equivalence/distinctiveness effects generated by such associations can influence subsequent discrimination learning. We have seen how, by processes akin to sensory preconditioning, associations between the critical stimuli and among the various components of each stimulus can play a role. Adding the associability changes inherent in latent inhibition, and the possibility that the state of habituation of a stimulus (i.e. its novelty or familiarity) can act as a cue in generalization and discrimination, gives us a set of processes capable of explaining all the experimental findings. These various processes are, unlike the differentiation notion, capable of explaining why pre-exposure should sometimes hinder later learning. The only 'perceptual' process for which a place was found was that responsible (possibly) for the formation of configures (should such learning occur). But this, of course, is the exact opposite of differentiation (rather than becoming capable of detecting extra features of the stimulus, these features are subsumed by some new whole); and even here an associative account of the basic phenomenon (SPC) is readily available.

The implication of this conclusion is that there may be no need to suppose that perceptual experience allows the formation of stimulus representations—or rather, that what it is to form a representation can be adequately accounted for in terms of the various associative and related processes described in the last few chapters. The final chapter attempts to address this issue directly.

8. Learning and the modification of stimulus representations

In the standard associative model described in Chapter 1, stimulus representations are treated as 'givens'. The event defined as a stimulus by the experimenter—a tone, light, food, a shock, and so on—is assumed to correspond exactly to a representation (or node) that it excites unconditionally. Learning consists of establishing excitatory and inhibitory links between such nodes. The model is neutral about how the representations come into being and makes no use of the notion that they might change as a consequence of experience.

Leaving aside, for the time being, questions about the particular developmental history that might be necessary to establish a representation, and the possibility that subsequent experience might change the nature of it, why should it be assumed that in a normal animal a stimulus such as a tone, say, has available to it a corresponding representation? The version of the standard model with which we have been working provides no account of the basis on which it comes to be assumed that certain representations do, in fact, exist.

Part of the answer to this question to be found in the pragmatic response that theorizing has to begin somewhere and that to assume the existence of nodes responsive to seemingly rather simple aspects of the stimulating environment is not a very contentious starting point. A related view (and one that seems to underlie, e.g. Hebb's approach (see Chapter 7, p. 236)) is that *perception* has to begin somewhere—that no matter how complex the representations that might ultimately be established, they can only be built on a basis supplied by pre-existing, simpler, perceptual abilities.

Based as they are on the intuitions of the experimenter, neither of these answers is likely to be wholly convincing. The experimenter perceives in the experimental situation a set of events that he assumes to be simple and basic, but the system of representation used by another individual (especially if that individual belongs to a different species) could well be quite different. No matter how sophisticated a theory of learning may be, it will be rendered impotent if it is unable to specify what environmental events have been learned about (see Taylor 1964). Certainly, prediction about when a learned pattern of behaviour is likely to recur will be impossible if we cannot specify what events tend to elicit it.

The solution to this problem traditionally adopted by learning theory has been to accept that the effective stimulus needs to be specified empirically.

When a subject shows a tendency, perhaps as a result of training, to do a given thing when confronted by a given set of environmental conditions, we can test this subject in a range of other conditions and note which do and which do not evoke the behaviour. The effective stimulus can be identified as some feature held in common by environments of the first sort and, with further tests, a process of elimination should allow this stimulus to be specified precisely. By our definitions, the animal must be assumed to be equipped with nodes or representations corresponding to the features of this stimulus. Satisfied that his subject can perceive a certain stimulus, the learning theorist could then devote his energies to determining the mechanisms by which this stimulus enters into associations, comes to control new responses, and so on. The issue of why these features should be effective as a stimulus when others are not could be left to the student of perception.

To accept that the effective stimulus can be defined empirically means that the issue of determining what nodes or representations exist for a given subject should not, in principle, constitute a major problem for the learning theorist. But this is to neglect the possibility of perceptual learning. Our strategy for determining the nature of stimulus representations will only be satisfactory if we can be sure that the relationship between the environmental input and the central representation is fixed. If, however, the nature of perceptual organization can change as a result of experience, a stimulus that was once effective may cease to be so, and vice versa. In such a case it will be necessary for the theorist to attempt to specify how representations can change—which brings us to the central issue of this chapter.

8.1. Revisions to the standard model

The version of the standard model presented in Chapter 1 treated stimulus representations as fixed and given. But this version has, to some extent, been overtaken by events. It is now necessary to restate and refine the characteristics of the model in the light of what has since transpired. The need to accommodate the data presented in subsequent chapters has led to a variety of amendments, some involving the addition of new assumptions, others revealing intricacies of the original model that were undeveloped. A summary of these additions and elaborations is presented next.

8.1.1. Additions

(a) Habituation

From the outset it was apparent that the phenomenon of habituation would constitute a challenge to standard associative learning theory, if only because there was no obvious associate for the target stimulus to become linked to. Wagner's (1976) attempt to give this role to the training context proved to be unsatisfactory, chiefly because habituation turns out not to be dependent on context—a stimulus that has become familiar in one context retains this property when it is encountered in another. No alternative associative interpretation has been offered and accordingly it seems necessary to graft a non-associative mechanism for habituation on to the standard model.

The review of the topic in Chapter 2 indicated what general form this mechanism must have. It was concluded that habituation occurs because the presentation of a given stimulus leaves some trace (modifies the state of a central representation). When an incoming stimulus matches the modified representation, it will fail to elicit its unconditioned response (UR). The evidence reviewed in Chapter 2 prompted the conclusion that, with repeated stimulation, not only the state but also the *nature* of the representation being activated will change. The latter part of the present chapter is concerned with the mechanisms responsible for this change in nature and raises the possibility that these may very well be associative. But however this may be, it remains the case that the fundamental process responsible for habituation itself (the change of state that reduces the likelihood that activation of a representation will evoke its UR) is essentially non-associative.

(b) Changes in associability

Attentional theories of the type discussed in Chapter 6 have proposed that in addition to associative learning there is a further learning process that produces changes in the attention paid to stimuli. These changes are revealed by modifications of the ease with which the stimulus in question is learned about, and are thus perhaps better described, to avoid surplus meanings conveyed by the term 'attention', as consisting of changes in conditionability or associability.

The conditions under which associability will change have been a matter for debate (see Chapter 6) but many, if not all, of the data can be accommodated by the view that the associability of a stimulus will be determined by how well it predicts its consequences. The associability of a novel stimulus will be high but will decline as the stimulus becomes securely associated with what follows it. Associability will be restored should the consequences of the stimulus be changed so that new associative learning is required. This mechanism for the loss of associability can be presumed to be in part responsible for the latent inhibition effect discussed in Chapters 3 and 4, although it seems certain that the effect is determined by more than one mechanism. (Chapter 4 presented evidence to suggest that associations formed during the pre-exposure phase of a latent inhibition experiment might directly interfere with that to be acquired during the conditioning phase.)

Although changes in associability are in a sense secondary to, or parasitic on, associative learning, being determined by how well associative links predict the consequence of the stimulus in question, the hypothesized mechanism is not in itself associative in nature. What changes when associability is modified is not the strength or nature of some association between nodes; rather the change is in the value of some parameter associated with a node that determines how readily changes in associative strength can occur. As was the case with habituation, the phenomena to be explained require that some further form of learning be added but the basic tenets of associative theory remain intact.

(c) Contextual control of retrieval

Chapters 3 and 4 described how conditioned responding (like the latent inhibition effect, but unlike habituation) will fail to transfer from one context to another. Straightforward associative explanations for this effect (that is, explanations that attempt to attribute context-specificity to direct association between the context and the conditioned stimulus (CS) or the context and the unconditioned stimulus (US)) were considered and rejected. Rather the context seems to exert its effect by controlling the activity of the CS–US association itself, an effect that I have tried to summarize by saying that appropriate contextual cues may be necessary for the efficient retrieval of associative information.

This topic is still the subject of intensive experimental investigation (work conducted for the most part with discrete events, 'occasion setters', rather than contexts as the conditional cues) and a consensus about the mechanisms involved has yet to be arrived at. These may operate by principles quite different from those governing simple associative learning. It could yet turn out, however, that associative principles have a part to play even here—one possibility (see e.g. Bonardi 1988, 1989) is that the conditional cue can be conceived of as entering into an association with some representation of the relationship between the CS and the US. But even if this latter formulation were found to be appropriate it would still remain the case that substantial additions would need to be made to the standard associative model in order to deal with the phenomena of contextual specificity and of conditional control more generally.

8.1.2. Elaborations

(a) Acquisition of stimulus features

The effective stimulus is the set of central processes or mechanisms (what we have sometimes referred to as 'nodes') that are activated when a given event occurs. Associative learning could act to add to the number of nodes that are activated by a given event. In particular, our analysis of excitatory conditioning holds that the conditioning procedure allows the CS node and the US node to become linked so that presentation of the CS will become able to generate activity in both nodes—in its own node directly; in the US node by way of the associative link. In most conditioning experiments the US is a motivationally significant event but our analysis is not restricted to such cases.

The precise nature of associatively generated activation is open to debate, although it has received little. The simplest interpretation (and that assumed when a theory does not specify otherwise) is that the activation in a node produced by direct presentation of an event is identical to that generated in the node by way of an excitatory associative link. The degree to which activation is aroused in the US node by presentation of a CS may well be rather less than that produced by the US itself, but the nature of the activation will be the same in the two cases. Associative learning, therefore, will effectively turn the CS into a more complex stimulus, one that possesses not only its own intrinsic features but also a set of features characteristic of the US— features corresponding to nodes that it has become able to excite associatively. Presentation of a tone, say, for a subject that has received prior tone–light pairings, will be effectively equivalent to presenting a version of the compound stimulus itself.

Wagner's 'standard operating procedures' (SOP) version of the standard model (e.g. Wagner 1981) is unusual in that it distinguishes two forms of activation: A1, produced by the stimulus itself, and A2, produced by an excitatory associative link. One of the reasons for making this distinction is that it allows for the possibility that the type of response elicited by direct application of a stimulus might be different from that elicited by presenting a signal for that stimulus. The fact that CR and UR can sometimes be quite different is certainly something that has been dealt with inadequately by simpler associative theories, and Wagner's suggestion seems to form the basis for an elegant solution to the problem. We can accept that the A1 and A2 states might generate different responses without supposing that they differ in other ways. In particular, we may want to reject the limitation imposed by Wagner's theory on the sort of associations a node in the A2 state can enter into. A node in the A1 state will form an excitatory association should a second node enter the A1 state. But the theory does not allow that a similar link will be formed when the first of these nodes is associatively activated and therefore in A2. (The theory allows the formation only of an inhibitory link in these conditions with the node that was in A1 coming to exert inhibitory control over that that was in A2.) We saw in Chapter 5, however, that this restriction is unjustified—that an associatively activated stimulus representation can act as CS and gain associative strength when paired with a US just as can a representation that is activated directly. Even if we accept Wagner's (1981) distinction between the A1 and A2 states, then, it still remains possible to maintain the view that the effective stimulus produced by the presentation of a given event will comprise not only the node or nodes that are unconditionally activated by that event but also those nodes with which that event has excitatory associations. The response elicited by a compound consisting of directly and associatively activated nodes may well be different from what would be elicited by a compound in which all the elements were physically present, but in other respects the two can be regarded as equivalent.

Acknowledging that the effective stimulus generated by an event with which the subject has received prior training is likely to include associatively activated features provides, as we saw in Chapter 5, an explanation for acquired equivalence and distinctiveness effects.

(b) Loss of stimulus features

Whatever the precise mechanism responsible for habituation, an implication of the phenomenon is that the stimulus complex evoked by the presentation of a given event will change with experience. I have sometimes referred to the change in the stimulus as being from novel to familiar, but a more concrete way of expressing just what this change involves (and the approach favoured in Chapter 7) is to note that with habituation a stimulus changes from being one that evokes its UR to one that does not. Thus the stimulus complex that constitutes an event on first presentation will include, for instance, the feedback cues generated by the occurrence of the UR; when the stimulus has become habituated these cues will be absent (replaced, perhaps, by the cues generated by whatever response now occurs). In applying associative theory to any training situation, then, it is important to take account of these facts. Differences in novelty/familiarity could provide a basis on which a discrimination might be formed; and, provided they evoke the same UR, generalization between ostensibly rather different events could be mediated by their sharing a common state of habituation. Incorporating these notions does not violate the basic principles of the standard model but it leads (as we saw in Chapter 7) to predictions about discrimination and generalization that would otherwise be unexpected.

(c) Within-stimulus learning

Even the simplest event that the experimenter refers to as 'a stimulus' can be conceived of as consisting of many different features or elements. Presentation of that event will mean, therefore, that the nodes corresponding to its various elements will be activated together. We must assume (as there is no reason to do otherwise) that the principles of associative learning will apply here just as they do to the case in which the event is a compound constructed by the experimenter from separable elements. Links will be formed among the nodes. The central representation of the frequency of a tone, say, will become connected with that of its intensity, its location, and so on. A novel tone would activate a set of separate nodes; for a familiar tone these nodes will be connected by a network of associations.

It will often be difficult, if not impossible, to present separately the various components of a simple stimulus (a tone of a given frequency must occur with at least some intensity, for instance). Accordingly it might appear that the associative analysis just offered is little more than fruitless speculation—difficult to test empirically and without worthwhile implications. We saw, however, in Chapter 7 that the formation of within-stimulus links (especially those involving elements that a given stimulus will hold in common with other similar stimuli) can have important implications for the outcome to be expected when subjects are required to learn a discrimination between stimuli to which they have been pre-exposed. And indeed, the degree of speculation is limited to that involved in identifying the notional elements of which a stimulus is composed. Suggestions about how and when associations will be formed among these elements are tightly constrained by the assumption that the same principles of associative learning as govern learning about orthodox stimuli presented together (see, e.g. Rescorla and Durlach 1981) will also govern learning about notional stimulus elements.

8.2. Applying the revised model

The revised version of the standard model (should the latter now be called the authorized version?) has proved capable of dealing with most of the phenomena of perceptual learning discussed in earlier chapters. In part this is because some of the revisions were directly determined by the findings. The non-associative learning mechanisms that have been added were forced on the theory by the empirical facts that demonstrate habituation, attentional learning, and conditional contextual control. But the other revisions, although made in response to challenging data, are better seen as developments of possibilities inherent in the standard model. Exploitation of these possibilities has allowed the development of associative explanations for the prime examples of perceptual learning—the acquired distinctiveness of cues, dnd the facilitation of subsequent discrimination by non-reinforced pre-exposure to the cues. This revised version of the standard model accepts that experience can produce changes in the representation activated by presentation of a given stimulus but offers an explanation for these changes in terms of associative mechanisms. The major phenomena of perceptual learning can then be explained associatively without appeal to the Gibsonian process of differentiation. There remains, however, a set of phenomena generated during our analysis of habituation for which a process of differentiation might well be the underlying mechanism.

According to one possible account of habituation the relevant stimulus representation is simply the set of S–R pathways that suffer a loss of effectiveness when the stimulus is presented; and the only way in which this representation changes with experience is that repeated presentation of the stimulus will cause these pathways to grow less and less effective.

Chapter 2 revealed, however, that the S–R theory of habituation is not fully secure. In particular, the notion of stimulus representation it assumes makes it difficult for the theory to supply a complete account of the dishabituation produced by various forms of stimulus change. Post-trial distractor effects and the results of studies of generalization after a retention interval and after extended training indicated that the *nature* of the representation activated by a given stimulus might change with experience. Now differentiation theory can accommodate these findings readily, given its assumption that repeated exposure to a stimulus will allow the development of an increasingly detailed (better differentiated) central representation of it. But the revised version of the standard model also allows the possibility that the nature of the representation can change. The question that must now be addressed, therefore, is how well the revised version of the model applies to these findings. Can it supply an account of the way in which representations change with experience that will accommodate those findings that might seem to demand a notion of differentiation?

8.2.1. Post-trial distractor effects

Following a target stimulus, T, by a distractor, D, will reduce the extent to which habituation is shown to T as assessed on a subsequent test trial with this stimulus. I argued in Chapter 2 that this result should be interpreted as being an instance of dishabituation produced by there being a mismatch between the test stimulus and the subject's memory of the stimulus experienced on the training trial. Stimulus T will be physically identical on the two occasions but the occurrence of D will modify the encoded representation established by the training trial. This latter process, it was suggested, seems to require us to assume that exposure to a stimulus induces the formation of a representation rather more complex than anything envisaged by the S–R, dual-process theory of habituation. We need to reconsider this suggestion in the light of the revised version of the associative model presented above.

One feature of the revised model was the assertion that the effective stimulus generated by the presentation of a given event consists not only of the node or nodes directly activated by that event but includes such other nodes as are activated associatively. The implications of this feature are best revealed by considering the simple case in which the subject receives one training trial with T followed by D and then one test trial with T represented alone. Now, habituation training in which stimulus T is followed by stimulus D should allow the formation of an associative link between them. On the training trial this link would not yet have been formed and so the subject would experience activation of the nodes corresponding to T and then, subsequently and separately, activation of the D nodes. On the test trial, however, presentation of T would produce direct activation of the T nodes, along with concurrent associative activation of the D nodes. The pattern of central activation would be different from that experienced during training.

It remains to specify why the central pattern so generated should be capable of evoking the response. Perhaps the simplest analysis available to the S–R theorist is to consider the event experienced on the test trial as consisting of two stimuli never experienced together before. Their interaction can be expected to generate new features (to produce generalization decrement), thus activating nodes not previously activated.* These nodes will then elicit their URs. We have already accepted in general terms that the effect of a distractor is to modify the representation produced by training, and that responding occurs because there is an imperfect match between input and representation on the subsequent test trial. The new suggestion is that the critical feature of the representation established by training might depend on an associative link between stimulus T and stimulus D.

There are no data that either require us to accept or force us to reject the associative interpretation of the post-trial distractor effect. One potential problem comes from the results of Kaye, Gambini, and Mackintosh (1988), who found that the interfering effect of a post-trial distractor on habituation disappeared when there was a relatively long retention interval before the test trial. In order to explain this effect within the associative framework it seems necessary to assume that the T–D association has decayed, been forgotten, or in some way rendered ineffective over the interval. Such a loss of effectiveness is neither impossible nor implausible but it is at variance with the assumption usually made by associative theorists, that associations, once formed, are more or less impervious to change with the mere passage of time. In this respect the alternative interpretation that makes use of the notion of differentiation may be at an advantage. The mechanism responsible for differentiation is not required to obey the rules that govern associative learning; and in the absence of such constraints it is open to the theorist to assume that brief exposure to a stimulus will (if no distractor occurs) allow the subject to encode many details, but that these will be lost so that only general features remain after a retention interval.

The effects of a retention interval are discussed further in the next section. But before turning to this it is perhaps worth mentioning that manipulation of the context might allow a direct test of the associative explanation for distractor effects. The retrieval of associative information, I have argued, is context-dependent. If the mismatch between the test stimulus and its central representation occurs because T associatively activates a representation of D, then no distractor effect should be evident when a change of context eliminates this associative process. If the distractor effect survives such a change

---

* This suggestion is not especially contentious. We can readily accept that presenting two environmental events, say a tone and a light together, might generate novel features in these stimuli if only because the peripheral adjustments evoked by the one may make the other impinge on the subject slightly differently. The argument is not different in principle when one of the events in question is an associatively produced pattern of activation.

of context then (as is the case with habituation itself) an associative explanation would seem unlikely. The relevant experiment remains to be done.

8.2.2. Generalization after a retention interval

Generalization gradients tend to be less sharp when the test is given after a retention interval rather than immediately after training. This flattening is the result of changes both at the training value and the test values. In the case of habituation (equivalent effects are reported for conditioning), the retention interval may produce some loss of habituation in the trained stimulus, and also an increase in the degree to which the test stimulus shows generalized habituation. One interpretation offered for this finding in Chapter 2 was based on the idea that differentiation might occur in reverse. It was suggested that initial training would allow a fairly complete representation of the stimulus to be formed but that the details would be lost from the representation over the retention interval. We must now consider whether our revised and extended associative theory can supply a mechanism for this effect. The aspect of the revised theory of relevance here is the suggestion that associations can be formed among the various elements that constitute any stimulus. Habituation training with stimulus A should allow associations between unique a elements and the c elements that it holds in common with generalization test stimulus B. Pursuing the suggestion put forward above, we may assume that associations lose effectiveness over a retention interval. The presence or absence of an effective c–a association may then be used to explain the degree of generalization evident to stimulus B (i.e. to stimulus elements b and c presented together).

Whenever stimulus B is presented its unique and novel b elements will tend to evoke the UR. The effect produced by the c elements will vary. When B is presented after a delay, the c elements will fail to produce their contribution to the UR and that is all. There will thus be some generalization of habituation from A to B but the effect will be incomplete. When B is presented immediately after training with A, the same processes will operate but in addition the presentation of the c elements will be able to activate the a elements associatively because, it is assumed, an effective c–a association will still be present. For the first time, then, the subject will experience the combination of a and b elements being activated together. To the extent that this novel combination means that new features are generated, there will be a second factor (in addition to the presence of b) tending to elicit a UR. Generalization of habituation should then be less evident with the immediate test procedure than with the delayed test.

As was the case for our proposed associative analysis of post-trial distractor effects, the theoretical analysis being considered here is similar in many important respects to the rival differentiation account. Both interpretations suppose that the nature of the central representation established by training changes with time. The way the two theories differ is in their suggestion about how the representation changes—in the one the details of the stimulus lose the ability to activate features of the central representation; in the other these features are activated but the links connecting them are no longer functional. Again, the evidence currently available does not allow a choice between these alternatives.

8.2.3. Generalization after extended training

The most direct approach to the issue of how a stimulus representation might change with experience comes from studies in which the amount of exposure to the stimulus is varied. We saw in Chapter 2 that an increase in training with a stimulus leads to an increase in the readiness with which that stimulus is discriminated from others, as evidenced by a sharpening of generalization gradients around it. This was true both when the behaviour under study was a conditioned response produced by reinforced training and when it was the loss of an unconditioned response engendered by habituation training. These results are consistent with the suggestion that differentiation occurs with extended training. How does the revised version of the standard model cope with them?

(a) The role of novelty/familiarity

The standard model needs no revision at all to deal with the effect seen after extended reinforced training. As we saw in Chapter 2, such training will increase the associative strength of the target stimulus and lead to a loss of such strength as may have been gained early in training by background cues. The result could be an increase in the tendency to respond at the training value and a reduction in the tendency to respond to generalization test stimuli.

The revised version of the model supplies a further reason for expecting a loss of generalization with extended training. When a generalization test is given after little training, both stimuli (the trained stimulus and the test stimulus) will be (fairly) novel. The test stimulus will never have been encountered before; the training stimulus, it may be assumed, will not have grown fully familiar and thus the cue of novelty should possess some associative strength. With extended training the trained stimulus will become familiar and (given certain assumptions) familiarity will gain strength at the expense of the novelty cue. One of the sources of generalization to the test stimulus will now be absent and, in consequence, the gradient will become steeper.

Whatever the merits of the argument just advanced, consideration of the role of novelty provides an uncomplicated explanation for the reduction in the extent of generalization that is produced by preliminary non-reinforced exposure to the generalization test stimulus—the observation that the conditioned responding generated by just a few reinforced trials generalizes much more readily to a novel test stimulus than to one that has received pre-exposure. Honey's (1990) explanation was that the cue of novelty that mediates generalization in the former case is ineffective in the latter case when the test stimulus has been allowed to acquire familiarity.

(b) Within-stimulus learning

Mediation by the cues of novelty and familiarity can help explain the generalization effects seen after extended reinforced training. They cannot apply, however, to the seemingly equivalent effects seen in habituation. Mediation by way of novelty occurs, I have suggested, because the cues associated with the tendency of a stimulus to evoke its UR can gain associative strength. This process becomes irrelevant when the likelihood of occurrence of the UR is itself the behaviour under investigation. The associative model can, however, fall back on the role played by within-stimulus associations. Just as the loss of these associations after a retention interval could lead to a flattening of the generalization gradient, so a strengthening of these associations with over-training might be expected to lead to a sharpening of the gradient. The argument is exactly analogous to that advanced above. Subjects given much training with stimulus A will have strong associations between the *a* and the *c* elements. Presentation of stimulus B (i.e. *b* and *c* elements) will evoke the UR both because the *b* elements are novel but also because the *a* elements will be activated (associatively) for the first time in combination with the *b* elements. In this way the omission of the *a* elements from the test stimulus will play a part in evoking the response.

Evidence relevant to this matter comes from the experiment by Gillette and Bellingham (1982). If we consider, for the sake of simplicity, a stimulus having just two components, X and Y, as the strength of the association between the two grows with repeated exposure, so the omission-induced responding produced by presenting just X on its own should grow in magnitude. In the experiment by Gillette and Bellingham, X and Y were the two components (saccharin and salt) of a compound flavour stimulus. Their results (see Fig. 2.12) were entirely in accord with the analysis just offered. Rats began to show the UR of suppressed consumption to salt (say) presented on its own the more frequently salt had been previously experienced in compound with saccharin.

(c) Configural learning

Once again it turns out that a pattern of results favourable to the analysis of perceptual learning offered by the differentiation theory can be explained by an elaborated version of the associative account. There are, however, reasons to doubt the interpretation just offered for the results of the Gillette and Bellingham experiment. But the alternative to the associative account prompted by these doubts is not necessarily a differentiation theory but could equally well be one that relies on the notion of 'configural' learning.

A problem for the associative analysis of the effect shown in Fig. 2.12 is that essentially identical results have been found in a procedure in which reinforced training with the compound is given. Bellingham and Gillette (1981*b*) gave different groups of subjects varying amounts of training in which a tone–light compound was followed by food. After extensive training it was found that the tone or the light when presented alone failed to evoke the conditioned response (see Fig. 2.16). This is not the outcome readily predicted by associative theory. The association between the tone and the light formed during compound training, although it might allow the occurrence of omission-induced responding on a test trial, should also act to foster the ability of an element to evoke the CR. Once the tone–light association has been formed, presentation of the tone, for example, will be able to contact a representation of the reinforcer both directly and by way of its ability to activate the light representation, which will also be associated with the reinforcer.

This problem prompts consideration of an alternative interpretation—that initially the subject is poor at discriminating the compound from its elements but that later, as a result of training, it becomes capable of doing so. Such an interpretation is compatible with differentiation theory but it is also what would be expected given the account favoured by Bellingham and Gillette (1981*b*) themselves. They suggest that repeated exposure to a compound stimulus causes that event to be perceived not as the sum of its elements but as a configural stimulus different from either. Assuming that the developing configural cue gains associative strength at the expense of the elements provides an explanation for the results displayed in Fig. 2.16.

There are few data that bear directly on this notion. It is certainly true that data on the ability of animals to learn a discrimination between a compound and its elements are nicely accounted for by the assumption that the compound consists not only of the original elements but also of some unique configural cue generated by their simultaneous presentation (e.g. Rescorla 1972, 1973). But the assumption carries no implication of perceptual learning; that is, these results can be explained given the assumption that the unique cue is present in the compound from the outset——they do not speak to the issue of whether the role by the unique cue tends to grow with extended experience of the compound.

In the absence of direct evidence on this issue we may consider the implications of an unpublished experiment by R.C. Honey using rats as the subjects and flavours as the stimuli. Subjects in one of the critical conditions received eight presentations of a compound flavour, AB. In another condition the subjects received four presentations of AB and four of AC. The effect of these compound trials was assessed by a second stage in which stimulus A was presented alone followed by an injection of LiC1. The extent to which latent inhibition occurs in this conditioning procedure can be taken as an index of the extent to which the target stimulus A was in fact perceived

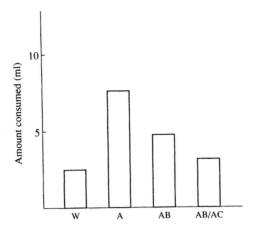

Fig. 8.1 Amount of fluid A consumed on a test session given after two conditioning trials in which A had been followed by an injection of LiCl. Prior to conditioning different groups had experienced just water (W); 8 presentations of A; 8 presentations of the compound AB; 4 presentations of AB and 4 of the compound AC (group AB/AC). Flavour A was sucrose. For half the subjects B was a dilute acid solution and C was saline; for the remainder this arrangement was reversed. (Data from an unpublished experiment by R. C. Honey.)

in the various forms of pre-training. Poor conditioning (i.e. good transfer of latent inhibition) would mean that A was 'abstracted' during pre-exposure.

The results are presented in Fig. 8.1. It shows, first, that latent inhibition occurs in this preparation, as a group given eight pre-exposure trials with A alone acquired the aversion much less readily than did control subjects (group W) given unflavoured water in pre-exposure. The other two groups both showed some latent inhibition but the effect was more marked in group AB than in the group AB/AC that experienced the varying concomitants.

This result lends no support to the notion that a configural cue tends to develop with exposure to these compound flavour stimuli. If extended training with a compound establishes a configure and eliminates the subject's ability to perceive the elements, then group AB (which has eight trials with the same compound) should have had the least opportunity to experience the A element during pre-exposure. For group AB/AC, which had only four trials with each compound, the process of configuring would not have proceeded so far with either of the compounds, thus ensuring that in this group the opportunity to experience the A element would be more extensive. It follows that, on these grounds, the extent of latent inhibition to A should be greater in group AB/AC than in group AB—the reverse of the result actually observed. In contrast, the pattern of results shown in Fig. 8.1 is what might be expected on the basis of differentiation. If it takes repeated exposure for a subject to become able to discriminate the various elements that make up a compound, then eight trials with one compound are more likely to allow the subject experience of the A element than are four trials with each of the two compounds.

It would be foolish to suggest that the experiment just described is in any sense critical. The generality of the effect it reveals needs to be established using different training procedures, subjects, and stimuli. And there are no doubt several, perhaps many, alternative explanations that need to be considered. It can stand, however, first as providing an indication that a place may yet be found for a process of stimulus differentiation, and second as an instance of the sort of study that is now required to resolve remaining issues in perceptual learning.

8.2.4. Conclusions

No lengthy summing up is needed at this point because the first section of this chapter has already presented an outline of how investigations of the phenomena of perceptual learning have interacted with, and required modifications in, our standard associative interpretation of learning. It will be worthwhile to summarize, however, the conclusions that have been generated by the discussion of this second part of the chapter.

My starting point is to restate that the pattern of activity evoked by a given environmental event will change with experience; that is, that the central representation of a stimulus is not fixed. Known mechanisms of habituation and associative learning are important in producing such change. Initially the representation will include features activated by the UR evoked by the stimulus, but as habituation occurs these elements will drop out, perhaps being replaced by features associated with such responses as a familiar stimulus evokes. A stimulus will also be able to acquire new features by a process of associative learning; by becoming linked associatively with other stimuli that occur along with it the central representation of the target, even when subsequently presented alone, will include features of its associates. Associations will also be formed among the various features that go to make up a complex stimulus and this too will produce a change in the pattern of central activity evoked by the stimulus.

Having said this we must now acknowledge that many of the data are also consistent with the possibility that the presentation initially activated by a stimulus might correspond only to gross features of that event, and that one effect of experience with it might be to allow more detailed features to be detected. For Gibson and Gibson (1955), such differentiation was the essence of perceptual learning and the possibility that an associative ('enrichment') mechanism might explain the phenomena was firmly denied. What we have seen is that that associative and related processes allow for more than just enrichment; and although we have acknowledged the possible contribution of a differentiation process, we have found that associative theory supplies powerful and satisfying explanations for a wide range of phenomena. In the process of meeting these explanatory challenges, the associative theory that we began with has been expanded and elaborated in a number of important ways. Some may object that what has emerged is no longer a purely associative theory but one that incorporates non-associative, perceptual mechanisms, but this is surely to be seen not as a shortcoming but as a worthwhile achievement.

References

Anderson, D.C., O'Farrell, T., Formica, R., and Caponigri, V. (1969). Preconditioning CS exposure: variation in place of conditioning and of presentation. *Psychonomic Science*, **15**, 54–5.

——, Wolf, D., and Sullivan, P. (1969). Preconditioning exposures to the CS: variation in place of testing. *Psychonomic Science*, **15**, 233–5.

Archer, T. and Sjödén, P.O. (1979). Neophobia in taste-aversion conditioning: individual differences and effects of contextual changes. *Physiological Physchology*, **7**, 364–9.

——, ——, Nilsson, L.G., and Carter, N. (1979). Role of exteroceptive background context in taste-aversion and extinction. *Animal Learning and Behavior*, **7**, 17–22.

——, ——, and —— (1985). Contextual control of taste-aversion conditioning and extinction. In *Context and learning* (ed. P D. Balsam and A. Tomie), pp. 225–71. Erlbaum, Hillsdale, N.J.

Arnoult, M.D. (1953). Transfer of predifferentiation training in simple and multiple shape discrimination. *Journal of Experimental Psychology*, **45**, 401–9.

—— (1957). Stimulus predifferentiation: some generalizations and hypotheses. *Psychological Bulletin*, **54**, 339–50.

Ayres, J.J.B., Moore, J.W., and Vigorito, M. (1984). Hall and Pearce negative transfer: assessments in conditioned suppression and nictitating membrane conditioning experiments. *Animal Learning and Behavior*, **12**, 428–38.

Babb, H. (1956). Proportional reinforcement of irrelevant stimuli and transfer value. *Journal of Comparative and Physiological Psychology*, **49**, 586–9.

Bainbridge, P.L. (1973). Learning in the rat: effects of early experience with an unsolvable problem. *Journal of Comparative and Physiological Psyochology*, **82**, 301–7.

Baker, A.G. (1976). Learned irrelevance and learned helplessness: rats learn that stimuli, reinforcers, and responses are uncorrelated. *Journal of Experimental Psychology: Animal Behavior Processes*, **2**, 130–41.

—— and Mackintosh, N.J. (1977). Excitatory and inhibitory conditioning following uncorrelated presentation of CS and US. *Animal Learning and Behavior*, **5**, 315–19.

—— and —— (1979). Preexposure to CS alone, US alone or CS and US uncorrelated: blocking by context or learned irrelevance. *Learning and Motivation*, **10**, 278–94.

—— and Mercier, P. (1982a). Prior experience with the conditioning events: evidence for a rich cognitive representation. In *Quantitative analyses of behavior*, Vol. 3 (ed. M. L. Commons, R. J. Herrnstein, and A. R. Wagner), pp. 117–43. Ballinger, Cambridge, MA.

—— and —— (1982b). Extinction of the context and latent inhibition. *Learning and Motivation*, **13**, 391–416.

——, Haskins, C., and Hall, G. (1990). Stimulus generalization decrement in latent inhibition to a compound following exposure to the elements or the compound. *Animal Learning and Behavior*, **18**, 162–70.

——, Singh, M., and Bindra, D. (1985). Some effects of contextual conditioning and US predictability on Pavlovian conditioning. In *Context and learning* (ed. P. D. Balsam and A. Tomie), pp. 73–103. Erlbaum, Hillsdale, NJ.

Baker, T.B. and Tiffany, S.T. (1985). Morphine tolerance as habituation. *Psychological Review*, **92**, 78–108.

Balaz, M.A., Capra, S., Hartl, P., and Miller. R.R. (1981). Contextual potentiation of acquired behavior after devaluing direct context–US associations. *Learning and Motivation*, **12**, 383–97.

——, ——, Kasprow, W.J., and Miller, R.R. (1982). Latent inhibition of the conditioning context: further evidence of contextual potentiation of retrieval in the absence of appreciable context–US associations. *Animal Learning and Behavior*, **10**, 242–8.

Barker, L.M. (1976). CS duration, amount, and concentration effects in conditioning taste aversions. *Learning and Motivation*, **7**, 265–73.

Basden, B.H. (1970). The effects of cue salience and overtraining on extradimensional shift learning. *Psychonomic Science*, **20**, 7–8.

Bateson, P.P.G. (1964). An effect of imprinting on the perceptual development of domestic chicks. *Nature*, **202**, 421–2.

—— (1966). The characteristics and context of imprinting. *Biological Reviews*, **41**, 177–220.

—— (1973). Internal influences on early learning in birds. In *Constraints on learning* (ed. R. A. Hinde and J. S. Hinde), pp. 101–16. Academic Press, London.

—— (1976). Psychology of knowing another side. *New Scientist*, **69**, 166–7.

—— and Chantrey, D.F. (1972). Retardation of discrimination learning in monkeys and chicks previously exposed to both stimuli. *Nature*, **202**, 421–2.

Batson, J.D. and Best, M.R. (1981). Single-element assessment of conditioned inhibition. *Bulletin of the Psychonomic Society*, **18**, 328–330.

Battig, W.F. (1956). Transfer from verbal pretraining to motor performance as a function of motor task complexity. *Journal of Experimental Psychology*, **51**, 371–8.

Bellingham, W.P. and Gillette, K. (1981*a*). Attenuation of overshadowing as a function of nondifferential compound conditioning trials. *Bulletin of the Psychonomic Society*, **18**, 218–20.

—— and —— (1981*b*). Spontaneous configuring to a tone–light compound using appetitive training. *Learning and Motivation*, **12**, 420–34.

Bennett, T.L. and Ellis, H.C. (1968). Tactual–kinesthetic feedback from manipulation of visual forms and nondifferential reinforcement in transfer of perceptual learning. *Journal of Experimental Psychology*, **77**, 495–500.

——, Rickert, E.J., and McAllister, L.E. (1970). Role of tactual–kinesthetic feedback in transfer of perceptual learning for rats with pigmented irises. *Perceptual and Motor Skills*, **30**, 916–18.

——, Anton, B.S., and Levitt, L. (1971). Stimulus relevancy and transfer of perceptual learning. *Psychonomic Science*, **25**, 159–60.

——, Levitt, L., and Anton, B.S. (1972). Effect of exposure to a single stimulus on transfer of perceptual learning. *Perceptual and Motor Skills*, **34**, 559–62.

Berlyne, D.E. (1960). *Conflict, arousal, and curiosity*. McGraw-Hill, New York.

Best, M.R. (1975). Conditioned and latent inhibition in taste-aversion learning:

clarifying the role of learned safety. *Journal of Experimental Psychology: Animal Behavior Processes*, **1**, 97–113.

—— and Barker, L.M. (1977). The nature of 'learned safety' and its role in the delay of reinforcement gradient. In *Learning mechanisms in food selection* (ed. L. M. Barker, M. R. Best, and M. Domjan), pp. 295–317. Baylor University Press, Waco, TX.

—— and Batson, J.D. (1977). Enhancing the expression of flavour neophobia: some effects of the ingestion–illness contingency. *Journal of Experimental Psychology: Animal Behavior Processes*, **3**, 132–43.

—— and Gemberling, G.A. (1977). Role of short-term processes in the conditioned stimulus preexposure effect and the delay of reinforcement gradient in long-delay taste-aversion learning. *Journal of Experimental Psychology: Animal Behavior Processes*, **3**, 253–63.

——, ——, and Johnson, P.E. (1979). Disrupting the conditioned stimulus preexposure effect in flavor-aversion learning: effects of interoceptive distractor manipulations. *Journal of Experimental Psychology: Animal Behavior Processes*, **5**, 321–34.

Bhatt, R.S. and Wasserman, E.A. (1989). Secondary generalization and categorization in pigeons. *Journal of Experimental Analysis of Behavior*, **52**, 213–24.

Billingsley, B.A., Feddersen, W.E., and Bitterman, M.E. (1954). Discrimination following nondifferential reinforcement with differential afferent consequences. *American Journal of Psychology*, **67**, 335–7.

Bitterman, M.E. and Elam, C.B. (1954). Discrimination following varying amounts of nondifferential reinforcement. *American Journal of Psychology*, **67**, 133–7.

—— and McConnell, J.V. (1954). The role of set in successive discrimination. *American Journal of Psychology*, **67**, 129–32.

——, Calvin, A.D., and Elam, C.B. (1953). Perceptual differentiation in the course of nondifferential reinforcement. *Journal of Comparative and Physiological Psychology*, **46**, 393–7.

——, Elam, C.B., and Wortz, E.C. (1953). Perceptual differentiation as a function of nondifferential reward and punishement. *Journal of Comparative and Physiological Psychology*, **46**, 475–8.

Blodgett, H.C. (1929). The effect of the introduction of reward upon the maze performance of rats. *University of California Publications in Psychology*, **4**, 113–34.

Boakes, R.A. and Thomas D. (1988). Generalization decrements with immediate versus delayed testing. Paper presented to the Experimental Analysis of Behavior Group, University of Leeds, April 1988.

Bolles, R.C. and Rapp, H.M. (1965). Readiness to eat and drink: effect of stimulus conditions. *Journal of Comparative and Physiological Psychology*, **60**, 93–7.

Bonardi, C. (1988). Associative explanations of discriminative inhibition effects. *Quarterly Journal of Experimental Psychology*, **40B**, 63–82.

—— (1989). Inhibitory discriminative control is specific to both the response and the reinforcer. *Quarterly Journal of Experimental Psychology*, **41B**, 225–42.

—— (1991). Blocking of occasion setting in feature-positive discriminations. *Quarterly Journal of Experimental Psychology*, (in press).

——, Honey, R.C., and Hall, G. (1990). Context specificity of conditioning in flavor-aversion learning: extinction and blocking tests. *Animal Learning and Behavior*, **18**, 229–37.

——, Guthrie, D., and Hall, G. (1991). The effect of a retention interval on habituation of the neophobic response. *Animal Learning and Behavior*, **19**, 11–17.

Bond, N. and DiGiusto, E. (1975). Amount of solution drunk is a factor in the establishment of taste aversion. *Animal Learning and Behavior*, **3**, 81–4.

Bond, N.W. and Westbrook, R.F. (1982). The role of amount consumed in flavor preexposure effects and neophobia. *Animal Learning and Behavior*, **10**, 511–15.

Booth, J.J. and Hammond, L.J. (1971). Configural conditioning: greater fear in rats to compound than component through overtraining of the compound. *Journal of Experimental Psychology*, **87**, 255–62.

Bouton, M.E. (1988). Context and ambiguity in the extinction of emotional learning: implications for exposure therapy. *Behaviour Research and Therapy*, **26**, 137–49.

—— (1990). Context and retrievcal in extinction and in other examples of interference in simple associative learning. In *Current topics in animal learning: Brain, emotion, and cognition* (ed. L. W. Dachowski and C. F. Flaherty), pp. 25–53. Erlbaum, Hillsdale, NJ.

—— and Bolles, R.C. (1979). Contextual control of the extinction of conditioned fear. *Learning and Motivation*, **10**, 445–6.

—— and King, D.A. (1983). Contextual control of the extinction of conditioned fear: tests for the associative value of the context. *Journal of Experimental Psychology: Animal Behavior Processes*, **9**, 248–65.

—— and Peck, C.A. (1989). Context effects on conditioning, extinction, and reinstatement in an appetitive conditioning preparation. *Animal Learning and Behavior*, **17**, 188–98.

—— and Swartzentruber, D. (1986). Analysis of the associative and occasion-setting properties of contexts participating in a Pavlovian discrimination. *Journal of Experimental Psychology: Animal Behavior Processes*, **12**, 333–50.

—— and —— (1989). Slow reacquisition following extinction: context, encoding, and retrieval mechanisms. *Journal of Experimental Psychology: Animal Behavior Processes*, **15**, 43–53.

Braveman, N.S. (1978). Preexposure to feeding-related stimuli reduces neophobia. *Animal Learning and Behavior*, **6**, 417–22.

—— and Jarvis, P.S. (1978). Independence of neophobia and taste aversion learning. *Animal Learning and Behavior*, **6**, 406–12.

Brodigan, D.L. and Peterson, G.B. (1976). Two-choice conditional discrimination performance as a function of reward expectancy, prechoice delay, and domesticity. *Animal Learning and Behavior*, **4**, 121–4.

Brogden, W.J. (1939). Sensory pre-conditioning. *Journal of Experimental Psychology*, **25**, 323–32.

Brown, B.L. (1970). Stimulus generalization in salivary conditioning. *Journal of Comparative and Physiological Psychology*, **71**, 467–77.

Calvin, A.D. (1953). The growth of learning during nondifferential reinforcement. *Journal of Experimental Psychology*, **46**, 248–54.

Cantor, G.N. (1955). Effects of three types of pretraining on discrimination learning in preschool children. *Journal of Experimental Psychology*, **49**, 339–42.

—— and Hottel, J.V. (1957). Psychomotor learning in defectives as a function of verbal pretraining. *Psychological Record*, **7**, 79–85.

Cantor, J.H. (1955). Amount of pretraining as a factor in stimulus predifferentiation and performance set. *Journal of Experimental Psychology*, **50**, 180–4.

—— (1965). Transfer of stimulus pretraining in motor paired-associate and discrimination learning tasks. In *Advances in child development and behavior*, Vol. 2, (ed. L. P. Lipsitt, and C. C. Spiker), pp. 19–58. Academic Press, New York.

Carlson, J.G. (174). Preconditioning the effects of shock-correlated reinforcement. *Journal of Experimental Psychology*, **103**, 409–13.

—— and Wielkiewicz, R.M. (1972). Delay of reinforcement in instrumental discrimination learning of rats. *Journal of Comparative and Physiological Psychology*, **81**, 365–70.

—— and —— (1976). Mediators of the effects of magnitude of reinforcement. *Learning and Motivation*, **7**, 184–96.

Carlton, P.L. and Vogel, J.R. (1967). Habituation and conditioning. *Journal of Comparative and Physiological Psychology*, **63**, 438–51.

Carr, A.F. (1974). Latent inhibition and overshadowing in conditioned emotional response conditioning in rats. *Journal of Comparative and Physiological Psychology*, **86**, 718–23.

Chamizo, V.D. and Mackintosh, N.J. (1989). Latent learning and latent inhibition in maze discriminations. *Quarterly Journal of Experimental Psychology*, **41B**, 21–31.

Channell, S. and Hall, G. (1981). Facilitation and retardation of discrimination learning after exposure to the stimuli. *Journal of Experimental Psychology: Animal Behavior Processes*, **7**, 437–46.

—— and —— (1983). Contextual effects in latent inhibition with an appetitive conditioning procedure. *Animal Learning and Behavior*, **1**, 67–74.

Chantrey, D.F. (1972). Enhancement and retardation of discrimination learning in chicks after exposure to the discriminanda. *Journal of Comparative and Physiological Psychology*, **81**, 256–61.

—— (1974). Stimulus preexposure and discrimination learning by domestic chicks: effect of varying interstimulus time. *Journal of Comparative and Physiological Psychology*, **87**, 517–25.

Chiszar, D.A. and Spear, N.E. (1969). Stimulus change, reversal learning and retention in the rat. *Journal of Comparative and Physiological Psychology*, **69**, 190–5.

Churchill, M., Remington, B., and Siddle, D.A.T. (1987). The effects of context change on long-term habituation of the orienting response in humans. *Quarterly Journal of Experimental Psychology*, **39B**, 315–38.

Collins, L. and Pearce, J.M. (1985). Predictive accuracy and the effects of partial reinforcement on serial autoshaping. *Journal of Experimental Psychology: Animal Behavior Processes*, **11**, 548–64.

——, Young, D.B., Davies, K., and Pearce, J.M. (1983). The influence of partial reinforcement on serial autoshaping with pigeons. *Quarterly Journal of Experimental Psychology*, **35B**, 275–90.

Corman, C.D. (1967). Stimulus generalization of habituation of the galvanic skin response. *Journal of Experimental Psychology*, **74**, 236–40.

Couvillon, P.A., Tennant, W.A., and Bitterman, M.E. (1967). Intradimensional vs. extradimensional transfer in the discriminative learning of goldfish and pigeons. *Animal Learning and Behavior*, **4**, 197–203.

Cross, H.A., Halcomb, C.G., and Matter, W.W. (1967). Imprinting or exposure learning in rats given early auditory stimulation. *Psychonomic Science*, **7**, 233–4.

Crowell, C.R. and Anderson, D.C. (1972). Variations in intensity, interstimulus interval and interval between CS exposure and conditioning with rats. *Journal of Comparative and Physiological Psychology*, 79, 291–8.

D'Amato, M.R., Salmon, D.P., and Colombo, M. (1985). Extent and limits of the matching concept in monkeys (*Cebus apella*). *Journal of Experimental Psychology: Animal Behavior Processes*, 11, 35–51.

Davis, M. (1970). Effects of interstimulus interval length and variability on startle response habituation. *Journal of Comparative and Physiological Psychology*, 72, 177–92.

Dawley, J.M. (1979). Generalization of the CS–preexposure effect transfers to taste-aversion learning. *Animal Learning and Behavior*, 7, 23–4.

DeLong, R.E., and Wasserman, E.A. (1981). Effects of differential reinforcement expectancies on successive matching-to-sample performance in pigeons. *Journal of Experimental Psychology: Animal Behavior Processes*, 7, 394–412.

Dember, W.N. and Earl, R.W. (1957). Analysis of exploratory, manipulatory, and curiosity behavior. *Psychological Review*, 64, 91–6.

Denenberg, V.A. (1964). Critical periods, stimulus input, and emotional reactivity: a theory of infantile stimulation. *Psychological Review*, 71, 335–51.

DeRivera, J. (1959). Some conditions governing the use of the cue producing response as an explanatory device. *Journal of Experimental Psychology*, 57, 299–304.

Desiderato, O., Butler, B., and Meyer, C. (1966). Changes in fear generalization gradients as a function of delayed testing. *Journal of Psychology*, 72, 678–82.

Dexter, W.R. and Merrill, H.K. (1969). Rate of contextual discrimination in fear conditioning. *Journal of Comparative and Physiological Psychology*, 69, 677–81.

Dickinson, A. (1976). Appetitive–aversion interactions: facilitation of aversive conditioning by prior appetitive training in the rat. *Animal Learning and Behavior*, 4, 416–20.

—— (1977). Appetitive–aversion interactions: superconditioning of fear by an appetitive CS. *Quarterly Journal of Experimental Psychology*, 29, 71–83.

—— and Dearing, M.F. (1979). Appetitive–aversive interactions and inhibitory processes. In *Mechanisms of learning and motivation* (ed. A. Dickinson and R. A. Boakes), pp. 203–31. Erlbaum, Hillsdale, NJ.

—— and Mackintosh, N.J. (1978). Classical conditioning in animals, *Annual Review of Psychology*, 29, 587–612.

—— and Pearce, J.M. (1977). Inhibitory interactions between appetitive and aversive stimuli. *Psychological Bulletin*, 84, 690–711.

Dollard, J. and Miller, N.E. (1950). *Personality and psychotherapy*, McGraw-Hill, New York.

Domjan, M. (1975). Poison-induced neophobia: role of stimulus generalization in conditioned taste aversions. *Animal Learning and Behavior*, 3, 205–11.

——, (1976). Determinants of the enhancement of flavored-water intake by prior exposure. *Journal of Experimental Psychology: Animal Behavior Processes*, 2, 17–27.

—— (1977). Attenuation and enhancement of neophobia for edible substances. In *Learning mechanisms in food selection* (ed. L. M. Barker, M. R. Best, and M. Domjan), pp. 151–79. Baylor University Press, Waco, TX.

—— and Gillan, D. (1976). Role of novelty in the aversion for increasingly concentrated saccharin solutions. *Physiology and Behavior*, **16**, 537–42.

—— and Siegel, S. (1971). Conditioned suppression following CS preexposure. *Psychonomic Science*, **25**, 11–12.

Durlach, P.J. and Mackintosh, N.J. (1986). Transfer of serial reversal learning in the pigeon. *Quarterly Journal of Experimental Psychology*, **38B**, 81–95.

Eck, K.O., Noel, R.C., and Thomas, D.R. (1969). Discrimination learning as a function of prior discrimination and nondifferential training. *Journal of Experimental Psychology*, **82**, 156–62.

Edwards, C.A., Jagielo, J.A., Zentall, T.R., and Hogan, D.E. (1982). Acquired equivalence and distinctiveness in matching to sample by pigeons: mediation by reinforcer-specific expectancies. *Journal of Experimental Psychology: Animal Behavior Processes*, **8**, 244–59.

Eikelboom, R. and Stewart, J. (1982). Conditioning of drug-induced physiological response. *Psychological Review*, **89**, 518–27.

Eisman, B.S. (1955). Attitude formation: the development of a colour preference response through mediated generalization. *Journal of Abnormal and Social Psychology*, **50**, 321–6.

Ellis, H.C. and Feuge, R.L. (1966). Transfer of predifferentiation training to gradients of generalization in shape recognition. *Journal of Experimental Psychology*, **71**, 539–42.

—— and Homan, L.E. (1968). Implicit verbal responses and the transfer of stimulus predifferentiation. *Journal of Experimental Psychology*, **76**, 486–9.

—— and Muller, D.G. (1964). Transfer in perceptual learning following stimulus predifferentiation. *Journal of Experimental Psychology*, **68**, 388–95.

——, Bessemer, D.W., Devine, J.W., and Trafton C.L. (1962). Recognition of random tactual shapes following predifferentiation training. *Perceptual and Motor Skills*, **10**, 99–102.

——, Feuge, R.L., Long, K.K., and Pegram, V.G. (1964). Evidence for acquired equivalence of cues in a perceptual task. *Perceptual and Motor Skills*, **19**, 159–62.

——, Muller, D.G., and Tosti, D.T. (1966). Stimulus meaning and complexity as factors in the transfer of stimulus predifferentiation. *Journal of Experimental Psychology*, **71**, 629–33.

Epstein, W. (1967). *Varieties of perceptual learning*, McGraw-Hill, New York.

Estes, W.K. (1950). Towards a statistical theory of learning. *Psychological Review*, **57**, 94–107.

Evans, J.G.M. and Hammond, G.R. (1983). Differential generalization of habituation across contexts as a function of stimulus significance. *Animal Learning and Behavior*, **11**, 431–4.

Fanselow, M.S. (1990). Factors governing one-trial contextual conditioning. *Animal Learning and Behavior*, **18**, 264–70.

Fedorchak, P.M. and Bolles, R.C. (1986). Differential outcome effect using a biologically neutral outcome difference. *Journal of Experimental Psychology: Animal Behavior Processes*, **12**, 125–30.

Forbes, D.T. and Holland, P.C. (1980). Positive and negative patterning after CS preexposure in flavour aversion conditioning. *Animal Learning and Behavior*, **8**, 595–600.

—— and —— (1985). Spontaneous configuring in conditioned flavor aversion. *Journal of Experimental Psychology: Animal Behavior Processes*, **11**, 224–40.

Foreman, N. and Thinus-Blanc, C. (1987). Weakness of the 'missing-stimulus effect' in hooded rats: gross asymmetry in the Sokolovian orienting response. *Psychobiology*, **15**, 265–71.

Forgus, R.H. (1956). Advantage of early over late perceptual experience in improving discrimination. *Canadian Journal of Psychology*, **10**, 147–55.

—— (1985a). The effect of different kinds of form preexposure on form discrimination learning. *Journal of Comparative and Physiological Psychology*, **51**, 588–91.

—— (1985b). The interaction between form preexposure and test requirements in determining form discrimination. *Journal of Comparative and Physciological Psychology*, **51**, 588–91.

Fowler, H., Fago, G.C., Domber, E.A., and Hochhauser, M. (1973). Signaling and affective functions in Pavlovian conditioning. *Animal Learning and Behavior*, **1**, 81–9.

——, Goodman, J.H., and Zanich, M.L. (1977). Pavlovian aversive to instrumental appetitive transfer: evidence for cross-reinforcement blocking effects. *Animal Learning and Behavior*, **5**, 129–34.

Franchina, J.J. and Fitzgerald, B.A. (1983). Poison-enhanced neophobia: effects of CS–UCS/UCS–CS procedures and long-delay training. *Learning and Motivation*, **14**, 351–66.

—— and Gilley, D.W. (1986). Effects of pretraining on conditioning enhanced neophobia: evidence for separable mechanisms of neophobia and aversion conditioning. *Animal Learning and Behavior*, **14**, 155–62.

Franken, R.E. and Bray, G.P. (1973). Prolonged duration of the 'novelty effect' following prolonged exposure to a single discrimination. *Animal Learning and Behavior*, **1**, 233–6.

Friedman, G.J. and Carlson, J.G. (1973). Effects of a stimulus correlated with positive reinforcement upon discrimination learning. *Journal of Experimental Psychology*, **97**, 281–6.

Frieman, J. and Goyette, C.H. (1973). Transfer of training across stimulus modality and response class. *Journal of Experimental Psychology*, **97**, 235–41.

Gabriel, M. and Vogt, J. (1972). Incubation of avoidance CRs in the rabbit produced by increase over time of stimulus generalization to apparatus. *Behavioral Biology*, **7**, 113–25.

Gagné, R.M. and Baker, K.E. (1950). Stimulus predifferentiation as a factor in transfer of training. *Journal of Experimental Psychology*, **40**, 439–51.

Galbraith, K. (1973). Fractional anticipatory goal responses as cues in discrimination learning. *Journal of Experimental Psychology*, **97**, 177–81.

Gallagher, M., Meagher, M.W., and Bostock, E. (1987). Effects of opiate manipulations on latent inhibition in rabbits: Sensitivity of the medial septal region to intracranial treatment. *Behavioral Neuroscience*, **101**, 315–24.

Ghiselli, W.B. and Fowler, H. (1976). Signaling and affective functions of the conditioned aversive stimuli in an appetitive choice discrimination: US intensity effects. *Learning and Motivation*, **7**, 1–16.

Gibbon, J., Farrell, L., Locurto, C.M., Duncan, H.J., and Terrace, H.S. (1980). Partial reinforcement in autoshaping with pigeons. *Animal Learning and Behavior*, **8**, 45–59.

Gibson, E.J. (1940). A systematic application of the concepts of generalization and differentiation to verbal learning. *Psychological Review*, 47, 196–229.

Gibson, E.J. (1969). *Principles of perceptual learning and development*. Appleton-Century-Crofts, New York.

—— and Levin, H. (1975). *The psychology of reading*. MIT Press, Cambridge, MA.

—— and Walk, R.D. (1956). The effect of prolonged exposure to visually presented patterns on learning to discriminate them. *Journal of Comparative and Physiological Psychology*, 49, 239–42.

—— and ——, Pick, H.L., and Tighe, T.J. (1958). The effect of prolonged exposure to visual patterns on learning to discriminate similar and different patterns. *Journal of Comparative and Physiological Psychology*, 51, 584–7.

——, ——, and Tighe, T.J. (1950). Enhancement and deprivation of visual stimulation during rearing as factors in visual discrimination. *Journal of Comparative and Physiological Psychology*, 52, 74–81.

Gibson J.J. and Gibson E.J. (1955). Perceptual learning—differentiation or enrichment? *Psychological Review*, 62, 32–41.

Gillette, K. and Bellingham, W.P. (1982). Loss of within-compound flavour associations: configural preconditioning. *Experimental Animal Behaviour*, 1, 1–17.

Gilley, D.W. and Franchina, J.J. (1985). Effects of preexposure flavor concentration on conditioned aversion and neophobia. *Behavioral and Neural Biology*, 44, 503–8.

Gisquet-Verrier, P. and Alexinsky, T. (1986). Does contextual change determine long-term forgetting? *Animal Learning and Behavior*, 14, 349–58.

Gluck, M.A. and Bower, G.H. (1988). From conditioning to category learning: an adaptive network model. *Journal of Experimental Psychology: General*, 117, 227–47.

Godden, D.R. and Baddeley, A.D. (1975). Context-dependent memory in two natural environments: on land and underwater. *British Journal of Psychology*, 66, 325–32.

—— and —— (1980). When does context influence recognition memory. *British Journal of Psychology*, 71, 99–104.

Goodman, J.H. and Fowler, H. (1976). Transfer of signaling properties of aversive CSs to an instrumental appetitive discrimination. *Learning and Motivation*, 7, 446–57.

Gordon, W.C., McCracken, K.M., Dess-Beech, N., and Mowrer, R.R. (1981). Mechanisms for the cueing phenomenon: the addition of the cueing context to the training memory. *Learning and Motivation*, 12, 196–211.

Goss, A.E. (1953). Transfer as a function of type and amount of preliminary experience with task stimuli. *Journal of Experimental Psychology*, 46, 419–28.

—— and Greenfield, N. (1958). Transfer to a motor task as influenced by conditions and degree of prior discrimination training. *Journal of Experimental Psychology*, 55, 258–69.

Graham, F.K. (1973). Habituation and dishabituation of responses innervated by the autonomic nervous system. In *Habituation*, Vol. 1, *Behavioral studies* (ed. H. V. S. Peeke and M. J. Herz), pp. 162–218. Academic Press, New York.

Grastyan, E. (1961). The significance of the earliest manifestations of conditioning in the mechanism of learning. In *Brain mechanisms and learning* (ed. A. Fessard), pp. 243–63. Blackwell, Oxford.

Gray, J.A. (1975). *Elements of a two-process theory of learning*. Academic Press, London.

Gray, T. and Lethbridge, D.A. (1976). Configural conditioning in the CER: loss of element strength after repeated reinforced compound CS trials. *Learning and Motivation*, 7, 532–9.

Green, K.F. and Parker, L.A. (1975). Gustatory memory: incubation and interference. *Behavioral Biology*, 13, 359–67.

Grice, G.R. (1965). Investigations of response-mediated generalization. In *Stimulus generalization* (ed. D. I. Mostofsky), pp. 373–82. Stanford University Press.

—— and Davis, J.D. (1958). Mediated stimulus equivalence and distinctiveness in human conditioning. *Journal of Experimental Psychology*, 55, 565–71.

—— and —— (1960). Effect of concurrent responses on the evocation and generalization of the conditioned eyeblink. *Journal of Experimental Psychology*, 59, 391–5.

—— and Hunter, J.J. (1963). Response mediation of the conditioned eyelid response. *Journal of Experimental Psychology*, 66, 338–46.

Groves, P.M. and Thompson, R.F. (1970). Habituation: a dual-process theory. *Psychological Review*, 77, 419–50.

Hake, H.W. and Eriksen, C.W. (1955). Effect of number of permissible response categories on learning of a constant number of visual stimuli. *Journal of Experimental Psychology*, 50, 161–7.

—— and —— (1956). Role of response variables in recognition and identification of complex forms. *Journal of Experimental Psychology*, 52, 235–43.

Halgren, C.R. (1974). Latent inhibition in rats: associative or nonassociative? *Journal of Comparative and Physiological Psychology*, 86, 74–8.

Hall, G. (1974). Transfer effects produced by overtraining in the rat. *Journal of Comparative and Physiological Psychology*, 87, 938–44.

—— (1975). An analysis of positive general transfer in discrimination learning in the rat. *Animal Learning and Behavior*, 3, 212–16.

—— (1979). Exposure learning in young and adult laboratory rats. *Animal Behaviour*, 27, 586–91.

—— (1980). Exposure learning in animals. *Psychological Bulletin*, 88, 535–50.

—— (1983). *Behaviour: an introduction to psychology as a biological science*. Academic Press, New York.

—— (1990). Reasoning and associative learning. In *Behaviour analysis in theory and practice*, (ed. D. E. Blackman and H. Lejeune) pp. 159–80. Erlbaum, Hillsdale, NJ.

—— and Channell, S. (1980). A search for perceptual differentiation produced by nondifferential reinforcement. *Quarterly Journal of Experimental Psychology*, 32, 185–95.

—— and —— (1983). Stimulus exposure and discrimination in rats: a test of a theory for the role of contextual factors. *Quarterly Journal of Experimental Psychology*, 35B, 135–47.

—— and —— (1985a). A comparsion of intradimensional and extradimensional shift learning in pigeons. *Behavioural Processes*, 10, 285–95.

—— and —— (1985b). Differential effects of contextual change on latent inhibition and on the habituation of an orienting response. *Journal of Experimental Psychology: Animal Behavior Processes*, 11, 470–81.

—— and —— (1985c). Latent inhibition and conditioning after preexposure to the conditioning context. *Learning and Motivation*, 16, 381–97.

—— and —— (1986). Context specificity of latent inhibition in taste aversion learning. *Quarterly Journal of Experimental Psychology*, 38B, 121–39.

—— and Honey, R.C. (1989*a*). Contextual effects in conditioning, latent inhibition, and habituation: associative and retrieval functions of contextual cues. *Journal of Experimental Psychology: Animal Behavior Processes*, **15**, 232–41.

—— and —— (1989*b*). Perceptual and associative learning. In *Contemporary learning theories: Pavlovian conditioning and the status of traditional learning theory* (ed. S. B. Klein and R. R. Mowrer), pp. 117–47. Erlbaum, Hillsdale, NJ.

—— and —— (1990). Context-specific conditioning in the conditioned-emotional-response procedure. *Journal of Experimental Psychology: Animal Behavior Processes*, **16**, 271–8.

—— and Minor, H. (1984). A search for context–stimulus associations in latent inhibition. *Quarterly Journal of Experimental Psychology*, **36B**, 145–69.

—— and Pearce, J.M. (1978). Transfer of learning across reinforcers: appetitive discrimination learning between stimuli previously associated with shock. *Quarterly Journal of Experimental Psychology*, **30**, 539–49.

—— and —— (1979). Latent inhibition of a CS during CS–US pairings. *Journal of Experimental Psychology: Animal Behavior Processes*, **5**, 31–42.

—— and —— (1982). Changes in stimulus associability during conditioning: implications for theories of acquisition. In *Quantitative analyses of behavior*, Vol. 3 (ed. M. L. Commons, R. J. Herrnstein, and A. R. Wagner), pp. 221–39. Ballinger, Cambridge, MA.

—— and Schachtman, T.R. (1987). Differential effects of a retention interval on latent inhibition and the habituation of an orienting response. *Animal Learning and Behavior*, **15**, 76–82.

——, Kaye, H., and Pearce, J.M. (1985). Attention and conditioned inhibition. In *Information processing in animals: conditioned inhibition* (ed. R. R. Miller and N. E. Spear), pp. 185–207. Erlbaum, Hillsdale, NJ.

Hamlin, P.H. (1975). Observing responses as an index of attention in chickens. *Journal of Experimental Psychology: Animal Behavior Processes*, **1**, 221–34.

Hearst, E. and Koresko, M.B. (1968). Stimulus generalization and amount of prior training on variable-interval reinforcement. *Journal of Comparative and Physiological Psychology*, **66**, 133–8.

Hebb, D.O. (1949). *The organization of behavior*, John Wiley, New York.

Hendrickson, L.N. and Muehl, S. (1962). The effect of attention and motor response pretraining on learning to discriminate b and d in kindergarten children. *Journal of Educational Psychology*, **53**, 236–41.

Hill, W.F. (1978). Effects of mere exposure on preferences in nonhuman mammals. *Psychological Bulletin*, **85**, 1177–98.

Hirsh, R. (1980). The hippocampus, conditional operations, and cognition. *Physiological Psychology*, **8**, 175–82.

Hoffeld, D.R. (1962). Primary stimulus generalization and secondary extinction as a function of strength of conditioning. *Journal of Comparative and Physiological Psychology*, **55**, 27–31.

Holder, M.D. (1988). Possible role of confounded taste stimuli in conditioned taste aversions. *Animal Learning and Behavior*, **16**, 231–4.

Holland, P.C. (1981). Acquisition of representation-mediated conditioned food aversions. *Learning and Motivation*, **12**, 1–18.

—— (1983). Occasion setting in Pavlovian feature positive discriminations. In *Quan-*

titative analyses of behavior, Vol. 4 (ed. M. L. Commons, R. J. Herrnstein, and A. R. Wagner), pp. 183–206. Ballinger, Cambridge, MA.

—— and Forbes, D.T. (1980). Effects of compound or element preexposure on compound flavor aversion learning. *Animal Learning and Behavior*, **8**, 199–203.

—— and —— (1982*a*) Control of conditional discrimination performance by CS-evoked event representations. *Animal Learning and Behavior*, **10**, 249–56.

—— and —— (1982*b*). Representation-mediated extinction of conditioned flavor aversions. *Learning and Motivation*, **13**, 454–71.

—— and Gory, J. (1986). Extinction of inhibition after serial and simultaneous feature negative discrimination training. *Quarterly Journal of Experimental Psychology*, **38B**, 245–65.

Holton, R.B. and Goss, A.E. (1956). Transfer to a discriminative motor task as a function of amount and type of preliminary verbalization. *Journal of General Psychology*, **55**, 117–26.

Honey, R.C. (1990). Stimulus generalization as a function of stimulus novelty and familiarity in rats. *Journal of Experimental Psychology: Animal Behavior Processes*, **16**, 178–84.

—— and Hall, G. (1988). Overshadowing and blocking procedures in latent inhibition. *Quarterly Journal of Experimental Psychology*, **40B**, 163–86.

—— and —— (1989*a*). Enhanced discriminability and reduced associability following flavor preexposure. *Learning and Motivation*, **20**, 262–77.

—— and —— (1989*b*). Attenuation of latent inhibition after compound preexposure: associative and perceptual explanations. *Quarterly Journal of Experimental Psychology*, **41B**, 355–68.

—— and —— (1989*c*). The acquired equivalence and distinctiveness of cues. *Journal of Experimental Psychology: Animal Behavior Processes*, **15**, 338–46.

——, Schachtman, T.R. and Hall, G. (1987). Partial reinforcement in serial autoshaping: the role of attentional and associative factors. *Learning and Motivation*, **18**, 288–300.

——, Willis, A., and Hall, G. (1990). Context specificity in pigeon autoshaping. *Learning and Motivation*, **21**, 125–36.

Honig, W.K. (1969). Attentional factors governing the slope of the generalization gradient. In *Animal discrimination learning*, (ed. R. M. Gilbert and N. S. Sutherland), pp. 35–62. Academic Press, London.

—— (1981). Working memory and the temporal map. In *Information processing in animals: memory mechanisms* (ed. N. E. Spear and R. R. Miller), pp. 167–97. Erlbaum, Hillsdale, N.J.

Hovland, C.I. (1937). The generalization of conditioned responses. IV. The effect of varying amounts of reinforcement upon the degree of generalization of conditioned responses. *Journal of Experimental Psychology*, **21**, 261–76.

Hull, C.L. (1939). The problem of stimulus equivalence in behavior theory. *Psychological Review*, **46**, 9–30.

—— (1943). *Principles of Behavior*. Appleton-Century, New York.

—— (1952). *A behavior system*. Yale University Press.

Jackson, D.E. (1974). CS-free food contingencies and subsequent acquisition of conditioned suppression: no transfer effect. *Bulletin of the Psychonomic Society*, **4**, 235–6.

James, J.H. and Wagner, A.R. (1980). One-trial overshadowing: evidence of distributive processing. *Journal of Experimental Psychology: Animal Behavior Processes*, **6**, 188–205.

James, J.P. (1971). Latent inhibition and the preconditioning–conditioning interval. *Psychonomic Science*, **24**, 97–8.

James, W. (1890). *The principles of psychology*, Holt, New York.

Jaynes, J. (1950). Learning a second response to a cue as a function of the magnitude of the first. *Journal of Comparative and Physiological Psychology*, **43**, 398–408.

Jeeves, M.A. and North, A.J. (1956). Irrelevant or partially correlated stimuli in discrimination learning. *Journal of Experimental Psychology*, **52**, 90–4.

Jeffrey, W.E. (1953). The effects of verbal and nonverbal responses in mediating an instrumental act. *Journal of Experimental Psychology*, **45**, 327–33.

Kalat, J.W. (1977). Status of 'learned safety' or 'learned noncorrelation' as a mechanism in taste-aversion learning. In *Learning mechanisms in food selection*, (ed. L. M. Barker, M. R. Best, and M. Domjan), pp. 273–93. Baylor University Press, Waco, TX.

—— and Rozin, P. (1973). 'Learned safety' as a mechanism in long-delay taste-aversion learning in rats. *Journal of Comparative and Physiological Psychology*, **83**, 198–207.

Kamin, L.J. (1968). 'Attention-like' processes in classical conditioning. In *Miami symposium on the prediction of behavior: aversive stimulation*. (ed. M. R. Jones), pp. 9–33. University of Miami Press.

—— and Idrobo, F. (1978). Configural conditioning and the CER: a possible artifact. *Animal Learning and Behavior*, **6**, 290–3.

Kasprow, W.J., Catterson, D., Schachtman, T.R., and Miller, R.R. (1984). Attenuation of latent inhibition by a post-acquisition reminder. *Quarterly Journal of Experimental Psychology*, **36B**, 53–63.

——, Schachtman, T.R., and Miller, R.R. (1985). Associability of a previously conditioned stimulus as a function of qualitative changes in the US. *Quarterly Journal of Experimental Psychology*, **37B**, 33–48.

Katz, P.A. (1963). Effects of labels on children's perception and discrimination learning. *Journal of Experimental Psychology*, **66**, 423–8.

Kawachi, J. (1965). Effect of previous preceptual experience of specific three-dimensional objects on later visual discrimination behavior in rats. *Japanese Journal of Psychological Research*, **7**, 20–7.

Kaye, H. and Mackintosh, N.J. (1990). A change of context can enhance performance of an aversive but not of an appetitive conditioned response. *Quarterly Journal of Experimental Psychology*, **42B**, 113–34.

Kaye, H. and Pearce, J.M. (1984). The strength of the orienting response during Pavlovian conditioning. *Journal of Experimental Psychology: Animal Behavior Processes*, **10**, 90–109.

—— and —— (1987). Hippocampal lesions attenuate latent inhibition and the decline of the orienting response in rats. *Quarterly Journal of Experimental Psychology*, **39B**, 107–25.

——, Preston, G.C., Szabo, L., Druiff, H., and Mackintosh, N.J. (1987). Context specificity of conditioning and latent inhibition: evidence for a dissociation of latent inhibition and associative interference. *Quarterly Journal of Experimental Psychology*, **39B**, 127–45.

——, Gambini, B., and Mackintosh, N.J. (1988). A dissociation between one-trial overshadowing and the effect of a distractor on habituation. *Quarterly Journal of Experimental Psychology*, **40B**, 31–47.

——, Swietalski, N., and Mackintosh, N.J. (1988*a*). Habituation as a function of similarity and temporal location of target and distractor stimuli. *Animal Learning and Behavior*, **16**, 93–9.

——, ——, and —— (1988*b*). Distractor effects on latent inhibition are a consequence of generalization decrement. *Quarterly Journal of Experimental Psychology*, **40B**, 151–61.

Keilitz, I. and Frieman, J. (1970). Transfer of training following errorless discrimination training. *Journal of Experimental Psychology*, **85**, 293–9.

Kelleher, R.T. (1956). Discrimination learning as a function of reversal and nonreversal shifts. *Journal of Experimental Psychology*, **51**, 379–84.

Kerpelman, L.C. (1965). Preexposure to visually presented forms and nondifferential reinforcement in perceptual learning. *Journal of Experimental Psychology*, **69**, 257–62.

Kimble, G.A. and Ost, J.W.P. (1961). A conditioned inhibitory process in eyelid conditioning. *Journal of Experimental Psychology*, **61**, 150–6.

Klosterhalfen, S., Fischer, W., and Bitterman, M.E. (1978). Modification of attention in honey bees. *Science*, **201**, 1241–3.

Konorski, J. (1967). *Integrative activity of the brain*. University of Chicago Press.

Kovach, J.K., Fabricius, E., and Falt, L. (1966). Relationship between imprinting and perceptual learning. *Journal of Comparative and Physiological Psychology*, **61**, 449–54.

Kraemer, P.J. and Ossenkopp, K-P. (1986). The effects of flavor preexposure and test interval on conditioned taste aversions in rats. *Bulletin of the Psychonomic Society*, **24**, 219–21.

—— and Roberts, W.A. (1984). The influence of flavor preexposure and test interval on conditioned taste aversions in the rat. *Learning and Motivation*, **15**, 259–78.

——, Hoffman, H., and Spear, N.E. (1988). Attentuation of the CS–preexposure effect after a retention interval in preweanling rats. *Animal Learning and Behavior*, **16**, 185–90.

Krank, M.D. (1985). Asymmetrical effects of Pavlovian excitatory and inhibiting aversive transfer on Pavlovian appetitive responding and acquistion. *Learning and Motivation*, **16**, 35–62.

Krank, M.P., Hinson, R.E., and Siegel, S. (1981). Conditioned hyperalgesia is elicited by environmental signals of morphine. *Behavioral and Neural Biology*, **32**, 148–57.

Kremer, E.F. (1972). Properties of preexposed stimulus. *Psychonomic Science*, **27**, 45–7.

Kurz, E.M., and Levitsky, D.A. (1982). Novelty of contextual cues in taste-aversion learning. *Animal Learning and Behavior*, **10**, 229–32.

Kurtz, K.H. (1955). Discrimination of complex stimuli: the relationship of training and test stimuli in transfer of discrimination. *Journal of Experimental Psychology*, **50**, 283–92.

—— and Hovland, C.J. (1953). The effect of verbalization during observation of stimulus objects upon accuracy of recognition and recall. *Journal of Experimental Psychology*, **45**, 157–64.

Lantz, A.E. (1973). Effect of number of trials, interstimulus interval, and dishabituation during CS habituation on subsequent conditioning in a CER paradigm. *Animal Learning and Behavior*, **1**, 273–7.

—— (1976). The effect of intensity of the preexposed stimulus on subsequent conditioning. *Bulletin of the Psychonomic Society*, **7**, 381–3.

Lashley, K.S. (1929). *Brain mechanisms and intelligence*, University of Chicago Press.

—— (1942). An examination of the continuity theory as applied to discriminative learning. *Journal of General Psychology*, **26**, 241–65.

Lawrence, D.H. (1949). Acquired distinctiveness of cues. I. Transfer between discriminations on the basis of familiarity with the stimulus. *Journal of Experimental Psychology*, **39**, 770–84.

—— (1950). Acquired distinctiveness of cues. II. Selective association in a constant stimulus situation. *Journal of Experimental Psychology*, **40**, 175–88.

—— (1952). The transfer of discrimination along a continuum. *Journal of Comparative and Physiological Psychology*, **45**, 511–16.

—— (1955). The applicability of generalization gradients to the transfer of a discrimination. *Journal of General Psychology*, **52**, 37–48.

—— (1963). The nature of a stimulus: some relationships between learning and perception. In *Psychology: a study of a science*, Vol. 5, (ed. S. Koch), pp. 179–212. McGraw-Hill, New York.

Lea, S.E.G. (1984). In what sense do pigeons learn concepts? In *Animal cognition* (ed. H. L. Roitblat, T. G. Bever, and H. S. Terrace), pp. 263–76. Erlbaum, Hillsdale, NJ.

—— and Morgan, M.J. (1972). The measurement of rate-dependent changes in responding. In *Reinforcement: behavioral analyses* (ed. R. M. Gilbert and J. R. Millenson), pp. 129–45. Academic Press, New York.

Leaton, R.N. (1974). Long-term retention of the habituation of lick suppression in rats. *Journal of Comparative and Physiological Psychology*, **87**, 1157–64.

Leeper, R.W. (1935). A study of a neglected portion of the field of learning—the development of sensory organization. *Journal of Genetic Psychology*, **46**, 41–75.

Levine, S. (1957). Infantile experience and resistance to psychological stress. *Science*, **126**, 405.

Liddell, H. (1950). The role of vigilance in the development of animal neurosis. In *Anxiety*, (ed. P. H. Hoch and J. Zubin), pp. 183–96. Hafner, New York.

Logan, F.A. (1966). Transfer of discrimination. *Journal of Experimental Psychology*, **71**, 616–18.

LoLordo, V.M. and Ross, R.T. (1987). Role of within-compound associations in occasion setting: a blocking analysis. *Journal of Experimental Psychology: Animal Behavior Processes*, **13**, 156–67.

Lovibond, P.F., Preston, G.C., and Mackintosh, N.J. (1984). Context specificity of conditioning and latent inhibition. *Journal of Experimental Psychology: Animal Behavior Processes*, **10**, 360–75.

Lubow, R.E. (1965). Latent inhibition: effects of frequency of nonreinforced preexposures to the CS. *Journal of Comparative and Physiological Psychology*, **60**, 454–7.

—— (1973). Latent inhibition. *Psychological Bulletin*, **79**, 398–407.

—— and Moore, A.U. (1959). Latent inhibition: the effect of nonreinforced preexposure to the conditional stimulus. *Journal of Comparative and Physiological Psychology*, **52**, 415–19.

——, Markman, R.E., and Allen, J. (1968). Latent inhibition and classical conditioning of the rabbit pinna response. *Journal of Comparative and Physiological Psychology*, **66**, 688–94.

——, Rifkin, B., and Alek, M. (1976). The context effect: the relationship between stimulus preexposure and environmental preexposure determines subsequent learning. *Journal of Experimental Psychology: Animal Behavior Processes*, **2**, 38–47.

——, Schnur, P., and Rifkin, B. (1976). Latent inhibition and conditioned attention theory. *Journal of Experimental Psychology: Animal Behavior Processes*, **2**, 163–74.

——, Weiner, I., and Schnur, R. (1981). Conditioned attention theory. In *The Psychology of learning and motivation*, Vol. 15 (ed. G. H. Bower), pp. 1–49. Academic Press, New York.

——, Wagner, M., and Weiner, I. (1982). The effects of compound stimulus preexposure of two elements differing in salience on the acquisition of conditioned suppression. *Animal Learning and Behavior*, **10**, 485–9.

McAllister, D.E. (1953). The effects of various kinds of relevant verbal pretraining on subsequent motor performance. *Journal of Experimental Psychology*, **46**, 329–36.

McAllister, W.R. and McAllister, D.E. (1963). Increase over time in the stimulus generalization of acquired fear. *Journal of Experimental Psychology*, **65**, 576–82.

McCollough, C. (1965). Color adaptation of edge-detectors in the human visual system. *Science*, **149**, 1115–16.

McCormack, P.D. (1958). Negative transfer in motor performance following a critical amount of verbal pretraining. *Perceptual and Motor Skills*, **8**, 27–31.

McIntosh, S.M. and Tarpy, R.N. (1977). Retention of latent inhibition in a taste-aversion paradigm. *Bulletin of the Psychonomic Society*, **9**, 411–12.

McLaren, I.P.L., Kaye, H., and Mackintosh, N.J. (1989). An associative theory of the representation of stimuli: applications to perceptual learning and latent inhibition. In *Parallel distributed processing: implications for psychology and neurobiology*, (ed. R. G. M. Morris), pp. 102–30. Clarendon Press, Oxford.

McNamara, H.J. (1959). Nonveridical perception as a function of rewards and punishments. *Perceptual and Motor Skills*, **9**, 67–80.

Mackintosh, N.J. (1962). The effects of overtraining on a reversal and a nonreversal shift. *Journal of Comparative and Physiological Psychology*, **55**, 555–9.

—— (1964). Overtraining and transfer within and between dimensions in the rat. *Quarterly Journal of Experimental Psychology*, **16**, 250–6.

—— (1965). Incidental cue learning in rats. *Quarterly Journal of Experimental Psychology*, **17**, 292–300.

—— (1969). Further analysis of the overtraining reversal effect, *Journal of Comparative and Physiological Psychology*, (Monograph supplement) **67**, No. 2, part 2.

—— (1973). Stimulus selection: learning to ignore stimuli that predict no change in reinforcement. In *Constraints on learning*, (ed. R. A. Hinde and J. S. Hinde), pp. 75–96. Academic Press, London.

—— (1974). *The psychology of animal learning*. Academic Press, London.

—— (1975). A theory of attention: variation in the associability of stimuli with reinforcement. *Psychological Review*, **82**, 276–98.

—— (1976). Overshadowing and stimulus intensity. *Animal Learning and Behavior*, **4**, 186–92.

—— (1977). Stimulus control: attentional factors. In *Handbook of operant behavior*, (ed. W. K. Honig and J. E. R. Staddon), pp. 481–513. Prentice-Hall, Englewood Cliffs, NJ.

—— (1983). *Conditioning and associative learning*. Clarendon Press, Oxford.

—— (1987). Neurobiology, psychology and habituation. *Behaviour Research and Therapy*, **12**, 81–97.

—— and Holgate, V. (1967). Effects of several pretraining procedures on brightness probability learning. *Perceptual and Motor Skills*, **25**, 629–37.

—— and Little, L. (1969). Intradimensional and extradimensional shift learning by pigeons. *Psychonomic Science*, **14**, 5–6.

—— and —— (1970). An analysis of transfer along a continuum. *Canadian Journal of Psychology*, **24**, 362–9.

—— and Reese, B. (1979). One-trial overshadowing. *Journal of Comparative and Physiological Psychology*, **31**, 519–26.

Macphail, E.M. (1982). *Brain and intelligence in vertebrates*. Clarendon Press, Oxford.

—— and Reilly, S. (1989). Rapid acquisition of novelty versus familiarity concept by pigeons. (*Columba livia*). *Journal of Experimental Psychology: Animal Behavior Processes*, **15**, 242–52.

Malloy, T.E. and Ellis, H.C. (1970). Attention and cue-producing responses in response-mediated stimulus generalization. *Journal of Experimental Psychology*, **83**, 191–200.

Mandler, J.M. (1966). Behavior changes during overtraining and their effects on reversal and transfer. *Psychonomic Monograph* (Supplement), **1**(6), 187–202.

—— (1968). Overtraining and the use of positive and negative stimuli in reversal and transfer. *Journal of Comparative and Physiological Psychology*, **66**, 110–15.

Marlin, N.A. (1982). Within-compound associations between context and the conditioned stimulus. *Learning and Motivation*, **13**, 526–41.

—— (1983). Second-order conditioning using a contextual stimulus as S1. *Animal Learning and Behavior*, **11**, 290–4.

—— and Miller, R.R. (1981). Associations to contextual stimuli as a determinant of long-term habituation. *Journal of Experimental Psychology: Animal Behavior Processes*, **7**, 313–33.

Marsh, G. (1969). An evaluation of three explanations for the transfer of discrimination effect. *Journal of Comparative and Physiological Psychology*, **68**, 268–75.

Matzel, L.D., Schachtman, T.R., and Miller, R.R. (1988). Learned irrelevance exceeds the sum of CS–preexposure and US–preexposure deficits. *Journal of Experimental Psychology: Animal Behavior Processes*, **14**, 311–19.

Mazur, J.E. and Wagner, A.R. (1982). An episodic model of associative learning. In *Quantitative analyses of Behavior*, Vol. 3 (ed. M. L. Commons, R. J. Herrnstein and A. R. Wagner), pp. 3–39. Ballinger, Cambridge, MA.

Mellgren, R.L., Hunsicker, J.R., and Dyck, D.C. (1975). Conditions of preexposure and passive avoidance behavior in rats. *Animal Learning and Behavior*, **3**, 147–51.

Mercier, P. and Baker, A.G. (1985). Latent inhibition, habituation, and sensory preconditioning: a test of priming in short-term memory. *Journal of Experimental Psychology: Animal Behavior Processes*, **11**, 485–501.

Miller, N.E. (1948). Theory and experiment relating psychoanalytic displacements to stimulus–response generalization. *Journal of Abnormal and Social Psychology*, **43**, 155–78.

—— and Dollard, J. (1941). *Social learning and imitation*. Yale University Press.

Miller R.R. and Holtzman, A.D. (1981). Neophobias and conditioned taste aversions in rats following exposure to novel flavors. *Animal Learning and Behavior*, 9, 89–100.

—— and Schachtman, T.R. (1985). The several roles of context at the time of retrieval. In *Context and learning* (ed. P. D. Balsam and A. Tomie), pp. 167–94. Erlbaum, Hillsdale, NJ.

—— and Springer, A.D. (1973). Amnesia, consolidation and retrieval. *Psychological Review*, 80, 69–70.

Misanin, J.R., Blatt, L.A., and Hinderliter, C.F. (1985). Age dependency in neophobia: its influence on taste-aversion learning and the flavor-preexposure effect in rats. *Animal Learning and Behavior*, 13, 69–76.

Mitchell, D., Kirschbaum, E.H., and Perry, R.L. (1975). Effects of neophobia and habituation on the poison-induced avoidance of exteroceptive stimuli in the rat. *Journal of Experimental Psychology: Animal Behavior Processes*, 1, 47–55.

——, Winter, W., and Moffitt, T. (1980). Cross-modality contrast: exteroceptive context habituation enhanced taste neophobia and conditioned taste aversion. *Animal Learning and Behavior*, 8, 524–8.

——, Koleszar, A.S., and Scopatz, R.A. (1984). Arousal and T-maze choice behavior in mice: a convergent paradigm for neophobia constructs and optimal arousal theory. *Learning and Motivation*, 15, 287–301.

Mullin, G.P. and Winefield, A.H. (1977). Immunization and helplessness. *Animal Learning and Behavior*, 5, 281–4.

—— and —— (1978). Helplessness in the rat: interfering response or motivational/cognitive deficit. *Perceptual and Motor Skills*, 47, 1059–680.

Murdock, B.B. (1958). Effects of task difficulty, stimulus similarity, and type of response on stimulus predifferentiation. *Journal of Experimental Psychology*, 55, 167–72.

Nachman, M. and Jones, D.R. (1974). Learned taste aversions over long delays in rats: the role of learned safety. *Journal of Comparative and Physiological Psychology*, 86, 949–56.

Neimark, E.D. and Estes, W.K. (1967). *Stimulus sampling theory*, Holden-Day, San Francisco.

Norcross, K.J. (1958). Effects of discrimination performance of similarity of previously acquired stimulus names. *Journal of Experimental Psychology*, 56, 305–9.

—— and Spiker, C.C. (1957). The effects of type of stimulus pretraining on discrimination performance in preschool children. *Child Development*, 28, 79–84.

Öhman, A. (1979). The orienting response, attention and learning: an information-processing perspective. In *The orienting reflex in humans*, (ed. H. D. Kimmel, E. H. van Olst, and J. F. Orlebeke), pp. 443–71. Erlbaum, Hillsdale, NJ.

—— (1983). The orienting response during Pavlovian conditioning. In *Orienting and habituation* (ed. D. Siddle), pp. 315–69. Wiley, Chichester.

Olson, G. and King, R.A. (1962). Stimulus generalization gradients along a luminosity continuum. *Journal of Experimental Psychology*, 63, 414–15.

O'Neill, W. and Beiderman, G.B. (1974). Avoidance conditioning as a function of appetitive stimulus pretraining: response and stimulus transfer effects. *Learning and Motivation*, 5, 195–208.

Oswalt, R.M. (1972). Relationship between level of visual pattern difficulty during rearing and subsequent discrimination in rats. *Journal of Comparative and Physiological Psychology*, 81, 122–5.

Overmier, J.B. and Payne, R.J. (1971). Facilitation of instrumental avoidance learning by prior appetitive Pavlovian conditioning to the cues. *Acta Neurobiologiae Experimentalis*, **31**, 341–9.

—— and Wielkiewicz, R.M. (1983). On unpredictability as a causal factor in 'learned helplessness'. *Learning and Motivation*, **14**, 324–37.

Paletta, M.S. and Wagner, A.R. (1986). Development of context-specific tolerance to morphine: support for a dual-process interpretation. *Behavioral Neuroscience*, **100**, 611–23.

Pavlov, I.P. (1927). *Conditioned reflexes*. Dover, New York (reprinted 1960).

Pearce, J.M. (1987). A model for stimulus generalization in Pavlovian conditioning. *Psychological Review*, **94**, 61–73.

—— and Hall, G. (1980). A model for Pavlovian learning: variations in the effectiveness of conditioned but not of unconditioned stimuli. *Psychological Review*, **87**, 532–52.

——, Kaye, H., and Hall, G. (1982). Predictive accuracy and stimulus associability: development of a model for Pavlovian learning. In *Quantitative analyses of behavior*, Vol. 3 (ed. M. L. Commons, R. J. Herrnstein, and A. R. Wagner), pp. 241–55. Ballinger, Cambridge, MA.

——, ——, and Collins, L. (1985). A comparison of the effects of partial reinforcement schedules using a within-subject serial autoshaping procedure. *Quarterly Journal of Experimental Psychology*, **37B**, 374–96.

——, Wilson, P., and Kaye, H. (1988). The influence of predictive accuracy on serial conditioning in the rat. *Quarterly Journal of Experimental Psychology*, **40B**, 181–98.

Peck, C.A. and Bouton, M.E. (1990). Context and performance in aversive-to-appetitive and appetitive-to-aversive transfer. *Learning and Motivation*, **21**, 1–31.

Peeke, H.V.S. and Veno, A. (1973). Stimulus specificity of habituated aggression in the stickleback. (*Gasterosteus aculeatus*). *Behavioral Biology*, **8**, 427–32.

Perkins, C.C. and Weyant, R.G. (1958). The interval between training and test trials as a determiner of the slope of generalization gradients. *Journal of Comparative and Physiological Psychology*, **51**, 596–600.

Peterson, G.B. and Trapold, M.A. (1980). Effects of altering outcome expectancies on pigeon's delayed conditional discrimination performance. *Learning and Motivation*, **11**, 267–88.

——, Wheeler, R.L., and Armstrong, G.D. (1978). Expectancies as mediators in the differential-reward conditional discrimination performance of pigeons. *Animal Learning and Behavior*, **6**, 279–85.

Pfafflin, S.M. (1960). Stimulus learning in stimulus predifferentiation. *Journal of Experimental Psychology*, **59**, 269–74.

Pfautz, R.L., Donegan, N.H., and Wagner, A.R. (1978). Sensory preconditioning versus protection from habituation. *Journal of Experimental Psychology: Animal Behavior Processes*, **4**, 286–95.

Phaup, M.R. and Caldwell, W.E. (1959). Perceptual learning: differentiation and enrichment of past experience. *Journal of General Psychology*, **60**, 137–47.

Polt, J.M. (1969). Effect of imprinting experience on discrimination learning in chicks. *Journal of Comparative and Physiological Psychology*, **69**, 514–18.

Postman, L. (1955). Association theory and perceptual learning. *Psychological Review*, **62**, 438–46.

Preston, G.C., Dickinson, A., and Mackintosh, N.J. (1986). Contextual conditional discriminations. *Quarterly Journal of Experimental Psychology*, **38B**, 217–37.

Pyles, M.K. (1932). Verbalization as a factor in learning. *Child Development*, **3**, 108–13.

Ramachandran, V.S. and Braddick, O. (1973). Orientation-specific learning in stereopsis. *Perception*, **2**, 371–6.

Randich, A. and LoLordo, V.M. (1979). Associative and nonassociative theories of the UCS preexposure phenomenon: implications for Pavlovian conditioning. *Psychological Bulletin*, **86**, 523–48.

—— and Ross, R.T. (1984). Mechanisms of blocking by contextual stimuli. *Learning and Motivation*, **15**, 106–17.

Ranken, H.B. (1963). Effects of name learning on serial learning, position learning, and recognition learning with random shapes. *Psychological Reports*, **13**, 662–780.

Razran, G. (1949). Stimulus generalization of conditioned responses. *Psychological Bulletin*, **46**, 337–65.

Reese, H.W. (1961). Level of stimulus pretraining and paired-associate training. *Child Development*, **32**, 89–93.

—— (1972). Acquired distinctiveness and equivalence of cues in young children. *Journal of Experimental Child Psychology*, **13**, 171–82.

Reid, L.S. (1953). The development of noncontinuity behavior through continuity learning. *Journal of Experimental Psychology*, **46**, 107–12.

Reiss, S. and Wagner, A.R. (1972). CS habituation produces a 'latent inhibition effect' but no active 'conditioned inhibition'. *Learning and Motivation*, **3**, 237–45.

Rescoria, R.A. (1967). Pavlovian conditioning and its proper control procedures. *Psychological Review*, **74**, 71–80.

—— (1968). Probability of shock in the presence and absence of CS in fear conditioning. *Journal of Comparative and Physiological Psychology*, **66**, 1–5.

—— (1969). Pavlovian conditioned inhibition. *Psychological Bulletin*, **72**, 77–94.

—— (1971). Summation and retardation tests of latent inhibition. *Journal of Comparative and Physiological Psychology*, **75**, 77–81.

—— (1972). 'Configural' conditioning in discrete-trial bar pressing. *Journal of Comparative and Physiological Psychology*, **79**, 307–17.

—— (1973). Evidence for 'unique stimulus' account of configural conditioning. *Journal of Comparative and Physiological Psychology*, **85**, 331–8.

—— (1979). Conditioned inhibition and extinction. In *Mechanisms of learning and motivation*, (ed. A. Dickinson and R. A. Boakes), pp. 83–110. Erlbaum, Hillsdale, NJ.

—— (1980). Simultaneous and successive associations in sensory preconditioning. *Journal of Experimental Psychology: Animal Behavior Processes*, **6**, 207–16.

—— (1981). Simultaneous associations. In *Advances in analysis of behavior*, Vol. 2, *Predictability correlation and contiquity* (ed. P. Harzem and M. Zeiler), pp. 47–79. Wiley, Chichester.

—— (1985). Inhibition and facilitation. In *Information processing in animals: conditioned inhibition* (ed. R. R. Miller and N. E. Spear), pp. 299–326. Erlbaum, Hillsdale, NJ.

—— (1986). Extinction of facilitation. *Journal of Experimental Psychology: Animal Behavior Processes*, **12**, 16–24.

—— and Cunningham, C.L. (1978). Within-compound flavor associations. *Journal of Experimental Psychology: Animal Behavior Processes*, **4**, 267–75.

—— and Durlach, P.J. (1981). Within-event learning in Pavlovian conditioning. In *Information processing in animals: memory mechanisms* (ed. N. E. Spear and R. R. Miller), pp. 81–111. Erlbaum, Hillsdale, NJ.

—— and Wagner, A.R. (1972). A theory of Pavlovian conditioning: variations in the effectiveness of reinforcement and nonreinforcement. In *Classical conditioning, II: Current research and theory* (ed. A. H. Black and W. F. Prokasy), pp. 64–99. Appleton-Century-Crofts, New York.

——, Durlach, R.J., and Grau, J.W. (1985). Contextual learning in Pavlovian conditioning. In *Context and learning* (ed. P. D. Balsam and A. Tomie), pp. 23–56. Erlbaum, Hillsdale, NJ.

Restle, F. (1958). Toward a quantitative description of learning set data. *Psychological Review*, **65**, 77–91.

Revusky, S. (1971). The role of interference in association over a delay, In *Animal Memory*, (ed. W. K. Honig and P. H. R. James), pp. 155–213. Academic Press, New York.

—— (1977). The concurrent interference approach to delay learning. In *Learning mechanisms in food selection*, (ed. L. M. Barker, M.R. Best and M. Domjan), pp. 319–66. Baylor Univesity Press, Waco, TX.

Riccio, D.C., Richardson, R., and Ebner, D.L. (1984). Memory retrieval deficits based upon altered contextual cues: a paradox. *Psychological Review*, **96**, 152–65.

Richardson, R., Williams, C., and Riccio, D.C. (1984). Stimulus generalization of conditioned taste aversion in rats. *Behavioral and Neural Biology*, **41**, 41–53.

Riley, D.A. (1968). *Discrimination learning*. Allyn and Bacon, Boston.

Rizley, R.C. and Rescorla, R.A. (1972). Associations in second-order conditioning and sensory preconditioning. *Journal of Comparative and Physiological Psychology*, **81**, 1–11.

Roberts, A.C., Robbins, T.W., and Everitt, B.J. (1988). The effects of intradimensional and extradimensional shifts on visual discrimination learning in humans and non-human primates. *Quarterly Journal of Experimental Psychology*, **40B**, 321–41.

Robertson, D. and Garrud, P. (1983). Variable processing of flavors in rat STM. *Animal Learning and Behavior*, **11**, 474–82.

Robinson, J.S. (1955). The effect of learning verbal labels of stimuli on their later discrimination. *Journal of Experimental Psychology*, **49**, 112–14.

Rodgers, J.P. and Thomas, D.R. (1982). Task specificity in nonspecific transfer and in extradimensional stimulus generalization in pigeons. *Journal of Experimental Psychology: Animal Behavior Processes*, **8**, 301–12.

Roitblat, H.L. (1987). *Introduction to comparative cognition*. Freeman, New York.

Ross, R.T. (1983). Relationships between the determinants of performance in serial feature-positive discriminations. *Journal of Experimental Psychology: Animal Behavior Processes*, **9**, 349–73.

—— and LoLordo, V.M. (1987). Evaluation of the relation between Pavlovian occasion-setting and instrumental discriminative stimuli: a blocking analysis. *Journal of Experimental Psychology: Animal Behavior Processes*, **13**, 3–16.

Rossman, I.L. and Goss, A.E. (1951). The acquired distinctiveness of cues: the role of discriminative verbal responses in facilitating the acquisition of discriminative motor responses. *Journal of Experimental Psychology*, **42**, 173–82.

Rudy, J.W., Krauter, E.E., and Gaffuri, A. (1976). Attentuation of the latent inhibition effect by prior exposure to another stimulus. *Journal of Experimental Psychology: Animal Behavior Processes*, **2**, 235–47.

Rumelhart, D.E., Hinton, G.E., and McCelland, J.L. (1986). A general framework for parallel distributed processing. In *Parallel distributed processing*, Vol. 1 (ed. D. E. Rumelhart and J. L. McCelland), pp. 45–76. MIT Press, Cambridge, MA.

Scavio, M.J. (1974). Classical–classical transfer: effects of prior aversive conditioning upon appetitive conditioning in rabbits. *Journal of Comparative and Physiological Psychology* **86**, 107–15.

—— and Gormezano, I. (1980). Classical–classical transfer: effects of prior appetitive conditioning upon aversive conditioning in rabbits. *Animal Learning and Behavior*, **8**, 218–24.

Schachtman, T.R., Channell, S., and Hall, G. (1987). Effects of CS preexposure on inhibition of delay. *Animal Learning and Behavior*, **15**, 301–11.

Schnur, P. and Lubow, R.E. (1976). Latent inhibition: the effects of ITI and CS intensity during preexposure. *Learning and Motivation*, **7**, 540–50.

Schull, J. (1979). A conditioned opponent theory of Pavlovian conditioning and habituation. In *The psychology of learning and motivation*, Vol. 13 (ed. G. H. Bower), pp. 57–90. Academic Press, New York.

Segal, E.M. (1964). Demonstration of acquired distinctiveness of cues using a paired-associate learning task. *Journal of Experimental Psychology*, **67**, 587–90.

Seraganian, P. (1979). Extradimensional transfer in the easy-to-hard effect. *Learning and Motivation*, **10**, 38–57.

Seward, J.P. (1949). An experimental analysis of latent learning. *Journal of Experimental Psychology*, **39**, 177–86.

Shalter, M.D. (1975). Lack of spatial generalization in habituation tests of fowl. *Journal of Comparative and Physiological Psychology*, **89**, 258–62.

Shanks, D.R., Preston, G.C., and Stanhope, K.J. (1986). Effects of distractor familiarity on habituation of neophobia. *Animal Learning and Behavior*, **14**, 393–7.

Sheldon, A.B. (1969). Preference for familiar versus novel stimuli as a function of the familiarity of the environment. *Journal of Comparative and Physiological Psychology*, **67**, 516–21.

Shepp, B.E. and Eimas, P.D. (1964). Intradimensional and extradimensional shifts in the rat. *Journal of Comparative and Physiological Psychology*, **57**, 357–61.

Siddle, D.A.T. (1985). Effects of stimulus omission and stimulus change on dishabituation of the skin conductance response. *Journal of Experimental Psychology: Learning, Memory, and Cognition*, **11**, 206–16.

——, Remington, B., Kuiack, M., and Haines, E. (1983). Stimulus omission and dishabituation of the skin conductance response. *Psychophysiology*, **20**, 136–45.

——, Stephenson, D., and Spinks, J.A. (1983). Elicitation and habituation of the orienting response. In *Orienting and habituation*, (ed. D. Siddle), pp. 109–82. Wiley, Chichester.

——, Booth, M.L., and Packer, J.S. (1987). Effects of stimulus preexposure on omission responding and omission dishabituation of the human electrodermal response. *Quarterly Journal of Experimental Psychology*, **39B**, 339–63.

——, Bond, N.W., and Packer, J.S. (1988). Comparator theories of habituation: a comment on Mackintosh's analysis. *Biological Psychology*, **27**, 59–63.

Sidman, M. and Tailby, W. (1982). Conditional discrimination vs. matching to sample: an expansion of the testing paradigm. *Journal of the Experimental Analysis of Behavior*, **37**, 5–22.

Siegel, S. (1967). Overtraining and transfer processes. *Journal of Comparative and Physiological Psychology*, **64**, 471–7.

—— (1969). Generalization of latent inhibition. *Journal of Comparative and Physiological Psychology*, **69**, 157–9.

—— (1970). Retention of latent inhibition. *Psychonomic Science*, **20**, 161–2.

—— (1972). Latent inhibition and eyelid conditioning. In *Classical conditioning II: current research and theory* (ed. A. H. Black and W. F. Prokasy), pp. 231–47. Appleton-Century-Crofts, New York.

—— (1974). Flavor preexposure and 'learned safety'. *Journal of Comparative and Physiological Psychology*, **87**, 1073–82.

—— (1977). Morphine tolerance acquisition as an associative process. *Journal of Experimental Psychology: Animal Behavior Processes*, **3**, 1–13.

—— (1979). The role of conditioning in drug tolerance and addiction. In *Psychopathology in animals: research applications* (ed. J. D. Keehn), pp. 143–68. Academic Press, New York.

—— and Allan, L.G. (1985). Overshadowing and blocking of the orientation-contingent color aftereffect: evidence for a conditioning mechanism. *Learning and Motivation*, **16**, 125–38.

—— and Domjan, M. (1971). Backward conditioning as an inhibitory procedure. *Learning and Motivation*, **2**, 1–11.

——, Hinson, R.E., and Krank, M.D. (1978). The role of predrug signals in morphine analgesic tolerance: support for a Pavlovian conditioning model of tolerance. *Journal of Experimental Psychology: Animal Behavior Processes*, **4**, 188–96.

——, ——, ——, and McCully, J. (1982). Heroin 'overdose' death: contribution of drug-associated environmental cues. *Science*, **216**, 436–7.

Singer, B., Zentall, T., and Riley, D.A. (1969). Stimulus generalization and the easy-to-hard effect. *Journal of Comparative and Physiological Psychology*, **69**, 528–35.

Sjödén, P.O. and Archer, T. (1988). Exteroceptive cues in taste-aversion learning, no artifact: reply to Holder. *Animal Learning and Behavior*, **16**, 235–9.

Skowbo, D. (1984). Are McCollough effects conditioned responses? *Psychological Bulletin*, **96**, 215–26.

Smith, B.D. and Council, J. (1978). Overhabituation and dishabituation responses as a function of stimulus intensity and amount of overhabituation training. *Psychophysiology*, **15**, 517–21.

Smith, M.P. and Means, J.R. (1961). Effects of type of stimulus pretraining on discrimination learning in mentally retarded. *American Journal of Mental Deficiency*, **66**, 259–65.

Smith, S.L. and Goss, A.E. (1955). The role of acquired distinctiveness of cues in the acquisition of a motor skill in children. *Journal of Genetic Psychology*, **87**, 11–24.

Sokolov, E.N. (1963). *Perception and the conditioned reflex*. Pergamon, Oxford.

Solomon, R.L. and Corbit, J.D. (1974). An opponent-process theory of motivation: 1. Temporal dynamics of affect. *Psychological Review*, **81**, 119–45.

Spear, N.E. (1973). Retrieval of memory in animals, *Psychological Review*, **80**, 163–75.

—— (1978). *The processing of memories: forgetting and retention*. Erlbaum, Hillsdale, NJ.

—— (1981). Extending the domain of memory retrieval. In *Information processing in animals: memory mechanisms* (ed. N. E. Spear and R. R. Miller), pp. 341–78. Erlbaum, Hillsdale, NJ.

—— and Molina, J.C. (1987). The role of sensory modality in the ontogeny of stimulus selection. In *Perinatal development: a psychobiological perspective* (ed. N. Krasnegor, E. M. Blass, M. A. Hofer, and W. P. Smotherman), pp. 83–110, Academic Press, Orlando, FL.

——, Kraemer, R.J., Molina, J.C., and Smoller, D.E. (1988). Developmental change in learning and memory: infantile disposition for unitization. In *Systems with learning and memory abilities* (ed. J. Delacour and J. C. S. Levy), pp. 27–52. Elsevier, Amsterdam.

Spence, K.W. (1936). The nature of discrimination learning in animals. *Psychological Review*, **43**, 427–9.

—— (1937). The differential response in animals to stimuli varying within a single dimension. *Psychological Review*, **44**, 430–44.

—— (1952). The nature of the response in discrimination learning. *Psychological Review*, **59**, 87–93.

Spiker, C.C. (1956a). The stimulus generalization gradient as a function of the intensity of stimulus lights. *Child Development*, **27**, 85–98.

—— (1956b). Experiments with children on the hypothesis of acquired distinctiveness and equivalance of cues. *Child Development*, **27**, 253–63.

—— (1956c). Stimulus pretraining and subsequent performance in the delayed reaction experiment. *Journal of Experimental Psychology*, **52**, 107–11.

—— and Norcross, K.J. (1962). Effects of previously acquired stimulus names on discrimination performance. *Child Development*, **33**, 859–64.

Stein, L. (1966). Habituation and stimulus novelty: a model based on classical conditioning. *Psychological Review*, **73**, 352–6.

Steinman, F. (1967). Retention of alley brightnes in the rat. *Journal of Comparative and Physiological Psychology*, **64**, 104–9.

Stephenson, D. and Siddle, D.A.T. (1976). Effects of 'below-zero' habituation on the electrodermal orienting response to a test stimulus. *Psychophysiology*, **13**, 10–15.

—— and —— (1983). Theories of habituation. In *Orienting and habituation*, (ed. D. Siddle), pp. 183–236. Wiley, Chichester.

Stewart, D.J., Capretta, P.J., Cooper, A.J., and Littlefield, V.M. (1977). Learning in domestic chicks after exposure to both discriminanda. *Journal of Comparative and Physiological Psychology*, **12**, 1095–109.

Sutherland, N.S. and Andelman, L. (1969). Effects of overtraining on intra- and extra-dimensional shifts. *Psychonomic Science*, **15**, 253–4.

—— and Mackintosh, N.J. (1971). *Mechanisms of animal discrimination learning*. Academic Press, New York.

Sutton, R.S. and Barto, A.G. (1981). Toward a modern theory of adaptive networks: expectation and prediction. *Psychological Review*, **88**, 125–70.

Svendsrød, R. and Ursin, H. (1974). A factor-analytic study of the acquisition of a conditioned emotional response in rats. *Journal of Comparative and Physiological Psychology*, **87**, 1174–9.

Swan, J.A. and Pearce, J.M. (1988). The orienting response as an index of stimulus associability in rats. *Journal of Experimental Psychology: Animal Behavior Processes*, **14**, 292–301.

Swartzentruber, D. and Bouton, M.E. (1986). Contextual control of negative transfer produced by prior CS–US pairings. *Learning and Motivation*, **17**, 366–85.

Szakmary, G.A. (1977). A note regarding conditioned attention theory. *Bulletin of the Psychonomic Society*, **9**, 142–4.

Tarpy, R.M. and McIntosh, S.M. (1977). Generalized latent inhibition in taste-aversion learning. *Bulletin of the Psychonomic Society*, **10**, 379–81.

Taus, S.E. and Hearst, E. (1972). Operant discrimination learning after different amounts of reinforced pretraining to the positive stimulus. *Journal of Experimental Psychology*, **94**, 33–40.

Taylor, C. (1964). *The explanation of behaviour*. Routledge and Kegan Paul, London.

Tees, R.C. (1976). Mammalian perceptual development. In *Studies in the development of behavior and the nervous system*, Vol. 3 (ed. G. Gottlieb), pp. 281–326. Academic Press, New York.

Tennant, W. and Bitterman, M.E. (1973). Some comparisons of intra- and extradimensional transfer in discriminative learning of goldfish. *Journal of Comparative and Physiological Psychology*, **83**, 134–9.

Testa, T.J. and Ternes, J.W. (1977). Specificity of conditioning mechanisms in the modification of food preferences. In *Learning mechanisms in food selection* (ed. L. M. Barker, M. R. Best, and M. Domjan), pp. 229–53. Baylor University Press, Waco, TX.

Tetewsky, S.J. and Garner, W.R. (1985). Perceptual learning: an analysis based on selective attention measurements. *Bulletin of the Psychonomic Society*, **24**, 375–8.

Thomas, D.A. and Riccio, D.C. (1979). Forgetting of a CS attribute in a conditioned suppression paradigm. *Animal Learning and Behavior*, **7**, 191–5.

Thomas, D.R. (1970). Stimulus selection, attention, and related matters. In *Current issues in animal learning* (ed. J. H. Reynierse), pp. 311–56. University of Nabraska Press, Lincoln.

—— and Burr, D.E.S. (1969). Stimulus generalization as a function of the delay between training and testing procedures: a reevaluation. *Journal of the Experimental Analysis of Behavior*, **12**, 105–9.

—— and Lopez, L.J. (1962). The effects of delayed testing on generalization slope. *Journal of Comparative and Physiological Psychology*, **55**, 541–4.

Thompson, R.F. (1958). Primary stimulus generalization as a function of acquisition level in the cat. *Journal of Comparative and Physiological Psychology*, **51**, 601–6.

—— (1959). Effect of acquisition level upon the magnitude of stimulus generalization across sensory modality. *Journal of Comparative and Physiological Psychology*, **52**, 183–5.

—— and Spencer, W.A. (1966). Habituation: a model phenomenon for the study of neuronal substrates of behavior. *Psychological Review*, **73**, 16–43.

——, Berry, S.D., Rinaldi, P.C., and Berger, T.W. (1979). Habituation and the orienting reflex: the dual-process theory revisited. In *The orienting reflex in humans* (ed. H. D. Kimmel, E. H. Van Olst, and J. R. Orlebeke), pp. 21–60. Erlbaum, Hillsdale, NJ.

Tighe, T.J., Brown, P.L., and Youngs, E.A. (1965). The effects of overtraining on the shift behavior of albino rats. *Psychonomic Science*, **2**, 141–2.

Tolman, E.C. (1932). *Purposive behavior in animals and men*. Century, New York.

Tomie, A. (1976). Retardation of autoshaping: control by contextual stimuli. *Science*, **192**, 1244–6.

Trapold, M.A. (1970). Are expectancies based upon different positive reinforcing events discriminably different? *Learning and Motivation*, **1**, 129–40.

Tulving, E. (1983). *Elements of episodic memory*. Clarendon Press, Oxford.

—— and Thompson, D.M. (1973). Encoding specificity and retrieval processes in episodic memory. *Psychological Review*, **80**, 352–73.

Turrisi, F.D., Shepp, B.E., and Eimas, P.D. (1969). Intra-and extra-dimensional shifts with constant- and variable-irrelevant dimensions in the rat. *Psychonomic Science*, **14**, 19–20.

Uhl, N.P. (1966). Intradimensional and extradimensional shifts as a function of amount of training and similarity between training and shift stimuli. *Journal of Experimental Psychology*, **72**, 429–33.

Vanderplas, J.M. (1958). Transfer of learning and its relation to perceptual learning and recognition. *Psychological Review*, **65**, 375–85.

—— (1963). Associative processes and task relations in perceptual learning. *Perceptual and Motor Skills*, **16**, 501–9.

—— and Garvin, E.A. (1959). Complexity, association value, and practice as factors in shape recognition following paired associates training. *Journal of Experimental Psychology*, **57**, 155–63.

——, Sanderson, W.A., and Vanderplas, J.N. (1964). Some task-related determinants of transfer in perceptual learning. *Perceptual and Motor Skills*, **18**, 71–80.

Voronin, L.G. and Sokolov, E.N. (1960). Cortical mechanisms of the orienting reflex and its relation to the conditioned reflex. *Electroencephalography and Clinical Neurophysiology*, **13**, 335–44.

Wagner, A.R. (1976). Priming in STM: an information-processing mechanism for self-generated or retrieval-generated depression in performance. In *Habituation: perspectives from child development, animal behavior, and neurophysiology* (ed. T. J. Tighe and R. N. Leaton), pp. 95–128. Erlbaum, Hillsdale, NJ.

—— (1979). Habituation and memory. In *Mechanisms of learning and motivation* (ed. A. Dickinson and R. A. Boakes), pp. 53–82. Erlbaum, Hillsdale, NJ.

—— (1981). SOP: A model of automatic memory processing in animal behavior. In *Information processing in animals: memory mechanisms* (ed. N. E. Spear and R. R. Miller), pp. 5–47. Erlbaum, Hillsdale, NJ.

—— and Larew, M.B. (1985). Opponents processes and Pavlovian inhibition. In *Information processing in animals: conditioned inhibition* (ed. R. R. Miller and N. E. Spear), pp. 233–65. Erlbaum, Hillsdale, NJ.

—— and Rescorla, R.A. (1972). Inhibition in Pavlovian conditioning: application of a theory. In *Inhibition and learning* (ed. R. A. Boakes and M. S. Halliday), pp. 301–36. Academic Press, London.

——, Logan, F.A., Haberlandt, K., and Price, T. (1968). Stimulus selection in animal discrimination learning. *Journal of Experimental Psychology*, **76**, 171–80.

Walk, R.D. (1978). Perceptual learning. In *Handbook of perception*, Vol. IX,

Perceptual processing (ed. E. C. Carerette and M. P. Friedman), pp. 257–97. Academic Press, New York.

——, Gibson, E.J., Pick, H.L., and Tighe, T.J. (1958). Further experiments on prolonged exposure to visual forrms: the effect of single stimuli and prior reinforcement. *Journal of Comparative and Physiological Psychology*, 51, 483–7.

——, ——, ——, and —— (1959). The effectiveness of prolonged exposure to cutouts vs. painted patterns for facilitation of discrimination. *Journal of Comparative and Physiological Psychology*, 52, 519–21.

Waller, T.G. (1970). Effect of irrelevant cues on discrimination acquisition and transfer in rats. *Journal of Comparative and Physiological Psychology*, 73, 477–80.

—— (1971). The effects of overtraining on two extradimensional shifts in rats. *Psychonomic Science*, 23, 123–4.

Waters, W.F. and McDonald, D.G. (1974). Effects of 'below-zero' habituation on spontaneous recovery and dishabituation of the orienting response. *Psychophysiology*, 11, 548–58.

Weiss, K.R. and Brown, P.L. (1974). Latent inhibition: a review and a new hypothesis. *Acta Neurobiologiae Experimentalis*, 34, 301–16.

Weiss, K., Friedman, R., and McGregor, S. (1974). Effects of spetal lesions of latent inhibition and habituation of the orienting response in rats. *Acta Neurobiologiae Experimentalis*, 34, 491–504.

Welker, W.I. (1959). Escape, exploratory, and food-seeking responses of rats in a novel situation. *Journal of Comparative and Physiological Psychology*, 52, 106–11.

Westbrook, F.R., Bond, N.W., and Feyer, A-M. (1981). Short- and long-term decrements in toxicosis-induced odor-aversion learning. *Journal of Experimental Psychology: Animal Behavior Processes*, 7, 362–81.

——, Provost, S.C., and Homewood, J. (1982). Short-term flavour memory in the rat. *Quarterly Journal of Experimental Psychology*, 34B, 235–56.

Wickens, D.D. and Briggs, G.E. (1951). Mediated stimulus generalization as a factor in sensory pre-conditioning. *Journal of Experimental Psychology*, 42, 197–200.

Wilson, B., Mackintosh, N.J., and Boakes, R.A. (1985). Transfer of relational rules in matching and oddity learning by pigeons and corvids. *Quarterly Journal of Experimental Psychology*, 37B, 313–32.

Winefield, A.H. (1978). The effect of prior random reinforcement on brightness discrimination learning in rats. *Quarterly Journal of Experimental Psychology*, 30, 113–19.

—— and Jeeves, M.A. (1971). The effect of overtraining on transfer between tasks involving the same stimulus dimension. *Quarterly Journal of Experimental Psychology*, 23, 234–42.

Wodinsky, J., Varley, M.A., and Bitterman, M.E. (1954). Situational determinants of the relative difficulty of simultaneous and successive discriminations. *Journal of Comparative and Physiological Psychology*, 47, 337–40.

Wohlwill, J.F. (1966). Perceptual learning. *Annual Review of Psychology*, 17, 201–32.

Woodbury, C.B. (1943). The learning of stimulus patterns by dogs. *Journal of Comparative Psychology*, 35, 29–40.

Woodworth, R.S. (1947). Reënforcement of perception. *American Journal of Psychology*, 60, 119–24.

Wright, A.A., Santiago, H.C., Urcuioli, P.J., and Sands, S.F. (1983). Monkey and pigeon acquisition of same/different concept using pictorial stimuli. In *Quantita-*

tive Analyses of Behavior, Vol. 4 (ed. M. L. Commons, R. J. Herrnstein, and A. R. Wagner), pp. 295–317. Ballinger, Cambridge, MA.

Wright, D.C. and Gustavson, K.K. (1986). Preexposure of the conditioning context and latent inhibition from reduced conditioning. *Bulletin of Psychonomic Society*, **24**, 451–2.

——, Skala, K.D., and Peuser, K.A. (1986). Latent inhibition from context-dependent retrieval of conflicting information. *Bulletin of the Psychonomic Society*, **24**, 152–4.

Young, A.W., Hay, D.C., and Ellis, A.W. (1985). The faces that launched a thousand slips: everday difficulties and errors in recognizing people. *British Journal of Psychology*, **76**, 495–523.

Zajonc, R.B. (1968). Attitudinal effects of mere exposure. *Journal of Personality and Social Psychology*, **9**, 1–29.

Author index

Subject index

298   *Subject index*

Printed in the United Kingdom
by Lightning Source UK Ltd.
107306UKS00001B/94